D1211816

THE MALTHUS LIBRARY CATALOGUE

THE MALTHUS LIBRARY CATALOGUE

The Personal Collection of Thomas Robert Malthus at Jesus College, Cambridge

with invited contributions by John Harrison, Ryotaro Minami, Patricia James, William Petersen, John Pullen, and a preface by Edward Gray

THOMAS ROBERT MALTHUS

PERGAMON PRESS

New York • Oxford • Toronto • Sydney • Paris • Frankfurt • Tokyo

Pergamon Press Offices:

U.S.A.	Pergamon Press Inc., Maxwell House, Fairview Park, Elmsford, New York 10523, U.S.A.
U.K.	Pergamon Press Ltd., Headington Hill Hall, Oxford OX3 0BW, England
CANADA	Pergamon Press Canada Ltd., Suite 104, 150 Consumers Road, Willowdale, Ontario M2J 1P9, Canada
AUSTRALIA	Pergamon Press (Aust.) Pty. Ltd., P.O. Box 544, Potts Point, NSW 2011, Australia
FRANCE	Pergamon Press SARL, 24 rue des Ecoles, 75240 Paris, Cedex 05, France
FEDERAL REPUBLIC OF GERMANY	Pergamon Press GmbH, Hammerweg 6, D-6242 Kronberg-Taunus, Federal Republic of Germany
JAPAN	Pergamon Press, Ltd., Matsuoka Central Building, 8F 7-1, Nishishinjuku 1-Chome, Shinjuku-ku, Tokyo 160, Japan

Library of Congress Cataloging in Publication Data

Jesus College (University of Cambridge)
The Malthus library catalogue.

1. Malthus, T.R. (Thomas Malthus), 1776-1834--
Library. I. Malthus, T.R. (Thomas Robert), 1766-1834.
II. Title.
Z7164.D3J47 1983 [HB861] 019'.1'0942659 82-24525
ISBN 0-08-029386-7

Printed in the United States of America

CONTENTS

PREFACE
by
Edward Gray*

The publication of this Catalogue of the library Malthus's heirs donated to his alma mater more than a century after his death is a preliminary step to the publication in microfiche of the full text of a large selection of the monographs which were the sources of information for his works.[1]

Considering the scope of the library inherited from Malthus, it appeared from the outset that, prior to reproducing his references, publishing a catalogue of this library was a most desirable preliminary undertaking, useful both for research and for achieving the next step of our program.

We have been most fortunate in this endeavour to have the understanding and invaluable help of Mr. D.J.V. Fisher, the Keeper of the Old Library at Jesus College. Mr. J. Harrison, formerly Senior Under-Librarian at Cambridge University College, had recently compiled the catalogue of the Malthus Collection, and agreed, at Mr. Fisher's suggestion, to prepare the Introductory Essay. The reading of Mr. Harrison's presentation is a must for the consideration of the Catalogue as a whole and of various groups of entries.

This Library Catalogue is published with invited contributions from distinguished Malthus scholars. Professor Ryozaburo Minami, undoubtedly the doyen of all Malthus scholars, contributed a thought-provoking essay. We believe Prof. Minami's analysis, as well as his suggestion to develop further research in population history and philosophy, are of particular interest.

Additional contributions to the Catalogue are by three other eminent scholars of Malthus: Mrs. Patricia James, who in 1979 published an exhaustive bio-

---

*Dr. Edward Gray is a director and Senior Vice President of Pergamon Press, Inc., and the President of Microforms International Marketing Corporation, its subsidiary. He concluded the agreement with Jesus College for the microfilming of Malthus's Library and has headed the editing and publishing of this Catalogue.

---

1 This catalogue is published as part of our History of Economics Series. Pergamon Press has already made available on microfiche the sources Adam Smith referred to in, or which have been established by scholarly research as being related to, his celebrated *Wealth of Nations*. Locating and reproducing some 200,000 pages, and presenting bibliographical information with concordance sketches for the monographs related to this project, was not an easy task. The famous catalogues of the library of Adam Smith prepared during the past century by Bonar, Yanaihara and, lately, by Professor Mizuta have, however, been immensely helpful. The present catalogue, in its preliminary presentation, has already helped Professor Minami to make an initial selection of monographs for micropublishing. Such reproductions can be converted, on demand, into conventional hard copies as well.

graphical monograph entitled *Population Malthus: His Life and Times* and was recently commissioned by Cambridge University Press to work on a variorum edition of the *Essay on Population*; Professor William Petersen, whose work *Malthus*, published in the same year by Harvard University Press, is a documented study which in many ways updates Mrs. James's work; and Professor John Pullen, a prominent Australian scholar who is about to complete a variorum editon of Malthus's *Principles of Political Economy*. We are grateful to them for their illuminating and thoughtful essays: Mrs. James's incisive placement of the library in a biographical-historical context, Professor Petersen's careful examination of the library as a reflection of Malthus's ubiquitous intellect, and Professor Pullen's exploration of fascinating questions raised by what the library does and does not contain.

Thomas Robert Malthus is certainly best known for *An Essay on the Principle of Population*, although the history of economic thought pays more attention—as it should—to his other writings. In addition to a few well-known pamphlets, Malthus's *Principles of Political Economy* (1820) and *Definitions in Political Economy* (1827), no less than his *Essay on Population*, triggered considerable controversy among his contemporaries. Marx, for example, was completely enraged. He labeled Malthus a plagiarist (of Ricardo, and earlier writers), a "miserable" who "draws only conclusions for the good use of the aristocracy against the bourgeoisie and for these two classes against the proletariat."[2] Despite their vilification by Marx and his followers, however, Malthus's theories were in time judged deserving of a prominent place among the economic classics. According to Schumpeter, Keynes found them unbiased, and even had the fortitude to claim Malthus as his own forerunner.[3]

Notwithstanding the impact of his other works on economic thought, for most people Malthus represents a demographer par excellence whose most enduring contribution is his *Essay on Population*. His principal thesis is tersely stated: "Population, when unchecked, increases in geometrical ratio and subsistence for man in an arithmetical ratio." Since the relation of population to subsistence has proved a recurrent theme throughout history, and most especially during the past century, it is not surprising to find Malthusianism a relevant school of thought to this day.

It is well to remember William Petty's apocalyptic vision of the consequences of population increase at a new rate. He wrote at the end of the 17th Century:

> "Memorandum, That if the People double in 360 Years, that the present 320 Millions computed by some learned Men, (from the Measures of all the Nations of the World, their Degrees of being peopled, and good Accounts of the People in several of them) to be now upon the Face of the Earth, will within the next 2000 Years, so increase, as to give one Head for every two Acres of Land in the habitable Part of the

---

2 *Histoire des Doctrines Economiques* (J. Molitor), Vol. IV, p. 13. Paris, 1947

3 *History of Economic Analysis*, Ch. 4(3), p. 481. NY/Oxford, 1980

> Earth. And then, according to the Prediction of the Scriptures, there must be Wars and great Slaughter, &c."[4]

Only three centuries later, we have seen this prophetic vision become reality in many parts of the world. While it is true that the United States—indeed much of the Western world—approaches zero population growth, vast areas of the world continue to experience an ever accelerating rate of growth. Those who study Malthus and his sources might well search for answers to some key questions as a result of these developments: for instance, does history teach us that a population explosion is the fundamental cause of war? And does the unchecked—or rather, apparently uncheckable—population growth in the poorest parts of the globe, with stagnation in such growth in the less populated, smaller and richer territories, mean the eventual ruin of the latter? Indeed, how close may we already be to William Petty's nightmare with nuclear capabilities fast spreading on both sides of the imagined fence separating the over-populated poor countries and the zero-growth rich ones?

A starting point might be to follow the pattern of population growth through recorded history. One must be struck by the view held by such an acknowledged genius as Montesquieu who, to the amazement of Robert Wallace and of David Hume, presumably said that in his time the population of the world was "the fiftieth part of mankind, which existed in the time of Julius Caesar."[5] Gibbon, too, concluded that the Roman World (which he estimated to have numbered 120 million people at its height) had a somewhat higher poplulation than Europe toward the end of the 18th Century.[6] Malthus showed that despite war, pestilence and famine, the number of people living two millennia earlier could not have been greater than during his time.[7] But even this is a frightening hypothesis, coming from Malthus: his principle, the tendency for population to increase at a geometric ratio, would suggest that the

4 *Several Essays in Political Arithemetick*, p. 18, written between 1671 and 1687, and published posthumously in London in 1699. In 1753, Robert Wallace, in his *Disertation on the Numbers of Mankind*, calculated that 384 people would—under fair developmental conditions—grow in just 1,000 years to exactly "412,316,860,416."

5 The citation is from Hume's essay "Of the Populousness of Ancient Nations" (*Political Discourses*, 1752), referring to *Lettres Persanes* and *L'Esprit des Loix*, Liv. xxiii cap. 17, 18, 19. In *A Disertation of the Number of Mankind* (1753), (submitted to Hume before the publication of his essay), Wallace made the following remark: "...what is much more surprising in so great a man, we find the learned author of *Lettres Persanes*, published some years ago (1721), giving it as his opinion, that there were fifty times in the world as many people in the days of Julius Caesar..." This estimate appears as cited in Letter 108 of the initial edition of *Lettres Persanes*. Its translation by John Ozell was first published in 1722. In the later editions, this estimate was substantially changed. Actually, in the text of Letter 112 which replaces Letter 108, the corresponding paragraph was modified and indicates that mankind had decreased only to one-tenth instead of a fiftieth part. Old text: "...I find there is hardly in the World the fiftieth part of the people that there was in *Caesar's* time." (1722 Ozell translation.) Latest text: "J'ai trouvé qu'il y a à peine sur la Terre la dixième partie des hommes qui y étoient dans les anciens temps." (Montesquieu, *Oeuvres Complètes*, Bibliothèque de la Pléiade, Paris, l949.)

6 *The Decline and Fall of the Roman Empire*, Ch. II. London, 1776/88

7 6th *Essay*, Bk. I, Ch. XIV. London, 1826

size of the world population 2,000 years before his time should have been but a tiny fraction of that in the 18th Century. If indeed only such "zero growth" was experienced, during all those centuries when contraceptives and other modern means of birth control did not exist, what can be the answer but never ending "Wars and...Slaughter."?

We believe that research into the historical and literary sources of Malthus's thought—even more than his own works—can be most profitable at the present historical crossroads since population and subsistence, directly or indirectly, must be triggering mankind's catastrophes. We need not reinvent the wheel—the Malthusian theories have generated invaluable thinking that we can apply to our present predicaments.

The Catalogue of Malthus's Library is intended as an inducement to proceed in that direction.

THE CATALOGUE

The present first-published Catalogue of the Malthus Library as established by Jesus College, Cambridge, reflects in fact the second cataloguing of the books that have survived in the collection which the celebrated author once possessed, including additions made by his heirs.

Mr. Harrison's tenure at Cambridge University Library enabled him to give an exceptional in-depth presentation as a contribution to this Catalogue. We only note here that the first cataloguing was arranged by James Bonar, and its manuscript is now with the Jesus College Library.[8] It is entitled: "Catalogue of Books (formerly belonging to Rev. H.R. Malthus, M.A.)[9] In the Library at Dalton Hill, Albury, Surrey. The Property of Sydenham Malthus, C.B., 1891."

The "Dalton Hill" Catalogue includes a number of items which were not in the collection when it was donated to Jesus College, but have been identified by Mr. Harrison and are presented separately herewith. This Catalogue has, therefore, two main parts:

The first part covers titles now in the possession of Jesus College. In addition to entries (marked with an asterisk) where the year of publication is after 1834 (the date of Malthus's death), that obviously did not reflect his acquisitions, Mr. Harrison has indicated that the titles catalogued with the mark MX were acquired by Jesus College after its receipt of the collection and added to it. Those marked ME were added to the Library after the Dalton Hill Catalogue was prepared, but before the collection was donated to Jesus College.

8 Its microfiche edition is now available from Pergamon Press.

9 Rev. H.R. Malthus, Vicar of Effingham, was the son of T.R. Malthus.

To the text of the original catalogue cards, we have added only the dates of birth and death of the authors, of interest especially for the more obscure writers. We have succeeded in completing this information in most instances.

In addition, for those books Malthus cited in his works, we have given in brackets useful cross-references and, in some cases, made annotations. Obviously a large number of the titles in Malthus's Library may be subject to annotations, a task we trust will be undertaken by some future Malthus scholars.

The second part is the Supplementary List of Books published before 1835 which were entered in the Dalton Hill Catalogue but do not form part of the Jesus College collection. The publication of this list might call attention to these books, and might help in establishing their present location.

To these two main listings we are adding two others which will be of obvious interest.

For the third part, as a result of our editorial work, we have compiled a preliminary listing of monographic sources to Malthus's specific main work, the *Essay on Population*. We did so by comparing the information on monographs Malthus referred to with bibliographical entries of (a) the actual Library holdings; (b) the National Union Catalog; (c) the Dictionary of National Biography; and (d) the world's major encyclopedias and other large bibliographical sources.

Among the monographs referred to by Malthus, we have identified most of the titles and have listed them with cross references to the *Essay*. As expected, quite a number of these cited monographs were not in the library donated to Jesus College, which gives additional importance to this section.

In the fourth part, we present a listing of references comprising articles in periodicals and non-monographic material, as well as a few remaining monographs for which bibliographic information could not be obtained before the conclusion of this work. This is followed by the listing of the few classics of antiquity cited in the *Essay*.

We believe the work now being prepared by Mrs. Patricia James for a variorum edition of the *Essay* will further complement and improve these listings.

Hartsdale, New York
June 1982

ACKNOWLEDGEMENTS

The reproduction of the Malthus Library collection project and, accordingly, the publication of this Catalogue, were made possible by the valued cooperation of D. J. V. Fisher, the Keeper of the Old Library at Jesus College, Cambridge University. We take this opportunity also to extend our heartiest thanks to Professor E. A. Wrigley of the London School of Economics and the Social Science Research Council, Cambridge Group for the History of Population and Social Structure, for the time spent with us in London and Cambridge and the valuable suggestions made when this project was initiated.

For his help, we wish to thank the actual cataloguer, John Harrison, for reviewing the entries as reproduced, and for his *Introductory Essay*. For their generous help, we extend our thanks to the other contributors to this Catalogue—Patricia James, Professor William Petersen, and Dr. John Pullen, as well as Professor Ryozaburo Minami.

The project has enjoyed the full support of *Robert Maxwell*, Chairman of Pergamon Press and of British Printing and Communication Corporation, and Jean Baddeley, Director of Information. Peter Ashby of Oxford Microform and Publishing Services Ltd., our associate in the U. K., was and is instrumental in all phases of this undertaking; the help of Yuki Hatori of Maruzen Company, Ltd. in Tokyo is also very much appreciated.

Continuous advice in preparing this Catalogue as well as editorial and technical assistance were received from the President of Pergamon Press, Inc., L. Straka, and from Pergamon's Directors and staff, especially Ian Maxwell, Basil Larthe, David Kellogg, Owen Elliott, Barbara Tilley, Ronnie Farina, Miriam Margoshes, Edmund Freundlich, and Emily Marothy.

Dr. E. Gray

* * * * * * * * * *

Most of the line drawings are reproduced with the permission of the publisher from *Larousse du XXe Siecle*. Color pictures of these authors can now be found in the new *Grand Dictionnaire Encyclopédique Larousse*, a work in progress.

The cartoon of Malthus by Richard Willson is reproduced with permission of the International Planned Parenthood Federation, the publishers of *People*.

The cover is from the collection *DIVINE COMEDY IN 600 IMAGES*, reproduced with the permission of Professor Eugen Ciuca, Sculptor and Painter (Venice and New York), founder of the "Fourth Dimension in Art."

INTRODUCTORY ESSAY
by
John Harrison

Within the field of historical bibliography there has appeared over the past few years a distinct movement towards attempting to approach and investigate a man's intellectual interests and pursuits by examining the books which once stood on his library shelves.[1] The content and range of the works therein show the items that he owned, whether by inheritance, purchase, or gift, and which (to put it at its lowest level) he thus had the opportunity to read. When we look at the 2,072 volumes (comprising 1,352 individual titles) of the Malthus Collection housed today in Jesus College Library, it is tempting to jump to speculative conclusions concerning the influence which some of the items might have exerted on Malthus. Their use and relevance within the context of the owner's writings, together with notations and other markings within the books themselves, help us to replace speculation or likelihood with certainty.

In the new edition, issued in 1803, of his *An Essay on the Principle of Population* Malthus's title-page claim that it was "very much enlarged" was no overstatement. The preface of the new version explains that "The Essay... which I published in 1798...was written on the spur of the occasion, and from the few materials which were within my reach in a country situation. The only authors from whose writings I had deduced the principle, which formed the main argument of the essay, were Hume, Wallace, Dr. Adam Smith, and Dr. Price...," but Malthus goes on to say that in his subsequent research he became aware that "The poverty and misery arising from a too rapid increase of population, had been distinctly seen, and the most violent remedies proposed, so long ago as the times of Plato and Aristotle. And of late years, the subject had been treated in such a manner, by some of the French Economists, occasionally by Montesquieu, and, among our own writers, by Dr. Franklin, Sir James Steuart, Mr. Arthur Young and Mr. Townsend..." Malthus had evidently been actively engaged between 1798 and 1802 in reading these authors, and many more, for the purpose of assembling the additional material which was to form the background to his completely new historical and world-wide introductory survey of social habits, customs and attitudes.

The original version of the *Essay*, an octavo volume of 396 pages, had been issued without footnotes. In contrast, the new edition, a bulky quarto of 610 pages, was liberally sprinkled with footnote references to 102 separate works. By the time the two-volume 6th edition (the last one published in Malthus's life-time) appeared in 1826, the number of works cited in the footnotes had risen to 163 and these yield an overall total of 1,054 individual

1 The present writer's earlier involvement in this area of study led to his co-authorship of *The Library of John Locke* (O.U.P. 1965, 2nd ed., 1971) and the authorship of *The Library of Isaac Newton* (C.U.P. 1978).

references. Books on history, social life and customs, geography and travel were the most prominently exploited areas of Malthus's formidable coverage. The 24 volumes of the *Lettres édifiantes et curieuses* of the Jesuit missionaries (MC.1.13-36)* led the way with 79 separate mentions, followed by Cook's *Voyages* with 57, Robertson's *History of America* (MF.5.5-8) 42, Süssmilch's *Die Göttliche Ordnung* 41, and so on down to just a single quote extracted from 66 separate titles. Of the 163 works to which Malthus referred his readers, I can trace no more than 49 in his final library, with another eight there present but not in the edition cited.

The amount of surviving Malthus manuscript material seems, unhappily, to be meagre. No autograph drafts of his published works appear to be in existence, no annotated or interleaved proof copies, no notebooks or documents showing how or where he gathered and recorded the vast amount of matter incorporated in the new edition of his *Essay*, and in its subsequent revisions and updatings.

The young Malthus had been brought up in a household where books were available to him. His father Daniel, a country gentleman of independent means, cultivated intellectual tastes and friendships. Within a fortnight of beginning residence at Jesus College, Malthus was discussing books in a letter to his father dated 14 November 1784.[2] "We begin," he wrote, "with mechanics and Maclaurin, Newton, and Keill's *Physics*. We shall also have lectures... in Duncan's *Logick* and in Tacitus's *Life of Agricola*... I have subscribed to a bookseller who has supplied me with all the books necessary." Malthus, then, had sufficient funds at his disposal to buy the works he required. Malthus *père* was quite prepared to discuss undergraduate reading with his son. In the course of a letter of 13 January 1786[3] Daniel enquired "Did not I ask you whether you had got my Theocritus with you? Have you got Rutherford's Philosophy, 2 vols. quarto? ...I recommend Sanderson's Optics to you, and Emerson's Mechanics; Long's Astronomy you certainly have." The certainty here expressed may well have been based on the knowledge that his son possessed both volumes of this particular work (ME.6.15-16), now in the Malthus Collection at Jesus College, which were specially bound with the College crest reproduced on their front and rear boards, having the appearance of a possible College prize. He goes on to ask "How do you manage about books? ...Have you seen Bougner's mensuration of the degree in South America? I suppose Sir I's Principia to be your chief classical book after the elementary ones..." Malthus's copy of the 3rd (1726) edition of Newton's *Principia* is also in Jesus College (ME.6.11), bound and embossed in similar style to Long's work.

* NOTE: These notations are the the shelf-marks at Jesus College.

2 James Bonar, *Malthus and his Work*, 2nd ed. London, 1924, pp. 408-9.

3 William Otter, *Memoir of Robert Malthus*. Publ. with the 2nd ed. of Malthus, *Principles of Political Economy*, London, 1836, pp. xxvi-xxvii.

The Library at Jesus College during Malthus's time there may not have been extensive by modern standards but examination of its registers of book-borrowing of those days shows that it was regularly used. The registers concern removal from the Library only, and though it is reasonable to assume that a number of works were consulted on the premises, there is no way of telling what they were or who read them. The procedure enabling undergraduates and Bachelors of Arts to borrow books required that their Tutor or some other resident Fellow should sign for the items on behalf of junior members. Thus in the *Register of Borrowers*, 1783-1790[4] we see that William Frend, his Tutor, usually signed on behalf of Malthus, with the Fellows Thomas Newton, Edward Otter and Thomas Bayley obliging occasionally. In early 1785 he borrowed (and I here reproduce the short-title versions as recorded) the College's copies of *Chesterfields Letters*; *Hooks Roman history vol. 2nd*; *Livy*; *Campbells Survey of Britain*, and later in that year, *Salmasius*.

In 1786 we notice *Gibbons Roman His^{t}.* [Vol. 1]; *Rapins History of England, 2 vol.*; *Emersons Syst of Astr^{y}.* [System of astronomy]. The year 1787 has no entries for Malthus. In 1788, however, he was reading *Pearce's Sermons, Vols. 1 & 2*; *Grosse's Antiquities of England & Wales* [Vols. 1-4]; *Gibbon's Decline and Fall of the Rom^{n}. Empire* [Vol. 1]; *Dunn's Atlas*, borrowed on two separate occasions. (Gibbon's work was taken out of the Library for Malthus on 28 March of that year and we can therefore recognize the tie-up with that part of the letter he wrote to his father less than a month later (17 April) in which he reported, "I have been lately reading Gibbon's *Decline of the Roman Empire*... I shall like much to see his next volumes."[5] Finally, in 1789, he began with *Smith's Wealth of Nations*; *Secker's Sermons*; following later with *Jortin's Sermons, Vols 1 & 2*, and in Midsummer ended with *Burnet on 39 Art^{s}.*

At first sight the titles suggest a variety of intellectual interests on Malthus's part, but too much should not be made of this. The selection of works was evidently not his own free choice but rather was made on the recommendation of his Seniors. The books that Malthus had from the College Library were also borrowed frequently on behalf of his student contemporaries.

Much more significant are the entries made by Malthus in the College's *Register of Borrowers*, 1791-1805,[6] showing him to have been in Cambridge, working, during the second half of November 1801. At this time Malthus was entitled to sign out books in his own right as a Fellow of the College. On 17 November he took (I transcribe his own brief titles) *Aristotelis opera*; *Homes* [i.e. Lord Kames's] *history of man* [Vol. 1]; *Platonis opera, 2 vols.* On the 18th he signed for *Gellius Aulus Beloe trans 3 vols*; *Livius* [recensuit J.B.L. Crevier]; *Tacitus Brotieri*; *Youngs travels*. On the 19th he collected *Pliny* [C. Plinii Cæcilii Secundi Epistolæ], and on the 26th, *Aristotle Gillies*. (All were duly

4 Jesus College Library, B.15.13.

5 Bonar, *Op. cit.*, p. 412.

6 Jesus College Library, B.15.14.

marked as returned, though without a date added.) From these books, Malthus can be seen actively gathering material for the greatly enlarged 1803 version of his *Essay*. Every work that he consulted on this visit to Jesus College is cited in the footnotes of that edition. All the borrowings made in both of the Library's Registers include shelf-marks at the end of their entries, which permit precise identification of works to be made. It is of interest that all the copies Malthus used in 1801 and the majority of those from the period 1785-9, are still on the Library shelves.

In addition to the immediate access he had to his own College Library during his time at Cambridge, Malthus may have obtained admission to other College Libraries, and to the collections of the Public Library of the University of Cambridge which became available to him as a Senior Member. We have the word of his friend William Otter that until Malthus forfeited his Fellowship on marriage in 1804, he was "occasionally residing in Cambridge upon his fellowship for the purpose of pursuing with more advantage that course of study to which he was attached."[7]

A plain pointer of the direction in which Malthus's researches had moved is given in the letter he wrote to his father on 4 February 1799, listing some books which he would like to get:[8] "Süssmilch's *Göttliche Ordnung*, Vol. 1, 3rd ed....Memoir of Mr. Wargenten [sic] in the *Mémoires abrégés de l'académie Royale de Sciences de Stockholm*, printed at Paris, 1772, Muret's *Memoir on Population in the Pays de Vaud*, Berne, 1766. Dr. Haygarth on the population and diseases of Chester (Chester, 1774). Kerseboom on the number of the people in Holland. Dr. Styles' *Discourse on Christian Union*. Also *The Interest of Gt. Britain considered with regard to her Colonies, together with Observations concerning the Increase of Mankind, Peopling of Countries, etc.*, 2nd ed., [By Benjamin Franklin] London, 1761." He added that "he is glad to have received Sir F.M. Eden. His book tends very much to confirm my opinion of the inefficiency of all regular establishments for the poor." A booklist of such variety illustrates the considerable familiarity Malthus possessed with the literature relating to historical demography. My guess is that he may already have used them, perhaps in the British Museum, and wished to have copies on his own shelves. In any event, with Daniel Malthus dying within a year of his son's request, it seems that he was unable to obtain any of the books, for none of them is known to have been present in Malthus's Library. Yet by 1803 he was quoting Süssmilch (41 times, as we have seen), Wargentin (9), Muret (27), Haygarth (2), and Eden (6), in the new edition of his *Essay*.

When he decided to join the Jesus College trio of Clarke, Otter and Cripps on their Scandinavian tour, lasting in the case of Malthus and Otter from May to November 1799, it was reported, again by William Otter, that "he [Malthus] was glad of the opportunity now afforded to procure, by actual observation and

7 Otter, *Memoir of Robert Malthus*, p. xxxv. In his *Essays in Biography*, London 1933, p. 113, J. M. Keynes states that 'after 1796 he divided his time between Cambridge and a curacy at Albury...Surrey.'

8 Bonar, *Op. cit.*, pp. 414-15.

inquiry, the materials of which he was in search. To this tour, therefore, the public are indebted for all that curious statistical information respecting Norway and Sweden, with which his quarto volume is enriched..."[9] The family tour in France and Switzerland in May to October 1802 was in part a further information-gathering expedition for Malthus. His manuscript travel diaries relating to the Scandinavian tour survive,[10] but there is no existing account of the French-Swiss journey. An examination of the books in his library leads me to conclude that though Malthus was able to gather material for his researches while travelling abroad, it did not take the form of printed matter. None of the books has any indication that it was acquired while Malthus was on his tours.

How large or comprehensive the Library of Daniel Malthus might have been is not known. We can guess that it contained a range of the classics, a selection of English and French literary works, historical and political items, some divinity—in short, the library of a late 18th century gentleman. We have his own word, however, about one section of his Library with his bequest: "To Mrs. Jane Dalton all my Botanical Books in which the Name of Rousseau is written..." As for the bulk of his books, we have no direct knowledge of his intentions regarding their future ownership. Daniel Malthus died in January 1800 and his wife Henrietta, who died in the following April, had been his executrix and legatee. The Library would then presumably have passed to his elder son Sydenham, and on the latter's death in 1821 the books (or at least some of them) may have passed to his younger brother Robert. But this is mere supposition, and is based on no firm evidence. Examination of the books surviving to form the Malthus Collection today shows a "DM" added on the title-page of Nelson's *Companion for the Festivals and Fasts of the Church of England*...1744 (MC.3.28), and the name of Daniel Malthus is on the printed list of subscribers to Beattie's *Essays*, 1776 (ME.6.14). These are the only suggestions of his ownership that I have seen. It would have helped had he indulged himself with a personal bookplate, but he did not, nor (and more important to us) did his son Robert.

I know of no documents, other than those already cited, which throw light on any systematic book collecting activities on Robert Malthus's part. I can trace no booksellers' accounts or reports, no accessions lists, no catalogues, no shelf-lists. He had no regular procedure for inscribing his name in the volumes, nor did he note the prices he paid. The books themselves carry no shelf-marks relating to Malthus's ownership of them. The conclusion to be drawn is that while he was a very active exploiter of books that served his immediate purpose, Malthus was not a specially keen collector or bibliophile. Even though he may have owned three works by the well-known bibliographer Dibdin (MG.1.7, MK.4.13, MK.4.14), there is not a single note or mark on any of them to suggest their possible use as aids to building up his

---

9 William Otter, *The Life and Remains of E.D. Clarke*, London, 1824, pp. 338-9.

10 Now in Cambridge University Library and published under the editorship of Patricia James as, *The Travel Diaries of T.R. Malthus*, Cambridge, 1966.

library. Malthus acquired no incunabula and few early printed works. Library catalogues and shelf arrangement were of no concern to the man who presumably knew where individual books stood and so could readily lay his hands on them.

We are forced, then, to rely to a very large extent on an examination of the books themselves comprising the Collection to help us to determine with certainty which ones Malthus owned. (Authenticating ownership of a book is, by itself, no guarantee that he ever read it, and conversely the absence of an item from his shelves did not mean that he was not thoroughly familiar with its content, as we have illustrated above.) That a book once belonged to Malthus is most reliably decided by the inscription on its title-page, fly-leaf or elsewhere. Sometimes it is simply his own signature, which could mean either a purchase or a gift. In other instances the inscription shows plainly the book to have been an author's presentation copy, with the recording made by Malthus or by the donor himself. Details of these categories are:

Malthus's signature only: 9

Adolphus, 3 vols. (MC.6.18-20), Arnay (MF.2.12), Harrington (MM.5.17), Jacob (MM.5.2), Lauderdale (MH.5.16), Milner (ME.2.9), Newton (ME.3.1), Pretyman, 2 vols. (ML.3.27-8), *Richesse*, 2 vols. (MA.3.3-4).

He styled himself "T.R. Malthus" five times; "T. Robt Malthus," "Rev. T.R. Malthus," and "T.R.M." each appear once, while on the fly-leaf of the Harrington volume he wrote "Malthus-3-10." No other price indications are given, and no acquisition dates are mentioned.

Malthus's inscription showing the book to have been a gift from its author: 5

Chalmers, 2 vols. (MC.4.18-19), Jevons, 2 vols. (MF.5.36-7), *Letter on ...Poor Rates in Scotland*[11] (MH.3.22^{9}), Parnell (MC.3.15), Whewell (MC.4.21).

The volumes given by Jevons and Whewell carry "The Rev. T.R. Malthus from the Author," the others have simply "From the Author."

Authors' presentation inscriptions in their own works: 30

Anderson (MH.5.15^{2}):	"D^{r}. Malthus from the Author"
Bell (MH.5.15^{5}):	"The Rev. T.R. Malthus from the Author"
Bertolacci (MB.7.32):	"The Rev^{d}. T.R. Malthus with the Author's Comps"
Burton (ME.1.40^{4}):	"From the Author"
Carpenter (MH.3.22^{8}):	"With the Author's Compliments"

11 Presumably Malthus knew who wrote this pamphlet; we do not.

Casa (MJ.1.28):	“To Mr. Rob. Malthus. Quamvis, Scaeva, satis &c.[12]”[from Richard Graves the translator, and Malthus's early tutor]
Chalmers (MH.1.15):	“To Professor Malthus with the authors best regards. St Andrews, June 29th 1826”
Chalmers (MH.1.16):	“To the Revd T.R. Malthus. With the authors profoundest admiration and esteem”
Dealtry (MC.4.7):	“Rev. T. R. Malthus, from his Friend the Author, 1827”
Findlater (ME.1.41):	“Mr T.R. Malthus in testimony of respect from the Author”
Godwin (MH.2.26):	“From the Author”
Gray (MK.4.19):	“The Rev. T.R. Malthus, with the author's most respectful compliments”
Haughton (MM.5.7^{1}):	“The Revd. T. Robert Malthus from the Author” *Hints* (MG.5.19^{1}): “To the Revd. T.R. Malthus from the Author”[13]
Jones (MH.1.17):	“The Rev. T.R. Malthus with the Author's Respects”
Mackintosh (MM.5.21):	“To Mr. Malthus from his Friend the Author”
Mathias (MK.3.20):	“Dall'Autore Napoli 1829”
Morse (MK.5.23):	“Rev. T. R. Malthus from the Author”
Owen (MM.5.5):	“To The Revd T. R. Malthus with the kind regards of The Author”
Penrose (MF.5.35):	“Mr Malthus from the Author”
Roscoe (MI.2.1^{3}):	“Rev. T. Malthus from the Author”
Roscoe (MI.2.1^{4}):	“Revd T. Malthus From the Author”
Secker (MB.6.19):	“From the Author”
Spenser, 2 works (ML.3.18-19):	“Dall'Autore” [i.e. the translator, T.J. Mathias, on both works]
Stewart, 2 vols. (MM.5.8-9):	“The Revd.T.R. Malthus From the Author” on both volumes
Thomson (ME.1.44):	“Dall'Autore” [i.e. the translator T. J. Mathias]
Tooke (MB.1.2):	“From the Author”
Weyland (MH.3.22^{7}):	“T. Robt. Malthus from the Author”
Weyland (MH.2.24):	“To the Rev. T.R. Malthus. From the Author”

12 Quoted from Horace, *Epistles* I, xvii, 1: 'Quamvis, Scaeva, satis tibi consulis...' ('Even though, Scaeva, you look after your own interests quite wisely...' Loeb translation.) I thank Dr. J. J. Hall for drawing my attention to this.

13 Identity not known to us.

It will be seen that among the authors who sent their books to Malthus were his critics William Godwin, John Gray (with his "most respectful compliments"), and John Weyland.

The Persian translation of the Book of Isaiah (MB.7.52), published by the British and Foreign Bible Society, was "Presented to the Rev^{d}. Prof^{r}. Malthus by the Com^{er}. of the Bible Society 17th May 1834." The copy of his revised edition (1803) of the *Essay* (ME.6.4) in the Malthus Collection offers a provenance puzzle. On the fly-leaf it has "From the Author" and marginal corrections in pencil have been made of misprints in the text of pages 313, 388, 415, 441, and 499. I do not identify the handwriting as that of Malthus, but wherever the book may have been sent originally on his behalf, it has now finished up in Jesus College.

A study of the books he owned shows Malthus to have been an infrequent annotator, disinclined to register agreement or disagreement with views stated, or to make other additional comments. Though Malthus's writing has no outstanding characteristics to make it instantly recognizable, I can with a fair degree of confidence attribute 47 separate instances of annotations to him. (The Collection as a whole consists of a high proportion of second-hand items in which there are a large number of notes and inscriptions by earlier owners.) It has to be said that none of the manuscript material added by Malthus sheds any really valuable new light on his life and thought. It falls into several different categories: bibliographical notes and page references, extracts from texts, indexes for personal use, corrections, queries and loose manuscript slips of paper. The fly-leaves or end-papers of twelve volumes were used by Malthus as blank space on which to make mathematical calculations or, in one case, to append a list of accounts. Among the more unusual features is the way Malthus shows how he set about reading the two formidable Greek tomes of Strabo's *Rerum geographicarum libri XVII* (MA.7.3-4). Besides supplying extensive page references and notes in Greek on the end-papers of both volumes, he also added a record of the time he spent on the books. In the margin of the first page of text of volume 1 he wrote "12 Decr. 1808" and "6th Jany. 1809" at the end, proceeding to volume 2 on the following day "7 Jany. 1809"; he finally reached the last page of the main text on "23rd Jany. 1809." The title-page of the first edition of his *Essay* begins *An Essay on the Principle of Population*, and after this phrase Malthus inserted, "Particularly addressed to Young Clergymen" in one of the surviving copies (MH.3.9).

Pencil sidelining of passages of books that attracted his attention and interest was a device which Malthus frequently used. Reading a work with a pencil ready at hand seems to have been a habit of his, and probably accounts for the majority of the annotations also being pencil-written. Though the books he consulted in his College Library carry no signs of his sideline markings, the span of the dates of publication of the items in his own library with these lines in their margins shows the practice to have been established early in his adult reading and continued for the rest of his life. During his later years works by McCulloch (MB.7.51) published in 1830, Sismondi (MB.1.32) of 1832, and Scrope (ML.2.22) of 1833 are all extensively sidelined, while examples arising as a result of Malthus's earlier work are discussed below. Simply to attribute the sidelining to Malthus without further evidence would be unacceptable: one person's vertical pencil lines are not normally distinguishable from another's, nor is such marking uncommon. An examination of the Jesus Collection, however, offers sufficiently powerful indication that Malthus was responsible for the sidelining there.

Of the 135 items marked in this manner, the majority relates to subjects covering his main field of study and writing, and to authors, mostly his contemporaries or nearly so, whose publications either provided background material for his *Essay* and for his work on political economy, or who participated in the controversy which he sparked off. Many tracts are sidelined; for example, three by Burke (MH.4.24[2], MH.4.24[3], MH.5.5[1]), one by Thomas Paine (MH.4.18[3]), as well as others treating of recent political history and dispute. The most numerous markings I have seen are in the two large volumes of Lord Kames's *Elements of Criticism* (MM.4.1-2) where well over a hundred pages have their margins pencil-lined. Richard Price's *Observations on Reversionary Payments* (MH.3.23-4) also has its two volumes extensively marked, and, not surprisingly, Ricardo's *On the Principles of Political Economy* (MH. 3.2) received similarly comprehensive treatment. What *is* perhaps surprising is to discover that the 24 volumes of his set of the Jesuit Fathers' *Lettres édifiantes et curieuses* (MC.1.13-36,), with, as we have seen, its 79 footnote references in the 1803 *Essay*, do not show a single trace of pencil having been put to marginal paper. Among other works in the Malthus Collection cited in the successively revised editions of the *Essay*, sidelining is present in Franklin (MH.1.23), Godwin, 2 vols. (MI.2.3-4), Harris, vol. 1 (MA.7.12), Juan and Ulloa, vol. 1 (ML.4.12), Montesquieu, vol. 3 (MA.5.5), Necker, vol. 1 (MB.2.21), Paley, vol. 1 (MB.4.37), Price, 2 vols. (MH.3.23-4) already mentioned, Robertson, vol. 1 (MF.5.1), Weyland (MH.2.24), and Young, vol. 1 (ME.6.9).

To find books with notes in them by Malthus along with pencil lines in their margins offers, I believe, sufficiently strong confirmation that the habit described above may be safely attributed to him. I have come across 19 volumes with the combination of annotations and markings. An additional device, very sparingly employed, is the sketching of a rough outline of a hand in the margin of a book, with the index finger pointing inwards to a particular line of text. In the only five examples I have seen, this pin-pointing is used along with sidelining.

Having expressed the opinion that Malthus was responsible for marking his books in this manner, I have to say that his son Henry who acquired the Collection after his father's death in 1834 appears to have adopted the same habit. The surviving copy of Babbage's *Ninth Bridgewater Treatise* (MC.4.30) carries a few pencil notes and sidelinings, and since it was not published until 1837, Henry Malthus was clearly responsible for them.

The run of volumes of pamphlets, some of them very rare, is an important and impressive feature of the Library. Their appearance and style of binding suggest that Malthus employed the same binder to bring together items of a similar nature in volumes containing anything from three to ten separate tracts, though the average number is six. In a few instances there is still to be seen a slip of paper pasted in at the beginning of the volume describing its general content and setting out for the binder the spine lettering to be used, thus 'Tracts on Ireland & West Indies,' 'Tracts on Currency,' 'Financial and Political Tracts,' 'Economical Tracts. Vol. 1' and so on. The Collection has 55 tract volumes containing 325 separate items. Some 46 of these volumes (270 items) are concerned directly with Corn Laws, Poor Laws, problems of rent, and a variety of social, economic and political questions of the late 18th and early 19th centuries. A dozen of the volumes each have several plays or poems bound together. In the absence of any convincing evidence from the books themselves it may well be that Malthus's father was just as likely as his son to have been responsible initially for acquiring this latter category of literature.

The researcher should consult the Catalogue below with a degree of caution in view of the elements of doubt relating to some books' early ownership and original acquisition. It would consequently be potentially misleading to attempt to make a very precise subject analysis of the Collection based solely on a list of book titles. On the other hand we need have no reservations about the authenticity of books containing Malthus's signature, his notes, his sidelinings, presentation inscriptions, copies of works cited in his footnotes, and the political-economic tracts. But for the scholar an examination of the surviving volume itself is likely to be the finally decisive and satisfying solution.

In order to determine the status and scope of the Malthus Collection in Jesus College it is helpful to consider an outline of the history of the descent of the books. We have already touched upon Malthus's use of his father's Library and his probable acquisition of at least some parts of it. After Malthus's death in December 1834 the Library passed to his son Henry who became Vicar of Effingham in Surrey the following year. The new owner was sufficiently proud of his inheritance to have a personal bookplate designed and pasted in the volumes. It reads 'Henry Malthus, Effingham Vicarage', and carries his motto 'Honor virtutis præmium'. The bookplate was evidently also inserted in the books which he had possessed before his father died, and thereby we are presented with a major problem of deciding whether a work was inherited or was already owned. It is clear from the subject matter of many of the volumes published after 1834 added to the Library by Henry Malthus that he shared several of his father's intellectual interests and continued to enlarge the Collection up to the end of his life in 1882. We cannot, therefore, attribute to Robert Malthus every book with a pre-1835 publication date, nor can we tell how many such items the 30-year-old Henry already possessed when his father's books came to him. We have outlined the relevant aids to authentication left in his books by Robert Malthus, but these occur only in a minority of the volumes. A salutary reminder of the caution required in this respect is provided by the copy of Bishop Burnet's *Exposition of the Thirty-nine Articles*, 5th ed., 1746 (MI.1.17) which might reasonably be assumed to have been owned by Robert Malthus, until we notice that the front paste-down has 'Henry Malthus 1830' inscribed on it . Similarly Law's *Serious Call to a Devout*

Life...16th ed., 1810 (ML.3.26), Mathias's anonymously published *Pursuits of Literature*, 14th ed., 1808 (MB.1.11), Watts's *Short View of the Whole Scripture History*... 19th ed., 1800 (MG.5.33), and Blanco White's *Letters from Spain*, 2nd ed., 1825 (MB.6.26) all carry Henry Malthus's signature.

In the absence of surviving children of Henry's marriage it is not clear whether his widow Sophia retained the Collection until her death in 1889 or whether—as seems more probable—it was left to Sydenham Malthus (Henry's cousin and grandson of Malthus's elder brother) on Henry's death in 1882. In any event the books were transferred from Effingham to the house called Dalton Hill at nearby Albury, Surrey. It was here that the first known documentation of the Collection was carried out in 1891. The 56 years intervening since Robert Malthus's death had doubtless given time for several 'intruders' to join his original Library. Equally there had been adequate time for books to display their unfortunate tendency to disappear (almost, it sometimes seems, of their own volition) from libraries both public and private, and this is likely to have happened in the case of the Collection under discussion. Losses of this nature may explain the absence of some items which Malthus is known to have received and to have been the subject of correspondence.

J. M. Keynes visited the Library in its Dalton Hill home when he was preparing the study of Malthus included in his *Essays in Biography*, London, 1933. I have not been able to determine the year of Keynes's visit but an early draft of his essay on Malthus is dated 1922. He wrote that 'This library...is the library of the Reverend Henry Malthus, T.R. Malthus's son. It includes, however, a considerable part of T. R. Malthus's library, as well as a number of books from Daniel's library. Dr. Bonar [author of *Malthus and his Work*, 1885 and 2nd ed., 1924] has had prepared a complete and careful catalogue of the whole collection.'[14] The manuscript catalogue, now in Jesus College, is a cloth-bound folio volume, lettered in gold on the front cover 'Catalogue of Books in the Library at Dalton Hill 1891'. The inside title is rather more explicit: 'Catalogue of Books (Formerly belonging to the Rev. H. R. Malthus, M.A.) In the Library at Dalton Hill, Albury, Surrey. The Property of Sydenham Malthus, C. B. 1891'. It consists of 57 leaves, with the first 38 setting out the contents of the Library in 10 separate subject divisions within which the component works are listed in alphabetical order of authors or, failing that, of titles. The sequence of subjects begins with Division I: 'Agriculture, Botany, Horticulture, Forestry &c', and ends with Division X: 'Politics & Political Economy, Commerce, Money & Tracts relating to foregoing'. The section with the most works is Division VI: 'Fiction, Drama, Novels, Poetry &c.' Each catalogue entry is preceded by a shelf-mark comprising two elements—a letter, followed by a number, denoting a book-case and one of its shelves, thus B3, E4, H2, etc. It will be seen, therefore, that the books were given a reference relating only to the shelf on which they were housed, and since they lack an

14 Keynes, *Op. cit.*, p. 104, n. 1. James Bonar was still a visitor to Dalton Hill in 1928 when he signed and dated a note on an envelope containing Malthus's annotations accompanying his *Principles of Political Economy*...1820, now in Cambridge University Library.

individual 'running' number, we usually find 20 to 30 volumes with the same shelf-mark. The range of letters given to the book-cases was originally A to H, and subsequently K was used. A variation in the number of shelves in the cases provides A1 to A9, B and C both 1 to 7, D, E and F all 1 to 9, G and H 1 to 10, and K1 to K6. The lower numbered shelves held the smaller books, while shelves 8, 9 and 10 normally had the larger ones. The shelf-mark was added in pencil in the volumes, usually on or near the top left-hand corner of the Henry Malthus bookplate, or, in the absence of a plate, towards the top of the front paste-down.

The compiler of the Catalogue wrote it out in a clear, regular hand and with a fair level of accuracy (though perhaps not as 'complete and careful' for my purpose as Maynard Keynes found it for his). Place and date of publication are given, except for works issued in London when the publisher's name only is stated. Problems of identification have arisen because of the shortening of book titles, sometimes with the omission of key words, in order to ensure that normally the entries ran to no more than a single line. Authors' names are occasionally mis-spelt, edition numbers and a book's format are never given. The most serious shortcoming of the Catalogue, however, is the manner in which it deals with the important tract volumes of the Collection. Though fortunately most of the volumes still survive, enabling the individual component items to be set out in detail in our Catalogue below, it is not possible to say with a high degree of certainty which works were concealed under such blanket entries as 'Political Tracts. Var^{s}. Auth^{rs}. 15 vols. Variously Publ^{d} & dated.'

The latest publication date among the books in the Dalton Hill Catalogue is 1882 and there are others of 1881 (including a Darwin item). Some years after the compilation of the Catalogue in 1891, a further 288 volumes were added to the Library. They were recorded on the blank pages within the author section, opposite the original 1891 listings. This supplementary material was presented by a different scribe whose handwriting is unclear at times and has the appearance of having been dashed off at high speed. Authors' names are given without initials, titles are extremely truncated, places and years of publication are not provided, so that final and positive identifications are not easy to make. I believe, for reasons that will be discussed later, that the 288 volumes added to the original Collection did not come from the Malthuses but stemmed from their relatives the Bray family.

From folios 39 to 57 the Dalton Hill Catalogue becomes an 'Index by cases and shelves' (or shelf-list) showing how the books were arranged. Starting at [case] A [shelf] 1 the titles are offered in a very brief form and without any imprint information. On the last folio (57) the compiler of the supplementary section added the items which he had inserted in the author sequence. He appears to have found some space for these extra volumes in D8, but the majority were allocated K1 to K6.

Following the death of Sydenham Malthus in 1916 the Library passed to his son Robert (1881-1972). Towards the end of the 1930's it seems that Robert

Malthus felt that the upkeep of Dalton Hill was more than he could sustain and so decided to live elsewhere. The resulting removal to smaller premises meant that a new home had to be found for the Malthus Library. With no direct descendants to consider, Robert Malthus was able to entrust the Library to the safe keeping of his relative Reginald Arthur Bray (a great grandson of T. R. Malthus's sister Mary Anne Catherine) who lived close by at Shere, near Guildford. It was, I believe, during R. A. Bray's custodianship that the 288 volumes already mentioned were added to the Library and duly registered in the Dalton Hill Catalogue.

Jesus College has 202 of the 288 volumes (all except five of them published before 1835), and most of them now stand together in the Library's class ME. Significantly only 12 of them carry a Henry Malthus bookplate. By contrast 22 of them have the bookplate of William Bray (1736-1832) with a further seven containing a note by him or his signature, three have a Mary Bray signature (one dated 1867), and H. M. Bray put his name in another. One of the Library's five copies of William Bray's *Sketch of a Tour into Derbyshire and Yorkshire* ...2nd ed., 1783 (MA.1.28) is inscribed 'From the Library of Reginald Bray Esqr, Shere 1879.' Bringing the Bray connection into the 20th century we find written in another copy of the same work (ML.5.25) a pencil note reading 'Given to Mr. Justice Reginald Bray by his nephew W. Cecil Harris. November 1911.' It would seem then, that most of the later additions to the Collection came from the Bray family—most, but not all. Others evidently contributed as can be evidenced from Bainbridge's *The Fly Fisher's Guide*...2nd ed., 1828 (ME.2.6) which bears on its end-paper 'S. Malthus 94th Foot,' Sydenham Malthus's Regiment in which he was a Colonel.

The final move of the Collection was completed in 1949 when Reginald Bray presented it to Jesus College, Cambridge, where it now stands, shelved and catalogued, in the Old Library. The College had a special bookplate printed reading 'Ex libris HENRICI MALTHUS/olim patris sui T.R. MALTHUS/COLLEGIO JESU CANTAB./R.A. BRAY. Armiger/d.d./1949,' and a copy was inserted in every volume even though the wording was not entirely applicable to all of them. The shelf-marks given to the books (and reproduced in the Main Catalogue below) consist of three elements—a letter (preceded by M for Malthus) indicating a book-case, the number of the shelf therein, and the individual location on the shelf, thus MB.2.18, MK.5.21, etc. The letters used go from MA to MM, the majority of the cases contain seven shelves, and the 'running' numbers vary from 1-11 to 1-71 depending on the size of the books. By the time the Malthus Collection reached Jesus College it is clear that over the intervening 155 years many volumes once on Malthus's shelves had been alienated and so did not arrive at the College. We can check back no further than 1891 when the Dalton Hill Catalogue established a basis on which a precise volume and title count can be made. Details of the pre-1835 works which formed part of the Collection in 1891 but were absent in 1949 are provided below in the Supplementary Catalogue. They number 369 volumes (178 titles). Particulars of any losses from the Library occurring between 1835 and 1891 inevitably remain unknown to us.

But over the years since Malthus's death there have been additions to the Library too. We have seen the contributions made by the Bray family and Sydenham Malthus, but they were not the only previous owners whose books found their way into the Library. The absence of Henry Malthus's personal bookplate from 510 of the surviving volumes cannot be readily explained as a mere oversight on his part, but would rather suggest that many of the books were late additions to the Library. This is not, however, likely to have been the reason why of the 105 volumes there with the bookplate of Jane Dalton present, only two also carry the Henry Malthus label. These books probably came to the Library soon after Jane's death in 1817 when her cousin Robert Malthus was one of her executors. It will be remembered that in 1800 Daniel Malthus had left Jane Dalton 'all my Botanical Books in which the Name of Rousseau is written'. How many was meant by 'all' is not known, but certainly two works with Rousseau's name on their title-pages, and both very extensively annotated by him, came to the Library from Jane Dalton, namely Boissier de Sauvages de la Croix: *Methodus Foliorum*...1751 (MK.3.15) and Ray: *Synopsis Methodica Stirpium Britannicarum*...Ed. 3ª, 1724 (MI.1.16). The items with Jane Dalton's bookplate range over a broad subject area, with literature (English, French and Italian), theology, and history predominating, and tailing down to two works on cookery and one on bakery. It is noticeable that all the volumes are quite small, and their size may have persuaded Henry Malthus that the one bookplate already occupying most of the paste-down was sufficient, and so he saw no point in attaching his own.

Jane Dalton's brother Henry, patron of the living at Walesby, Lincolnshire where Malthus became Rector in 1804, has his name inscribed on nine of the books in Jesus College. In addition a copy of the first edition of Malthus's *Principles of Political Economy*...1820, now in Cambridge University Library[15], has 'Hʸ Dalton Esqʳ. from the Author' on the title-page, as well as numerous notes by the author in the text. With the death of Dalton in 1821 the volume presumably was returned to Malthus who then made several more corrections and additions for incorporation in the second edition of 1836. Other members of the Malthus family, their relatives, and their friends, also contributed to the Collection. Florian's *Les Six Nouvelles*, 1784 (MM.1.15) has the signature 'H. Eckersall' (the maiden name of Malthus's wife Harriet) and *The Guardian*, 1729 (MG.5.42) formerly had belonged to the unidentified 'S. C. Eckersall.' Koch's *Tableau des Révolutions de l'Europe*...3 vols, 1807 (MA.3.5-7) was presented 'To Mʳˢ. Malthus from J. Mackintosh 15ᵗʰ Feby 1818.' The Otter family is represented by William Otter (Malthus's life-long friend) with his name written in four books, his wife with her maiden name 'N.S. Bruere 1802' on two volumes, 'N.S. Otter' on two more, and 'Mrs. Otter' on another. Their daughter, later to become Mrs. Henry Malthus, appears on Sir Henry Taylor's dramatic romance *Philip van Artevelde*...2 vols., 1834 (MB.2.16-17) as 'Sophia Otter,' and, more fully, as 'Sophia M. F. Otter' in Burns's *Poems*...1802 (ML.2.28) which came to her as a gift from 'her

15 Shelf-mark Marshall. c. 29.

affectionate Father.' The set of Spenser's *The Faerie Queene*...1758 (ML.3.4-7) has 'EMM' on the fly-leaves of each of its four volumes: these were probably the property of Malthus's second sister Elizabeth Maria. Lightfoot's *Works*...2 vols., 1684 (MA.6.6-7), besides carrying the impressive bookplate of Gilbert Burnet, Bishop of Salisbury, also has at the foot of the title-page of each volume: 'This book belongs to the Vicars Library at Effingham in Surrey 1740.' Henry Malthus as Rector of Effingham refrained from inserting his bookplate in the work, even if it was through him that it joined the Collection. The *Baskerville Bible* of 1769 (MA.7.6) was plainly first acquired by Sydenham Malthus (the third Sydenham, 1801-68) who used it as his family Bible, recording his marriage in July 1829 and the births of his children from 1830-1845. Contrasting with the large number of books showing very distinct signs of use, often by more than one owner, the doubtful distinction of keeping its pages uncut right down to the present day belongs to Hodgson's *An Account of the Augmentation of Small Livings*...1826 (MG.7.19).

The habit of pressing flowers between the pages of a book was indulged in by some member or members of the family during the early Malthuses's ownership. Flowers or ferns or leaves are all still present in one or other of seven volumes in the Library, though I cannot offer any reason that might make the host books appear especially appropriate homes for them. The authors in question are Bausset, Vol. 2, 1817 (MA.4.22), Fréart, 1723 (MC.7.10), Kaempfer, Vol. 1, 1727 (MA.6.9), Robertson, Vol. 1, 1794 (MF.4.32), Rollin's *The Ancient History*...Vols. 1 & 3, 1804 (MG.2.6 & 8), and his *De la Manière d'Enseigner*...Vol. 2, 1748 (MB.2.19). It would be nice to think that these botanical survivals were once something more than mere book-marks.

The foregoing sketch of the Library's history affords a background against which the size of the Collection may be seen during its descent to the present day. An analysis of the Dalton Hill Catalogue and of the surviving books themselves provides the following statistics:

		Volumes	Titles
A.	Works in the Dalton Hill Catalogue of the Malthus Collection.	3011	1844
B.	Division of above by date of publication:		
	i. Pre-1835 works	2370	1492
	ii. Post-1834 works	641	352
C.	Works from A above presented to Jesus College by R.A. Bray in 1949	2215	1421
D.	Division of above by date of publication:		
	i. Pre-1835 works	2001	1314
	ii. Post-1834 works	214	107

		Volumes	Titles
E.	Sale of post-1834 works from above by Jesus College[16]	140	66
F.	Works in Jesus College in 1982[17]	2072	1352
G.	Division of above by date of publication:		
	i. Pre-1835 works	1999	1312
	ii. Post-1834 works	73	40
H.	Works in the Dalton Hill Catalogue which were not given to Jesus College	796	423
I.	Division of above by date of publication:		
	i. Pre-1835 works[18]	369	178
	ii. Post-1834 works	427	245

At first glance the totals in category B.i. might give some idea of the size of Malthus's Library, and it would be fair to say that they provide an upper limit. But the pre-1835 works which Henry Malthus and others added to the Collection cannot be disregarded, and such 'intruders' probably outnumbered any losses incurred from 1834 up to the making of the Dalton Hill Catalogue in 1891. My guess, a very rough one, is that Malthus's Library when he died consisted of about 2,000 volumes.

The Main Catalogue below lists the works in category F, that is the whole Jesus College holding irrespective of dates of publication, including the works in class MX which did not stem from the Malthus Collection, and is based on the books themselves. For the Supplementary Catalogue, comprising items in category I.i., their recordings in the Dalton Hill Catalogue have been expanded by examining copies of the works in Cambridge University Library (whose forms of author or other relevant headings I have adopted throughout) or by consulting the published catalogues of other libraries. In the six instances where I have not been able to identify a work or its edition with certainty I have

16 The works sold consisted largely of historical and theological books which duplicated works already in the College Library.

17 Over the period 1949-1982 three single-volume titles (two pre-1835 and one post-1834) have disappeared from the Collection. In fairness to the College it should be added that over the same period it has extended its rich coverage of works written by Malthus. While still not possessing copies of every item that he published, the College now owns a complete set of all six editions of the *Essay* issued during Malthus's lifetime, having acquired copies of the 3rd, 4th, and 5th editions (1806, 1807, 1817), as well as the 1809 French version of Pierre Prévost. These works are in class MX.

18 Present location of all unknown except for Malthus's annotated copy of his *Principles of Political Economy*, 1820, now in Cambridge University Library.

added a note to that effect. In both sequences a shelf-mark is reproduced to stand directly below the author or other appropriate heading, the first being those of Jesus College Library, and those in the Supplement relate to the shelves at Dalton Hill. The latter Catalogue offers a check-list of books whose whereabouts is currently unknown (except for one) but which may surface in the second-hand market at some future date when the shelf-mark with (or even without) the Henry Malthus bookplate may serve to establish an item's provenance. I have tried to keep cross-references down to the bare minimum, with headings for editors used very sparingly. Anonymous works will normally be found under the first word of their title, with a reference supplied under the author's or editor's name, unless the authorship is so widely known, even if not stated originally on the title-page, that a title entry would not be helpful or necessary, as, for example, in the case of the first edition of Malthus's *Essay*.

Two manuscripts are included in the Catalogues below. One describing itself *Armes of Surrey taken 1662*, is in Jesus College (ME.5.59), and consists of ink sketches of coats of arms of Surrey families. It was added to the Dalton Hill Catalogue after the main 1891 listing, and it does not carry a Henry Malthus bookplate. I think, therefore, that it was one of the Bray family items, even if the manuscript does not contain their coat of arms (nor, for that matter, any mention of the Malthuses). I am puzzled by the other manuscript whose entry reads 'Malthus H. M.S. Notes. 1822' in the Dalton Hill Catalogue where it appears in the Subject Division V: 'Encyclopædic, Educational & general, Magazines, Dictionaries, Lexicons &c.' Born in December 1804 Henry Malthus would have been 17 (or just possibly 18) in 1822, and though it is not impossible that the manuscript was his work, it seems far more likely to have originated with his father and I have treated it so in the Supplementary Catalogue. Its subject matter is beyond my speculation.

At the risk of repetition I would issue a gentle reminder to readers to avoid passing snap judgements, especially if they suit one's pre-conceived ideas, based on the scanning of the Catalogue of a Library such as that of Malthus, which has travelled down to us through four separate later owners. Very occasionally examination of the books themselves will show how misleading such judgements of an individual title may be. A pertinent illustration is provided by the Collection's copy of Beckford's *Thoughts on Hunting*...1820 (MA.4.5) which at first sight could be assumed to be wholly relevant as a pointer to Malthus's enjoyment of country pursuits. It is a surprise, then, to find that Malthus did not even own the book. It bears the signature and date 'A.F. Cooper, 1838,' together with the bookplate of Henry Malthus who evidently obtained the volume second-hand. The Catalogue can reflect Malthus's special interests and studies with a reasonable degree of accuracy in the great majority of cases, but at times it should serve as a stepping-stone to the perusal of individual books within the Collection.

T.R. MALTHUS AS POPULATION SCIENTIST

by
Ryozaburo Minami*
Former President, Population Association of Japan

1. THE MALTHUS COMMEMORATIVE IN JAPAN AND THE MALTHUS CONFERENCE IN PARIS

In 1916 (5th year of Taisho) the 150th anniversary of Malthus's birth was celebrated on a grand scale at Kyoto University (then the Kyoto Imperial University), and the university press published a special commemorative monograph of collected papers. Later, in 1934 (9th year of Showa), a seminar at the Otaru Higher Commercial School (the present Otaru University of Commerce) in Hokkaido sponsored a collective work to commemorate the 100th anniversary of Malthus's death. At the same time, the Population Problems Research Foundation sponsored an exhibition of Malthus-related documents, and in 1966 (41st year of Showa) the nationwide Population Association of Japan sponsored an exhibition of Malthus manuscripts at Chuo University in Kanda. One can see from these events the level of respect that the Japanese scholarly community holds for Thomas Robert Malthus as a population scientist.

In the beginning, however, many Japanese economists were only studying Malthus within the framework of political economics, and they had not yet begun to study specifically Malthus's main work, *An Essay on the Principle of Population*, and weave an independent scholarly field around it. There were many excellent economists in Japan from the end of Meiji to the beginning of Taisho, but there were none who concerned themselves solely with population.

Much later, in May of 1980 (55th year of Showa), a grand-scale Malthus Conference was organized over several days at the UNESCO Hall in Paris. It was co-sponsored by the International Union for the Scientific Study of Population, and the International Union for Economic Research, but I understand that it was planned by the then-newly-established French Societé de4Démographie Historique. Although this conference was entitled "Malthus: Yesterday and Today," it was different from commemorative meetings celebrating Malthus's birth or death, such as we had seen in Japan. It was international in scope, and it was purely scholarly. It considered Malthusian

* "Professor Minami," writes Mrs. Patricia James, "is the doyen of living Malthusians, and I am proud to regard myself as one of his pupils: it was his bibliography (mercifully printed in English and not Japanese) which launched my researches into Malthus's life and times. I have always felt ashamed of the contrast between Professor Minami's enthusiasm and the indifference of Malthus's own countrymen."

theories that have spread throughout the world, and thoroughly examined the truth of these theories. Attending this meeting, I felt that Malthus is indeed not just a subject for economists, and that the greatness of his thoughts still lives on.

Of the classical British economists, Malthus is the only one whose collected works were not published after his death. Adam Smith has his collected works, as do Ricardo and J.S. Mill, but as for Malthus, his treatment is such that parts of his letters are even included in Ricardo's collected works as being Ricardo's. And yet, he has become the focus of international interest, nearly 150 years after his death, and is seriously discussed in various fields.

There are no similar examples. Malthus, from his upbringing and college education, like Stanley Jevons who was to appear later, did not at first wish to pursue the course of economics. After writing his *Essay on Population*, however, at the East India College Malthus became England's first—and therefore the world's first—professor of economics and history. His main work is also a source of development for all fields of learning, not just economics or demography, and has as its ultimate aim the happiness of human society.

2. GENERATION AND AMPLIFICATION OF THE MALTHUSIAN PRINCIPLE OF POPULATION

Over 50 years ago, I examined in detail the Malthusian principle of population. Indeed, there have been throughout history many and varied scholars who have speculated on population, so that we find ideas on population dating from ancient times. In the ages before Christ, we have Plato and Aristotle. Their conceptions, however, were all either fragmentary or supplementary to other subjects, and there are no consistent efforts to discuss population phenomena. Further, their views of a nation's population are almost the opposite of Malthus's. The idea that "population is the source of riches" is popular. One must upend this view and deal with population as it is. Malthus started on his path by following such predecessors as Townsend. Karl Marx, who later was to criticize Malthus, praised Sir James Steuart's opposing population theory, which Malthus himself severely criticized.

After Malthus died, Darwin and Wallace announced a new theory in the field of biology (theory of biological development through natural selection). It is known that both theorists, as if by mutual agreement, had read Malthus's main work before announcing their new theories. There must be various opinions as to the true reason for this, and I myself would not say that Malthus was at the basis of their new theories. This is, however, an interesting point. Malthus was truly a "seed-sower of thoughts," said James Alfred Field (the American Malthus scholar who died young).

This recurs in various areas of learning. It cannot be forgotten that political economics, sociology, statistics, ethnology, and biology all built new fields of learning on the foundation of the Malthusian principle of population. I have just discussed the development of biology, but let me discuss the development of sociology as well. What Franz Oppenheimer *et alia* discussed as the "law of blood veins" and the "law of social currents" were nothing but the concept of class intercourse that Georg Hansen published as *Die drei Bevölkerungsstufen* at the end of the 1880's. When one examines Hansen's new theories of sociology, however, they are clearly based on Malthus's *An Essay on the Principle of Population.* Malthus was indeed a person who disseminated a wealth of ideas.

3. THE TWO PRINCIPLES OF MALTHUS: THE REGULATING PRINCIPLE AND THE PRINCIPLE OF INCREASE

The basic title of Malthus's main work is *The Principle of Population.* It is clearly intended to be in the singular, but I think that there are actually two principles there. A principle in human society, which W. Godwin discusses in his *Political Justice*, points to the regulating effect on the increase in population of the level of food production. In response to this, Malthus pronounced the principle of population that tends to overcome the range of food production and tries to surpass the regulating effect (or law). I call the former the regulating principle and understand the latter as the principle of increase. This interpretation of definition is not clear in the 1798 first edition of Malthus's *Essay*, but becomes clear in the later editions (starting with the 2nd edition of 1803). In any case, Malthus's main work covers the interaction of these two principles and allows for the progressive and retrogressive oscillations of population in society.

No one will doubt the regulating principle. Food is indispensable for the survival of humankind, and there is a limit to the area of land that can be utilized for the production of food. Naturally, depending on the age or the stage of development of the economy, there may be surplus food in a nation, or it may be that food may be purchased from other countries. Also, people who are overly confident in human technology may be convinced of the excellence of human adaptation, and deny the regulating effect of food on population. Human beings as a whole, however, are still ruled, and will be permanently ruled, by the regulating effect.

On the other hand, the principle of increase more clearly reflects the age. The age of Malthus was during the progress and the beginnings of the English industrial revolution, with population escaping from the stagnation of the middle ages and steadily increasing. It was not incredible, therefore, that there were areas of the newly discovered American continent where the population doubled every 25 years. And it was also at this time that Francis Place, who started the labor movement in London in the 1820's, conceived of a way to regulate the principle of increase; in other words, through birth control. In speaking of leaders of the labor movement, we cannot ignore the position of Karl Marx, who made his name at the end of that century. Marx was also active at the time when the principle of increase was rampant, at the same period of time as Malthus, and his thought was also, to a large extent, influenced by the outburst of population, but his approach was different.

The fecundity of human beings as living organisms actually increases with civilization, but various artificial and effective means are invented so that the actual population shrinks and stagnates. It has come to such a state that in the advanced nations of Europe and the U.S. especially, there is great anxiety for the future population. It is understandable then that there is the urge once again to study Malthus, and in that sense, Malthus must be permanently and seriously remembered.

4. POPULATION HISTORY OR POPULATION PHILOSOPHY

In this paper, I referred earlier to Malthus as a "seed-sower of thoughts." The development and expansion of various sciences have taken lavish advantage of his *Essay on Population*—economics and sociology are but two examples. The effect of Malthus's *Essay* has even extended to such areas of natural sciences as biology.

It might therefore appear that Malthus's main work came down the ages with little resistance. That was never the case. Years ago, I learned of the strenuous criticism and opposition that the *Essay* met at the time and searched for the outstanding examples, mainly at the Menger Library of the Tokyo University of Commerce (presently Hitotsubashi University). Later, I came to want to collect those original works of Malthus's detractors and, partly supplemented by reprints of economic classics, I was able to collect most of them. Among just those that were published when Malthus was alive— properly the 36 years from publication of the first edition of the main work in 1798 till Malthus's death in 1834—there were works by Charles Hall, Thomas Jarrold, William Hazlitt, Simon Gray, James Grahame, George Ensor, William Godwin, Piercy Ravenstone, John McIniscon, Michael Thomas Sadler and various others. Among these, there were some that Malthus answered in appendices of later editions of the *Essay*, but now we cannot know how or in what form and on what occasion Malthus replied to other detractors. There must have been some that he also ignored. There were none that I have seen who insulted him as much as the author of *Das Kapital* did, by calling his work "a monkish plagiarism." But on meeting such opposition and criticism, an ordinary person would immediately abandon the theory or would become ill and collapse. At the same time I am surprised that English publishers continued to publish such detractors of Malthus. In one respect it goes to show how great a shock Malthus's theory was to English society.

Nevertheless, Malthus has lived on. Even 150 years after his death, his theories are valued highly. It was a long, strenuous course, but it is a deep-rooted theory. It was for this that I called him a person who sowed seeds of thoughts.

I believe that in future years, a unique view of history will evolve out of Malthus's theories. An historical view that is adjacent to, but completely different from, Marx or Engels's historical view will probably be established. I would like to refer to the "population interpretation of history" and base this view on the "Produktion und Reproduktion des Lebens" passage in the unpublished "Deutsche Ideologie" that Marx and Engels conceived of when they were young and in exile, and incorporate Malthus's thoughts with that. By doing this, the anti-Malthus atmosphere in Japanese scholarly circles, where there are many Marxian economists, might change somewhat. This is to be desired.

At the same time, I would like to conceive of something called "population philosophy" as a parting gift. Especially when population becomes an object of artificial policies, such as happens with research in other fields, then "population philosophy" should become the last deciding factor. I would like to advance our theories into the new world of the "population interpretation of history" and "population philosophy," which even Malthus himself did not deal with.

I would like to add, finally, that the first (1798) edition of Malthus's *Essay on the Principle of Population* is translated and published by two or three publishers in Tokyo. This must be because it is small and convenient. Malthus himself, however, made this edition go out-of-print several months after it was printed. This was probably because he did not like it. The editions starting with the second *Essay* of 1803 are the proper work. Revisions and processing were continued until the 6th edition of 1826. With respect to the 6th edition, there was a Japanese translation published in Tokyo at one time, and there was also a scholar named Hideo Yoshida who had published several volumes of a parallel translation (translation and text side-by-side) of the various editions, but such Japanese translations are probably no longer on the market. I think it is necessary now to popularize and continually translate the 6th edition in Japan in a form that is convenient for readers.

Tokyo, Japan
June 1982

INTRODUCTORY REMARKS

by

Patricia James*

The mere perusal of this catalogue is a liberal education in miniature, and every reader will be struck by it in different ways. Some may be surprised to learn that Latin was by no means a dead language in the eighteenth century, and that the British middle classes in Georgian times were far more European in outlook than their Victorian descendants; other readers may be impressed by the number of rare sixteenth and seventeenth century books in the collection.

Malthus was neither methodical nor businesslike, and one cannot picture him, like John Locke, carefully noting the date and price on page 11 of each volume acquired. Some of the books are inscribed, but it is impossible to determine exactly whether others were bought by Malthus himself, or inherited from his father or other members of an exceptionally well-read and affectionate family. That Malthus was afflicted with bibliomania is shown by the presence in this catalogue of three works by Thomas Dibdin, despised as a bibliographer, but certainly a benefactor to the book trade; he set a fashion for "rare and valuable editions of the Greek and Latin classics," and his *Library Companion (or The Young Man's Guide and the Old Man's Comfort, in the Choice of a Library)* needs no comment.

Shortly after the publication of the anonymous first *Essay on Population*, in 1798, Malthus wrote in a long letter to William Godwin that "Moderate cloathing, moderate houses, the power of receiving friends, the power of purchasing books, and particularly the power of supporting a family, will always remain objects of rational desire among the majority of mankind." It is therefore pathetic to find that he was obviously lacking a proper library of his own during the five years which elapsed between the first and second versions of the *Essay*; his parents' deaths early in 1800 had deprived him of a settled home and he was without an income to support a family. He rented a "garret in town" near the London house of a married sister, and travelled about visiting friends and relations. The reference notes in the great quarto on *Population*, published in 1803, sometimes give two different editions of the same work, and a few are quite confused; these are sad indications of a peripatetic life and much unsatisfactory book-borrowing.

---

* Mrs. Patricia James is one of the most prolific contemporary scholars of Malthus. She is the editor of his *Travel Diaries* (1966), and the author of the outstanding monograph, *Population Malthus: His Life and Times* (1979). Mrs. James was commissioned by Cambridge University Press to work on a long-awaited variorum edition of the *Essay on Population* which is expected to be published in 1985.

It is pleasant to know that Malthus's moderate ambitions were to be fulfilled. He had great hopes for the United States, and never spoke of them, unlike many English people, as "our revolted colonies"; later in life he was to refer to his "friends in America," and was particularly fond of Charles Wilkes of New York, father-in-law of another friend, Francis Jeffrey, the celebrated editor of the *Edinburgh Review*. Thus it is fitting that American enterprise should make Malthus's library known to the academic world at large, through technical processes he could never have imagined. A devoted younger colleague, William Empson, wrote that Mr. Malthus "was far from being indifferent to fame," but he had an underlying modesty, and might well have been somewhat amused by the solemnity with which we search his books for clues to his life and character.

Pedanius Dioscorides' *De Materia Medica*, published in Basle in 1529, reminds us that Malthus was descended on both sides from apothecaries, so successful in their business that they attended royalty—Queen Anne and the first three Georges. Malthus's maternal uncle, Richard Graham, kept up the fashionable family shop in Pall Mall, at the sign of the Pestle and Mortar, until 1800.

On the other side of the family, Malthus's father had inherited enough money, from his own lawyer father and apothecary grandfather, to embark on the leisured life of an eccentric and literary country gentleman. Daniel Malthus was a passionate admirer of Jean Jacques Rousseau, and his neighbours enjoyed his "highly cultivated mind and very fascinating manners"; yet he seems to have been a selfish tyrant at home, fond only of his eldest daughter and his second son, Thomas Robert. His relationship with his "dear Bob" (Malthus was never called Tom) appears to have been especially happy, mainly because they shared the same literary tastes, but perhaps also because Robert was born on 13th February 1766—with a severe handicap, a cleft palate and hare-lip. The lip was sutured, but at that period nothing could be done about the palate; although Robert was a handsome man, his snuffly, "crawky" voice was to annoy and distress other people all his life.

His life ended on 29th December 1834, so that Malthus lived almost exactly 69 years, nearly thirty-five of them in the eighteenth century and thirty-four in the nineteenth.

Young Bob's education began in an attractive eighteenth-century setting, in the rectory of the Rev. Richard Graves at Claverton, near Bath; he was another eccentric, but a delightful schoolmaster all the same. Three of his books appear in this catalogue, including the "comic romance" called *The Spiritual Quixote* which was first published in 1772. It is very crude: the Sancho Panza of the story is Jerry Tugwell, a cobbler, whose mouth always seems to be wide open when he and his master, Mr. Geoffrey Wildgoose, are being pelted with horse dung or similar organic material.

The elegances of urban Bath were within walking distance of rural Claverton, and it seems likely that here Malthus acquired his lifelong love of the theatre, perhaps after watching the young Mrs. Siddons play Juliet, and applauding her as she was carried away in a sedan chair after the performance. Malthus may also have acquired in Bath his charming manners, which were commented upon again and again by all sorts of people, even when he had grown into "a polite, handsome, kind old man," as one little girl described him. It is important to remember that at this period the children of well-to-do English people were not imprisoned in their nurseries or schoolrooms: "young ladies and gentlemen under the age of twelve years" were welcomed at the Bath Assemblies, provided they were introduced by a subscriber. Young gentlemen in those days were as brightly dressed as young ladies, in velvet and lace, and it was not considered foppish or effeminate for boys to learn to dance really well—there were few alternative forms of exercise—any more than it was considered unmanly for them to learn drawing and French with their sisters. The segregation of the sexes, like the separation of children and adults, was a phenomenon of the nineteenth century.

When he was sixteen, Robert was removed from Richard Graves's tuition and the beauties of Somerset, to the industrial town of Warrington, between Liverpool and Manchester, to "read" with Gilbert Wakefield; perhaps this gave Malthus his distaste for "unwholesome manufactures," which it took him some years to overcome. Later he boarded at the Wakefields' home near Nottingham, and it might have seemed a lonely and austere life after his jolly little school. The list of Wakefield's works in the catalogue is in marked contrast to Richard Graves's light-hearted satire and versifying. Did Daniel Malthus arrange all this deliberately, giving his son first a social training, to help him with the difficulties occasioned by his hare-lip and cleft palate, and then a bout of steady work to qualify him for Cambridge?

In any event, Robert was obviously fond of his second eccentric mentor, and a loyal friend to the family after his early death. His tutor at Jesus College, William Frend, was yet a third unusual character, although the choice in this case was probably a matter of chance, and not Daniel Malthus's. Both Wakefield and Frend were Unitarians, and both attacked the establishment for political as well as religious reasons—Wakefield spent two years in gaol, Frend was expelled from the college. Frend also maintained close links with Malthus, as is shown in his daughter's memoirs, but only two of his many pamphlets, one duplicated, are in this collection.

A more imposing souvenir of Malthus's time at Cambridge is the gorgeously bound quarto volume of Newton's *Principia Mathematica.* There is also an elementary work on mathematics, published in 1762, by Richard Ramsbottom, which is called *Fractions anatomized: or, The doctrine of parts made plain and easy to the meanest capacity.* Pedagogues today might envy this unknown Mr. Ramsbottom, who felt no need to make professional concessions to humbug.

During Malthus's time at Cambridge, his family moved from Berkshire to Surrey, and the country round Albury and Shere is still the home base of his youngest sister's descendants. Daniel Malthus was not an orthodox Christian, but he rented an appropriate number of seats in Shere church for his household; one of his granddaughters wrote that he expected his children to attend religious services with reverence, and reprimanded them severely if they gossiped about the congregation afterwards. In 1788 Robert became an ordained minister of the Church of England, and in this connection it is particularly tantalising not to know which of the older theological works, listed in the catalogue, were bought by Malthus himself, and which were inherited. Sermons at that time were published and criticised like any other branch of contemporary literature, along with history or biography, books of verse or books of travel. They were read aloud, particularly on Sundays, as a matter of custom rather than piety, while the ladies—if they sewed at all—worked on garments for the poor.

What this catalogue does show very clearly, however, is that Malthus went on buying books on religion and ethics all through his life. He was not one of those clergymen, common in the eighteenth century, who took orders simply to obtain a college fellowship or a comfortable living. As the first *Essay on Population* demonstrates, Malthus was perplexed, and probably at times overwhelmed, by the problems of theodicy: how could a benevolent deity allow so much suffering in the world? The *Essay* of 1798 also shows that, like his tutor Frend, he found it impossible to believe that a loving God could consign any of His creatures to everlasting torture in hell. As one of the ordained professors, Malthus preached in rotation as a matter of course in the chapel of the East India College, and those who knew him praised both his sermons and his deep but unassertive piety.

It seems incredible to us, but Malthus had no scruples about becoming the absentee rector of a good family living in Lincolnshire, with a poor curate to do all the work. There was nothing remarkable about this in an era (rapidly coming to an end) when non-residence was so general that the parsons who excited comment were those who remained in their parishes all the time, year in and year out. His becoming rector of Walesby enabled Malthus to marry his cousin Harriet Eckersall, in 1804, and in 1805 he was appointed Professor of History and Political Economy at the East India College, founded in that year for the training of the East India Company's civil servants. Here he stayed for the rest of his life, first in the country town of Hertford, then on the college's own beautiful campus at Haileybury. He may not have lived altogether "happily ever after," as in fairy-tales, but he came very near to it.

Just as this catalogue reminds us forcibly that Malthus was a sincere minister of religion, it also shows us Malthus as a professor of history. The economists have taken him over so thoroughly that this aspect of his life is almost forgotten; Malthus wrote no historical works himself, but the study of them undoubtedly influenced his theoretical economics. Here, as with the books on theology, the catalogue makes it plain that Malthus took this half of his job as seriously as the other, new works on history being purchased over the years to bring his lectures up to date, just as he presumably quoted new theological works in his sermons. In both cases he would have been bringing his own ideas up to date, at least as far as increasing age enabled him to do so. Old Pop, as his students called him, was never a good lecturer, but it is impossible to imagine him guilty of any kind of perfunctory teaching. Like St. Paul, whatever he did, he was incapable of doing less than heartily.

But then comes the amazing revelation that the Rev. Professor Malthus possessed volume after volume of frivolous plays, including the most bawdy of Restoration comedies. It is clear from Malthus's correspondence with his publisher John Murray, as well as from his and his wife's travel diaries, that they both loved the theatre and were experienced critics of the technique of acting. It is also apparent from the catalogue that, although we know the Malthuses kept up to date with the London stage (rather insipid at this period), most of the plays they possessed must either have been bought second-hand or inherited from the eighteenth century—in which latter case they might well have been used for lighting fires in some clerical households.

Malthus acknowledged that he owed his position at the East India College mainly to Charles Grant. Grant was one of the most prominent of what were called the "Clapham Sect" of the Anglican Evangelical movement, to which many of Malthus's colleagues and friends were attached. The Evangelicals were foremost in campaigns for the improved study of the Bible, the abolition of slavery, and the education of poor children, all of which Malthus supported, as this catalogue indicates; but they were also introducing into the Church of England a Puritanism which we were later to designate "Victorian," and which must have been quite uncongenial to him. Some of Malthus's visitors may have chalked up his galaxy of licentious drama as yet another black mark against the author of the *Essay on Population*.

The same strictures might have been applied to Malthus's fondness for Byron in particular and poetry in general, and certainly this catalogue must dispel for ever the idea that he was a cold, hard man.

Too much importance should not be attached to old books on the indoor feeding of cattle[1] or "the manures most advantageously applicable to the various sorts of soils."[2]

At this time the occupants of a country house, even a rented one, took it for granted that they would be self-sufficient in milk and eggs, pork and bacon, as well as in fruit and vegetables. Nor should we assume that Malthus had any special interest in horses merely because he possessed Youatt's well known book on their care and management, even though he did boast to Ricardo that he had driven his mare, in his low gig, "ten years without a fall." It is possible, of course, that he made a journey in a railway train, drawn by a steam locomotive, but there is no evidence for this; we know that he enjoyed travelling by steamboat in Scotland in 1826.

Indications of the new age can be found in plenty. Malthus's travel diaries show that he was interested in geology, and here again he kept up to date, with Lyell's seminal *Principles of Geology* (1830) and de la Beche's *Geological Manual* (1832) and *Researches in Theoretical Geology* (1834). *The Origin of Species*, sparked off by the *Essay on Population*, was not to appear until a

1 Tschifelli, J. R. *Lettres sur la nourriture des bestiaux à l'établie*, Berne, 1775.

2 Kirwan, R. *The manures most advantageously applicable...*, London, 1796.

quarter of a century later, but when Malthus died the young Charles Darwin had already been away with the *Beagle* for three years.

Less well known today, for obvious reasons, are the *Bridgewater Treatises*, yet they were important in their time, and especially to Malthus. Francis Henry Egerton, eighth and last Earl of Bridgewater, died in 1829, and in his will left £8,000 for the best essay on "The Goodness of God as manifested in the Creation," the President of the Royal Society to be the judge. He wisely decided to divide the money among eight writers, of whom at least three were known to Malthus: his younger friend William Whewell of Trinity College, Cambridge, whose work was entitled *Astronomy and General Physics considered with reference to Natural Theology*; Malthus's disciple as regards economic theory, Thomas Chalmers, wrote *On the power, wisdom and goodness of God as manifested in the adaptation of external nature to the moral and intellectual constitution of man*; Peter Mark Roget, of *Thesaurus* fame, a nephew of Sir Samuel Romilly, preferred the simpler title, *Animal and Vegetable Physiology considered with reference to Natural Theology*. All eight treatises are in this catalogue, and it is easy to see how the subject appealed to Malthus, related as it was to his concern for the theodicy of his principle of population.

All this takes us well into the nineteenth century, when the Princess Victoria's Uncle Leopold was already planning her marriage to Prince Albert. But what may be the most fascinating volumes in this collection, for many of us, belong to an earlier period—the books of travel and adventure of characters as diverse as the Jesuit missionaries and Captain Cook. Some of these works Malthus quoted in Books I and II of the second version of the *Essay on Population*, but we know that he bought a number of them second-hand much later on. While he was adrift in his London garrets, as we noted before, he had to make use of whatever authorities he could borrow. Clearly, in the course of his reading, he was enthralled by the records of long journeys into the unknown; the maps and pictorial engravings, sometimes mounted on fine linen, which unfolded right across his desk; the stories of faith and courage, determination and practical skill, and—above all—of curiosity, curiosity at once enthusiastic and cerebral, with which he was himself so splendidly endowed. Then, when he had the longed-for "power of purchasing books," and a home to put them in, he could buy such treasures as Frezier's *Voyage to the South-Sea, and along the coasts of Chili and Peru in the years 1712, 1713 and 1714*. Malthus was the archetypal home-lover who delighted in foreign travel, his own and other people's.

Specialists will study this catalogue through different spectacles: there is, for instance, an interesting number of pamphlets of the early 1790's, mainly in protest against the French revolutionary war and the repression of civil liberty in Britain. One is entitled *The Crisis Stated: or, Serious and Seasonable Hints upon War in General and upon the Consequences of a War with France.*[3] This is reminiscent of the pamphlet which Malthus himself wanted to add to the overflowing market in 1796, to be called simply *The Crisis*, but it was never published, and only a few second-hand quotations remain.

3 Listed in the Malthus Catalog under "Crisis"

What will puzzle economists about this catalogue are the books which we know Malthus possessed, and in some cases valued, but which are "missing," if that be the appropriate word. To give but two examples: even in his unsettled days, Malthus had his own copy of Adam Smith's *Wealth of Nations*, the sixth edition of 1791 in three volumes; this is the one he quoted in all his works. In this catalogue, the only edition listed is McCulloch's annotated version of 1828, in four volumes; there is no mention of Garnier's French edition of 1802, Playfair's of 1805, or Buchanan's of 1814, although we have Malthus's comments on all three of them. Again, the only translation of the *Essay on Population* in the catalogue is that of Hegewisch, in German, a language which Malthus could not read. Malthus's French translator, Pierre Prévost, was a personal friend, and in the 1817 edition of *Population*, Malthus quoted one of Prévost's notes with approval; yet this important book is no longer in the Malthus library.

Old Pop may well have given away some of his books during his life-time. His widow probably presented others to particular friends, colleagues and pupils. When she left Hertfordshire with her surviving daughter to join her unmarried sisters in Bath, she no doubt took with her the novels of Jane Austen and Sir Walter Scott; we know from the diary of a colleague's daughter, Fanny Mackintosh, that these two writers were greatly appreciated by both sexes at the East India College. Somebody, somewhere, may yet have the good fortune to pick up a book which once belonged to Malthus.

The subsequent history of this library is not without pathos. Malthus's son Henry married a daughter of his father's old friend, William Otter, and died childless in 1882. He was the vicar of Effingham, in Surrey, not far away from his cousin Colonel Malthus, who lived at Albury, and to whom he bequeathed his library. This cousin was descended from Robert's elder brother, Sydenham Malthus II, who lived from 1754 to 1821, and who seems to have been an unimpressive character. His only surviving son, Sydenham III (1801-1868) is said to have inherited the eccentricity of his grandfather Daniel: in spite of having eleven children, or perhaps because of this, he admired his uncle but long postponed buying an engraving of Linnell's portrait of Malthus "on account of the price"; he finally ordered Linnell to send him a print "*immediately*, as I am leaving for the Continent." There is a tradition that some of his younger children were slung in baskets under the family coach on these occasions, as there was no room for them inside.

Two of Sydenham II's sons emigrated to New Zealand, where the Malthus family flourished exceedingly, now numbering about four hundred, the adults working mainly in the learned professions, as one might expect. The eldest son, Sydenham IV (1831-1916) is still remembered by those who saw him when they were very little children, "an old man with rosy cheeks and a big, white beard, looking like Father Christmas." He was Colonel of the 94th Regiment of Foot, and made a Companion of the Bath for his services. A cousin wrote that "a hill somewhere in Africa was *nearly* called Mount Malthus after him"; it is probably as well that the mountain was named after another soldier, for it would inevitably have been associated with Population Malthus, and there might have been much confusion and bewilderment.

Colonel Malthus was born in a charming house in Albury known as The Cottage, although we should not so describe a dwelling with two staircases and ten acres of land attached to it. On some of these acres in 1871, shortly after his marriage, Colonel Malthus built what an agent might have advertised as an imposing family residence, called Dalton Hill. Here Malthus's books were housed after Henry's death, and for this reason the collection was called the Dalton Hill Library for many years.

John Maynard Keynes visited Dalton Hill when he was working on his biographical sketch of Robert Malthus. The owner was then Colonel Malthus's only surviving son, another Robert, who lived from 1881 to 1972; he was educated at Winchester and Trinity College, Cambridge, and became the first graduate apprentice ever to be employed by a British railway company. He spent his working life overseas, managing railways in Trinidad, Sierra Leone, and Ceylon—now Sri Lanka. At first, during his long retirement in the Isle of Wight, he enjoyed sailing and gardening; the increasing interest in Old Pop (whose portrait, with "Mrs. Pop," had a place of honour in his sitting-room) was a source of gentle amusement, and he welcomed with endearing modesty the visits of two prominent Malthusians, Dr. McCleary and Professor Minami of Tokyo. Later he bore with courage the amputation of both legs, on account of his diabetes, and took to making rugs, the most useful employment possible for "an old buffer in a wheel-chair."

The late Mr. Malthus never grumbled over the social changes in England which completely altered the life-style of the professional classes. On his retirement, it was obvious that Dalton Hill could no longer be kept up, nor could room be found for a library in the much smaller houses to which he and his wife had to move for their last years. Mr. and Mrs. Malthus had no children, and so another cousin, the late Mr. Reginald Bray, agreed to keep the books in the family; he did not want them, but he had space for them in his servant's hall. Here they remained until after the second world war, when it became impossible to preserve them there any longer, and Jesus College agreed to accept the collection.*

Both Malthus's family and his college have been censured for what appears to be their casual attitude towards the library of a very great man, one whose name has added a new word to a number of languages. This criticism is unjust. The

---

* Note: Since the information from Jesus College indicates that the donation was made by Edward Bray rather than Reginald Bray, Mrs. James gives the following explanation:

"I certainly understood that Reginald Bray gave the books to the College, 'just in time,' before he died in 1950. On the other hand, it is quite possible that Edward 'wrote the letters.' Sir Edward Bray (born 1874) was five years younger than Reginald; I don't know when he died, but in 1944 he was living at Rye in Sussex. I cannot imagine that the library—its accretions and remains—would have been given to the College without consultation amongst the family."

Malthus family belonged to a caste who believed in carrying their worldly successes as lightly as they carried their learning, without pomposity or swagger: to them, any kind of showing-off was bad form, and to swank about distinguished relations was the most reprehensible of all types of boastfulness; to sell the books would have been unthinkable. The Master and Council of Jesus College understood the family's point of view. They did not really want a higgledy-piggledy accumulation of assorted literature, at an uneasy period of postwar readjustment. However, they did their immemorial duty as an ancient seat of learning, and kept the books safe through what might be called the Dark Ages, as far as interest in Malthus was concerned.

Now in 1982, nearly 150 years after Malthus's death, America has come to the rescue, and the high-principled tenacity of family and college are justified. Scholars in many fields should be grateful to all of them, the Pergamon Press, Jesus College, the Malthus family and, of course, to Old Pop himself, who made such good use of his moderate power of purchasing books.

Chipping Norton
March 1982

INTRODUCTORY REMARKS

by

William Petersen*

Most people know that Reverend Thomas Malthus predicted that the world's population would outgrow its food supply, and some specialists are able to supplement this statement with such telling details as that he was born on St. Valentine's Day or that, contrary to his advice to others, he produced a family of truly prodigious size. The only thing not generally known is that all of this is fiction—his name, his birthday, his family, his occupation, and his theory. Legends propounded during his lifetime have spread to the most prestigious places. The wrong date of birth is chiseled on the memorial tablet in Bath Abbey; the introduction to the Everyman edition of the *Essay on Population* repeats the myth that Malthus had eleven daughters. For decades the adjective "Malthusian" labeled a movement to spread a doctrine that Malthus had specifically opposed. Currently phrases like "Malthusian pressure" unknowingly refer to the first of seven editions of the *Essay*, ignoring the crucial emendations in the other six. As I wrote in my recent book on Malthus, "If we adopt the cynical definition of a classic, a work that everyone cites and no one reads, then the *Essay on Population* must be designated a superclassic—written by a man whose name has entered all the Western languages but whose central ideas are often not accurately known even by professional demographers."

Happily, at long last this neglect and misunderstanding are being dissipated. In 1979 there appeared the first biography ever—*Population Malthus: His Life and Times*, by Patricia James. My own *Malthus* (1979) was the first book in English to relate his theories to current issues since James Bonar's work, published in 1885 and in a second edition in 1924. Also in that year there was a conference on Malthus in Paris, with mostly appreciative papers by scholars from around the world. In short, the man whose work on population marked the beginning of modern demography, whose analysis of economics is no less significant than Ricardo's, is being given some of the recognition long due him.

As Mrs. James noted repeatedly, the difficulties in writing a biography a century and a half after its subject's death are stupendous. He led an active life, but many of the extant documents of his scholarship are no more than tantalizing. Mrs. James spent years traveling about England, visiting every surviving descendant of Malthus's brother and sister-in-law (there are no direct

---

* William Petersen is Robert Lazarus Professor of Social Demography Emeritus at Ohio State University, and the author of the 1979 monograph *Malthus*, published by Harvard University Press.

descendants) and every place where he lived or worked. For the second edition of the *Essay*, a quarto volume of 610 pages, Malthus consulted 102 works, and Mrs. James tried to track down and read all of them, some in "delightful seventeenth-century Latin," some "leather-bound books with the long *s*," the maps mounted on fine linen, showing gaps marked "Great Space of Land Unknown." She believed, and I agree, that an excellent way of coming to understand a man's ideas is to trace the path he took in arriving at his conclusions.

In that respect, too, there has been a marked change in the past several years. I was in England in the winter of 1976 doing research for my book, and I planned to visit Malthus's alma mater, Jesus College, Cambridge, to which a later member of the family donated his library. Setting aside several days for what I anticipated would be profitable and pleasant research, I arrived in Cambridge and, by appointment, met one of the librarians. She took me through several locked doors along a corridor to the end of one building's wing, where in a cold and gloomy room there was stored, uncatalogued, the personal library of one of the college's most famous graduates. A few small bulbs hung from the ceiling, and to read the title of a book taken at random from the shelves, I had to carry it over to one of these skimpy lights. It was impossible to reach the top shelves, for no stools or ladders were available. Bundled up in my overcoat, I asked the librarian how one could work under such conditions, and she suggested that I might return on a pleasant summer day.

Now, a few short years later, the mountain has come to Mohammed. This book gives a full listing of the works in the Malthus library, which any reader is free to peruse at any season whatever in the comfort of his own home. In Malthus's day it was usual, because often necessary, that each man doing research on any topic would collect his own reference works, and a list of a scholar's complete holdings gives a relatively full view of what engaged his mind. Of course, such an indicator cannot be perfect, and in this instance some of the imperfections are manifest. Some of the works that Malthus consulted and cited are not included; if he owned them once, much could have happened to them in the long interval before the library was catalogued. Jesus College acquired the collection only in 1949, and it contains quite a number of volumes published after 1834, when Robert Malthus died. The several novels of Dickens, for instance, must represent later purchases, for Dickens's first book, *Sketches by Boz*, was published in 1836-37. A number of works, as those on gardening and cooking, can be identified by their bookplates as the property of other persons, which by various routes ended up as part of this collection. Even with such faults, the list of Robert Malthus's library affords an illuminating view of the man.

That Malthus was well read in his professional specialties we know without circumstantial corroboration. It is no surprise that there are pamphlets and books on taxes, grain imports, the state of Ireland and of the poor, the nature of value and the meaning of currency, and population. The classics are represented: Adam Smith, David Ricardo, and Jean-Baptiste Say, William

Petty and Francis Place, as well as most of the works of William Godwin, Malthus's perennial adversary. These represented sectors of his learning most manifest in his writings, and the more general works that underlay them are in some respects more revealing. Malthus owned several books by Thomas Frognall Dibdin, librarian to Lord Spencer at Althorp and a noted bibliomaniac (for the cure of that disorder he recommended the study of bibliography). To suggest purchases of books outside his immediate professional interests, Malthus may have used a book that he owned, Dibdin's *Library Companion; or, The Young Man's Guide, and the Old Man's Comfort, in the Choice of a Library*. In any case, his collection was wide in its range and discriminating in its taste. The one notable lacuna is mathematics. At Jesus, Malthus graduated as Ninth Wrangler (meaning, he received honors in mathematics), and in the occasional passages in his writings using the discipline he showed a continuing competence. Perhaps works on mathematics were some of those that were not retained in the library after Malthus's death.

Of the first ten books in the list, three are in French and two in Latin (including a Latin dictionary), and this proportion is more or less maintained throughout. Many of the Latin classics are represented, as well as Greek ones translated into Latin; these may be the remnants from Malthus's early schooling or undergraduate studies rather than what he read in his mature years. French, on the contrary, was evidently a true second language, and Italian a third one. But the only works in German are two dictionaries by Christian Ludwig—little used, one would guess.

Hobbes, Hume, and Locke are in the library, as well as Machiavelli complete in Italian, Descartes in the original Latin, Blackstone's *Commentaries*, the basic works of James Mill (as well as those of John Stuart Mill, purchased after 1834). These are what one might expect in the holdings of a professor of political economy, and the more personal choices reflect Malthus's predilection for rebellious spirits. William Frend, Malthus's tutor at Jesus until he was "banished" from the college after a notorious eight-day trial, has three of his works included. More significant is the list of Thomas Paine's pamphlets, not only *Common Sense* and *Rights of Man*, but relatively fugitive commentaries on Britain's army and system of finance. Though today Edmund Burke is seen as the prototypical conservative, at that time his defense of the American revolution, as a prime instance, was not well regarded in official circles; Malthus owned a complete 16-volume set of his writings, as well as many of them in duplicate copies. In the first third of the nineteenth century Malthus was England's most persistent and probably most influential proponent of free universal primary education, that most fundamental social reform. Joseph Lancaster founded a system of education based on "general Christian principles"—that is, not tied to the Anglican church; and Malthus owned one of the books describing his plan. Hannah More wrote poems and plays and then, in a more serious vein, expositions that led to the founding of the Religious Tract Society. Malthus owned none of the tracts, but his holdings did include the two-volume *Strictures on the Modern System of Female Education*.

At the time that Malthus attended Jesus College, Cambridge and Oxford were still partly Anglican seminaries, only partly the seats of secular learning that they would become. Like many other graduates, Malthus became a curate and for a while had a living at Okewood, Surrey, a village "truly remarkable throughout the eighteenth century," as Patricia James noted, "for its enormous number of baptisms and its small number of burials." Some volumes of sermons are in the library, but here too the level is far higher than the dull norm. Consider some authors of Malthus's books on religion: Richard Bentley, who had the assistance of Isaac Newton in writing *A Confutation of Atheism*; George Berkeley, one of the principal English philosophers of the eighteenth century; Thomas Arnold, who as head master raised Rugby to the rank of a great public school, later appointed Regius professor of modern history at Oxford; Thomas Chalmers, a professor of divinity at Edinburgh and an active pioneer in the formation of Scotland's Free Church; Jonathan Edwards, the American preacher and philosopher whose unorthodox teachings led to his dismissal from his church in Northampton, Massachusetts; Fénelon, archbishop of Cambrai, whose so-called Quietist doctrine of "interior inspiration" was condemned by the Vatican; and the eight distinguished authors of the *Bridgewater Treatises*, written in competition for a prize on the best demonstration of "the goodness of God manifested in the Creation." These were not the standard reading matter of the conventional Anglican cleric, and they were supplemented by such other works as the Koran, Henry Hart Milman's *History of the Jews*, Sydney Smith's eloquent pleas for Catholic emancipation, and authoritative works by Henry Thomas de la Beche on geology, which in the early nineteenth century was (what biology would become after Darwin's *Origin of Species*) the focus of antireligious argumentation. Malthus was for all his life a pious member of the Anglican church, but his writings were constructed on a foundation of empirical evidence. After he had been repeatedly attacked as an atheist or worse, he signed the later editions of the *Essay on Population* "Rev. T. R. Malthus"; but in fact he was professor of history and political economy, in the latter discipline the first such professor in Britain and probably in the world.

Economics may or may not be the dismal science that Carlyle termed it, but treatises in the subject are often dismally written, hardly less so a century and a half ago than now. Malthus's books, pamphlets, and articles are typically a pleasure to read. His cogently marshaled arguments indicate not only a mastery of the facts and a fine logical mind but also a sense of style. We should not be surprised, then, that the library is full of fine works of literature—Rabelais in French, Boccaccio in both Italian and French, *The Thousand and One Nights* in French, *Don Quixote*, Dante in Italian and English, Chaucer. He had a particular liking for poetry—from Milton through Byron, Pope to Coleridge and Cowper. It is even more evident that he enjoyed reading plays—Congreve, Molière in French, both Garrick's plays and a biography by Thomas Davies, the works of Beaumont and Fletcher, Samuel Ayscough's *Index to the Remarkable Passages and Words Made Use of by Shakespeare*. There are also names that fewer today would recognize—Mark Akenside, a distinguished physician who as an avocation wrote two volumes of poetry; Robert Bloomfield, a shoemaker who wrote *The Farmer's Boy*, among other poems; James Macpherson, who ostensibly translated *Fingal* from the Gaelic but in fact wrote most of it himself. The one literary form not well represented is the novel; Sterne's *Tristram Shandy* may be the only one in the library. Walter Scott's *Letters on Demonology and Witchcraft* one finds, but none of the Waverley novels or, for that matter, of his poetry. It is most remarkable, also, that there is nothing of Jane Austen, whose picture of middle-class country life so resembles what we imagine Malthus's must have been like that Mrs. James used some of her passages to fill in gaps in his biography.

The greatest difference between the first edition of the *Essay on Population* (1798) and the second (1803) is that in the first, population growth was held in check by an increase in mortality, in the second also by a reduction in fertility. In the following editions Malthus increasingly stressed the second factor: man can evade the lamentable consequences of too numerous a progeny by exercising self-control and reducing the size of his family. Another difference between the first and the second edition is in sheer size, from a mainly deductive book of some 55,000 words to a work of some 200,000 words in which the argument was illustrated by examples from around the world, roughly divided between what we would call developed and less developed countries. When present-day scholars undertake this kind of comparative analysis of social life, they usually collate a number of prior studies to bring them into the same framework. It was quite different at the beginning of the nineteenth century.

After the 1798 edition appeared Malthus traveled in Norway, and what he found there was an important stimulus to the revisions he made. Later he travelled whenever he could to the Continent, but generally his account of how the checks to population work in various societies was culled from a wide variety of travel books or memoirs concerning distant places. Some are well known: Captain James Cook's *A Voyage towards the South Pole, and Round the World*, Bougainville's *Voyage around the World*, Washington Irving's *A History of New-York*. George Barrington, whose real name was Waldron, was a famous pickpocket who ultimately was transported to Botany Bay; Malthus owned his account of the voyage to New South Wales and the natives "in the vicinity of Botany Bay." Sir John Barrow accompanied Lord Macartney on missions to China and the Cape of Good Hope, later writing a history of voyages to the Arctic region and other books of travel; Malthus had his account of treks into the interior or Southern Africa. *A Short Account of the Marratta State, Written in Persian by a Munshy* was translated by William Chambers, one of the two brothers who founded the famous *Chambers's Encyclopaedia*. Finally, one should note a book by the famous chemist and inventor of the miner's safety lamp, Sir Humphry Davy—*Consolations in Travel, or the Last Days of a Philosopher*, published posthumously in 1830, or only four years before Malthus's own death.

Another work by Davy has often been compared with Izaak Walton's famous disquisition—*Salmonia: or Days of Fly Fishing*. It was one of two books on fly fishing that Malthus owned, and he also had works on hunting and rural sports generally, not to mention *The Manures Most Advantageously Applicable to the Various Sorts of Soils*. If the two-volume *Ornithological Dictionary; or, Alphabetical Synopsis of British Birds* can be taken as evidence, Malthus was a bird watcher; and he also owned the equally serious four-volume *Introduction to Entomology; or, Elements of the Natural History of Insects*, as well as a work by one Jacques Barbut illustrating Linnaeus's classic exposition on insects. The region where Malthus lived was indeed England's green and pleasant land, and we can imagine him strolling along country lanes and seeking out details of the natural world. The library also gives us hints about indoor diversions. Two books on chess by the grand master Philidor suggest how some evenings were spent.

If a man has written important works but otherwise maintained his private life away from prying eyes, how can we many generations later get an inkling about how he lived, what he did other than working at his desk and teaching students? Few modes of investigation are likely to be so rewarding as a perusal of his library, for a person whose life is centered on intellectual pursuits will buy a book on anything he does or thinks about, whether it is political issues, travel to the places he never got to, or watching butterflies on his daily walk.

Carmel, California
March 1982

INTRODUCTORY REMARKS

by

John Pullen*

In publishing this Catalogue of the Malthus Library and in proposing to microfilm the contents of the Library, Jesus College and Pergamon Press have opened up a wonderful opportunity for further research into the life and thought of Malthus in particular, and into the intellectual history of his times in general.

Until now research on the Malthus Library has involved either a personal visit to Jesus College, or an enquiring letter to the Keeper of the Old Library. The former alternative is not always practicable, especially for antipodean students of Malthus; but when the pilgrimage is undertaken, the experience of working with Malthus's own books in the old-world atmosphere of the College Library is memorable and rewarding. The latter alternative produces a detailed response, but is hardly a fair and viable procedure, given the increasing output of Malthus studies. This microfilming project will give worldwide accessibility to the Malthus Library, and will greatly facilitate and stimulate research into its contents.

Some caution needs to be exercised if the Malthus Library as it now stands is to be used as evidence of Malthus's reading habits and personal interests, and as an indication of the authors who might have influenced the development of his thought. One would first need to know which items in the Malthus Library as it now stands were originally acquired by Malthus for his own use, and whether there are any items which were once part of the library that Malthus used but are no longer. Unfortunately these questions are very difficult, and will probably never be satisfactorily answered.

The surviving correspondence of Malthus and his father reveals some information about books owned and read, and it is to be hoped that further information about ownership and use will come from a search of the Library for book-plates, inscriptions, and manuscript annotations. If an energetic Malthus scholar has already undertaken this search, the results will be awaited with great interest.

Even if it becomes possible to identify the books held by Malthus himself, it still would not be legitimate to conclude that those books, and those books alone, influenced Malthus. Such a conclusion would involve an unacceptable

---

* Dr. John Pullen is Professor of Economics at the University of New England in Armidale, Australia and is nearing completion of a variorum edition of Malthus's *Principles of Political Economy.*

degree of bibliographical determinism. It is conceivable that he was influenced by sources other than his books. It is also conceivable that he did not read all the books he possessed, or that he did not remember all that he read.

We know that Malthus was acquiring books on his own account when he entered Jesus College at the end of 1784. In a letter to his father, Daniel Malthus, of November 14, 1784, the day before his first lecture, he said: "I have subscribed to a bookseller who has supplied me with all the books necessary."[1] We could assume that his book-acquiring period began at the latest at the end of 1784, and lasted for fifty years until his death in 1834. However, it is possible that part—perhaps even a large part—of the Library was initially acquired by Malthus's father. As a landowner of considerable wealth, with scientific and intellectual interests, and himself an author,[2] it is quite likely that Daniel Malthus possessed a good library. A brief glimpse of a part of his library is provided in his letter of 13 January 1786 to Malthus at Cambridge, in which he recommended that his son read "Rutherford's *Philosophy*, ... Sanderson's *Optics*, Emerson's *Mechanics*, Long's *Astronomy* [which] you certainly have, ... and Bouguer's *Mensuration of the degree in South America*"; from which we can assume that these works were part of Daniel's library. In the same letter Daniel enquired, "Did not I ask you whether you had got my Theocritus with you?" from which we can assume that Malthus was in the habit of making good use of his father's library.[3]

When Daniel Malthus and his wife died in 1800, did the Library pass to Malthus, and was it taken by him to the East India College in 1805? Or did it pass first of all to Malthus's elder brother, Sydenham, and did Malthus's personal ownership of it commence only after Sydenham's death in 1821?

After Malthus's death in 1834 the Library apparently passed to his son, Henry, Vicar of Effingham. A book plate reads "Ex libris Henrici Malthus olim patris sui T.R. Malthus Collegio Jesus Cantab.," with the motto "Honor virtutis praemium. Henry Malthus. Effingham Vicarage." And after Henry's death in 1882, or perhaps after the death of Henry's wife, Sophia, in 1889, the Library seems to have passed to Colonel Sydenham Malthus, C.B. (1831-1916), who was the grandson of Malthus' brother, Sydenham (1754-1821).[4] A MS. catalog of the Library was prepared in 1891, and its title page reads:

---

1 See J. Bonar, *Malthus and His Work*, ed. 2, 1924, pp. 407-8. The identification of 1784-1834 as his book-acquiring period does not of course mean that he did not acquire books published before 1784.

2 Malthus said that the pieces written by his father came from "the original copious source of his own fine understanding and genius." See [W. Otter], *Memoir of Robert Malthus*, in T.R. Malthus, *Principles of Political Economy*, ed. 2, 1836; reprinted A. M. Kelley, New York, 1968, p. xxii.

3 See Otter, *op.cit.*, p. xxvi. The Malthus Library contains Roger Long's *Astronomy*, and *Theocriti quae extant*, but not the other works recommended by Daniel.

4 See the family tree in Mrs. Patricia James, *The Travel Diaries of T.R. Malthus*, Cambridge University Press, 1966, facing p. 316.

"Catalogue of Books,/(Formerly belonging to the Rev. H.R. Malthus, M.A.)/In the Library at/Dalton Hill,/Albury, Surrey./ The Property of Sydenham Malthus. C.B./1891."[5]

The Library no doubt passed from Henry to Colonel Sydenham because Henry and Sophia had no surviving children, and because, following the rules of primogeniture, Colonel Sydenham was the eldest grandson of Malthus's elder brother.

At some time after the death of Colonel Sydenham Malthus in 1916, the Library passed to Reginald Arthur Bray, 1869-1950, the great-grandson of Malthus's sister, Mary Anne Catherine (1771-1852), and Edward Bray (d. 1814). The following letter[6] was written by J.M. Keynes to R.A. Bray in 1938:

Kings College, Cambridge.
November 11, 1938

R.A. Bray Esq.,
The Manor House
Shere,
Guildford.

Dear Mr. Bray,

I am interested to hear what you tell me about the Malthus Library, and very glad to learn that it is passing into secure hands.
As the Malthus family are leaving the district, it will be useful to have a record as to what is happening to the portraits, particularly the two small ones of Malthus and his wife which hung, I think, in the Library. There was another one of Malthus's son, but, of course, that is only of secondary interest.

Many thanks for writing and letting me know.

Yours sincerely,
(signed) J.M. KEYNES

In 1949 R.A. Bray offered the economics section of the Malthus Library to the Marshall Library of Economics at the University of Cambridge, but because of limited space at the Marshall Library, the complete Malthus Library was given, on the suggestion of Mr. P. Sraffa, to Jesus College.

---

5 A copy of this 1891 Catalogue was kindly supplied by Mr. D.J.V. Fisher, Keeper of the Old Library, Jesus College, Cambridge. The 1891 Catalogue contains many pre-1835 items that are not in the current Catalogue, and only about one-half of the items in the current Catalogue are in the 1891 catalogue. A more complete picture of Malthus's library will be provided when the two catalogues are published and collated, and when a full list of all the authors cited by Malthus in all his publications and correspondence is prepared.

6 A photocopy of this letter was supplied by the County Archivist, Guildford Muniment Room, Guildford, England. Acknowledgement is made to Mrs. Handa Bray, High House, Shere, the present owner of the Bray papers.

It is only to be expected that during these changes of ownership and location some of the contents of Malthus's library would go astray, and also that some subsequent users after Malthus might add pre-1835 items.

Of the scores of books cited by Malthus in his various publications—and therefore presumably owned by him—many have unfortunately not survived in the Malthus Library today. For example, there are no holdings of Barton, Buchanan, Garnier, Humboldt, Pitkin, Senior, Shuckburgh, Sinclair, Storch, T.P. Thompson, Torrens, and West, all of whom Malthus cited in his *Principles of Political Economy*. And those authors who figure in the Library are not always represented by the books one would expect. For example, there is McCulloch's edition of the *Wealth of Nations*, but not the sixth edition of 1791 which Malthus quoted frequently in his *Principles*, nor the single volume edition published by Thomas Nelson and Peter Brown, Edinburgh, which was used by Malthus's students at the East India College—for example, J.D. Inverarity (1829 ed.). There is the third edition (1821) of Ricardo's *Principles*, but not the first and second editions. There is Lauderdale's *Observations...on the Review of his Inquiry*, 1804, but not his *Inquiry*, 1804. There is one book by F.M. Eden, but it is not *The State of the Poor* whose statistics Malthus used in extensive calculations of average wheat prices. There are two historical books by Simonde de Sismondi, but not his *De la Richesse Commerciale*, 1803, nor his *Nouveaux Principes d'Economie Politique*, 1819 and 1827, which were used by Malthus. Say's *Cours Complet*, 1828-29, is there, but not his *Traité d'Economie Politique* (Malthus referred to the second, fourth and fifth editions of the *Traité*), nor his *Lettres à M. Malthus*. Even Malthus's own works are not complete—in particular, his *Definitions in Political Economy*, 1827, is missing.

Also, some books received by Malthus as gifts and acknowledged (usually belatedly) in his correspondence are no longer in the Library. For example, in a letter of January 31, 1815, he thanks Sir John Sinclair for his gift of the *General Report of the Agricultural State and Political Circumstances of Scotland*, 1814, and states that he had already read Sinclair's *Husbandry of Scotland*, but neither is in the Library.[7]

Even though the Library is not now exactly as Malthus left it, it will still be of great value to researchers. But if we wish to use the Library as evidence of Malthus's personal and intellectual life, it will be important to avoid the argument that, because a particular pre-1835 book is in the Library, therefore Malthus must have used it and been influenced by it; and that because a particular pre-1835 book is not in the Library, therefore Malthus did not own it or use it, and was not influenced by it.

With these reservations in mind, the Library opens up many interesting avenues of speculation concerning Malthus's personal life, his family environment, and the development of his ideas. Perhaps the most striking feature of the Library for the reader glancing through this Catalogue for the first time, is the breadth of its contents, and by implication the breadth of

7 See *The Correspondence of the Right Honourable Sir John Sinclair,* Bart., 1831, Vol. I, pp. 391-92.

interest of its owners.[8] In addition to the large number of books on political economy and history that one would expect in the library of a Professor of those two subjects, it includes books in theology, ethics, philosophy, classical literature, modern literature, politics, law, geology, geography, ornithology, fishing, cooking, art, architecture, horticulture, landscaping, education, as well as many books of travels and miscellaneous works too varied to categorise. A considerable number of the books are in foreign languages— Latin, Greek, French, Italian and German.

In political economy there are books by James Anderson, Bailey, Baring, Beeke, Burke, Thomas Chalmers, Child, Colquhoun, Crumpe, Eden, Frend, Ganilh, Godwin, John Gray, Simon Gray, Hume, Jones, Lauderdale, Mably, Mercier de la Rivière, McCulloch, James Mill, Mun, Mushet, Necker, Owen, Paine, Petty, Place, Price, Ravenstone, Ricardo, Rooke, Sadler, Say, Scrope, Adam Smith, Charles Smith, Spence, Steuart, Tooke, Turgot, Weyland, Young, and others, as well as most of Malthus's own works. In all there are about 150 books on political economy, about 10 per cent of the total.[9]

A major section of the Library consists of books by or on classical Greek and Roman authors, their number exceeding the works on political economy. Some of these books date from the seventeenth and sixteenth centuries—for example, a 1567 edition of *Tragoediae selectae Aeschyli, Sophoclis, Euripidis*—and suggest the interest of a bibliophile, as well as a classical scholar. This is confirmed by the presence of several works on book collecting by Thomas Dibdin—for example, *An introduction to the knowledge of rare and valuable editions of the Greek and Latin Classics*, 1804.

In addition to classical literature the Library contains a large collection of modern literature—novels, plays and poetry.[10] They represent as much as one-fifth of the total and exceed the number of books on political economy. They include the *Works* of a number of authors—for example, Robert Burns (1808), Byron (two sets, 1827 and 1832-33),[11] Chaucer (two sets, 1602 and 1782), Fielding (1767), Milton (two sets, 1753 and 1776), Pope (1797), Ben Johnson (1816), Molière (two sets, 1750 and 1773), Rabelais

8 It is possible that some of the pre-1835 works now in the Library were acquired, not by Malthus for his own use and interest, but by or on behalf of various members of the households using the Library—for example, Malthus's mother, sisters, wife and daughters. Malthus might or might not have shared their interests. And after Malthus's death, pre-1835 books could have been added to cater for the interests of the later households in which the Library resided. Mrs. Patricia James has already noted that the Library includes a number of books—including French cookery books—owned by Jane Dalton, a cousin of Daniel Malthus. (*Population Malthus: His Life and Times*, Routledge & Kegan Paul, 1979, pp. 12, 78.)

9 Bentham, Cazenove, Cobbett, Condorcet, de Quincey, Everett, Hodgskin, Thompson, Quesnay, Whewell (on economics), and Whately are further notable omissions.

10 In his *Memoir of Robert Malthus*, William Otter said that Malthus "found sufficient time for the cultivation of history and general literature, particularly of poetry, of which he was always a great admirer and discerning judge." See Otter, *op.cit.*, p. xxxv; quoted by Mrs. James (1979), p. 27.

11 The presence of two sets of the *Works* of a number of authors could mean either that the second set was acquired as part of a bibliophile's collection, or that the Library as it now stands is a combination of two or more libraries.

(1675), and Thomas Southerne (1721). Other authors represented include Boccaccio, Samuel Butler, Cervantes, Chateaubriand, Congreve, George Crabbe, Dryden, Goethe (in French), Samuel Johnson, La Fontaine, Petrarca, Racine, Samuel Richardson, Schiller, Smollett, Spenser, Sterne, Swift and Voltaire; as well as many minor authors, including Maria Edgeworth's *Tales and Novels*, 18 volumes, 1832-33. There is only one book by Sir Walter Scott in this current Catalogue but there are over thirty pre-1835 books of Scott in the 1891 Catalogue. It is clear that the owners and users of this Library had more than a casual interest in literature.

An interesting sub-category of the literature section is a collection of contemporary theatrical plays, of a light or even frivolous nature; for example, Susannah Centlivre, *The Wonder: A Woman Keeps a Secret, a Comedy, as it is now acted at the Theatre-Royal in Drury-Lane*, 1758; Hannah Cowley, *A Bold Stroke for a Husband, a Comedy, as acted at the Theatre-Royal in Covent-Garden*, 1784; Mrs. Elizabeth Inchbald, *Wives As They Were, and Maids As They Are, A Comedy, in 5 Acts, performed at the Theatre Royal, Covent-Garden*, 1797. One would not expect to find such works in the library of the "Parson" who founded the "Dismal Science." Were they purchased by Malthus or by his father? Was Malthus a regular patron of the modern theatre during the period that Mrs. James has called his "fallow decade," 1788-1798? Some of the works were published in the 1790's. However there are very few dated after 1800 (the year of his father's death), and this might suggest that the lighter sort of drama was an interest of Daniel rather than Robert. But even if Malthus did not purchase them, or attend the performances, did he read them? Did he enjoy them? James Bonar has stated: "Among [Daniel's] occasional relaxations the drama, with Mrs. Siddons and Kemble to play, was evidently a favourite, as it was with his son Robert." (*Op.cit.*, p. 403)

In contrast with these light plays, the Library also contains a large number of theological and ethical books. One would expect to find a certain number of such books in a library used by two clergymen—the Reverend Robert Malthus and the Reverend Henry Malthus—but the number and intellectual depth of the theological books in this Library suggest a more than normal interest in that field.

Did any of the theological books belong to Daniel Malthus? His granddaughter Louisa Bray wrote of him in her *Recollections* (1857) that he "was not a religious man, but he had a respect for religion, and would never allow light conversation on such a subject in his presence," (quoted by Mrs. James [1979], p.13). But Daniel's action in sending Malthus for part of his schooling to the Dissenting Academy in Warrington—founded to provide a liberal education for the sons of dissenters and particularly of dissenting ministers—suggests that he was concerned about religious issues, and partial towards radical theology. Is it no more than a coincidence that the number of theological and ethical books is almost exactly the same (about 150) as the number of books in political economy? It would be hazardous to draw any definite conclusion from this fact, given the reservations that need to be borne in mind in interpreting the contents of the Library. But it remains nevertheless an interesting fact, particularly for any interpreter who sees the first edition of the *Essay on Population* as not merely a work on demography in the modern narrow sense, but also as a work in natural theology. Even if it could be shown that the majority of the theological books were acquired by Daniel Malthus—and indeed the bulk of them pre-date 1785—it is quite possible that Malthus would have been familiar with them. Were any of these theological writers responsible for the radical, if not heretical, views on hell, annihilationism,[12] and divine omnipotence expressed by Malthus in the first edition of the *Essay*? Who was it who was sufficiently interested in Fenelon to buy his complete *Works*? The sixty or so theological books dated 1784-1834 fall mainly into two distinct intervals, viz. the first ten years of that period, and the last ten years. Does this suggest that Malthus's interest in theological questions waxed from 1784-1794 and from 1824-1834, but waned in the thirty years in between?

The Library contains also a smattering of scientific books, about thirty in all, on a variety of topics including entomology, botany, astronomy, chemistry, physiology, medicine, ornithology, geology, and geography. Malthus's interest in geology was indicated in his letter to William Whewell of Februry 28, 1831, where he stated that he had read Whewell's review of Lyell's *Geology* in the *British Critic* "with very great gratification and instruction."[13] The works on geology in the Library include Sir Charles Lyell, *Principles of Geology*, 3 volumes, 1830. Malthus's interest in geography and chemistry was indicated in a letter of April 17, 1788, (after his graduation) to his father where he said, "I have laid aside my chemistry for a while and am at present endeavouring to get some knowledge of general history and geography."[14] But one would have expected to find in the Library a greater collection of books on botany. Malthus's father was a keen botanist, an interest he derived from Rousseau. Malthus's comments on the flora of Scandinavia in a letter to his father from Stockholm, dated 18th August 1799, show that he shared this interest.[15] The small number of books on botany might be explained by the fact that in his will Daniel Malthus left to Jane Dalton "all my Botanical Books in which the Name of Rousseau is written, likewise a Box of Plants given me by Mons. Rousseau."[16] Although some of Jane Dalton's cookery books became part of the Library, some or all of her inherited botany books apparently went elsewhere.

The Library is remarkable also for its lack of books on mathematics, given that Malthus was Ninth Wrangler in his year. There is Newton's *Principia*

---

12 Malthus in 1798 was apparently unconvinced by Philip Burton, *Annihilation no punishment to the wicked after the day of judgement*, 1792.

13 See N.B. de Marchi and R.P. Sturges, *Malthus and Ricardo's Inductionist Critics: Four Letters to William Whewell, Economica*, N.S., Vol. 40, 1973, p. 390.

14 See Bonar, *op.cit.*, p. 412.

15 See Bonar, *op.cit.*, pp. 415-16.

16 See Bonar, *op.cit.*, p. 402.

Mathematica, 1726;[17] Euclid's *Elements*, two copies, 1660 and 1756; and a set of log tables. A letter from Malthus to Macvey Napier of August 28, 1822, about the article on population that Malthus was writing for the *Encyclopaedia Britannica* implies that Malthus would have used logarithms in the article if Macvey Napier had thought the readers could understand them.[18] This comparative absence of books on mathematics suggests either that subsequent users of the Library removed them or that Malthus lost interest in mathematics. He believed that political economy was closer to ethics and politics than to mathematics. There is very little mathematics in his published works, and what there is, is not very sophisticated. In his letters to Whewell of May 26, 1829, and May 31, 1831, he had to admit that he had never been very familiar with algebra and had not had the occasion to use it for many years.[19] He referred to fluxions (calculus) in several places, particularly in relation to his "doctrine of proportions," but his colleague at the East India College, William Dealtry, is represented in the library by his *Sermons*, not by his *Fluxions*.

The large number of books in French (about 170, or one-eighth of the total) comes as no surprise. Malthus's quotations from French works show that he read French easily. Henry Malthus spent holidays in France, and Daniel Malthus corresponded (in French) with Rousseau. It is surprising however that there is only one book by Rousseau (*Emile*, 1762) in the Library.

The twenty or so books in Italian in the Library raise the question of whether Malthus could read Italian. Bonar stated that although there is no record of Malthus having studied Italian as a student, he "certainly knew [Italian] afterwards."[20] Were the Italian books bought and read by Malthus, or were they added to the Library by Malthus's brother, Sydenham, who spent a number of years with his family in Italy?[21] Several of the Italian books were published after Sydenham's death in 1821.

By contrast with the French and Italian books, there are only six books in German, including two dictionaries and a translation of Malthus's *Essay*. In a letter to his father of February 4, 1799, Malthus referred to his own inability to read German. He expressed interest in obtaining several books, including Süssmilch's *Göttliche Ordnung*, but added that it would have to be in a French or English translation.[22] He subsequently quoted Süssmilch in his *Essay on Population* and his *Principles of Political Economy*, but there is no copy of

---

17 Mrs. James (1979) has noted (p. 29) that Malthus bought this work second-hand and embossed it with his College Arms.

18 See British Museum, Add. MSS. 34613, f.96.

19 See de Marchi and Sturges, *op.cit.*, pp. 387, 390.

20 Bonar, *op.cit.*, p.407.

21 See letter of Malthus to Prevost October 13, 1815, and March 30, 1818, in G.W. Zinke, *Six Letters from Malthus to Pierre Prevost*, *Journal of Economic History*, Vol. 2, 1942, pp. 174-189.

22 See Bonar. *op.cit.*, pp. 414-15. It is possible of course that Malthus learned German after 1799.

Süssmilch in the Library. This supports Mrs. James's view (1979, p.471) that Malthus quoted Süssmilch indirectly from a secondary source. But if Malthus could not read German, who acquired the German books for the Library? The pre-1800 German books might have been bought by Daniel Malthus. When an obituary writer said that Daniel had translated Goethe's *Werther*, Malthus denied it on the grounds that the work of a mere translator was unworthy of his father's abilities, but in denying it he did not say that his father was incapable of translating German, which if it had been the case would have been the obvious reply.[23]

Malthus's tutors—Richard Graves, Gilbert Wakefield and William Frend—are well represented with four, eleven and three works respectively. Was Graves's translation of Giovanni della Casa, *Galateo: or, A treatise of politeness and delicacy of manners*, 1774, required reading for the young Malthus and his fellow pupils?

The Library also reveals something of the pastimes and leisure activities of those who used it. For the hobby-farmer there were Thomas Bucknall's *The Orchardist: or, a system of close pruning and medication, for establishing the science of orcharding*, 1797; John Evelyn's *Silva: or A discourse of forest-trees...*, 1776; and Richard Kirwan's *The manures most advantageously applicable to the various sorts of soils*, 1796.

For the gourmet members of the Malthus households, there were Brillat-Savarin, *Physiologie du goût, ou Meditations de gastronomie transcendante*, 1828; Menon, *La cuisinière bourgeoisie*, 1775; Parmentier, *Le parfait boulanger, ou Traité complet sur la fabrication et le commerce du pain*, 1778; and for the perfect host, Grimod de la Reynière, *Manuel des amphitryons; contenant un traité de la dissection des viandes à table*, 1808.

For the outdoor sportsman, there were *The Fly Fisher's Guide illustrated by coloured plates*, 1828, by George Bainbridge; *Rural Sports*, 1801-2, by William Daniel; and *Salmonia; or Days of Fly Fishing*, 1832, by Sir Humphry Davy; while for indoor activities, there were several books on chess.

The Malthus Library as it now exists cannot be regarded as, and does not pretend to be, the exact library used by Malthus. But it is nevertheless an important collection of books that are interesting both in themselves and as suggestions for further speculation and research into the life and thought of Malthus. A very remarkable feature of the Library is the fact that it has survived as a distinct collection, despite the fact that over the last 150 years its increasing commercial value, and the cost and inconvenience of caring for it, must have on occasions been an argument for its dispersal. Its survival is a tribute to Malthus, to the subsequent generations of the Malthus family, and to Jesus College.

Armidale, Australia
April 1982

23 See Otter, *op.cit.*, p. xxii, and Bonar, *op.cit.*, p. 403.

THE MALTHUS LIBRARY CATALOGUE

ABERCROMBIE, John (1780-1844)
MB.5.26 Inquires concerning the intellectual powers and the investigation of truth. 3rd ed. 8°, Edinburgh, 1832.

ABREGE
ME.2.22 Abrégé de l'histoire ancienne, en particulier de l'histoire grecque, suivi d'un abrégé de la fable... 12°, Londres, 1802.

ABU TALIB IBN MUHAMMAD KHAN (1752-1806)
MB.1.7-8 The travels of Mirza Abu Taleb Khan, in Asia, Africa, and Europe, during the years 1799-1803...Translated by C. Stewart. 2 vols. 8°, London, 1810.

ACADEMIE ROYALE DES INSCRIPTIONS ET BELLES-LETTRES
MF.6.5-7 Choix des Mémoires de l'Académie Royale des Inscriptions et Belles-Lettres. 3 vols. 4°, Londres, 1777.

ACCARIAS DE SERIONNE, JACQUES (1706-1792)
MA.3.3-4 See RICHESSE
La richesse de la Hollande, ouvrage dans lequel on expose l'origine du commerce & de la puissance des Hollandois...[By J. Accarias de Sérionne.] 2 vols. 1778.

[ED. NOTE: Malthus cited this work in Bk. III, Ch. IX of his later *Essay*.]

NOTE: Titles obviously added to Malthus's Library after his death in 1834 are indicated with an asterisk (*).
Most of the items prefixed with ME are titles which were added to the "Dalton Hill" Collection after the original 1891 listing was compiled. Items prefixed MX are titles added to the Collection by Jesus College after it was donated to them in 1949 and are indicated with two asterisks (**).

ACCOUNT

MH.5.7[3] An account of the proceedings, intentions, rules, and orders, of the Society for the Encouragement of Agriculture and Industry, instituted at Odiham in Hampshire... 8°, London, [1785].

ACHILLES TATIUS, Alexandrinus (fl. 2nd C.)

MF.1.19 Achillis Tatii de Clitophontis & Leucippes amoribus lib. VIII. Longi Sophistæ de Daphnidis & Chloes amoribus lib. IV. (Item Laurentij Gambaræ expositorum ex Longo libri IV. heroico carmine liberius redditi. Parthenij Nicæensis de amatoriis affectibus liber. I. Cornario interprete.) [Ed. by J. and N. Bonnuitius.] (Greek & Latin.) [Wants title-page.] 8°, [Heidelberg] 1601.

ADAIR, James Makittrick (1728-1802)

ML.3.12 A philosophical and medical sketch of the natural history of the human body and mind... 8°, Bath, 1787.

ADAM, Alexander (1741-1809)

MI.1.18 A compendious dictionary of the Latin tongue: for the use of schools. 2nd ed. 8°, Edinburgh, 1814.

ADDISON, Joseph (1672-1719)

MG.5.39 See FREE-HOLDER

The Free-holder, or political essays. (December 23, 1715 - June 25, 1716.) [A periodical, ed. by J. Addison.] 1716.

ADDISON, Joseph (1672-1719)

MG.5.42 See GUARDIAN

The Guardian. [A periodical by Sir. R. Steele, J. Addison and others.] 5th ed. Vol. 1. (March 12 to June 15, 1713.) 1729.

ADDISON, Joseph (1672-1719)

The lucubrations of Isaac Bickerstaff [i.e. Sir Richard Steele, J. Addison, and others.] [Other editions called The Tatler.] See TATLER.

ADDISON, Joseph (1672-1719)

For the Spectator, by J. Addison, Sir R. Steele, and others, See SPECTATOR.

ADDRESS

MH.3.21[1] An address to those citizens who, in their public and private capacity, resisted the claim of the late House of Commons to nominate the Ministers of the Crown. 3rd ed. 8°, London, 1788.

ADOLPHUS, John (1768-1845)

MC.6.18-20 The history of England, from the accession of King George the Third, to...1783. 2nd ed. 3 vols. 8°, London, 1805.

ÆLIANUS, Claudius (c. 170-235)
MI.2.8-9 Varia historia, ad MStos codices nunc primum recognita & castigata, cum versione J. Vulteji...et perpetuo commentario J. Perizonii. (Greek & Latin.) 2 vols. 8°, Lugduni in Batavis, 1701.

ÆSCHINES, the Orator (c. 397-c. 322 B.C.)
MF.3.30-31 See DEMOSTHENES

Δημοσθένους καί Αἰσχίνου οἱ περί τῆς παραπρεσβείας, κατά κτησιφωτός, καί περί τοῦ στεφάνου λόγοι ἀντίπαλοι

Graece et Latine [in the translation of H. Wolfius]. Edidit I. Taylor. 2 vols., 1769.

AESCHYLUS (525/4-458 B.C.)
MF.1.22-3 Tragœdiæ quae extant septem. Cum versione Latina, et lectionibus variantibus. 2 vols. 8°, Glasguæ, 1746.

AESCHYLUS (525/4-458 B.C.)
MM.1.38-40 Tragœdiæ selectæ Aeschyli, Sophoclis, Euripidis. Cum duplici interpretatione Latina, una ad verbè, altera carmine. Ennianae interpretationes locorè aliquot Euripidis. 3 vols. 16°, [Paris] 1567.

AESCHYLUS (525/4-458 B.C.)
MF.1.17-18 Tragœdiæ septem, cum versione Latina. [Ed. by R. Porson.] 2 vols. 8°, Oxoniae, 1806.

AIKIN, John (1747-1822)
MK.3.16 A view of the character and public services of the late John Howard, Esq. LL.D. F.R.S. 8°, London, 1792.

AIKIN, John (1747-1822)
MB.7.33 See SELECT
Select works of the British poets. With biographical and critical prefaces. By D[r]. Aikin. 1820.

AIKIN, John (1747-1822)
ME.5.31-40 See SELECT
Select works of the British poets. With biographical and critical prefaces. By D[r]. Aikin. 10 vols., 1821.

AKBAR, Emperor of Hindostan (1542-1605)
ML.5.5-6 Ayeen Akbery; or, The institutes of the Emperor Akber. Translated from the original Persian by F. Gladwin.
2 vols. 8°, London, 1800.

AKENSIDE, Mark (1721-1770)
ME.4.39 Poetical works. With the life of the author. 2 vols. in 1. (Bell's Edition. The Poets of Great Britain.) 12°, Edinburg, 1781.

ALCIPHRON
MI.4.10-11 Alciphron: or, The minute philosopher. In seven dialogues. Containing an apology for the Christian religion...[By G. Berkeley.] 2 vols. 8°, London, 1732.

ALDEBURGH, Edward Stratford, Second Earl of (d. 1801)
MH.4.29[8] See ESSAY
An essay on the true interests and resources of the Empire of the King of Great Britain and Ireland, &c. &c. &c. By the Earl of A—-H. [Aldeburgh.] 1783.

ALEMBERT, Jean Le Rond d' (1717-1783)
MB.2.28-9 See MELANGES
Mélanges de littérature, d'histoire, et de philosophie. [By J. Le R. d'Alembert.] Nouvelle éd., augmentée...Vols. 1, 2. 1763.

ALFRED
MH.5.7[4] Alfred, or A narrative of the...measures to suppress a pamphlet intituled, Strictures on the declaration of Horne Tooke, Esq. respecting...Mrs. Fitzherbert...[By P. Withers.] 4th ed. [Imperfect: wants all after p. 46.] 8°, London, 1789.

ALFRED
MH.4.21[1] Alfred unmasked: or, The new Cataline, intended as a pair of spectacles for the short-sighted politicians of 1789. [A reply to Philip Withers' pamphlet 'Alfred'.] 8°, London, 1789.

ALGAROTTI, Francesco, conte (1712-1764)
MK.2.28 Dialoghi sopra la luce, i colori, e l'attrazione. 8°, Napoli, 1752.

ALPHABETUM
MB.6.52[1] Alphabetum Græcum Regiis trium generum characteribus postremo excusum. 8°, Lutetiæ, 1566.

ALPHABETUM
MB.6.52[2] See also CEVALLERIUS
Alphabetum Hebraicum, in quo literæ Hebraicæ describuntur...Ex Antonii Ceuallerii recognitione. 8°, [Paris] 1566.

AMMIANUS MARCELLINUS (c. 330-395)
MC.7.3 Ammiani Marcellini rerum gestarum qui de XXXI. supersunt, libri XVIII. Ope MSS. codicum emendati ab H. Valesio...Ed. posterior...(2 pts.) F°, Parisiis, 1681.

AMSTERDAM

MJ.1.44 Le guide, ou Nouvelle description d'Amsterdam; enseignant aux voyageurs, et aux négocians, son origine, ses agrandissemens & son état actuel... 8°, Amsterdam, 1753.

ANACREON (560?-c. 475 B.C.)

ME.2.17 Anacreontis carmina. Accedunt selecta quædam e lyricorum reliquiis. Ed. 3ª locupletior. (Greek.) 12°, Argentorati, 1786.

ANDERSON, James (1739-1808)

MH.5.15[2] A calm investigation of the circumstances that have led to the present scarcity of grain in Britain... 2nd ed. 8°, London, 1801.

[ED. NOTE: In 1903, J.H. Hollander had the following comment regarding the views of James Anderson as expressed in "A Calm Investigation...," "Recent critical study has made clear that James Anderson, often urged as the real author of the Ricardian law of rent, strenuously insisted that a law of increasing, not of diminishing returns prevailed in intensive cultivation. The first edition of Malthus's 'Essay on the Principle of Population' (London, 1798) contained no explicit statement of a law of diminishing returns. But before the second edition of the *Essay* appeared in 1803, Malthus had read Anderson's 'A Calm Investigation of the Circumstances that have led to the Present Scarcity of Grain in Britain' (London, 1801), if no other of his writings, and had noted its characteristic assertion that increased population will always result in increased relative production. A criticism so fundamental of Malthus's own theory that population tended to outrun subsistence could not be neglected, and the second edition of the *Essay* contained (p. 473) a long note in reply to Anderson, while the text of the *Essay* thenceforth intimated a law of diminishing returns in unmistakable terms. We have no means of knowing whether Malthus was familiar with other of Anderson's writings in which rent was clearly explained as a consequence of differential costs in extensive cultivation, nor of the extent to which any such acquaintance may have influenced Malthus's thinking. Even more, the nature of the Haileybury lectures and their precise relation to the published essay on rent are uncertain. The most that can be hazarded is a reasonable likelihood that some part of the clear statement of the law of diminishing costs and of the co-ordination of extensive and intensive cultivation, which appeared in the tract on rent, figured in the Haileybury lectures, and that James Anderson is to be counted among the influences which may have affected Malthus's academic exposition." (From the Introduction to the reprint of Malthus's "The Nature and Progress of Rent" of 1815). In the later *Essay* the note on Anderson appears in Bk. III, Ch. XIV.—General Observations.]

ANDREWS, John (18th C.)

MC.4.6 The scripture-doctrine of grace. In answer to a treatise on the doctrine of grace by William [Warburton], Lord Bishop of Gloucester... 8°, London, 1763.

ANIMADVERSIONS

MH.5.23.[3] Animadversions on a Reverend Prelate's [Bishop Thomas Sherlock's] remarks upon the Bill now depending in Parliament: entitled A Bill to prevent suits for tythes...By a Member of the House of Commons [William Arnall]... 8°, London, 1731.

ANSON, Admiral George Anson, Baron (1697-1762)

MG.7.13 A voyage round the world in the years MDCCXL, I, II, III, IV. By G. Anson...Compiled from his papers and materials, by R. Walter. 5th ed. 4°, London, 1749.

ANSTEY, Christopher (1724-1805)

MK.3.34 See NEW

The new Bath guide: or, Memoirs of the B——-r——-d [i.e. Blunderhead] family. In a series of poetical epistles. [By C. Anstey.] 4th ed., 1767.

ANSTEY, Christopher (1724-1805)

ME.2.34 See NEW

The new Bath guide: or, Memoirs of the B—n—r—-d [i.e. Blunderhead] family. In a series of political epistles. [By C. Anstey.] 10th ed., 1776.

ANSTEY, John (d. 1819)

MC.1.1 See PLEADER'S

The pleader's guide: a didactic poem...By the late J.J.S. Esquire [i.e. J. Anstey.] New ed., 1803.

ANSWER

MH.5.23[6] An answer to a pamphlet, entitled, Considerations on the Bill to permit persons professing the Jewish religion to be naturalized...2nd ed. 8°, London, 1753.

ANTHOLOGIA

MF.7.18 Anthologia veterum Latinorum epigrammatum et poëmatum. Sive, Catalecta poëtarum Latinorum in VI. libros digesta...cura P. Burmanni Secundi qui perpetuas adnotationes adjecit. Vol. 1. (Vol. 2 wanting.) 4°, Amstelaedami, 1759.

ANTIGONUS, Carystius (fl. 240 B.C.)

MG.6.15 Historiarum mirabilium collectanea, explicata a I. Beckmann. Additis annotationibus G. Xylandri [etc.]...cum interpretatione G. Xylandri...(Greek & Latin.) 4°, Lipsiæ, 1791.

ANTI-JACOBIN, The

MG.5.40 Poetry of the Anti-Jacobin. 8°, London, 1799.

ANTI-JACOBIN, The
ME.2.20&21, [2 copies.] Poetry of the Anti-Jacobin. 6th ed. 8°, London, 1813.

ANTONINUS, Marcus Aurelius (c. 83 B.C.-31 B.C.)
MG.7.17 Marci Antonini Imperatoris, de rebus suis, sive de eis quæ ad se pertinere censebat libri XII. ...Versione insuper Latina nova ...Studio operâque T. Gatakeri ...(Greek & Latin.) (2 pts.) 4°, Londini, 1697.

APOLLONIUS, Rhodius (3rd C. B.C.)
MM.5.4 The loves of Medea and Jason. A poem, in 3 books: translated from the Greek of Apollonius Rhodius's Argonautics, by J. Ekins. 4°, London, 1771.

APPIANUS (b.c 123 A.D.)
MG.1.1-2 Romanarum historiarum pars prior (& pars altera). A. Tollius...correxit & H. Stephani...annotationes adjecit. (Greek & Latin.) 2 vols. 8°, Amstelodami, 1670.

ARBUTHNOT, John (1667-1735)
ML.1.36-7 Miscellaneous works. 2nd ed., with additions. 2 vols. 8°, Glasgow, 1751.

ARBUTHNOT, John (1667-1735)
MK.5.22 See MISCELLANIES
Miscellanies. [By J. Arbuthnot, A. Pope, J. Swift, and others.] Vol. 2. 1727.

ARBUTHNOT, John (1667-1735)
MF.6.18 Tables of ancient coins, weights and measures, explain'd and exemplify'd in several dissertations. 4°, London, 1727.

ARGUMENT
MH.3.20^{3} An argument, &c. [Not identified, wants title-page.] [A work of 89 pages, with running title at top of page 3 'An argument, &c.', about the war with France and the desirability of peace. The printed date May, 25, 1795 appears on the last page.] 8°, [London?, 1795?.]

ARGUMENTORUM
ML.2.31 Argumentorum ludicrorum et amoenitatum scriptores varij. In gratiam studiosæ juventutis collecti & emendati. (2 pts.) 8°, two works. Lugduni Batavorum, 1623.

ARIOSTO, Lodovico (1474-1533)
MA.6.3,4,4^{a},5 Orlando furioso. 4 vols. (Baskerville printing). 8°, Birmingham, 1773.

ARIOSTO, Lodovico (1474-1533)
MA.2.8-11 Roland furieux, poëme héroïque. Traduction nouvelle par M. d'Ussieux. 4 vols. 8°, Paris, 1775-83.

ARISTÆNETUS (5th or 6th C.)
MM.3.4

'Αριοταινέτου 'Επιστολαί ἐρωτικαί Τινά τῶν παλαιῶν ἡρώων ἐπιταφια

E Bibliotheca C. V. Ioan Sambuci. 4°, Antverpiae, 1566.

ARISTIDES, Aelius (c. 129-81 B.C.)
MG.7.11-12 Opera omnia Graece & Latine...cum notis & emendationibus G. Canteri [etc.]...recensuit & observationes suas adjecit S. Jebb. 2 vols. 4°, Oxonii, 1722-30.

ARISTOPHANES (c. 445-385 B.C.)
MG.5.23 The clouds: a comedy. Written...against Socrates... Now first intirely translated into English, with the principal scholia, and notes...[by J. White]. 12°, London, 1759.

ARMATA
MH.1.25 Armata: a fragment. [By Thomas, Lord Erskine.] (2 pts.) 8°, London, 1817.

ARMES
ME.5.59 Armes of Surrey taken 1662. [A manuscript, titled thus, comprising ink sketches of the coats of arms of Surrey families, with index. Provenance and compiler not known.]

ARNALL, William (1699 or 1700-1736)
MH.5.23[3] See ANIMADVERSIONS
Animadversions on a Reverend Prelate's [Bishop Thomas Sherlock's] remarks upon the Bill now depending in Parliament: entitled A Bill to prevent suits for tythes...By a Member of the House of Commons [William Arnall]...1731.

ARNALL, William (1699 or 1700-1736)
MH.5.23[1] See LETTER
A letter to the Reverend Dr. Codex [i.e. E. Gibson], on the subject of his modest instruction to the Crown...[By W. Arnall.] 2nd ed., 1734.

ARNAY, Jean Rodolphe d' (fl. 1757)
MF.2.12 De la vie privée des Romains. Nouvelle éd. 12°, Lausanne, 1760.

ARNOLD, Thomas (1795-1842)
MC.4.34 Christian life, its hopes, its fears, and its close. Sermons... 8°, London, 1842.

ARNOLD, Thomas (1795-1842)
MC.4.31[1],32,33 Sermons...3 vols. 8°, London, 1829-34.

ARNOLD, Thomas (1795-1842)
MC.4.31[2] Two sermons on the interpretations of prophecy...2nd ed. 8°, London, 1844.*

ASTLEY, Philip (1742-1814)
MH.5.13[4] A description and historical account, of the places now the theatre of war in the Low Countries... Embellished with...plans of those places... 4th ed. 8°, London, 1794.

ATHENAEUS, Naucratita (fl. c. 200 A.D.)
MC.7.7 Athenæi Deipnosophistarum libri XV. Cum I. Dalechampii Latina interpretatione...Ed. postrema...I. Casaubonus recensuit... F°, Lugduni, 1612.

ATTERBURY, Francis, Bp of Rochester (1662-1732)
MG.3.8-9 Sermons and discourses upon several subjects and occasions. 2 vols. 8°, London, 1723.

AUCKLAND, William Eden, 1st Baron (1744-1814)
MH.4.19[1] Four letters to the Earl of Carlisle...2nd ed. 8°, London, 1779.

AUCKLAND, William Eden, 1st Baron (1744-1814)
MH.4.27[4] Letter to the Earl of Carlisle, on the subject of the late arrangement. 8°, London, 1786.

AUSONIUS, Decius Magnus (d. c. 395 A.D.)
MI.2.13 Opera, I. Tollius recensuit... 8°, Amstelodami, 1671.

AUTHENTIC
MB.6.61[7] An authentic account of forgeries and frauds of various kinds committed by...Charles Price. Otherwise Patch... 8°, London, 1786.

[ED. NOTE: Richard Patch (1770?-1806) was a notorious English criminal.]

AUTHENTIC
MH.5.3[5] An authentic copy of the French Constitution, as revised and amended by the National Assembly, and presented to the King on the Third of September, 1791. Translated from the original... 8°, London, 1791.

AYSCOUGH, Samuel (1745-1804)
MG.7.14 An index to the remarkable passages and words made use of by Shakespeare... 8°, London, 1790.

FRANCIS BACON

BABBAGE, Charles (1792-1871)
MC.4.30 The Ninth Bridgewater treatise. A fragment. 8°, London, 1837.*

BACON, Francis, Viscount St. Albans (1561-1626)
MH.4.5 Essays, or Councils, civil and moral...To this edition is added The Character of Queen Elizabeth... 8°, London, 1696.

BACON, Francis, Viscount St. Albans (1561-1626)
MK.3.24 The two bookes of S^r. Francis Bacon. Of the proficience and advancement of learning, divine and humane. 4°, London, 1629.

BAILEY, Nathan (d. 1742)
MI.1.6 An universal etymological English dictionary... 13th ed., with considerable improvements. 8°, London, 1747.

BAILEY, Samuel (1791-1870)
MH.3.5 See CRITICAL
A critical dissertation on the nature, measures, and causes of value; chiefly in reference to the writings of Mr. Ricardo and his followers...[By S. Bailey.] 1825.

[ED. NOTE: Ch. VII. of this monograph is entitled "On the Measure of Value proposed by Mr. Malthus." In his work "Definitions in Political Economy," Malthus discusses the views of the "anonymous writer" of this monograph. Actually Ch. VIII. of Malthus's "Definitions" is entitled "On the Definition and Use of Terms by the author of 'A Critical Dissertation on the Nature, Measure, and Causes of Value.'"]

BAILEY, Samuel (1791-1870)
MH.3.3 See ESSAYS
Essays on the formation and publication of opinions, and on other subjects. [By S. Bailey.] 1821.

BAILEY, Samuel (1791-1870)
MH.3.4 See QUESTIONS
Questions in political economy, politics, morals, metaphysics, polite literature...[By S. Bailey.] 1823.

BAINBRIDGE, George Cole
ME.2.6 The fly fisher's guide, illustrated by coloured plates...2nd ed., with additions. 8°, Liverpool, 1828.

BAKER, Henry (1698-1774)
ME.4.4-7 The universal spectator. By H. Stonecastle [i.e. H. Baker and others]. 3rd ed., 4 vols. 12°, London, 1756.

BALE, John, Bp of Ossory (1495-1563)
ME.1.37 A declaration of Edmonde Bonners articles, concerning the cleargye of London Dyocese...[With the text of the articles.] 8°, (London, 1561).

BALGUY, Thomas (1716-1795)
ML.3.30[1] Discourses on various subjects. 8°, Winchester, 1785.

BALGUY, Thomas (1716-1795)
ML.3.30[2] Divine benevolence asserted; and vindicated from the objections of ancient and modern sceptics. 8°, London, 1781.

BARBAULD, Anna Laetitia (1743-1825)
MK.5.15[3] Epistle to William Wilberforce, Esq. on the rejection of the Bill for abolishing the slave trade. 2nd ed. 4°, London, 1791.

BARBAULD, Anna Laetitia (1743-1825)
ME.1.40[1] Remarks on Mr. Gilbert Wakefield's Enquiry into the expediency and propriety of public or social worship. 2nd ed. 8°, London, 1792.

BARBAULD, Anna Laetitia (1743-1825)
MH.4.25[7] See SINS
Sins of government, sins of the nation; or, A discourse for the fast, appointed on April 19, 1793. By a volunteer [i.e. A.L. Barbauld]. 2nd ed. 1793.

BARBUT, Jacques
ME.6.2 Les genres des insectes de Linné; constatés par divers échantillons d'insectes d'Angleterre, copiés d'après nature. (Parallel English & French texts). 4°, Londres, 1781.

BARING, Sir Francis (1740-1810)
MH.3.18[2] Observations on the publication of Walter Boyd, Esq. M. P. [i.e. on his 'Letter on the influence of the stoppage of issues in specie']. 8°, London, 1801.

BARLOW, Joel (1754-1812)
MH.5.25[3] A letter to the National Convention of France, on the defects in the Constitution of 1791... 8°, London, 1792.

BARRINGTON, Hon. Daines (1727-1800)
MB.6.27 The possibility of approaching the North Pole asserted. A new ed. With an appendix...by Colonel Beaufoy. 8°, London, 1818.

BARRINGTON, George (b. 1755)
MH.5.7[7] A voyage to New South Wales; with a description of the country; the manners...of the natives, in the vicinity of Botany Bay. 8°, [London] 1795.

BARROW, Isaac (1630-1677)
MM.2.9-16 Theological works. (With Some account of the life of I. Barrow, by A. Hill). 8 vols. 8°, Oxford, 1830.

BARROW, Sir John, Bart (1764-1848)
MF.7.3-4 An account of travels into the interior of Southern Africa, in the years 1797 and 1798...2 vols. 4°, London, 1801-4.

BASTIDE, Jean François de (1724-1798)
MK.2.3 See RESSOURCES
Les ressources de l'amour. [By J. F. de Bastide.] (4 pts.) 1752.

BAUSSET, Louis François de, Cardinal (1748-1824)
MA.4.21-4 Histoire de Fénélon, archevèque de Cambrai, composée sur les manuscrits originaux. 3e éd., revue, corrigée et augmentée. 4 vols. 8°, Versailles, 1817.

BAXTER, William (1650-1723)
MI.1.5 Glossarium antiquitatum Britannicarum, sive Syllabus etymologicus antiquitatum veteris Britanniæ atque Iberniæ, temporibus Romanorum...[Ed. by M. Williams.] Ed. 2^{a}. 8°, Londini, 1733.

BEARCROFT, Philip (1697-1761)
MM.3.18 An historical account of Thomas Sutton Esq., and of his foundation in Charter-House. 8°, London, 1737.

BEATTIE, James (1735-1803)
ME.6.14 Essays... 4°, Edinburgh, 1776.

BEAUMONT, Francis (1584-1616)
MI.4.7[6] Philaster, a tragedy. Written by Beaumont and Fletcher. With alterations [by G. Colman]. As it is acted at the Theatre-Royal in Drury-Lane. 8°, London, 1763.

BEAUMONT, Francis (1584-1616)
MF.1.8-9 Select plays of Beaumont and Fletcher. 2 vols. 8°, Glasgow, 1768.

BEAUMONT, Francis (1584-1616)
MI.3.7-20 The works of Beaumont and Fletcher: with an introduction and explanatory notes, by H. Weber. 14 vols. 8°, Edinburgh, 1812.

BECKFORD, Peter (1740-1811)
MA.4.5 Thoughts on hunting, in a series of familiar letters to a friend. 8°, London, (1820).

BECKMANN, Johann (1739-1811)
MF.4.3-5 A history of inventions and discoveries. Translated from the German, by W. Johnston. 3 vols. 8°, London, 1797.

BEDA (673-735)
MF.7.19 Ecclesiasticæ historiæ gentis Anglorum libri V diligenti studio à mendis, quibus hactenus scatebant, vindicati. 4°, Antverpiæ, 1550.

BEDDOES, Thomas (1760-1808)
MB.6.61[3] See HISTORY
The history of Isaac Jenkins, and Sarah his wife and their three children. [By T. Beddoes.] 2nd ed., 1793.

BEDFORD, Francis Russell, 5th Duke of (1765-1805)
MB.6.53[1] See DESCRIPTIVE
A descriptive journey through the interior parts of Germany and France, including Paris...By a young English Peer [Francis Russell, 5th Duke of Bedford]...1786.

BEEKE, Henry (1751-1837)
MH.3.20[1] Observations on the produce of the income tax, and on its proportion to the whole income of Great Britain. A new and corrected ed. ... 8°, London, 1800.

BEHN, Aphra (1640-1689)
ML.1.17-20 Plays. 3rd ed. 4 vols. 12°, London, 1724.

BELL, Archibald (1755-1854)
MH.5.15[5] An inquiry into the policy and justice of the prohibition of the use of grain in the distilleries... 8°, Edinburgh, 1808.

BELL, Sir Charles (1774-1842)
MC.4.22 The hand, its mechanism and vital endowments as evincing design. (Bridgewater Treatises, 4). 8°, London, 1833.

BELLEGARDE, Jean Baptiste Morvan de
See MORVAN DE BELLEGARDE, Jean Baptiste.

BELSHAM, William (1752-1827)
ME.3.26-7 History of Great Britain, from the Revolution to the accession of the House of Hanover. 2 vols. 8°, London, 1798.

BELSHAM, William (1752-1827)
ME.3.28-9 History of Great Britain, from the Revolution, 1688, to the conclusion of the Treaty of Amiens, 1802. Vols. 3,4. (Vols. 1,2,5-12 wanting.) 8°, London, 1805.

BENTLEY, Richard (1662-1742)
MI.1.23 Eight sermons preach'd at the Honourable Robert Boyle's lecture, in the first year MDCXCII. 6th ed. ... 8°, Cambridge, 1735.

BENTLEY, Thomas Richard (1748 or 1749-1831)
MH.5.10[5] See SECOND
A second letter to the Rt. Hon. Charles James Fox, upon the dangerous and inflammatory tendency of his late conduct in Parliament...By the author of the First letter [T.R. Bentley?]. 1793.

BERKELEY, George, Bp of Cloyne (1685-1753)
MI.4.10-11 See ALCIPHRON
Alciphron: or, The minute philosopher. In seven dialogues. Containing an apology for the Christian religion...[By G. Berkeley.] 2 vols., 1732.

BERKELEY, George, Bp of Cloyne (1685-1753)
ML.3.9 Memoirs. 2nd ed., with improvements. 8°, London, 1784.

BERKELEY, George, Bp of Cloyne (1685-1753)
MG.5.10 A miscellany, containing several tracts on various subjects. 12°, Dublin, 1752.

BERKELEY, George, Bp of Cloyne (1685-1753)
ML.3.33[1] Siris: a chain of philosophical reflexions and inquiries concerning the virtues of tar water...2nd ed., improved and corrected... 8°, London, 1744.

BERKELEY, George, Bp of Cloyne (1685-1753)
MI.1.9 A treatise concerning the principles of human knowledge... 8°, London, 1734.

BEROALDE DE VERVILLE, François (1556-ca. 1621)
ME.1.34-6 See MOYEN
Le moyen de parvenir. [By F. Béroalde de Verville.] Nouvelle éd. augmentée...3 vols. 1781-6.

BERTIE, Rt. Hon. Willoughby (1740-1799)
MH.5.6[2] See LETTER
A letter to the Right Honourable Willoughby Bertie, by descent Earl of Abingdon, by descent Lord Norreys...In which His Lordship's ... treatment of the now Earl of Mansfield is fully vindicated. [By J. Lind.] 1778.

BERTOLACCI, Anthony (18th C.-1833)
MB.7.32 A view of the agricultural, commercial, and financial interests of Ceylon... 8°, London, 1817.

BERWICK, James FitzJames, 1st Duke of (1670-1734)
MM.2.1-2 Memoirs of the Marshal Duke of Berwick. Written by himself...Translated from the French. 2 vols. 8°, London, 1779.

BETTER
MH.5.12[2] Better late than never! An impartial review of Mr. Pitt's administration...By An enemy to the War... Addressed to the Hon. C. Jenkinson. 8°, London, 1794.

BEXLEY, Nicholas Vansittart, Baron (1766-1851)
MH.4.24[4] See REFLECTIONS
Reflections on the propriety of an immediate conclusion of peace. [By N. Vansittart, Lord Bexley.] 1793.

BHAGVAT - GEETA
See MAHABHARATA. Bhagavadgita.

BIBLE. English
MA.7.6 The Holy Bible, containing the Old Testament and the New, with the Apocrypha...with annotations. (The Baskerville Bible.) F°, Birmingham, 1769.

[ED. NOTE: In Bk. I, Ch. VI. of the later *Essay*, Malthus cited Ch. XIII. of Genesis.]

BIBLE. French
MD.1.8-9 La Sainte Bible contenant l'Ancien et le Nouveau Testament; traduite en françois...par M. Le Maistre de Saci. 2 vols. 4°, Paris, 1701.

BIBLE. Greek. Old Testament
MK.4.8 Vetus Testamentum Græcum ex versione Septuaginta interpretum, juxta exemplar Vaticanum Romæ editum...(With In Sacra Biblia Græca ex versione LXX. interpretum scholia...) (2 pts.) 4°, Londini, 1653.

BIBLE. Greek. New Testament
ML.2.9 Novum Testamentum, versiculis distinctum. Ex Regiis aliisque optimis editionibus accuratè expressum. 16°, Parisiis, 1721.

BIBLE. Greek. New Testament
MI.2.19

Τῆς Καινῆς Διαθήκης ἅπαντα

Novum Testamentum. 8°, Londini, 1728.

BIBLE. Greek. New Testament
ML.3.20-23 Novum Testamentum Græcum Domini Nostri Jesu Christi; cum scholiis theologicis et philologicis...[by] S. Hardy. 2 vols. in 4. [Interleaved.] 8°, Londini, 1820.

BIBLE. Greek. New Testament
MG.3.3 Novum Testamentum. Textum Græcum Griesbachii et Knappii denuo recognovit...adnotatione...instruxit J. S. Vater. 8°, Halis Saxonum, 1824.

BIBLE. Greek. New Testament
MF.2.1 Novum Testamentum. Ed. nova, denuo recusa studio & labore S. Curcellæi. (2 pts.) 12°, Amstelodami, 1675.

BIBLE. Italian
MC.7.11 La Sacra Bibbia, tradotta in lingua italiana, e commentata da G. Diodati. 2[a] ed., migliorata, ed accresciuta... F°, Geneva, 1641.

BIBLE. Persian. Isaiah
MB.7.52 Sahifat Ishaya al-Nabi. [The Book of Isaiah translated into Persian by Muhammad Ibrahim, and edited by F. Johnson.] (British & Foreign Bible Society.) 8°, London, 1834.

BICKERSTAFF, Isaac, pseud.
For Sir Richard Steele, J. Addison, and others, when writing under this pseudonym in The Tatler, see TATLER. The lucubrations of Isaac Bickerstaff.

BIGLAND, John (1750-1832)
MF.5.10-11 A sketch of the history of Europe, from the Peace of 1783 to the present time...2 vols. 8°, London, 1810.

BIOGRAPHICAL
MH.1.24[1] A biographical memoir of the late Right Honourable William Windham. [By E. Malone.] 8°, London, 1810.

BIOGRAPHICAL
MJ.1.1-2 Biographical peerage of the Empire of Great Britain: in which are memoirs and characters of the most celebrated persons of each family. [By Sir S. E. Brydges.] 2 vols. 12°, London, 1808.

BION, Smyrnaeus (fl. c. 100 B.C.)
MG.6.16 Musæi, Moschi & Bionis quæ extant omnia: quibus accessere quædam selectiora Theocriti Eidyllia...Autore D. Whitfordo. (Greek & Latin.) 4°, Londini, 1659.

BIRCH, Thomas (1705-1766)
MD.1.15 The heads of illustrious persons of Great Britain, engraven by Mr. Houbraken, and Mr. Vertue. With their lives and characters. F°, London, 1743.

BIRD, Henry Merttins (end 18th-start 19th C.)
MH.3.20[2] Proposals for paying off the whole of the present National Debt, and for reducing taxes immediately. 3rd ed. 8°, London, 1803.

BLACK, William (1749-1829)
MH.5.13[3] Reasons for preventing the French, under the mask of liberty, from trampling upon Europe. 2nd ed. 8°, London, 1793.

BLACKSTONE, Sir William (1723-1780)
ML.3.11 An analysis of the laws of England...4th ed. 8°, Oxford, 1759.

BLACKSTONE, Sir William (1723-1780)
MH.1.3-6 Commentaries on the laws of England. In 4 books. 9th ed. ... by R. Burn. 4 vols. 8°, London, 1783.

BLACKWELL, Thomas (1701-1757)
MM.3.21 See ENQUIRY
An enquiry into the life and writings of Homer. [By T. Blackwell.] 2nd ed., 1736.

BLANE, William
MH.5.24[4] An account of the hunting excursions of Asoph Ul Doulah, Visier of the Mogul Empire, and Nabob of Oude. 8°, London, 1788.

BLIN DE SAINMORE, Adrien Michel Hyacinthe (1733-1807)
MF.7.6 Histoire de Russie, représentée par figures, accompagnées d'un précis historique; les figures gravées par F.A. David...le discours par Blin de Sainmore. 3 vols. in 1. 4°, Paris, 1813.

BLOOMFIELD, Robert (1766-1823)
MG.5.20^{2} The banks of Wye; a poem. In 4 books. 2nd ed., corrected. 12°, London, 1813.

BLOOMFIELD, Robert (1766-1823)
MG.5.20^{1} The farmer's boy; a rural poem. 13th ed. 12°, London, 1815.

BLUNT, John James (1794-1855)
MA.3.29 Vestiges of ancient manners and customs, discoverable in modern Italy and Sicily. 8°, London, 1823.

BOADEN, James (1762-1839)
MI.4.5^{5} Fontainville Forest, a play in 5 acts—founded on the Romance of the forest [by A. Radcliffe]—, as performed at the Theatre-Royal Covent-Garden. 8°, London, 1794.

BOCCACCIO, Giovanni (1313-1375)
MM.1.4-14 Contes; traduction nouvelle, augmentée...Par A. Sabatier de Castres. 11 vols. 12°, Paris, 1801.

BOCCACCIO, Giovanni (1313-1375)
MF.2.6 Il Decamerone. Nuovamente corretto, historiato, & con diligenza stampato. 8°, Venetia, 1545.

BŒTHIUS, Anicius Manlius Severinus (c. 480-524 A.D.)
MJ.1.31 Consolationis philosophiæ libri V. 12°, Glasguae, 1751.

BOIARDO, Matteo Maria (1441-1494)
ME.5.65-6 Orlando innamorato...rifatto da F. Berni. 2 vols. 12°, Venezia, 1740.

BOISSIER DE SAUVAGES DE LA CROIX, François (1706-1767)
MK.3.15 Methodus foliorum, seu Plantæ floræ Monspeliensis, juxta foliorum ordinem, ad juvandam specierum cognitionem, digestæ. 8°, La Haye, 1751.

[ED. NOTE: This monograph is from the Library of Malthus's father and is from Jean-Jacques Rousseau who probably reciprocated for the English botanical books sent to him by Daniel Malthus. It is heavily annotated by Rousseau.]

BOLINGBROKE, Henry St. John, 1st Viscount (1678-1751)
MH.4.23 See COLLECTION
A collection of political tracts. [By H. St. John, Viscount Bolingbroke.] 2nd ed. 1748.

BOLINGBROKE, Henry St. John, 1st Viscount (1678-1751)
MK.5.13-14 Letters and correspondence, public and private, during the time he was Secretary of State to Queen Anne...By G. Parke. 2 vols. (Works, 6, 7.) 4°, London, 1798.

BOLINGBROKE, Henry St. John, 1st Viscount (1678-1751)
MK.5.8-14 Works. 7 vols., (Vols. 1-5 published by D. Mallet, Vols. 6, 7 by G. Parke). 4°, London, 1777-98.

BOLINGBROKE, Henry St. John, 1st Viscount (1678-1751)
MM.3.13 See MEMOIRS.
Memoirs of the life and ministerial conduct, with some free remarks on the political writings, of the late Lord Visc. Bolingbroke. 1752.

BONAR, James (1852-1941)
MX.1.8 Malthus and his work. 8°, London, 1885.**

[ED. NOTE: James Bonar's basic comprehensive account of Malthus's life and work was published in 1885 and further expanded in 1924 (see below). A new impression appeared in 1966. He started his Introduction by underlining that "Of the three English writers whose work has become a portion of Political Economy, Malthus is the second in time and in honour. His services to general theory are at least equal to Ricardo's; and his full illustration of one particular detail will rank with the best work of Adam Smith."] See ED. NOTE under MALTHUS [ME.6.4].

BONAR, James (1852-1941)
MX.1.9 Malthus and his work. (2nd ed.) 8°, London, (1924).** See ED. NOTE under MALTHUS.

BONAR, James (1852-1941)
MX.1.15 See RICARDO, David.
Letters of David Ricardo to T.R. Malthus, 1810-23; ed. by J. Bonar. 1887.** See ED. NOTE under RICARDO.

BOOK OF COMMON PRAYER. Greek
MJ.1.12

Λειτουργία Βρεττανική ἤχουν Βίβλος δημοσίων εὐχῶν καί διακονήσεως μυστηφίων καί τῶν ἄλλων θεσμῶν καί τελετῶν ἐν τή 'Εκκλησία ἡμῶν 'Αγγλικάνη είς τήν τῶν φιλελλήνων νέων χάριν ἐλληνιστὶ ἐκδοθεῖσα ---

Opera et studio E. Petilli. (2 pts.) 8°, Londini, 1638.

BOOK OF HOURS
ML.2.8 See HEURES
Heures nouvelles dédiées au Roy, contenant les offices qui se disent dans l'Eglise pendant l'année. En latin & en françois...Nouvelle éd., augmentée...1760.

BOOTH, Joseph
MH.5.24[6] A treatise explanatory of the nature and properties of pollaplasiasmos; or, The original invention of multiplying pictures in oil colours... 8°, [London, 1784.]

BOSSUET, Jacques Bénigne, Bp of Meaux (1627-1704)
MJ.2.23-4 Histoire universelle, à Monseigneur Le Dauphin. Pour expliquer la suite de la religion, & des changements des Empires. 2 vols. 12°, Amsterdam, 1763.

BOSSUET, Jacques Bénigne, Bp of Meaux (1627-1704)
MK.1.21 Recueil des oraisons funébres...Nouvelle éd., revue... 12°, Paris, 1762.

BOSWELL, James (1740-1795)
MB.4.4-13 The life of Samuel Johnson, LL.D., including a journal of his tour to the Hebrides. New ed....by J.W. Croker...10 vols. 8°, London, 1839.*

BOUGAINVILLE, Louis Antoine de (1729-1811)
ML.4.17 Voyage autour du monde, par la frégate du Roi La Boudeuse, et la flute L'Etoile; en 1766, 1767, 1768 & 1769. 4°, Paris, 1771.

[ED. NOTE: Referred to in Malthus's later *Essay*, Bk. I, Ch. V.]

BOULAINVILLIERS, Henri,comte de Saint Saire (1658-1722)
MK.2.4 Lettres sur les anciens Parlemens de France que l'on nomme Etats-Généraux. 3 vols. in 1. 12°, Londres, 1753.

BOURNE, Vincent (1695-1747)
MF.1.27 Poematia. Latinè partim reddita, partim scripta: a V. Bourne. 5ª ed. 12°, Londini, 1764.

BOWDLER, John (1783-1815)
MB.1.9-10 Select pieces in verse and prose. 4th ed.
2 vols. 8°, London, 1820.

BOWLES, William Augustus (1763-1805)
MB.6.61[5] Authentic memoirs of William Augustus Bowles, Esquire, Ambassador from the united nations of Creek and Cherokees, to the Court of London. 8°, London, 1791.

BOWLES, William Lisle (1762-1850)
MK.5.15^{2} Sonnets, written chiefly on picturesque spots, during a tour. 2nd ed., corrected, with additions. 4°, Bath, 1789.

BOYD, Walter (1754?-1837)
MH.3.18^{1} A letter to the Right Honourable William Pitt, on the influence of the stoppage of issues in specie at the Bank of England; on the prices of provisions, and other commodities. 8°, London, 1801.

BOYER, Abel (1667-1729)
ML.4.18 The Royal dictionary, French and English, and English and French...New ed. revised... 4°, London, 1729.

BRABANT
ML.3.14^{5} See PROJET
Projet de requête à présenter à Sa Majesté par les Tiers-Etat de sa province de Brabant. Au sujet des refus de subsides, impôts &c. 1789.

BRAY, William (1736-1832)
MA.1.28; ME.3.23-5; ML.5.25 [5 copies] Sketch of a tour into Derbyshire and Yorkshire...2nd ed. 8°, London, 1783.

BRIDGEWATER
MC.4.18-30 The Bridgewater treatises on the power, wisdom and goodness of God as manifested in the Creation. 9 treatises in 13 vols. (Treatises 5, 7, 2nd ed.). 8°, London, 1833-7. [Treatises 6, 7, 9.]*

BRIEF
ME.5.16^{2} A brief character of the Low-Countries under the States...[By O. Feltham.] 12°, London, 1660.

BRIEF
MH.5.20^{6} A brief narrative of the late campaigns in Germany and Flanders. In a letter to a Member of Parliament. 8°, London, 1751.

BRIGHTON
MB.6.53^{4} See DESCRIPTION
A description of Brighthelmstone, and the adjacent country...[1788.]

BRILLAT-SAVARIN, Jean Anthelme (1755-1826)
MA.3.1-2 Physiologie du goût, ou Méditations de gastronomie transcendante...2e éd. 2 vols. 8°, Paris, 1828.

BRISSOT DE WARVILLE, Jacques Pierre (1754-1793)
MH.5.12^{3} J.P. Brissot, Deputy of Eure and Loire, to his constituents, on the situation of the National Convention...Translated from the French... 8°, London, 1794.

BRISTOL. Prudent Man's Friend Society
MG.5.19^{2} See PROPOSALS
Proposals for the establishment of a society in Bristol, for the suppression of mendicity, and the promotion of economy and prudence among the labouring classes, to be called The Prudent Man's Friend Society. [c. 1812.]

BRISTOW, William
MB.6.61^{2} See GENUINE
The genuine account of the trial of Eugene Aram, for the murder of Daniel Clark...[By W. Bristow.] 8th ed. 1792.

BRITANNIA
ME.6.1^{3} Britannia in tears: an elegaic pastoral, on the death of Frederic Prince of Wales. 4°, London, 1751.

BRODIE, George (1786?-1867)
MC.6.14-17 A history of the British Empire, from the accession of Charles I. to the Restoration...4 vols. 8°, Edinburgh, 1822.

BROOME, Ralph
MH.4.18^{8} Observations on Mr. Paine's pamphlet, entitled The decline and fall of the English system of finance... 8°, London, [1796].

BROSSES, Charles de (1709-1777)
ML.4.14-15 See HISTOIRE
Histoire des navigations aux Terres Australes. Contenant ce que l'on sçait des mœurs & des productions des contrées découvertes jusqu'à ce jour...[By C. de Brosses.] 2 vols. 1756.

BROTHERS
MI.4.7^{5} The brothers, a comedy as it is performed at the Theatre-Royal in Covent-Garden. [By R. Cumberland.] 8°, London, 1770.

BROUGHAM AND VAUX, Henry Brougham, 1st Baron (1778-1868)
MH.3.20^{4} See INQUIRY
An inquiry into the state of the nation, at the commencement of the present administration. [By Lord Brougham.] 1806.

BROWN, Thomas, M.D. (1778-1820)
ML.5.26 Observations on the Zoonomia of Erasmus Darwin, M.D. 8°, Edinburgh, 1798.

BROWN, Thomas, of Shifnal (1663-1704)
MC.1.9-12 Works. 4 vols., (Vols. 2-4, 8th ed., carefully corrected.) 8°, London, 1744.

BRUCKER, Jakob (1696-1770)
MG.4.7-8 The history of philosophy...drawn up from Brucker's Historia critica philosophiæ. By W. Enfield. 2 vols. 8°, London, 1819.

BRUSLE DE MONTPLEINCHAMP, Jean Chrysostome (1641-1724)
ML.2.10-11 See LUCIEN
Lucien en belle humeur. Ou Nouvelles conversations des morts. [By J.C. Bruslé de Montpleinchamp.] Nouvelle éd., augmentée & corrigée. 2 vols. 1701.

BRUZEN DE LA MARTINIERE, Antoine Augustin (1662-1746)
MF.2.10-11 See NOUVEAU
Nouveau recueil des épigrammistes françois, anciens et modernes...Par Mr. B.L.M. [i.e. A.A. Bruzen de la Martinière.] 2 vols. 1720.

BRYAN, Michael (1757-1821)
ME.7.12-13 A biographical and critical dictionary of painters and engravers...2 vols. 4°, London, 1816.

BRYAN, William
MH.5.10[1] A testimony of the spirit of truth, concerning Richard Brothers...in an address to the People of Israel, &c. ... 8°, London, 1795.

BRYANT, Jacob (1715-1804)
ML.5.7-12 A new system; or, An analysis of antient mythology...3rd ed. 6 vols. 8°, London, 1807.

BRYDGES, Sir Samuel Egerton (1762-1837)
MJ.1.1-2 See BIOGRAPHICAL
Biographical peerage of the Empire of Great Britain: in which are memoirs and characters of the most celebrated persons of each family. [By Sir S.E. Brydges.] 2 vols. 1808.

BUCKINGHAM, George Villiers, 2nd Duke of (1628-1687)
MF.1.10 Genuine works. 8°, Glasgow, 1752.

BUCKINGHAM, John Sheffield, 1st Duke of (1648-1721)
MJ.1.26-7 Works. 2 vols. 8°, London, 1726.

BUCKLAND, William (1784-1856)
MC.4.25-6 Geology and mineralogy considered with reference to natural theology. 2 vols. (Bridgewater Treatises, 6.) 8°, London, 1836.*

BUCKNALL, Thomas Skip Dyot
MG.5.24[1]; MH.5.11[1] [2 copies.] The orchardist: or, A system of close pruning and medication, for establishing the science of orcharding... 8°, London, 1797.

BUDGELL, Eustace (1686-1737)
MI.1.4 A letter to Cleomenes King of Sparta; being an answer...to his Spartan Majesty's Royal Epistle...(3 pts.) 8°, London, (1731).

BURDON, William (1764-1818)
MI.2.1^{2} See OBSERVATIONS
Observations suggested by a pamphlet entitled 'The question, why do we go to war? temperately discussed...' [by W. Burdon]. In a letter to a friend. 1803.

BURDON, William (1764-1818)
MI.2.1^{1} See QUESTION
The question, why do we go to war? temperately discussed, according to the official correspondence. [By W. Burdon.] 1803.

BURGESS, Thomas, Bp of Salisbury (1756-1837)
MH.5.24^{8} See MORAL
Moral annals of the poor, and middle ranks of society, in various situations, of good and bad conduct. [By T. Burgess.] 1793.

BURKE, Rt. Hon. Edmund (1729-1797)
MH.4.24^{2} A letter from the Right Honourable Edmund Burke to a Noble Lord, on the attacks made upon him and his pension, in the House of Lords, by the Duke of Bedford and the Earl of Lauderdale... 8°, London, 1796.

BURKE, Rt. Hon. Edmund (1729-1797)
MH.4.24^{3} A letter from the Rt. Honourable Edmund Burke to His Grace the Duke of Portland, on the conduct of the minority in Parliament. Containing fifty-four articles of impeachment against the Rt. Hon. C.J. Fox... 8°, London, 1797.

BURKE, Rt. Hon. Edmund (1729-1797)
MH.5.5^{1} Speech on American taxation, April 19, 1774. 4th ed. 8°, London, 1775.

BURKE, Rt. Hon. Edmund (1729-1797)
MH.5.3^{3} Speech, on presenting to the House of Commons, on the 11th of February, 1780, a plan for the better security of the independence of Parliament... 8°, London, 1780.

BURKE, Rt. Hon. Edmund (1729-1797)
MH.5.3^{2} Substance of the speech, in the debate on the Army Estimates...the 9th of February, 1790...3rd ed. 8°, London, 1790.

BURKE, Rt. Hon. Edmund (1729-1797)
MH.4.16^{1} Thoughts and details on scarcity, originally presented to the Right Hon. William Pitt...1795. 8°, London, 1800.

BURKE, Rt. Hon. Edmund (1729-1797)
MH.2.1-16 Works. New ed. 16 vols. 8°, London, 1815-27.

[ED. NOTE: Malthus refers to "Burke's America" in Bk. I, Ch. IV. and Bk. III, Ch. IV. of his later *Essay*.]

BURKE, Rt. Hon. Edmund (1729-1797)
MH.4.26^4 See LETTER
A letter to the Right Hon. Edmund Burke, in reply to his 'Reflections on the Revolution in France, &c' 2nd ed., with considerable additions...By a Member of the Revolution Society [i.e. J. Scott, afterwards Scott Waring]. 1790.

BURKE, Rt. Hon. Edmund (1729-1797)
MH.4.26^2 See OBSERVATIONS
Observations on the Reverend Doctor Hurd's, now Lord Bishop of Worcester's, two dialogues on the constitution of the English government, addressed in a letter to the Right Hon. E. Burke. 1790.

BURKE, Rt. Hon. Edmund (1729-1797)
MH.4.21^7 See PARAPHRASE
A paraphrase in rhyme of the poetical beauties and spirit exhibited in a letter from the Right Hon. Edmund Burke to a Noble Lord. 1796.

BURKE, Rt. Hon. Edmund (1729-1797)
MK.5.15^4 See POETICAL
A poetical and philosophical essay on the French Revolution. [By J. Courtenay.] Addressed to the Right Hon. E. Burke. 1793.

BURLAMAQUI, Jean Jacques (1694-1748)
MA.3.21 The principles of natural law. In which the true systems of morality and civil government are established... Translated into English by Mr. Nugent. 8°, London, 1752.

BURMAN, Pieter (1668-1741)
MF.7.18 See ANTHOLOGIA
Anthologia veterum Latinorum epigrammatum et poëmatum. Sive, Catalecta poëtarum Latinorum in VI. libros digesta...cura P. Burmanni Secundi qui perpetuas adnotationes adjecit. Vol. 1. (Vol. 2 wanting.) 1759.

BURNABY, Andrew (1734?-1812)
MH.5.4^2 Travels through the middle settlements in North-America. In the years 1759 and 1760...2nd ed. 8°, London, 1775.

BURNET, Gilbert, Bp of Salisbury (1643-1715)
MK.2.32 The abridgment of the History of the Reformation of the Church of England. (2 pts.) 8°, London, 1682.

BURNET, Gilbert, Bp of Salisbury (1643-1715)
MI.1.17 An exposition of the Thirty-nine articles of the Church of England. 5th ed. corrected. 8°, London, 1746.

BURNET, Gilbert, Bp of Salisbury (1643-1715)
ML.2.12 The lives of Sir Matthew Hale and John Earl of Rochester. (2 pts.) 12°, London, 1820.

BURNET, Thomas (1635?-1715)
MA.3.22-3 The sacred theory of the earth...4th ed., 2 vols. 8°, London, 1719.

BURNS, Robert (1759-1796)
MG.5.28 Poetical works; with his life [by J. Currie]. 2 vols. in 1. [Vol. 1, pp. 1-48 (The life of Burns) misbound at the beginning of vol. 2.] 8°, Alnwick, 1808.

BURNS, Robert (1759-1796)
ML.2.28 Poems: with his life and character [by J. Currie], and a complete glossary. 12°, Edinburgh, 1802.

[ED. NOTE: The "Life of Burns" written by James Currie (M.D.), was referred to by Malthus in his later *Essay*, Bk. IV, Ch. II, for the prefixed observations on the character and conditions of the Scotch peasantry.]

BURTON, John Hill (1809-1881)
MF.5.38-9 See HUME, David
Life and correspondence of D. Hume...By J.H. Burton. 2 vols. 1846.*

BURTON, John Hill (1809-1881)
MM.3.11 See LETTERS
Letters of eminent persons addressed to David Hume. [Ed. by J.H. Burton.] 1849.*

BURTON, Philip
ME.1.40[4] Annihilation no punishment to the wicked after the day of judgment... 4°, London, [1792].

BURTON, Robert (1577-1640)
MB.5.24-5 The anatomy of melancholy...13th ed. corrected...2 vols. 8°, London, 1827.

BUTLER, Charles (1750-1832)
MB.7.42 Horæ Biblicæ; being a connected series of notes on the...Bibles...2nd ed., Vol. 2. (Vol. 1 wanting.) 8°, London, 1807.

BUTLER, Joseph, Bp of Durham (1692-1752)
MA.1.23-4 The analogy of religion, natural and revealed, to the constitution and course of nature...A new ed....by S. Halifax. 2 vols. 8°, Oxford, 1820.

BUTLER, Joseph, Bp of Durham (1692-1752)
MG.3.28 Fifteen sermons preached at the Rolls Chapel... 8°, London, 1726.

BUTLER, Samuel, Bp of Lichfield (1744-1839)
ML.5.13 A sketch of modern and antient geography, for the use of schools. 4th ed., considerably enlarged and improved. 8°, London, 1818.

BUTLER, Samuel, poet (1612-1680)
MB.7.41 Genuine poetical remains. With notes, by R. Thyer...[New ed.] 8°, London, 1827.

BUTLER, Samuel, poet (1612-1680)
MA.1.21-2 Hudibras, in 3 parts...With large annotations and a preface. By Z. Grey. 2 vols. 8°, London, 1806.

BUTLERD, Fanni, pseud.
MJ.1.15 See LETTRES
Lettres de Mistriss Fanni Butlerd, à Milord Charles Alfred de Caitombridge, comte de Plisinte, duc de Raslingth, écrites en 1735, traduites de l'Anglois en 1756, par A. de Varançai. [By M.J. Riccoboni.] 1759.

BYRON, George Gordon Noel Byron, 6th Baron (1788-1824)
MB.7.44 Works, including his suppressed poems. 8°, Paris, 1827.

BYRON, George Gordon Noel Byron, 6th Baron (1788-1824)
MB.1.12-28 Works: with his letters and journals, and his life, by T. Moore. 17 vols. 8°, London, 1832-3.

BYRON, Hon. John (1723-1786)
ML.5.22 The narrative of the Honourable John Byron, Commodore in a late expedition round the world, containing an account of the great distresses suffered...on the coast of Patagonia...1740, till...1746. With a description of St. Jago de Chili...2nd ed. 8°, London, 1768.

BYSSHE, Edward (fl. 1702-1712)
ME.4.29-30 The art of English poetry...(With A dictionary of rhymes.) 8th ed. corrected and enlarged. (3 pts.) 2 vols. 12°, London, 1737.

BYSSHE, Edward (fl. 1702-1712)
MM.2.23 The art of poetry...4th ed. (3 pts.) 8°, London, 1710.

CÆSAR, Gaius Julius (100-44 B.C.)
MG.1.6 C. Julii Cæsaris quæ extant...Accesserunt annotationes Samuelis Clarke... 8°, Londini, 1720.

[ED. NOTE: Malthus refers to Cæsar's "De Bello Gallico" in his later *Essay*, Bk. I, Ch. VI.]

CALABER, Quintus
See QUINTUS, Smyrnaeus

CALIDAS
See KALIDASA

CALLIMACHUS (c. 310-235 B.C.)
MG.1.26 Hymni, epigrammata et fragmenta: ejusdem poëmatium...Cum notis A. Tanaquilli Fabri Filiæ. (Greek & Latin.) 4°, Parisiis, 1675.

CALLIMACHUS (c. 310-235 B.C.)
MG.1.27 Hymni et epigrammata: quibus accesserunt Theognidis Carmina: nec non Epigrammata...Notas addidit, atque omnia emendate imprimenda curavit [R. Bentley] editor...(Greek & Latin.) (2 pts.) 8°, Londini, 1741.

CALLIOPE
MM.1.30 Calliope, a selection of ballads, legendary & pathetic. 12°, London, 1816.

CALPURNIUS FLACCUS (2nd C.)
MG.7.10 See QUINTILIANUS, Marcus Fabius
M. Fabii Quinctiliani, ut ferunt Declamationes XIX majores, et quae ex CCCLXXXVIII. supersunt CXLV minores. Et Calpurnii Flacci Declamationes. Cum notis doctorum virorum; curante P. Burmanno. 1720.

CAMBRIDGE

MA.6.2 The Cambridge concordance to the Holy Scriptures, together with the Books of the Apocrypha...[By S. Newman.] 5th ed.; very accurately corrected. F°, London, 1720.

CAMDEN, William (1551-1623)

MA.7.9 Britannia, newly translated into English: with large additions and improvements. Publish'd by E. Gibson. F°, London, 1695.

CAMPBELL, Colin (1676-1729)

MD.1.13 Vitruvius Britannicus, or The British architect, containing the plans...of the regular buildings, both publick and private, in Great Britain...Vol. 1. (Vols. 2 & 3 wanting.) F°, London, 1715.

CAMPBELL, George (1719-1796)

MC.3.30 The Four Gospels, translated from the Greek; with preliminary dissertations, and notes...by G. Campbell. 2nd ed. Vol. 1 [consisting of Cambell's dissertations]. (Vol. 2 wanting.) 8°, London, 1825.

CAROLINE

MM.1.31-3 Caroline de Lichtfield, par Madame de *** [i.e. the Baronne de Montolieu]. Publié par le traducteur de Werther. 3 vols. 12°, Paris, an II-III [1795].

CARPENTER, Daniel

MH.3.22[8] Reflections suggested by Mr. Whitbread's Bill, and by several publications...on the subject of the Poor-Laws, particularly by...T.R. Malthus, G. Rose, J. Weyland, and P. Colquhuon... 8°, London, 1807.

[ED. NOTE: One of the books which rather defends Malthus's views regarding the Poor-Laws.]

CARTWRIGHT, John (1740-1824)

MH.4.27[5] See HARTLEY, David

An address to the Right Worshipful the Mayor and Corporation...of the town of Kingston-upon-Hull, containing...arguments in favour of a Parliamentary reform...To which is added a letter to...C.J. Fox, by J. Cartwright. 1784.

CASA, Giovanni della, Abp of Benevento (1503-1556)

MJ.1.28 Galateo: or, A treatise of politeness and delicacy of manners. Addressed to a young nobleman. From the Italian...[by R. Graves]. 8°, London, 1774.

CASAUBON, Isaac (1559-1614)
MC.7.8 Animadversionum in Athen. Dipnosophistas libri XV...2ª ed. postrema. F°, Lugduni, 1621.

CASE
MH.5.20[8] The case of the Hessian forces, in the pay of Great Britain, impartially and freely examin'd...[By Horatio, Lord Walpole.] 8°, London, 1731.

CATECHISM
MK.2.29 The Catechism for the curats, compos'd by the decree of the Council of Trent, and publish'd by command of Pope Pius the Fifth. Faithfully translated into English. 8°, London, 1687.

CATULLUS, Gaius Valerius (c. 84-c.54 B.C.)
MI.1.2 Carmina varietate lectionis et perpetua adnotatione illustrata a F.G. Doering. 2 vols. in 1. 8°, Lipsiae, 1788-92.

CENTLIVRE, Susannah (1667?-1723)
ML.1.29[1] A bold stroke for a wife. A comedy. 8°, London, 1755.

CENTLIVRE, Susannah (1667?-1723)
ML.1.29[3] The busie body, a comedy. 8°, London, 1757.

CENTLIVRE, Susannah (1667?-1723)
ML.1.29[2] The wonder: a woman keeps a secret. A comedy. As it is now acted at the Theatre-Royal in Drury-Lane, by His Majesty's servants. 5th ed. 8°, London, 1758.

CENTLIVRE, Susannah (1667?-1723)
ML.1.26-8 Works. With a new account of her life. 3 vols. 8°, London, 1760-61.

CERVANTES SAAVEDRA, Miguel de (1547-1616)
ME.5.50-52 Don Quichotte de la Manche, traduit de l'Espagnol par Florian; ouvrage posthume. 6 vols. in 3. 12°, Paris, 1809.

CERVANTES SAAVEDRA, Miguel de (1547-1616)
MB.3.24-6 The history and adventures of the renowned Don Quixote: from the Spanish...By T. Smollett. To which is prefixed a memoir of the author, by T. Roscoe. 3 vols. 8°, London, 1833.

CEVALLERIUS, Antonius Rodolphus
MB.6.52[2] See ALPHABETUM
Alphabetum Hebraicum, in quo literæ Hebraicæ describuntur...Ex Antonii Ceuallerii recognitione. 1566.

CHALMERS, George (1742-1825)
MH.4.29^{6} See DEFENCE
Defence of Opposition with respect to their conduct on Irish affairs...By an Irish gentleman, a member of the Whig Club [i.e. G. Chalmers?]. (With Appendix.) (2 pts.) 1785.

CHALMERS, Thomas (1780-1847)
MH.1.15 An enquiry into the extent and stability of national resources. 8°, Edinburgh, 1808.

CHALMERS, Thomas (1780-1847)
MH.1.16 On political economy, in connexion with the moral state and moral prospects of society. 8°, Glasgow, 1832.

CHALMERS, Thomas (1780-1847)
MC.4.18-19 On the power, wisdom and goodness of God as manifested in the adaptation of external nature to the moral and intellectual constitution of man. 2 vols. (Bridgewater Treatises, 1.) 8°, London, 1833.

CHAMBERS, William (1787-1860)
MH.4.28^{3} See SHORT
A short account of the Marratta State. Written in Persian by a Munshy, who accompanied Col. Upton...Translated by W. Chambers. To which is added The voyages and travels of M. Cæsar Fredericke...1787.

CHARACTER
ME.5.16^{1} A character of England, as it was lately presented in a letter, to a noble man of France. With reflections upon Gallus Castratus. [By J. Evelyn.] 3rd ed. 12°, London, 1659.

CHARACTER
MH.4.15^{5} Character of the late Lord Viscount Sackville. [By R. Cumberland.] 8°, London, 1785.

CHATEAUBRIAND, François René, vicomte de (1768-1848)
MM.1.42 Atala, ou Les amours de deux sauvages dans le désert. 3e éd., revue et corrigée. 12°, Paris, 1801.

[ED. NOTE: In his 1802 major work "Génie du Christianisme," a romantic account of Christianity, Chateaubriand's view was that an excessive population is the calamity of Empires. He refers especially to China where children were thrown to the pigs! Apparently Chateaubriand was familiar with Malthus's *Essay* on Population.]

CHATHAM, William Pitt, 1st Earl of (1708-1778)
MH.5.6[1] Genuine abstracts from two speeches of the Earl of Chatham: and his reply to the Earl of Suffolk...[Ed. by H.M. Boyd.] 8°, London, 1779.

CHATHAM, William Pitt, 1st Earl of (1708-1778)
MH.5.6[5] See LETTER
A letter to the Earl of Chatham on the Quebec Bill. [By Sir W. Meredith.] 5th ed. 1774.

CHAUCER, Geoffrey (1340?-1400)
ME.4.9-15 Poetical works. 14 vols. in 7. (Bell's Edition. The Poets of Great Britain.) 12°, Edinburg, 1782.

CHAUCER, Geoffrey (1340?-1400)
MM.5.15 The workes of our ancient and learned English poet, Geffrey Chaucer, newly printed. [Ed. by T. Speght.] F°, London, 1602.

CHESTERFIELD, Philip Dormer Stanhope, 4th Earl of (1694-1773)
MH.2.17-20 Miscellaneous works...To which are prefixed, memoirs of his life...By M. Maty. [Ed. by J.O. Justamond.] 2nd ed. 4 vols. 8°, London, 1779.

CHILD, Sir Josiah (1630-1699)
MF.1.1 A new discourse of trade...4th ed. 12°, London, [1740?].

CHILLINGWORTH, William (1602-1644)
MD.1.11 Works. 7th ed. ...made more correct. F°, London, 1719.

CHOMEL, Noel (1632-1712)
MA.6.1 Dictionaire oeconomique. Or, The family dictionary...Done into English, from the 2nd ed. ...Revised and recommended by R. Bradley. 2 vols. in 1. F°, London, 1725.

CHRESTOMATHIA
MJ.2.38 Chrestomathia patristica Græca sive Loci illustres ex antiquissimis patribus Græci selecti, ac nova versione Latina scholiisque Latinis...Cum præfatione J.F. Birgii. (6 pts.) 8°, Vratislaviæ, 1739-45.

CHRYSAL
MC.2.38-9 Chrysal: or, The adventures of a guinea...By an adept [i.e. C. Johnstone]. 4th ed., greatly inlarged and corrected. 2 vols. 12°, London, 1764.

CHRYSAL
ME.2.12-15 Chrysal: or, The adventures of a guinea...By an adept [i.e. C. Johnstone]. 4 vols. (Vols. 1, 2, 5th ed.) 12°, London, 1766-7.

CHURCHILL, Charles (1731-1764)
ME.5.4-5 Poetical works. With the life of the author. 3 vols. in 2. (Bell's Edition. The Poets of Great Britain.) 12°, Edinburg, 1779.

CIBBER, Colley (1671-1757)
MB.2.1-5 Dramatic works. 5 vols. 12°, London, 1777.

CICERO, Marcus Tullius (106-43 B.C.)
MK.1.26-31 Lettres à Atticus. Avec des remarques, et le texte latin de l'édition de Græevius. Par L. Mongault. 6 vols. 12°, Paris, 1714.

CICERO, Marcus Tullius (106-43 B.C.)
MK.1.22-5 Lettres à ses amis. Traduits en françois [by L. Maumenet], le latin à côté suivant l'édition de Græevius...4 vols. 12°, Paris, 1725.

CICERO, Marcus Tullius (106-43 B.C.)
MF.3.14-21 Opera omnia ex recensione I.A. Ernesti cum eiusdem notis et Clave Ciceroniana. 8 vols. 8°, Halis Saxonum, 1773-7.

CIVIL
MI.1.11 Civil polity. A treatise concerning the nature of government...[By P. Paxton.] 8°, London, 1703.

CLARK, Hugh
MG.5.36 A short and easy introduction to heraldry, in two parts. By H. Clark and T. Wormull. 6th ed., with considerable improvements. 8°, London, 1788.

CLARKE, Edward Daniel (1769-1822)
ML.5.17 See TOUR
A tour through the South of England, Wales, and part of Ireland, made during the summer of 1791. [By E.D. Clarke.] 1793.

[ED. NOTE: Clarke studied at Jesus College at the same time as Malthus and became his lifetime friend. Clarke travelled for 13 years with rich students and persuaded William Otter and Malthus to accompany him in his travels in Northern Europe.]

CLARKE, Samuel (1675-1729)
MK.4.6 A collection of papers, which passed between the late learned Mr. Leibnitz, and Dr. Clarke, in the years 1715 and 1716. Relating to the principles of natural philosophy and religion... 8°, London, 1717.

CLARKE, Samuel (1675-1729)
MG.3.17 A discourse concerning the Being and attributes of God, the obligations of natural religion, and the truth and certainty of the Christian Revelation...3rd ed., corrected. (2 pts.) (Boyle Lectures, 1704, 1705.) 8°, London, 1711.

CLARKE, Samuel (1675-1729)
MK.3.17 A letter to Mr. Dodwell; wherein all the arguments in his Epistolary discourse against the immortality of the soul are particularly answered...5th ed. 8°, London, 1718.

CLARKE, Samuel (1675-1729)
MG.3.5 The scripture-doctrine of the Trinity. In 3 pts. ... 8°, London, 1712.

CLARKE, Samuel (1675-1729)
ME.1.25, 25a-33,33a Sermons. With a preface...by Benjamin [Hoadly], now Lord Bishop of Winchester. 7th ed. 11 vols. 12°, London, 1749.

CLARKE, Samuel (1675-1729)
ML.2.23 Three practical essays, on baptism, confirmation, and repentance...4th ed. 12°, London, 1721.

CLUVERIUS, Philipp (1580-1622)
MG.7.15 Introductio in universam geographiam tam veterem quam novam, tabulis geographicis XLVI ac notis olim ornata a J. Bunone...additamentis & annotationibus J.F. Hekelii & J. Reiskii... 4°, Londini, 1711.

COBBETT, William (1763-1835)
MH.4.21^{2} See OBSERVATIONS
Observations on the emigration of Dr. Joseph Priestley...[By W. Cobbett.] New ed. 1794.

COCHRAN, Sir Robert (d. 1482)
MH.5.19^{7} See LIFE
The life of Sir Robt. Cochran, Prime-Minister to King James III. of Scotland. 1734.

COCKBURN, Henry, Lord Cockburn (1779-1854)
ME.3.14-15 Life of Lord Jeffrey with a selection from his correspondence. 2 vols. 8°, Edinburgh, 1852.*

CODE
ME.7.14 A code of Gentoo laws, or, ordinations of the Pundits, from a Persian translation, made from the original, written in the Shanscrit language. [Translated and ed. by N.B. Halhed.] 4°, London, 1776.

COLBERT, Jean Baptiste, Marquis of Torcy (1665-1746)
ML.2.17-19 Mémoires, pour servir à l'histoire des négociations depuis le Traité de Ryswyck jusqu'à la Paix d'Utrecht. 3 vols. 8°, Londres, 1757.

COLERIDGE, Samuel Taylor (1772-1834)
MH.1.28[1] A lay sermon, addressed to the higher and middle classes, on the existing distresses and discontents. 8°, London, 1817.

COLERIDGE, Samuel Taylor (1772-1834)
MB.1.29-31 Poetical works. 3 vols. 8°, London, 1835-6.*

COLERIDGE, Samuel Taylor (1772-1834)
MH.1.28[2] The statesman's manual; or The Bible the best guide to political skill and foresight: a lay sermon...(2 pts.) 8°, London, 1816.

COLLECTION
MC.2.27-32 A collection of poems. By several hands. [Ed. by R. Dodsley.] 6 vols. (Vols. 1-3, 5th ed.; vol. 4, 2nd ed.) 8°, London, 1758.

COLLECTION
MH.4.23 A collection of political tracts. [By H. St. John, Viscount Bolingbroke.] 2nd ed. 8°, London, 1748.

COLLECTION
MM.2.17-22 A collection of theological tracts. [Ed.] By R. Watson. 6 vols. 8°, Cambridge, 1785.

COLLECTION
MA.6.14 A collection of two hundred original etchings; consisting of 7 original plates, by Rembrandt [etc.]... F°, London, [ca. 1820].

COLMAN, George (1762-1836)
ME.4.16-19 See CONNOISSEUR
The Connoisseur. By Mr. Town, critic and censor-general [i.e. G. Colman and B. Thornton]. [A periodical, 1754-6.] 2nd ed. 4 vols. 1755-7.

COLMAN, George (1732-1794)
MK.3.10-13 Dramatick works. 4 vols. 8°, London, 1777.

COLQUHOUN, Patrick (1745-1820)
MH.1.20 See TREATISE
A treatise on the police of the Metropolis...By a magistrate [i.e. P. Colquhoun]. 3rd ed., revised and enlarged. 1796.

[ED. NOTE: Malthus refers to and cites from this Treatise in his *Essay*, Bk. IV, Ch. IV. Colquhoun had a good knowledge of the poor people, and suggested various institutions for public relief.]

COLQUHOUN, Patrick (1745-1820)
MM.5.18 A treatise on the wealth, power, and resources, of the British Empire...2nd ed., with additions and corrections. 4°, London, 1815.

[ED. NOTE: Malthus refers to this work in his "Principles of Political Economy" (1820 ed. p. 171). He also refers to this work in his Tract of 1815, "An Inquiry into the Nature and Progress of Rent."]

COMBE, William (1741-1823)
MK.5.15[7] See DIABOLIAD
The Diaboliad, a poem. Dedicated to the worst man in His Majesty's dominions. [By W. Combe.] New ed., with large additions. 1677 [or rather 1777].

COMBE, William (1741-1823)
MK.5.15[9] See FIRST
The First of April: or, The triumphs of folly: a poem. Dedicated to the celebrated Dutchess. By the author of The Diaboliad [i.e. W. Combe]. 1777.

COMBE, William (1741-1823)
MK.5.15[8] See JUSTIFICATION
The justification: a poem. By the author of The Diaboliad [i.e. W. Combe]. 1777.

COMBE, William (1741-1823)
MK.5.15[1]0 See LETTER
A letter to Her Grace the Duchess of Devonshire. [By W. Combe.] 1777.

COMBE, William (1741-1823)
MG.7.8[5] See POETICAL
A poetical epistle to Sir Joshua Reynolds, Knt. and President of the Royal Academy. [By W. Combe.] 1777.

COMBER, William Turner
MH.1.2 An inquiry into the state of national subsistence, as connected with progress of wealth and population. (2 pts.) 8°, London, 1808.

COMINES, Philippe de, sire d'Argenton (c. 1445-1511)
MA.7.14 Mémoires, contenans l'histoire des roys Louys XI. & Charles VIII. ...Revues & corrigez...Augmentez...Par D. Godefroy. F°, Paris, 1649.

COMMENTS
MH.5.13[2] Comments on the proposed war with France, on the state of parties, and on the new Act respecting aliens...By a lover of peace. 8°, London, 1793.

COMPLAINT
MK.5.20 The complaint: or, Night-thoughts on life, death, and immortality. [By E. Young.] (Nights 5-8.) (4 pts.) [Misbound.] 4°, London, 1743-5.

COMTE, François Charles Louis (1782-1837)
MM.5.7[2] Notice historique sur la vie et les travaux de M. Thomas-Robert Malthus. (Extr. from Académie des Sciences Morales et Politiques. Recueil des lectures...1836.) 4°, [Paris, 1837].*

[ED. NOTE: In 1833, Malthus was elected as the fifth foreign associated member of the Académie. Comte, its secretary, read this notice on Malthus's life in the public meeting of Dec. 28, 1836.]

CONANT, John (1608-1694)
MG.3.18-23 Sermons preach'd on several occasions. Published by Dr. J. Williams. 6 vols. (Vol. 1, 2nd ed. corrected.) 8°, London, 1697-1722.

CONGLETON, Henry Brooke Parnell, 1st Lord (1776-1842)
MH.3.18[5] Observations upon the state of currency in Ireland, and upon the course of exchange between Dublin and London. 8°, Dublin, 1804.

CONGLETON, Henry Brooke Parnell, 1st Lord (1776-1842)
MC.3.15 On financial reform. 2nd ed. 8°, London, 1830.

CONGREVE, William (1670-1729)
ML.1.32-4 Works. Consisting of his plays and poems. 6th ed. 3 vols. 12°, London, 1753.

CONNOISSEUR
ME.4.16-19 The Connoisseur. By Mr. Town, critic and censor-general [i.e. G. Colman and B. Thornton]. [A periodical, 1754-6.] 2nd ed. 4 vols. 12°, London, 1755-7.

CONSIDERATIONS
MH.5.25[1] Considerations on Lord Grenville's and Mr. Pitt's Bills, concerning treasonable and seditious practices, and unlawful assemblies. By a lover of order [i.e. W. Godwin]. 8°, London, [1795].

CONSIDERATIONS
MH.5.21[2] Considerations on several proposals, lately made, for the better maintenance of the poor. [By C. Gray.] 8°, London, 1751.

CONSIDERATIONS
MH.5.23[8] Considerations on the Bill for preventing clandestine marriages. By a freeholder. 8°, London, 1753.

CONSIDERATIONS
MH.5.23[5] Considerations on the Bill to permit persons professing the Jewish religion to be naturalized by Parliament. In several letters from a merchant... 8°, London, 1753.

CONSIDERATIONS
MH.4.27[2] Considerations on the present state of East-India affairs. By a member of the last Parliament. 2nd ed. 8°, London, 1784.

CONSOLATION
ME.6.1[1] The consolation. Containing, among other things, I. A moral survey of the nocturnal heavens. II. A night-address to the Deity...[By E. Young.] 4°, London, 1745.

CONYBEARE, William Daniel (1787-1857)
ML.3.34 Outlines of the geology of England and Wales...By W.D. Conybeare and W. Phillips. Pt. 1. [No more published.] 8°, London, 1822.

COOK, James (1728-1779)
MK.5.3-4 A voyage towards the South Pole, and round the world. Performed in His Majesty's ships the Resolution and Adventure, in the years 1772, 1773, 1774, and 1775...2 vols. 4°, London, 1777.

[ED. NOTE: Malthus refers to Cook's voyages in his later *Essay*, Bk. I, Ch. III, IV. & V.]

COOKE, William (d. 1824)
MJ.1.17-19 Memoirs of Samuel Foote, Esq. With a collection of his genuine bon-mots, anecdotes, opinions, &c. mostly original...3 vols. 8°, London, 1805.

COOPER, John Gilbert (1723-1769)
MM.3.19 The life of Socrates, collected from the Memorabilia of Xenophon and the Dialogues of Plato...3rd ed. 8°, London, 1750.

COPLESTON, Edward, Bp of Llandaff (1776-1849)
ML.3.25 An enquiry into the doctrines of necessity and predestination in four discourses preached before the University of Oxford...2nd ed. 8°, London, 1821.

COUNTRY
ML.5.29[8] A country curate's observations on the advertizement...from the Leeds Clergy, relative to the Test Act, &c. ...[By G. Wakefield?]. 8°, [London, 1790].

COURTENAY, John (1741-1816)
MH.4.21[5] Courtenay's Four patriotic songs. Addressed to the British sailors, soldiers, and volunteers. 8°, London, 1803.

COURTENAY, John (1741-1816)
MK.5.15[4] See POETICAL
A poetical and philosophical essay on the French Revolution. [By J. Courtenay.] Addressed to the Right Hon. E. Burke. 1793.

COURTENAY, John (1741-1816)
MH.4.21[3] See TWO
Two apologetical odes, and an elegy. [By J. Courtenay.] (Privately pr.) 1808.

COUSIN, Victor (1792-1867)
MC.3.14 Report on the state of public instruction in Prussia...Translated by S. Austin. 8°, London, 1834.

COVELLE, Robert
MB.2.34[3] Robert Covelle, citoyen de Genève [a letter] à Monsieur de Voltaire gentilhomme ordinaire de la Chambre du Roi, à Fernex. 12°, [Geneva? 1767.]

COWLEY, Abraham (1618-1667)
ME.5.2-3 Poetical works. From the text of Dr. Sprat, &c. With the life of the author. 4 vols. in 2. (Bell's Edition. The Poets of Great Britain.) 12°, Edinburg, 1777.

COWLEY, Abraham (1618-1667)
MM.3.23-4 Works. Consisting of those which were formerly printed; and those which he design'd for the press...11th ed. 2 vols. 8°, London, 1710.

COWLEY, Abraham (1618-1667)
MM.3.25 The third and last volume of the works of Mr. A. Cowley: being the second and third parts thereof... 8°, London, 1711.

COWLEY, Hannah [Parkhouse] (1743-1809)
MI.4.8[1] The belle's stratagem, a comedy as acted at the Theatre-Royal in Covent-Garden. 8°, London, 1782.

COWLEY, Hannah [Parkhouse] (1743-1809)
MI.4.8[2] A bold stroke for a husband, a comedy, as acted at the Theatre Royal in Covent Garden. 2nd ed. 8°, London, 1784.

COWLEY, Hannah [Parkhouse] (1743-1809)
MI.4.8^{3} More ways than one, a comedy, as acted at the Theatre Royal in Covent Garden. 2nd ed. 8°, London, 1784.

COWLEY, Hannah [Parkhouse] (1743-1809)
MI.4.8^{4} Which is the man? A comedy, as acted at the Theatre-Royal in Covent-Garden. 5th ed. 8°, London, 1785.

COWLEY, Hannah [Parkhouse] (1743-1809)
MI.4.8^{5} Who's the dupe? A farce: as it is acted at the Theatre-Royal in Drury-Lane. 3rd ed. 8°, London, 1780.

COWPER, William (1731-1800)
MI.4.12-13 Poems. 4th ed. 2 vols. 8°, London, 1788.

COWPER, William (1731-1800)
ME.5.48-9 Poems. 2 vols. (University ed.) 16°, London, 1826.

COX, Sir Richard, 2nd Bart. (1702-1766)
MH.5.22^{2} See PROCEEDING
The proceeding of the honourable House of Commons of Ireland, in rejecting the altered Money-Bill, on December 17, 1753, vindicated...[By Sir Richard Cox.] [1754].

COXE, William (1747-1828)
MH.5.24^{1} A letter on the Secret Tribunals of Westphalia, addressed to Elizabeth, Countess of Pembroke. (Signed: W. Coxe.) 4°, Salisbury, 1796.

[ED. NOTE: In 1781, Coxe published *Nouvelles découvertes de Russes...*, which is apparently part of the "Découvertes Russes" Malthus refers to in Bk. I of his *Essay on Population*. In 1784, Coxe published an account of "Travels into Poland, Russia, Sweden and Denmark..." The account given for Sweden (Bk. VII.) was a guide for the preparation of the journey of Malthus and Clarke in that country. From this journey Malthus got basic information which he covered in the second and later editions of his *Essay* on Population.]

CRABBE, George (1754-1832)
MG.5.1 The Borough: a poem, in twenty-four letters. 2nd ed., revised. 8°, London, 1810.

CRABBE, George (1754-1832)
MG.5.2 Poems. 3rd ed. 8°, London, 1808.

CRABBE, George (1754-1832)
MG.5.3 Tales. 8°, London, 1812.

CRABBE, George (1754-1832)
MG.5.4-5 Tales of the Hall. New ed. 2 vols. 8°, London, 1819.

CREBILLON, Claude Prosper Jolyot de (1707-1777)
MF.1.16 Lettres de la Marquise de M***, au Comte de R***. 2 vols. in 1. 12°, La Haye, 1761.

CRISIS
MH.4.25[4] The crisis stated; or, Serious and seasonable hints upon war in general, and upon the consequences of a war with France. 8°, London, 1793.

CRITICAL
MH.3.5 A critical dissertation on the nature, measures, and causes of value; chiefly in reference to the writings of Mr. Ricardo and his followers...[By S. Bailey.] 8°, London, 1825.

[ED. NOTE: Ch. VII of this monograph is entitled "On the Measure of Value proposed by Mr. Malthus." In his work "Definitions in Political Economy," Malthus discusses the views of the "anonymous writer" of this monograph. Actually Ch. VIII of Malthus's "Definitions" is entitled "On the Definition and Use of Terms by the author of 'A Critical Dissertation on the Nature, Measure and Causes of Value.'"]

CROKER, Rt. Hon. John Wilson (1780-1857)
MH.3.17[3] See SKETCH
A sketch of the state of Ireland, past and present. [By J.W. Croker.] 1808.

CROWE, William (1745-1829)
MK.5.15[1] See LEWESDON
Lewesdon Hill; a poem. [By W. Crowe.] 1788.

CRUMPE, Samuel (1766-1796)
MH.1.18 An essay on the best means of providing employment for the people... 8°, Dublin, 1793.

[ED. NOTE: "Dr. Crumpe's Prize Essay on the best means of finding employment for the people is an excellent treatise..." Malthus's *Essay*, Bk. IV, Ch. X. (older ed.), or Ch. XI, latest ed.]

CRUSIUS, Lewis (1701-1775)
MG.5.26-7 The lives of the Roman poets...2 vols. 12°, London, 1733.

CUDWORTH, Ralph (1617-1688)
MD.1.12 The true intellectual system of the Universe; the first part... F°, London, 1678.

CUISINIERE
MB.3.13 La cuisinière bourgeoise, suivie de l'office...[By Menon.] Nouvelle éd., augmentée... 12°, Paris, 1775.

CUMBERLAND, Richard (1732-1811)
ML.2.15 Anecdotes of eminent painters in Spain, during the Sixteenth and Seventeenth centuries...2 vols. in 1. 8°, London, 1782.

CUMBERLAND, Richard (1732-1811)
MI.4.7^{5} See BROTHERS
The brothers, a comedy as it is performed at the Theatre-Royal in Covent-Garden. [By R. Cumberland.] 1770.

CUMBERLAND, Richard (1732-1811)
MH.4.15^{5} See CHARACTER
Character of the late Lord Viscount Sackville. [By R. Cumberland.] 1785.

CUMBERLAND, Richard (1732-1811)
MI.4.7^{4} See FASHIONABLE
The fashionable lover; a comedy: as it is acted at the Theatre-Royal in Drury-Lane. [By R. Cumberland.] 2nd ed. 1772.

CUMBERLAND, Richard (1732-1811)
MI.4.5^{2} The Jew: a comedy. Performed at the Theatre-Royal, Drury-Lane. 3rd ed. 8°, London, 1795.

CUMBERLAND, Richard (1732-1811)
MI.4.7^{2} See WEST INDIAN
The West Indian: a comedy. As it is performed at the Theatre-Royal in Drury-Lane. By the author of The Brothers [R. Cumberland]. 1771.

CUMBERLAND, Richard (1732-1811)
MI.4.5^{1} The wheel of fortune: a comedy. Performed at the Theatre-Royal, Drury-Lane. 2nd ed. 8°, London, 1795.

CURRAN, William Henry (1789?-1858)
MM.3.9-10 The life of the Right Honourable John Philpot Curran, late Master of the Rolls in Ireland. 2 vols. 8°, London, 1819.

CURRIE, James (1756-1805)
MH.5.25^{2} A letter, commercial and political, addressed to the R^{t}. H°nble. William Pitt: in which the real interests of Britain, in the present

crisis, are considered...By Jasper Wilson [i.e. James Currie]. 2nd ed., corrected and enlarged. 8°, London, 1793.

CURRIE, James (1756-1805)
For the Life of Burns by J. Currie, published with the Poems of Burns, see BURNS, Robert.

CURTIS, William (1746-1799)
MG.7.21^{3} A short history of the brown-tail moth... 4°, London, 1782.

CURTIUS RUFUS, Quintus (41?-79 A.D.?)
MG.1.23 Historia Alexandri Magni. Cum notis selectiss. variorum, Raderi, Freinshemii, Loccenii, Blancardi, &c. Ed. novissima. 8°, Amstelodami, 1684.

CYDER
MJ.1.48^{2} Cyder. A poem in two books. [By J. Philips.] 4th ed. 12°, London, 1744.

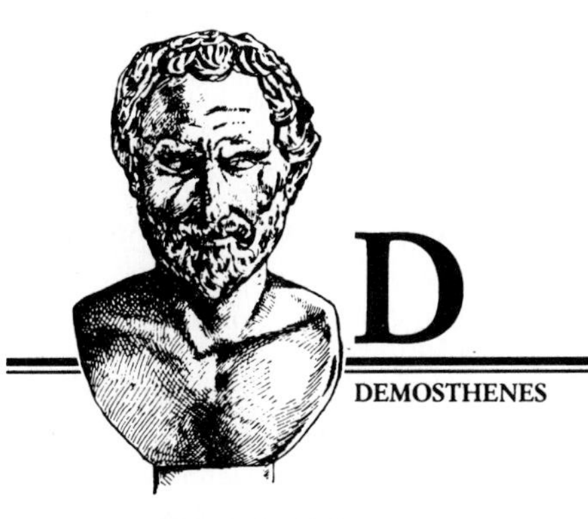

DALRYMPLE, Sir John (1726-1810)
ME.6.3 Memoirs of Great Britain and Ireland. From the dissolution of the last Parliament of Charles II. until the sea-battle of La Hogue. (2 pts.) 4°, Edinburgh, 1771.

DAMM, Christian Tobias (1699-1778)
MG.6.8 Novum lexicon Græcum etymologicum et reale...Ed. de novo instructa...cura J.M. Duncan. 4°, Glasguæ, 1824.

DANCE OF DEATH
ML.3.17 La danse des morts, comme elle est dépeinte dans la louable et célebre ville de Basle, pour servir de miroir de la nature humaine. Dessinée et gravée sur l'original de M. Merian...(German & French.) 4°, Basle, 1789.

DANIEL, William Barker (1753?-1833)
ME.3.9-11 Rural sports. 2 vols. in 3. 8°, [London, 1801-2].

DANTE ALIGHIERI (1265-1321)
MJ.1.3-4 La Divina Commedia, col comento del P. Pompeo Venturi...Vols. 1, 3. (Vol. 2 wanting.) 12°, Firenze, 1826.

DANTE ALIGHIERI (1265-1321)
MB.6.22-4 The vision; or Hell, purgatory, and paradise. Translated by H.F. Cary. 2nd ed. corrected. 3 vols. 8°, London, 1819.

DARU, Pierre Antoine Noël Bruno, comte (1767-1829)
MA.1.1-8 Histoire de la république de Venise. 2e éd., revue et corrigée. 8 vols. 8°, Paris, 1821.

DARWIN, Erasmus (1731-1802)
ME.6.17[1] Phytologia; or The philosophy of agriculture and gardening... 4°, London, 1800.

DARWIN, Erasmus (1731-1802)
ME.6.17[2] A plea for the conduct of female education, in boarding schools. 4°, Derby, 1797.

DARWIN, Erasmus (1731-1802)
ME.7.1-2 Zoonomia; or, The laws of organic life. 2 vols. 4°, London, 1794-6.

DAVID, François Anne (1741-1824)
MF.7.6 Histoire de Russie, représentée par figures, accompagnées d'un précis historique; les figures gravées par F.A. David...le discours par Blin de Sainmore. 3 vols. in 1. 4°, Paris, 1813.

DAVIES, Thomas (1712?-1785)
MM.3.29-30 Memoirs of the life of David Garrick, Esq. ... 2 vols. 8°, London, 1780.

DAVILA, Enrico Caterino (1576-1631)
MD.1.10 The historie of the civill warres of France, written in Italian. Translated out of the original [by W. Aylesbury]. F°, London, 1647.

DAVY, Sir Humphry (1778-1829)
MB.2.11 Consolations in travel, or The last days of a philosopher. 8°, London, 1830.

DAVY, Sir Humphry (1778-1829)
MB.2.12 See SALMONIA
Salmonia: or Days of fly fishing. In a series of conversations...By an angler [Sir Humphry Davy]. 3rd ed. 1832.

DAY, Thomas (1748-1789)
MH.5.3[4] Two speeches at the general meetings of the Counties of Cambridge and Essex, held March 25, and April 25, 1780. 8°, [London] 1780.

DEALTRY, William (1775-1847)
MC.4.7 Sermons, chiefly practical, preached in the Parish Church of Clapham, Surrey. 8°, London, 1827.

DEFENCE
MH.4.29[6] Defence of Opposition with respect to their conduct on Irish affairs...By an Irish gentleman, a member of the Whig Club [i.e. G. Chalmers?]. (With Appendix.) (2 pts.) 8°, London, 1785.

DE LA BECHE, Sir Henry Thomas (1796-1855)
MK.1.19 A geological manual. 2nd ed., corrected and enlarged. 12°, London, 1832.

DE LA BECHE, Sir Henry Thomas (1796-1855)
MC.3.9 Researches in theoretical geology. 8°, London, 1834.

DELILLE, Jacques (1738-1813)
MM.1.41 La pitié, poëme. 12°, Paris, 1803.

DEMETRIUS, Cydonius (c. 1384)
MG.1.15 Opusculum De contemnenda morte Græce et Latine, recensuit, emendavit, explicavit C.T. Kuinoel. 8°, Lipsiae, 1786.

DEMOSTHENES (384-322 B.C.)
MF.3.30-31

Δημοσθένους καί Αισχίνου οἱ περί τῆς παραπρεσβείας, κατά κτησιφωτός, καί περί τοῦ στεφάνου λόγοι ἀντίπαλοι

Græce et Latine [in the translation of H. Wolfius]. Edidit I. Taylor. 2 vols. 8°, Cantabrigiæ, 1769.

DEMOSTHENES (384-322 B.C.)
ML.2.41-2 Demosthenis Orationum pars prima (and secunda). (Corrigente P. Manutio.) [Part 3 wanting.] 8°, Venetiis, 1554.

DESCARTES, René (1596-1650)
MG.6.12 Opera philosophica. 3 pts. (Principia philosophiæ). Ultima ed. ...Specimina philosophiæ: seu Dissertatio de methodo...dioptrice et meteora. Ex Gallico translata...Ultima ed. ...Passiones animæ, per Renatum Descartes: Gallicè ab ipso conscriptæ, nunc autem in exterorum gratiam Latina civitate donatae. Ab H.D.M.I.V.L.). 4°, (Amstelodami, 1677-92).

DESCRIPTION
MB.6.53[4] A description of Brighthelmstone, and the adjacent country... 8°, Brighthelmstone [1788].

DESCRIPTIVE
MB.6.53[1] A descriptive journey through the interior parts of Germany and France, including Paris...By a young English Peer [Francis Russell, 5th Duke of Bedford]... 8°, London, 1786.

DES MAIZEAUX, Pierre (1673?-1745)
MM.2.8 An historical and critical account of the life and writings of W. Chillingworth, Chancellor of the Church of Sarum. (By P. Des Maizeaux.) 8°, London, 1725.

DEVONSHIRE, Georgina [Spencer Cavendish], Duchess of (1757-1806)
MK.5.15[1]0 See LETTER
A letter to Her Grace the Duchess of Devonshire. [By W. Combe.] 1777.

DIABOLIAD
MK.5.15[7] The Diaboliad, a poem. Dedicated to the worst man in His Majesty's dominions. [By W. Combe.] New ed., with large additions. 4°, London, 1677 [or rather 1777].

DIALOGUE
MI.2.2[8] A dialogue between an associator and a well-informed Englishman, on the grounds of the late associations, and the commencement of a war with France. [By J. Towers.] 8°, London, 1793.

DIAZ DEL CASTILLO, Bernal (1496-1584)
MF.7.12 The true history of the conquest of Mexico, written in the year 1568. Translated from the original Spanish, by M. Keatinge. 4°, London, 1800.

DIBDIN, Thomas Frognall (1776-1847)
MK.4.14 Bibliomania; or Book madness: a bibliographical romance, in 6 parts. 8°, London, 1811.

DIBDIN, Thomas Frognall (1776-1847)
MG.1.7 An introduction to the knowledge of rare and valuable editions of the Greek and Latin classics...2nd ed., enlarged and corrected. 8°, London, 1804.

DIBDIN, Thomas Frognall (1776-1847)
MK.4.13 The library companion; or, The young man's guide, and the old man's comfort, in the choice of a library. 8°, London, 1824.

DICEY, Thomas
ME.2.40 An historical account of Guernsey, from its first settlement...to the present time... 12°, London, 1751.

DICKENS, Charles (1812-1870)
MG.4.19 The adventures of Oliver Twist; or, The Parish boy's progress. With 24 illustrations on steel, by G. Cruikshank. New ed., revised and corrected. 8°, London, 1846.*

DICKENS, Charles (1812-1870)
MG.4.20 Bleak House. With illustrations by H.K. Browne. 8°, London, 1853.*

DICKENS, Charles (1812-1870)
MG.4.15 Dombey and Son. With illustrations by H.K. Browne. 8°, London, 1848.*

DICKENS, Charles (1812-1870)
MG.4.18 The life and adventures of Martin Chuzzlewit. With illustrations by Phiz. 8°, London, 1844.*

DICKENS, Charles (1812-1870)
MG.4.16 The life and adventures of Nicholas Nickleby. With illustrations by Phiz. 8°, London, 1839.*

DICKENS, Charles (1812-1870)
MG.4.21 Little Dorrit. With illustrations by H.K. Browne. 8°, London, 1857.*

DICKENS, Charles (1812-1870)
MG.4.23 Master Humphrey's clock. With illustrations by G. Cattermole and H. Browne. [Includes 'The Old Curiosity shop' and 'Barnaby Rudge'.] 3 vols. in 1. 8°, London, 1840-41.*

DICKENS, Charles (1812-1870)
MG.4.17[2] The mystery of Edwin Drood. With twelve illustrations by S.L. Fildes. 8°, London, 1870.*

DICKENS, Charles (1812-1870)
MG.4.12-13 Our mutual friend. With illustrations by M. Stone. 2 vols. 8°, London, 1865.*

DICKENS, Charles (1812-1870)
MG.4.14 The personal history of David Copperfield. With illustrations by H.K. Browne. 8°, London, 1850.*

DICKENS, Charles (1812-1870)
MG.4.22 The posthumous papers of the Pickwick Club. With 43 illustrations, by R. Seymour and Phiz. 8°, London, 1837.*

DICKENS, Charles (1812-1870)
MG.4.24 Sketches by Boz illustrative of every-day life and every-day people. With 40 illustrations by G. Cruikshank. New ed., complete. 8°, London, 1863.*

DICKENS, Charles (1812-1870)
MG.4.17[1] A tale of two cities. With illustrations by H.K. Browne. 8°, London, 1859.*

DICTIONARY. Biography
MM.4.15-26 See NEW
A new and general biographical dictionary; containing an historical and critical account of the lives and writings of the most eminent persons in every nation...New ed., greatly enlarged and improved. 12 vols. 1784.

DICTIONNAIRE
MA.4.9 Dictionnaire philosophique, portatif. [By F.M.A. de Voltaire.] 8°, [London] 1765.

DIEZ, Franz Maximilian
ML.5.1 Post- und Reise-Karte von Deutschland und den anliegenden Ländern...[Single sheet folded.] Gotha, 1827.

DIODORUS, Siculus (fl. c. 60-30 B.C.)
MK.1.8-14 Histoire universelle. Traduite en françois par M. l'Abbé Terrasson. 7 vols. (Vol. 1, Nouvelle éd.) 12°, Paris, 1737-77.

DIOSCORIDES (fl. middle 1st C.)
MK.4.18 (Pedacij Dioscoridis De materia medica libri VI. Eiusdem de venenatis animalibus libri II...[Ed. by J. Cornarius].) (Greek.) 8°, Basileae, 1529.

DISCOURS
ML.3.14[4] Discours d'un Syndic de***, prononcé le 4 décembre 1788, &c. 2e éd. 8°, [Paris?] 1789.

DISCOURSE
MH.5.21[4] A discourse concerning some of the most important branches, and parts, of the Office of the Justices of the Peace...With proposals for their better reparation and amendment. 12°, [London? c. 1750.]

DISCOURSE
MH.5.24[7] A discourse concerning the Resurrection bodies...By Philalethes [i.e. J. Gough]. 8°, London, 1788.

DISSERTATION
MH.1.21 A dissertation on the numbers of mankind in antient and modern times: in which the superior populousness of antiquity is maintained...[By R. Wallace.] 8°, Edinburgh, 1753.
See ED. NOTE under R. Wallace.

DIVITIO, Bernardo, Cardinal (1470-1520)
See DOVIZI, Bernardo, Cardinal.

DOBLADO, Leucadio, pseud.
See WHITE, Joseph Blanco.

DODD, Thomas (1771-1850)
MF.7.15 A catalogue of the extensive and choice collection of prints, formed by the late Robert Morse, Esq. ...and a matchless collection of the works of J.G. Wille...Sold by auction, by Mr. Thomas Dodd, at no. 42, Old Bond Street, on Wednesday, May 15, 1816, & twenty-seven following days... 4°, [London, 1816].

DODDRIDGE, Philip (1702-1751)
MM.3.5-6 A course of lectures on the principal subjects in pneumatology, ethics, and divinity...To which are added a great number of references...By A. Kippis. 4th ed., 2 vols. 8°, London, 1799.

DODSLEY, Robert (1703-1764)
MC.2.27-32 See COLLECTION
A collection of poems. By several hands. [Ed. by R. Dodsley.] 6 vols. (Vols. 1-3, 5th ed., vol. 4, 2nd ed.). 1758.

DODSLEY, Robert (1703-1764)
ME.2.32-3 See FUGITIVE
Fugitive pieces on various subjects. By several authors. [Ed. by R. Dodsley.] [2nd ed.] 2 vols. 1765.

DORSET, Charles Sackville, 2nd Duke of (1711-1769)
MH.5.17[4] See TREATISE
A treatise concerning the Militia, in 4 sections...By C.S. [i.e. Charles Sackville, Duke of Dorset.] 1752.

DOVIZI, Bernardo, Cardinal [Dovizi da Bibbiena, B.] (1470-1520)
ML.2.3 Calandra; comedia. Di nuovo con somma diligenza corretta et ristampata. 12°, Vinegia, 1562.

DRYDEN, John (1631-1700)
MC.2.33, 33a-37 Dramatick works. [Dedication by Congreve.] 6 vols. (Vol. 2 an earlier ed. of 1735). 12°, London, 1735; 1762-3.

DRYDEN, John (1631-1700)
MF.1.2-6 See MISCELLANY
Miscellany poems. Containing variety of new translations of the ancient poets: together with several original poems. By the most eminent hands. Publish'd by Mr. Dryden. Pts. 1-3, 5, 6. (Pts. 1, 2, 4th ed.) (Pt. 4 wanting.) 5 vols. 1716.

DUBOIS, Edward (1774-1850)
MB.4.25 See MY
My pocket-book; or, Hints for 'A ryghte merrie and conceitede' tour...By a Knight errant [i.e. E. Dubois]. 3rd ed. With various additions... 12°, London, 1808.

DU CANGE, Charles du Fresne, Sieur (1610-1688)
MA.7.10-11 Glossarium ad scriptores mediæ & infimæ Latinitatis...Vols. 1, 2. (Vol. 3 wanting.) F°, Lutetiæ Parisiorum, 1678.

DUDLEY, Sir Henry Bate (1745-1824)
MH.3.17[4] A short address to...William, Lord Primate of all Ireland; recommendatory of some commutation, or modification of the tythes of that country...3rd ed. 8°, London, 1808.

DUFRESNOY, Lenglet (1674-1755)
See LENGLET DU FRESNOY, Pierre Nicolas.

DUNCAN, William (1717-1760)
MG.5.32 The elements of logick. In four books. 3rd ed. 12°, London, 1752.

DURAND, François Jacques (1727-1816)
MK.1.15-18 Statistique élémentaire, ou Essai sur l'état géographique, physique et politique de la Suisse. 4 vols. 8°, Lausanne, 1795-6.

DUTENS, Louis (1730-1812)
MA.2.7 Œuvres mélées de M.L. Dutens. (Nouvelle éd.) 8°, Genève, 1784.

[ED. NOTE: Reference by Malthus to this work in later *Essay*, Bk. II, Ch. V.]

DUVAL, Valentin Jamerai
See JAMERAI-DUVAL, Valentin.

DYER, John (1700?-1758)
MK.3.14 Poems. Viz. I. Grongar Hill. II. The ruins of Rome. III. The fleece, in four books. 8°, London, 1770.

E

THOMAS ERSKINE

EAST INDIA COMPANY
MH.3.21[2] See SHORT
Short state of the present situation of the India Company, both in India and in Europe...1784.

EDEN, Sir Frederick Morton (1766-1809)
MH.3.17[6] Address on the maritime rights of Great Britain. 2nd ed. 8°, London, 1803.

EDEN, Rt. Hon. William
See AUCKLAND, William Eden, 1st Baron.

EDGEWORTH, Maria (1767-1849)
MC.2.9-26 Tales and novels. 18 vols. 8°, London, 1832-3.

EDWARDS, Jonathan (1629-1712)
ML.3.2 An inquiry into the modern prevailing notions respecting that freedom of will which is supposed to be essential to moral agency...New ed. ...(2 pts.) 8°, London, 1831.

EGMONT, John Perceval, 2nd Earl of (1711-1770)
MH.5.20[1] See EXAMINATION
An examination of the principles, and an enquiry into the conduct of the two B*****rs [Brothers: The Duke of Newcastle and The Hon. Henry Pelham]; in regard to the establishment of their power...[By the Earl of Egmont.] 3rd ed., reviewed and corrected. 1749.

EGMONT, John Perceval, 2nd Earl of (1711-1770)
MH.5.22[1] See SOME
Some observations on the present state of Ireland, particularly with relation to the woollen manufacture...[By John Perceval, Earl of Egmont.] 1731.

EIKON BASILIKE
ME.2.23 Εἰκών Βασιλική The pourtraicture of His Sacred Maiestie in his solitudes and sufferings. 8°, [London] 1648.

ELEGANT
ME.3.2-3 Elegant extracts: or, Useful and entertaining passages in prose...[Compiled by V. Knox.] 4 books. 2 vols. 8°, London, 1808.

ELEGANT
ME.3.4-5 Elegant extracts: or, Useful and entertaining pieces of poetry...[Compiled by V. Knox.] 4 books. 2 vols. 8°, London, 1809.

ELIAS, Levita (1469-1549)
MB.6.52[3] Nomenclatura Hebraica... 8°, Impressum Isne, 1542.

ELITE
ME.5.67-8 Elite de bon mots, pensées choisies, histoires singulières, & autres petites pièces...Nouvelle éd., augmentée...2 vols. 12°, Amsterdam, 1731.

EMMIUS, Ubbo (1547-1625)
MC.3.10-12 Vetus Græcia illustrata...3 vols. 8°, Lugduni Batavorum, 1626.

ENFIELD, William (1741-1797)
MG.4.7-8 See BRUCKER, Jacob
The history of philosophy...drawn up from Brucker's Historia critica philosophiæ. By W. Enfield. 2 vols. 1819.

ENQUIRY
MM.3.21 An enquiry into the life and writings of Homer. [By T. Blackwell.] 2nd ed. 8°, London, 1736.

ENQUIRY
MH.5.20[5] An enquiry into the reasons of the conduct of Great Britain, with relation to the present state of affairs in Europe. [By B. Hoadly.] 8°, London, 1727.

ENTHUSIASM
MF.5.30-31 The enthusiasm of Methodists and Papists compared. [By G. Lavington.] (3 pts.) 2 vols. (Vol. 1, 2nd ed.) 8°, London, 1749-51.

EPICTETUS (c. 55-c. 135 A.D.)
MK.2.22-3 All the works of Epictetus, which are now extant...Translated from the original Greek, by E. Carter...3rd ed. 2 vols. 12°, London, 1768.

EPICTETUS (c. 55-c. 135 A.D.)
ML.2.13 Epicteti Enchiridion, Cebetis Thebani Tabula, Theophrasti Characteres ethici, Prodici Hercules, et M.T. Ciceronis de exilio dialogus. Cum versione Latina. Denuo recognita & notis illustrati. 12°, Oxonii, 1680.

EPICTETUS (c. 55-c. 135 A.D.)
MH.1.22 Epicteti Manuale, Cebetis Thebani Tabula, Prodici Hercules, et Theophrasti Characteres ethici, Græce et Latine, notis illustrati a J. Simpson. (4 pts.) 8°, Oxonii, 1739.

EPICTETUS (c. 55-c. 135 A.D.)
MK.4.16-17 Epicteti quæ supersunt disseratationes ab Arriano collectæ nec non Enchiridion et fragmenta Græcè et Latinè. Cum integris J. Schegkii et H. Wolfii...recensuit, notis & indice illustravit J. Uptonus. 2 vols. 4°, Londini, 1741.

EPISTLE
MK.5.15[6] Epistle from the Honourable Charles Fox, partridge-shooting, to the Honourable John Townshend, cruising. [By R. Tickell.] 4°, London, 1779.

EPISTOLÆ OBSCURORUM VIRORUM
ML.2.21 Duo volumina epistolarum obscurorum virorum, ad Dominum M. Ortuinum Gratium, Attico lepôre referta, denuo excusa, & à mendis repurgata...[By U. von Hutten and others.] (2 pts.) 8°, Francoforti ad Moenum, 1581.

ERMENONVILLE, René Louis Girardin, vicomte de
See GIRARDIN, René Louis, marquis de.

ERSKINE, Thomas Erskine, 1st Baron (1750-1823)
MH.1.25 See ARMATA
Armata: a fragment. [By Thomas, Lord Erskine.] (2 pts.) 1817.

ERSKINE, Thomas Erskine, 1st Baron (1750-1823)
MH.5.25[6] A view of the causes and consequences of the present War with France. 13th ed. 8°, London, 1797.

ERSKINE, Thomas Erskine, 1st Baron (1750-1823)
MH.5.7[5] See SKETCHES
Sketches of the characters of the Hon. Thomas Erskine, and James Mingay, Esq. interspersed with anecdotes and professional strictures. [Wants title-page.] 1794.

ESSAI
MA.4.10[2] Essai contre l'abus du pouvoir des souverains, et juste idée du gouvernement d'un bon prince...Par M**, avocat. 8°, Londres, 1776.

ESSAI
MI.2.20[1] Essai sur la Secte des Illuminés. [By J.P.L. de La Roche du Maine, marquis de Luchet.] 8°, Paris, 1789.

ESSAY
MH.5.15[4] An essay of the impolicy of a bounty on the exportation of grain; and on the principles which ought to regulate the commerce of grain...[By James Mill.] 8°, London, 1804.

ESSAY
MH.4.29[8] An essay on the true interests and resources of the Empire of the King of Great-Britain and Ireland, &c. &c. &c. By the Earl of A———-h [Aldeburgh]. 8°, London, 1783.

ESSAY
MH.5.22[5] An essay towards a method of speedily manning a fleet upon any sudden emergency. 8°, London, 1754.

ESSAYS
MB.6.8 Essays and reviews. 8°, London, 1860.*

ESSAYS
MH.3.3 Essays on the formation and publication of opinions, and on other subjects. [By S. Bailey.] 8°, London, 1821.

ESSENTIAL
MH.5.15[1] The essential principles of the wealth of nations, illustrated, in opposition to some false doctrines of Dr. Adam Smith, and others. [By John Gray.] (2 pts.) 8°, London, 1797.

ETAT
MB.2.30-33 L'état et les délices de la Suisse, ou Description helvétique historique et géographique. Nouvelle éd. corrigée...[A translation of A. Stanyan's Account of Switzerland, together with Les délices de la Suisse, by A. Ruchat. Ed. by J.G. Altmann.] 4 vols. 12°, Basle, 1764.

ETHEREGE, Sir George (1635?-1691)
ML.1.16 Works. Containing his plays and poems. 12°, London, 1735.

EUCLIDES (c. 300 B.C.)
MJ.1.14 Euclide's Elements; the whole 15 books compendiously demonstrated by Mr. Isaac Barrow. And translated out of the Latin. 8°, London, 1660.

EUCLIDES (c. 300 B.C.)
MG.7.5 The Elements of Euclid, viz. the first six books, together with the eleventh and twelth...By R. Simson. 4°, Glasgow, 1756.

EUPHROSYNE
MK.2.31 Euphrosyne: or, Amusements on the road of life. By the author of The spiritual Quixote [i.e. Richard Graves]. 8°, London, 1776.

EURIPIDES (c. 480 or 485-406, or 407 B.C.)
MG.1.28 Supplices mulieres (and Iphigenia in Aulide et in Tauris) cum notis J. Marklandi integris et aliorum selectis ...(Greek). 2 vols. in 1. 8°, Oxonii, 1811.

EURIPIDES (c. 480 or 485-406, or 407 B.C.)
MM.1.38-40 See AESCHYLUS
Tragœdiæ selectæ Aeschyli, Sophoclis, Euripidis. Cum duplici interpretatioae Latina, una ad verbu, altera carmine. Ennianæ interpretationes locoru aliquot Euripidis. 3 vols. 1567.

EUSTACE, John Chetwode (1762?-1815)
MF.6.1-2 A classical tour through Italy. An, MDCCCII. 2nd ed., revised and enlarged...2 vols. 4°, London, 1814.

EUSTACE, John Chetwode (1762?-1815)
MH.1.7[4] Letter from Paris, to George Petre, Esq. 8°, London, 1814.

EUSTATHIUS, Macrembolita (fl. 12th C.)
MF.1.25 De Ismeniæ et Ismenes amoribus, libri XI. G. Gaulminus primus Græcè ex Regia Bibliotheca edidit, & Latinè vertit. (Parallel texts.) (2 pts.). 8°, Lutetiæ Parisiorum, 1618.

EUTROPIUS (fl. 2nd half of 4th C.)
ML.3.10 Historiæ Romanæ Breviarium. Notis et emendationibus illustravit A. Tanaquilli Fabri Filia. In usum Serenissimi Delphini. 8°, Londini, 1755.

EVANS, John (1767-1827)
MC.1.8 A sketch of the denominations of the Christian world...14th ed. 12°, London, 1821.

EVELYN, John (1620-1706)
ME.5.16[1] See CHARACTER
A character of England, as it was lately presented in a letter, to a noble man of France. With reflections upon Gallus Castratus. [By J. Evelyn.] 3rd ed. 1659.

EVELYN, John (1620-1706)
MM.5.1 Silva: or, A discourse of forest-trees, and the propagation of timber in His Majesty's dominions...With notes by A. Hunter. 4°, York, 1776.

EXAMINATION
MH.5.20[1] An examination of the principles, and an enquiry into the conduct of the two B*****rs [Brothers: The Duke of Newcastle and The Hon. Henry Pelham]: in regard to the establishment of their power...[By the Earl of Egmont.] 3rd ed., reviewed and corrected. 8°, London, 1749.

EXPLANATION

MH.4.22[4] Explanation of the view of the interior of the City of Paris, now exhibiting in the Large Circle, Barker's Panorama, Strand, near Surrey-Street. 8°, [London] 1815.

EXPOSITION

MH.5.17[5] Exposition of the motives, founded upon the universally received laws of nations, which have determined the King, of Prussia, upon the repeated instances of his subjects trading by sea...(English & French.) 8°, London, (1752).

F

J. FLETCHER

FABLE

MG.5.21-2 The fable of the bees: or, Private vices, public benefits. With, An essay on charity and charity-schools; and, A search into the nature of society. [By B. Mandeville.] 2 vols. (Vol. 1, 9th ed.) 12°, Edinburgh, 1755.

FALCONER, William (1732-1769)

ME.7.3 An universal dictionary of the marine...New ed., corrected. 4°, London, 1789.

FARMER, Hugh (1714-1787)

MI.2.21 An essay on the Demoniacs of the New Testament. 8°, London, 1775.

FARQUHAR, George (1678-1707)

ML.1.14-15 Dramatick works. 7th ed. 2 vols. 12°, London, (1733-) 1736.

FASHIONABLE

MI.4.7[4] The fashionable lover; a comedy: as it is acted at the Theatre-Royal in Drury-Lane. [By R. Cumberland.] 2nd ed. 8°, London, 1772.

FAWCETT, C.
MH.5.22[6] See LETTER
A letter to the late Recorder of N[ewcastle, C. Fawcett]. From an old friend. [1754.]

FEARON, Henry Bradshaw (1770?-?)
MH.1.24[2] Sketches of America. A narrative of a journey of five thousand miles through the Eastern and Western states of America...2nd ed. 8°, London, 1818.

FELTHAM, Owen (1602?-1668)
ME.5.16[2] See BRIEF
A brief character of the Low-Countries under the States...[By O. Feltham.] 1660.

FENELON, François de Salignac de la Mothe, Abp of Cambrai (1651-1715)
ME.2.35-6 The adventures of Telemachus, the son of Ulysses. From the French...by J. Hawkesworth. 2 vols. 8°, London, 1808.

FENELON, François de Salignac de la Mothe, Abp of Cambrai (1651-1715)
ME.2.37 Les aventures de Télémaque, fils d'Ulysse. Nouvelle éd. ...par N. Wanostrocht. 12°, Londre, 1813.

FENELON, François de Salignac de la Mothe, Abp of Cambrai (1651-1715)
ML.2.2 De l'éducation des filles. Dernière éd. reveuë, corrigée, & augmentée. 12°, Bruxelles, 1705.

FENELON, François de Salignac de la Mothe, Abp of Cambrai (1651-1715)
MK.2.13-14 Dialogue des morts anciens et modernes, avec quelques fables, composez pour l'éducation d'un prince. 2e éd. revûë & corrigée. 2 vols. 12°, Paris, 1725.

FENELON, François de Salignac de la Mothe, Abp of Cambrai (1651-1715)
MK.2.18 Dialogues sur l'éloquence en général, et sur celle de la chaire en particulier. Avec une lettre écrite à l'Académie Françoise. 8°, Paris, 1718.

FENELON, François de Salignac de la Mothe, Abp of Cambrai (1651-1715)
MJ.1.43 Explication des maximes des Saints sur la vie intérieure. 12°, Paris, 1697.

FENELON, François de Salignac de la Mothe, Abp of Cambrai (1651-1715)
MA.4.25-34 Œuvres. Nouvelle éd., revue et corrigée avec soix. 10 vols. 8°, Paris, 1822.

FENELON, François de Salignac de la Mothe, Abp of Cambrai (1651-1715)
MK.2.9 Œuvres philosophiques. 2 pts. 12°, Paris, 1718.

FENELON, François de Salignac de la Mothe, Abp of Cambrai (1651-1715)
MK.2.10-11 Œuvres spirituelles. 2 vols. 12°, Anvers, 1718.

FERGUSON, James (1710-1776)
MG.7.21[8] A plain method of determining the parallax of Venus, by her transit over the sun... 4°, London, 1761.

FICORONI, Francesco de' (1664-1747)
MF.6.16 Le vestigia, e rarità di Roma antica (& moderna) ricercate, e spiegate. 2 pts. 4°, Roma, 1744.

FIELDING, Henry (1707-1754)
MB.3.22 The adventures of Joseph Andrews. 8°, London, 1832.

FIELDING, Henry (1707-1754)
MG.5.41 An enquiry into the causes of the late increase of robbers, &c. ...[Wants title-page and all before sign. B1 and after p. 202.] 12°, [London, 1751.]

FIELDING, Henry (1707-1754)
MB.3.18-19 The history of Amelia. 2 vols. 8°, London, 1832.

FIELDING, Henry (1707-1754)
MB.3.20-21 The history of Tom Jones, a foundling. With a memoir of the author by T. Roscoe. 2 vols. (The Novelist's Libr., 5, 6). 8°, London, 1831.

FIELDING, Henry (1707-1754)
MG.5.35 The journal of a voyage to Lisbon. 12°, London, 1755.

FIELDING, Henry (1707-1754)
MH.5.21[5] A proposal for making an effectual provision for the poor... 8°, London, 1753.

FIELDING, Henry (1707-1754)
MK.3.6-9 Works. With the life of the author [by A. Murphy]. 4th ed. Vols. 1-4. (Plays.) (Vols. 5-12 wanting.) 8°, Edinburgh, 1767.

FIFTH
ME.2.7[5] A fifth letter to the people of England, on the subversion of the Constitution: and, the necessity of its being restored. [By J. Shebbeare.] 2nd ed. 8°, London, 1757.

FINDEN, Edward (1791-1857)
MB.7.53-4 Finden's illustrations of the life and works of Lord Byron. [An issue consisting of the illustrations only, without title-page or text.] 2 vols. 8°, [London, 1832-4.]

FINDEN, Edward (1791-1857)
ME.3.6-8 Finden's illustrations of the life and works of Lord Byron. With original and selected information...by W. Brockedon. 3 vols. 4°, London, 1833-4.

FINDLATER, Charles (1754-1838)
ME.1.41 General view of the agriculture of the County of Peebles... 8°, Edinburgh, 1802.

FINGAL
MF.7.7 Fingal, an ancient epic poem...together with several other poems, composed by Ossian the Son of Fingal. Translated [or rather, largely composed] from the Galic language, by J. Macpherson. 2nd ed. 4°, London, 1762.

FIRST
ME.2.7[1] A first letter to the people of England. On the present situation and conduct of national affairs. [By J. Shebbeare.] 4th ed. 8°, London, 1756.

FIRST
MK.5.15[9] The First of April: or, The triumphs of folly: a poem. Dedicated to the celebrated Dutchess. By the author of the Diaboliad [i.e. W. Combe]. 4°, London, 1777.

FITZ-ADAM, Adam, Pseud.
See MOORE, Edward.

FLAMINIUS, Marcus Antonius (1498-1550)
ML.2.25 De rebus divinis carmina. 8°, London, 1834.

FLEETWOOD, Everard, pseud.
MH.5.23[2] An enquiry into the customary-estates and tenant-rights of those who hold lands of Church and other foundations...By E. Fleetwood [i.e. S. Burroughs]. 8°, London, 1731.

FLETCHER, Andrew (1655-1716)
MI.1.15 Poetical works. 8°, London, 1732.

FLETCHER, John (1579-1625)
MI.4.7[6] Philaster, a tragedy. Written by Beaumont and Fletcher. With alterations [by G. Colman]. As it is acted at the Theatre-Royal in Drury-Lane. 8°, London, 1763.

FLETCHER, John (1579-1625)
MF.1.8-9 Select plays of Beaumont and Fletcher. 2 vols. 8°, Glasgow, 1768.

FLETCHER, John (1579-1625)
MI.3.7-20 The works of Beaumont and Fletcher: with an introduction and explanatory notes, by H. Weber. 14 vols. 8°, Edinburgh, 1812.

FLORIAN, Jean Pierre Claris de (1755-1794)
MM.1.29 Estelle, pastorale. 3e éd. 12°, Paris, 1793.

FLORIAN, Jean Pierre Claris de (1755-1794)
MM.1.17 Fables. (Œuvres de M. de Florian.) 12°, Paris, 1792.

FLORIAN, Jean Pierre Claris de (1755-1794)
MM.1.21 Galatée, pastorale; imitée de Cervantes. 5e éd. (Œuvres de M. de Florian.) 12°, Paris, 1788.

FLORIAN, Jean Pierre Claris de (1755-1794)
MM.1.22-4 Gonzalve de Cordoue ou Grenade reconquise. 2e éd. 3 vols. (Œuvres de M. de Florian.) 12°, Paris, 1792.

FLORIAN, Jean Pierre Claris de (1755-1794)
MM.1.16 Mélanges de poésie et de littérature. (Œuvres de M. de Florian.) 12°, Paris, 1787.

FLORIAN, Jean Pierre Claris de (1755-1794)
MM.1.28 Nouvelles nouvelles. (Œuvres de M. de Florian.) 12°, Paris, 1792.

FLORIAN, Jean Pierre Claris de (1755-1794)
MM.1.18-19 Numa Pompilius, second Roi de Rome. 2e éd. 2 vols. (Œuvres de M. de Florian.) 12°, Paris, 1786.

FLORIAN, Jean Pierre Claris de (1755-1794)
MM.1.15 Les six nouvelles. 12°, Paris, 1784.

FLORIAN, Jean Pierre Claris de (1755-1794)
MM.1.20 Les six nouvelles. (Œuvres de M. de Florian.) 12°, Paris, 1786.

FLORIAN, Jean Pierre Claris de (1755-1794)
MM.1.25-7 Théâtre. 4e éd. 3 vols. (Œuvres de M. de Florian.) 12°, Paris, 1791.

FLORIO
MG.7.8^2 Florio: a tale, for fine gentlemen and fine ladies: and The Bas Bleu; or, Conversation: two poems. [By H. More.] 4°, London, 1786.

FONTENELLE, Bernard Le Bovier de (1657-1757)
MK.2.7-8 Histoire du renouvellement de l'Académie Royale des Sciences en M.DC.XCIX. Et les éloges historiques...2 vols. 8°, Paris, 1708-17.

FONTENELLE, Bernard Le Bovier de (1657-1757)
MJ.2.15-21 Œuvres diverses. Nouvelle éd. augmentée. 7 vols. 12°, Paris, 1715.

FOOTE, Samuel (1720-1777)
MG.4.29-30 Works. 2 vols. 8°, Edinburgh, 1798.

FORD, John (1586-1640)
MI.3.21-2 Dramatic works. With an introduction and explanatory notes, by H. Weber. 2 vols. 8°, Edinburgh, 1811.

FORDYCE, George (1736-1802)
MH.5.11[5] Elements of agriculture and vegetation...3rd ed. (2 pts.) 8°, London, 1779.

FORTESCUE, Sir John (c. 1394-c. 1476)
MJ.1.5 De laudibus legum Angliæ. Hereto are added the two sums of Sir Ralph de Hengham...With notes on Fortescue and Hengham, by J. Selden. (3 pts.) 8°, London, 1672.

FOURTH
ME.2.7[4] A fourth letter to the people of England. On the conduct of the M——rs in alliances, fleets, and armies...[By J. Shebbeare.] 2nd ed. 8°, London, 1756.

FOX, Rt. Hon. Charles James (1749-1806)
MH.5.2[1] Fox against Fox!!! or Political blossoms of the Right Hon. C.J. Fox; selected from his speeches in the House of Commons... 8°, London, 1788.

FOX, Rt. Hon. Charles James (1749-1806)
MH.4.25[2] A letter, to the worthy and independent electors of the City and Liberty of Westminster. 8°, London, 1793.

FOX, Rt. Hon. Charles James (1749-1806)
MH.4.29[1] Mr. Fox's Reply to Mr. Pitt, upon reporting the fourth proposition of the Irish system...1785. 8°, London, [1785].

FOX, Rt. Hon. Charles James (1749-1806)
MK.5.15[6] See EPISTLE
Epistle from the Honourable Charles Fox, partridge-shooting, to the Honourable John Townshend, cruising. [By R. Tickell.] 1779.

FOX, Rt. Hon. Charles James (1749-1806)
MH.5.10[5] See SECOND
A second letter to the Rt. Hon. Charles James Fox, upon the dangerous and inflammatory tendency of his late conduct in Parliament...By the author of the First letter [T.R. Bentley?]. 1793.

FOX, William (1736?-1826?)
MH.4.25[8] A discourse on national fasts, particularly in reference to that of April 19, 1793, on occasion of the war against France. 3rd ed. 8°, London, 1793.

FRANCE. Constitution
MH.5.3[5] See AUTHENTIC
An authentic copy of the French Constitution, as revised and amended by the National Assembly, and presented to the King on the Third of September, 1791. Translated from the original...1791.

FRANCKLYN, Gilbert (fl. end of 18th C.)
MH.5.10[7] Observations occasioned by the attempts made in England to effect the abolition of the slave trade; shewing the manner in which Negroes are treated in the West-Indies... [Imperfect, wants all after p. 72.] 8°, London, 1789.

FRANKLIN, Benjamin (1706-1790)
MH.1.23 Political, miscellaneous, and philosophical pieces... 8°, London, 1779.

[ED. NOTE: Franklin's writings referring to population are first mentioned by Malthus in the Preface to the second edition of his *Essay*. In the later *Essay* reference to this work is made by Malthus in Bk. III, Ch. IV "Of Emigration."]

FREART, Roland, sieur de Chambray (1606-1676)
MC.7.10 A parallel of the antient architecture with the modern...[ed.] by J. Evelyn. 3rd ed....(3 pts.) F°, London, 1723.

FREDERICK, Louis, Prince of Wales (1707-1751)
ME.6.1[3] See BRITANNIA
Britannia in tears: an elegaic pastoral, on the death of Frederic Prince of Wales. 1751.

FREDERICK II, the Great, King of Prussia (1712-1786)
MB.6.55[1] See LETTERS
Letters on patriotism. Translated from the French original printed at Berlin. [By Frederick II, the Great.] 1780.

FREE-HOLDER
MG.5.39 The Free-holder, or political essays. (December 23, 1715 - June 25, 1716.) [A periodical, ed. by J. Addison.] 12°, London, 1716.

FREE-HOLDER
ME.2.41-3 Selections from the Spectator, Tatler, Guardian, and Freeholder: with a preliminary essay by A.L. Barbauld. 3 vols. 12°, London, 1804.

FREND, William (1757-1841)
MH.3.18^{3} The effect of paper money on the price of provisions... 8°, London, 1801.

FREND, William (1757-1841)
MH.4.25^{5} Peace and Union recommended to the associated bodies of Republicans and Anti-Republicans. 8°, St Ives, 1793.

FREND, William (1757-1841)
MH.5.7^{2} Peace and Union recommended to the associated bodies of Republicans and Anti-Republicans. 2nd ed. 8°, Cambridge, 1793.

FRERE, Rt. Hon. John Hookham (1769-1846)
MB.6.58 See MONKS
The monks and the giants: prospectus and specimen of an intended national work, by William and Robert Whistlecraft [i.e. J.H. Frere]. 4th ed. 1821.

FREZIER, Amédée François (1682-1773)
MG.7.9 A voyage to the South-Sea, and along the coasts of Chili and Peru, in the years 1712, 1713, and 1714... (Translated from the French.) With a postscript by E. Halley... 4°, London, 1717.

FUGITIVE
ME.2.32-3 Fugitive pieces on various subjects. By several authors. [Ed. by R. Dodsley.] [2nd ed.] 2 vols. 8°, London, 1765.

FULLER, Thomas (1608-1661)
ME.7.9 The historie of the Holy Warre. 4th ed. F°, [Cambridge] 1651.

FUNERAL
MH.5.2^{5} The funeral procession of Mrs. Regency. To which is added, the sermon; with the last will and testament. 8°, London, 1789.

GAISFORD, Thomas (1779-1855)
MF.3.28-9 See POETÆ
Poetæ minores Græci. Præcipua lectionis varietate et indicibus locupletissimis instruxit T. Gaisford. Vols. 1, 2. (Vols. 3, 4 wanting.) 8°, Oxonii, 1814-16.

GALE, Thomas (1635?-1702)
MI.2.7 See OPUSCULA
Opuscula mythologica physica et ethica. Græce et Latine...[Ed. by T. Gale.] 1688.

GALLAND, Antoine (1646-1715)
ML.2.34-40 See MILLE
Les mille et une nuits; contes arabes, traduits en français par M. Galland. Nouvelle éd., corrigée...7 vols. 1811.

GALLY, Henry (1696-1769)
MH.5.17[3] Some considerations upon clandestine marriages. 2nd ed. with additions. 8°, London, 1750.

GANILH, Charles (1758-1836)
MA.2.24-5 Des systèmes d'économie politique...2e éd., avec de nombreuses additions relatives aux controverses recéntes de MM. Malthus, Buchanan, Ricardo...2 vols. 8°, Paris, 1821.

[ED. NOTE: "One of the most able impugners of the doctrine of Adam Smith respecting productive labour is Mr. Ganilh, in his valuable work on the various systems of political economy," said Malthus in his "Principles" (1820 ed. p. 33 n.). Obviously he referred to the 1809 edition of Ganilh. The listed edition is the second which brings into focus the historical controversies in political economy between Malthus, Buchanan and Ricardo.]

GARDINER, William
MK.3.33 Tables portatives de logarithmes, publiées à Londres par Gardiner, augmentées, et perfectionnées dans leur disposition par M. Callet... 12°, Paris, 1783.

GARRICK, David (1717-1779)
MB.2.6-8 Dramatic works. To which is prefixed a life of the author. 3 vols. 12°, London, 1798.

GARRICK, David (1717-1779)
MI.4.9[7] Lethe. A dramatic satire. As it is performed at the Theatre-Royal in Drury-Lane, by His Majesty's Servants. 2nd ed. 8°, London, 1749.

GAY, John (1685-1732)
ML.1.12 Fables. 8°, London, 1769.

GAY, John (1685-1732)
ML.1.10-11 Poems on several occasions. 2 vols. 12°, London, 1767.

GAY, John (1685-1732)
ME.4.41[1] Poetical works. Including his fables. With the life of the author. Vol. 3. (Vols. 1, 2 wanting.) (Bell's edition. The Poets of Great Britain.) 12°, Edinburg, 1777.

GELL, Sir William (1777-1836)
MA.5.1-2 Pompeiana: the topography, edifices and ornaments of Pompeii, the result of excavations since 1819. 2 vols. 8°, London, 1832.

GELLIUS, Aulus (c. 130-180 A.D.)
MF.3.22-3 Noctium Atticarum libri XX sicut supersunt editio Gronoviana, praefatus est et excursus operi adiecit I.L. Conradi. 2 vols. 8°, Lipsiae, 1762.

[ED. NOTE: From Gellius's Noctium Atticarum, Malthus cited a paragraph of the speech of Metellus Numidicus, who speculates that "If it were possible, entirely to go without wives, we would deliver ourselves at once from this evil..." Malthus's comment was: "It is impossible to read the speech of Metellus Numidicus in his censorship without indignation and disgust," later *Essay*, Bk. I, Ch. XIV.]

GENERAL
MG.7.21[7] A general and particular account of the annular eclipse of the sun, which will happen on Sunday, April 1, 1764, in the forenoon... 4°, London, 1764.

GENLIS, Stéphanie Félicité Ducrest de Saint-Aubin, comtesse de (1746-1830)
MK.1.3, 5-7 Les annales de la vertu, ou Histoire universelle, iconographique et littéraire...Nouvelle éd. Vols. 1, 3-5. (Vol. 2 wanting.) 12°, Paris, 1811.

GENLIS, Stéphanie Félicité Ducrest de Saint-Aubin, comtesse de (1746-1830)
MB.3.14-16 Les chevaliers du Cygne, ou La cour de Charlemagne. Conte historique et moral...3 vols. 12°, Hambourg, 1795.

GENUINE
MB.6.61[2] The genuine account of the trial of Eugene Aram, for the murder of Daniel Clark...[By W. Bristow.] 8th ed. 8°, York, 1792.

GEOPONICA
MG.1.12 Geoponicorum, sive De re rustica, libri XX. Cassiana Basso Scholastico collectore. Antea C. Porphyrogenneto a quibusdam adscripti. Græce & Latine...prolegomena, notulas, & indices adjecit P. Needham. 8°, Cantabrigiæ, 1704.

GEORGE IV, King of England (1762-1830)
MI.2.2[7] See LETTER
A letter most humbly and respectfully addressed to His Royal Highness the Prince of Wales [George IV], upon the present state of Ireland...1798.

GEORGE IV, King of England (1762-1830)
MI.2.2[6] See LETTER
A letter to the Prince of Wales [George IV], on a second application to Parliament, to discharge debts wantonly contracted since May, 1787. 10th ed. enlarged ...[1795.]

GERMAN
MC.1.2-7 The German theatre, translated by B. Thompson. 4th ed. 6 vols. 12°, London, 1811.

GIBBON, Edward (1737-1794)
MG.2.20-31 The history of the decline and fall of the Roman Empire. New ed. 12 vols. 8°, London, 1783-90.

[ED. NOTE: Referred to by Malthus in his later *Essay*, Bk. I, Ch. VI. & VII.]

GIBBON, Edward (1737-1794)
ME.6.6-8 Miscellaneous works. With memoirs of his life and writings, composed by himself... with occasional notes and narrative, by John, Lord Sheffield. 3 vols. (Vol. 3, a later ed.) 4°, London, 1796-1815.

GIBBON, Edward (1737-1794)
MJ.1.20[1] See OBSERVATIONS
Observations on the three last volumes of the Roman history, by E. Gibbon. [By H.J. Pye?] 1788.

GIBSON, Edmund, Bp of London (1669-1748)
MH.5.23[1] See LETTER
A letter to the Reverend Dr. Codex [i.e. E. Gibson], on the subject of his modest instruction to the Crown...[By W. Arnall.] 2nd ed. 1734.

GILPIN, William (1724-1804)
MB.7.49-50 Observations, relative chiefly to picturesque beauty, made in the year 1776, on several parts of Great Britain; particularly the High-lands of Scotland. 2nd ed. 2 vols. 8°, London, 1792.

GINGUENE, Pierre Louis (1748-1816)
MI.4.19-24 Histoire littéraire d'Italie. Vols. 1-6. (Vols. 7-14 wanting.) 8°, Paris, 1811-13.

GIRARD, Pierre Jacques François
MK.5.16 Traité des armes, dédié au Roy: enseignant la manière de combattre de l'épée...Obl. 4°, Paris, 1737.

GIRARDIN, René Louis, marquis de (1735-1808)
MJ.1.24 & 25 [2 copies] An essay on landscape...Translated from the French [by D. Malthus?]. 8°, London, 1783.

[ED. NOTE: In May 1778, Jean Jacques Rousseau moved to Girardin's estate at Ermenonville, where he died on July 2, and was buried on the 'Ile des Peupliers'. Girardin erected a tomb on this island for Rousseau but his remains were moved to the Panthéon in Paris during the Revolution. "An Essay on Landscape" by Girardin was published with a frontispiece showing Rousseau's tomb on the island at Ermenonville. The translation is attributed to Daniel Malthus who was both a friend of Rousseau and corresponded with him on botanical matters. (See Patricia, James, *Population Malthus*, pp. 77/78).]

GLADWIN, Francis (d. 1813)
ML.5.5-6 See AKBAR, Emperor of Hindostan. Ayeen Akbery: or, The institutes of the Emperor Akber. Translated from the original Persian by F. Gladwin. 2 vols. 1800.

GLOVER, Richard (1712-1785)
MH.5.5[2] The substance of the evidence on the petition presented by the West-India planters and merchants to the House of Commons...16th of March, 1775. 8°, London, [1775].

GODSCHALL, William Man (d. 1802)
MX.1.22 A general plan of parochial and provincial police. With instructions to Overseers and Constables, for better regulating their respective parishes... 8°, London, 1787.**

GODWIN, Mary Wollstonecraft (1759-1797)
MG.5.14-17 Posthumous works of the author of A vindication of the rights of woman [i.e. M.W. Godwin. Ed. by W. Godwin]. 4 vols. 12°, London, 1798.

GODWIN, William (1756-1836)

MH.5.25[1] See CONSIDERATIONS

Considerations on Lord Grenville'snd Mr. Pitt's Bills, concerning treasonable and seditious practices, and unlawful assemblies. By A lover of order [i.e. W. Godwin]. [1795.]

GODWIN, William (1756-1836)

MI..5 The enquirer. Reflections on education, manners, and literature. In a series of essays. 8°, London, 1797.

[ED. NOTE: In one of the collected essays which comprises "The Enquirer" of 1797 entitled "Of Avarice and Profusion," Godwin continued his examination which first appeared in his influential "Political Justice" of 1793. Malthus and "a friend" (actually his father) read Godwin's essay which triggered the famous "Essay on Population." As described in the first sentence of the preface to the 1798 edition, "The following *Essay* owes its origin to a conversation with a friend, on the subject of Mr. Godwin's Essay, on avarice and profusion, in his Enquirer."]

GODWIN, William (1756-1836)

MI.2.3-4 Enquiry concerning political justice, and its influence on morals and happiness. 2nd ed. corrected. 2 vols. 8°, London, 1796.

[ED. NOTE: "Political Justice" 1796, 2nd edition is the actual book referred to, and cited by Malthus in his later edition of the *Essay*. Bk. III, Ch. II. of the later *Essay* is entitled "Of Systems of Equality. Godwin." Malthus discusses Godwin from his early preface to his late edition's appendix. As it was remarked by Mrs. Margaret Smith, Malthus might have used the first and third edition of "Political Justice" for his first *Essay*.]

GODWIN, William (1756-1836)

MG.5.18 Memoirs of the author of A vindication of the rights of woman (M.W. Godwin). 8°, London, 1798.

GODWIN, William (1756-1836)

MH.2.26 Of population. An enquiry concerning the power of increase in the numbers of mankind, being an answer to Mr. Malthus's Essay on that subject. 8°, London, 1820.

[ED. NOTE: It was 20 years before Godwin replied to Malthus, and this was his "Documented" reply which would (he thought) annihilate for good the author of the *Essay* (Margaret Smith, et al.]

GOETHE, Johann Wolfgang von (1749-1832)

MJ.1.16 Werther, traduit [by G. Deyverdun] de l'allemand. (2 pts.) 12°, Maestricht, 1776.

GOLDSMITH, Oliver (1728-1774)
MM.3.26[1] The good-natur'd man: a comedy. As performed at the Theatre-Royal in Covent-Garden. 8°, Perth, 1792.

GOLDSMITH, Oliver (1728-1774)
MM.3.27-8 Poetical and dramatic works. New ed. With an account of the life and writings of the author. 2 vols. 8°, London, 1791.

GOLDSMITH, Oliver (1728-1774)
MM.3.26[2] She stoops to conquer: or, The mistakes of a night. A comedy. As performed at the Theatre-Royal in Covent-Garden. 8°, Perth, 1792.

GOLDSMITH, Oliver (1728-1774)
MB.3.23[1] The Vicar of Wakefield. A tale. 8°, London, 1832.

GORDON, Thomas (d. 1750)
MM.4.10-12 See INDEPENDENT
The independent Whig: or, A defence of primitive Christianity...[By J. Trenchard and T. Gordon.] (Nos. 1-74.) 6th ed. With additions and amendments. 3 vols. 1735.

GOUGH, John (1721-1791)
MH.5.24[7] See DISCOURSE
A discourse concerning the Resurrection bodies...By Philalethes [i.e. J. Gough]. 1788.

GRANGER, James (c. 1723-1776)
MM.2.5-7 See NOBLE, Mark
A biographical history of England, from the Revolution to the end of George I's reign; being a continuation of J. Granger's work...Editor, M. Noble. 3 vols. 1806.

GRANVILLE, John Carteret, 2nd Earl (1690-1763)
MH.5.20[4] See STATE
The state of the Nation for the year 1747, and respecting 1748. Inscribed to a Member of the present Parliament. [By John Carteret, Earl of Granville.] 3rd ed. 1748.

GRATIUS, Faliscus (16th C.?)
ML.2.24 Cynegeticon, cum pœmatio cognomine M.A. Olympii Nemesiani: notis perpetuis, variisq; lectionibus adornavit T. Johnson. Accedunt Hier. Fracastorii Alcon, Carmen pastoritium: Jo. Caii, de canibus libellus: ut et Κυνοσόφιον ...incerto auctore. 8°, Londini, 1699.

GRAVES, Richard (1715-1804)
MK.2.31 See EUPHROSYNE
Euphrosyne: or, Amusements on the road of life. By the author of The spiritual Quixote [i.e. R. Graves]. 1776.

GRAVES, Richard (1715-1804)
MH.5.14[2] See LETTER
A letter from a father to his son at the University: relative to a late address to young students, &c. [By R. Graves.] 1787.

GRAVES, Richard (1715-1804)
MM.4.6-8 See SPIRITUAL
The spiritual Quixote; or, The summer's ramble of Mr. Geoffry Wildgoose. A comic romance. [By R. Graves.] (New ed.) 3 vols. 1792.

GRAY, Charles (1695-1782)
MH.5.21[2] See CONSIDERATIONS
Considerations on several proposals, lately made, for the better maintenance of the poor. [By C. Gray.] 1751.

GRAY, John (end of 18th C.)
MH.5.15[1] See ESSENTIAL
The essential principles of the wealth of nations, illustrated, in opposition to some false doctrines of Dr. Adam Smith, and others. [By J. Gray.] (2 pts.) 1797.

GRAY, John (end of 18th C.)
MK.4.19 The social system: a treatise of the principle of exchange. [Chapter X, a criticism of the principle of Malthus.] 8°, Edinburgh, 1831.

GRAY, Simon (18th & 19th C.)
MH.2.27 Gray versus Malthus. The principles of population and production investigated...By George Purves [i.e. Simon Gray]. 8°, London, 1818.

[ED. NOTE: A famous book in The Population Controversy. Gray wrote under the pen name, George Purves.]

GRAY, Thomas (1716-1771)
ME.6.12 Poems. To which are prefixed Memoirs of his life and writings by W. Mason. 2nd ed. 4°, London, 1775.

GRECIAN
MI.4.7[3] The grecian daughter: a tragedy: as it is acted at the Theatre-Royal in Drury-Lane. [By A. Murphy.] 8°, London, 1772.

GREG, Thomas
MH.4.22[6] See HIGGINS, John
Report upon the farm of Thomas Greg, Esq. at Coles in Hertfordshire. (Signed J. Higgins, T. Wilson, J. Foster.) 1811.

GRETSERUS, Jacobus (1562-1625?)
ME.5.71 Rudimenta linguæ Græcæ, ex primo libro Institutionum Jacobi Gretseri... 12°, Florentiæ, 1717.

GRIMOD DE LA REYNIERE, Alexandre Balthasar Laurent (1758-1838)
MI.4.18 See MANUEL
Manuel des amphitryons; contenant un traité de la dissection des viandes à table...Par l'auteur de l'Almanach des gourmands [A.B.L. Grimod de la Reynière]. 1808.

GROSE, Francis (1731?-1791)
ML.5.24 A provincial glossary, with a collection of local proverbs, and popular superstitions. 8°, London, 1787.

GROTIUS, Hugo (1583-1645)
MM.5.16[2]-3 Hugonis Grotii Annotationum in Novum Testamentum pars 3[a] ac ultima. Cui subiuncti sunt eiusdem auctoris libri Pro veritate religionis Christianæ...(2 pts.) F°, Parisiis, 1650.

GROTIUS, Hugo (1583-1645)
ML.2.30 De veritate religionis Christianiæ. Ed. novissima... 12°, Amstelodami, 1680.

GUARDIAN
MG.5.42 The Guardian. [A periodical by Sir R. Steele, J. Addison and others.] 5th ed. Vol. 1. (March 12 to June 15, 1713.) 12°, London, 1729.

GUARDIAN
ME.5.15 A general index to the Spectators, Tatlers and Guardians. 12°, London, 1757.

GUARDIAN
ME.2.41-3 Selections from the Spectator, Tatler, Guardian, and Freeholder: with a preliminary essay by A.L. Barbauld. 3 vols. 12°, London, 1804.

GUESSES
MB.2.9-10 Guesses at truth by two brothers [i.e. J.C. and A.W. Hare]. 2 vols. 8°, London, 1827.

GUIDE
MJ.1.44 See AMSTERDAM
Le guide, ou Nouvelle description d'Amsterdam...1753.

GUIZOT, François Pierre Guillaume (1787-1874)
MA.1.25 Histoire générale de la civilisation en Europe. (Cours d'histoire moderne.) 8°, Paris, 1828.

GURNEY, Joseph John (1788-1847)
MK.1.32 Essays on the evidences, doctrines, and practical operation, of Christianity. 3rd ed. 12°, London, 1827.

H

DAVID HUME

HALHED, Nathaniel Brassey (1751-1830)
MH.5.10^2 Testimony of the authenticity of the prophecies of Richard Brothers... 8°, London, 1795.

HALHED, Nathaniel Brassey (1751-1830)
MH.5.24^2 Testimony of the authenticity of the prophecies of Richard Brothers...2nd ed. 8°, London, 1795.

HALHED, Nathaniel Brassey (1751-1830)
ME.7.14 See CODE
A code of Gentoo laws, or, ordinations of the Pundits, from a Persian translation, made from the original, written in the Shanscrit language. [Translated and ed. by N.B. Halhed.] 1776.

HALL, Robert (1764-1831)
MB.5.15-20 Works. With a brief memoir of his life by Dr. Gregory...Published under the superintendence of O. Gregory. 6 vols. 8°, London, 1832.

HALLAM, Henry (1777-1859)
MF.6.12-13 The constitutional history of England from the accession of Henry VII. to the death of George II. 2 vols. 4°, London, 1827.

HALLAM, Henry (1777-1859)
MF.6.14-15 View of the state of Europe during the Middle Ages. 2 vols. 4°, London, 1818.

[ED. NOTE: Referred to by Malthus in his "Principles of Political Economy," 1820 ed., p. 273.]

HAMILTON, Antoine, comte (1646?-1720)
ML.4.16 Mémoires. Nouvelle éd. augmentée de notes & d'éclaircissemens nécessaires, par H. Walpole. 8°, Londres, 1783.

HAMILTON, Antoine, comte (1646?-1720)
MA.2.12-14 Œuvres. (Nouvelle éd. [by] A.A. Renouard.) 3 vols. 8°, Paris, 1812.

HAMILTON, Antoine, comte (1646?-1720)
ME.1.38 Suite des Quatre Facardins et de Zeneyde, contes d'Hamilton terminés par M. de Levis. 8°, Paris, 1813.

HAMILTON, Robert (1743-1829)
MC.6.13 An inquiry concerning the rise and progress, the redemption and present state, and the management, of the National Dept of Great Britain. 2nd ed., enlarged. 8°, Edinburgh, 1814.

HAMILTON, Robert (1743-1829)
MA.3.31 The progress of society. [Chapter XVIII, 'Population,' discusses Malthus.] 8°, London, 1830.

HAMILTON, Walter
MB.6.25 The East India gazetteer... 8°, London, 1815.

HANWAY, Jonas (1712-1786)
MI.1.7-8 Letters on the importance of the rising generation of the laboring part of our fellow-subjects...2 vols. 8°, London, 1767.

[ED. NOTE: In the later *Essay*, Bk. III., Ch. VI., Malthus wrote: "The dreadful account given by Jonas Hanway of the treatment of parish children in London is well known."]

HANWAY, Jonas (1712-1786)
MH.5.23[4] See REVIEW
A review of the proposed naturalization of the Jews...By a merchant [J. Hanway]...1753.

HARE, Augustus William (1792-1834) & Julius Charles (1795-1855)
MB.2.9-10 See GUESSES
Guesses at truth by two brothers [i.e. J.C. and A.W. Hare]. 2 vols. 1827.

HARRINGTON, James (1611-1677)
MM.5.17 The Oceana of James Harrington, and his other works...The whole collected...with an exact account of his life prefix'd, by J. Toland. F°, London, 1700.

HARRIS, James (1709-1780)
MM.3.22 Hermes: or, A philosophical inquiry concerning language and universal grammar. By J.H(arris). 8°, London, 1751.

HARRIS, John (1666?-1719)
MA.7.12-13 Navigantium atque itinerantium bibliotheca: or, A compleat collection of voyages and travels...2 vols. F°, London, 1705.

[ED. NOTE: Referred to by Malthus in the later *Essay*, Bk. I., Ch. V, VII, X. However, he cites the 1744 folio edition.]

HARTLEY, David (1705-1757)
MM.3.1-3 Observations on man, his frame, his duty, and his expectations...2 vols. (With Notes and additions to Dr. Hartley's Observations on man; by H.A. Pastorius, translated from the German original...) (3 vols.). 8°, London, 1791.

HARTLEY, David (1732-1813)
MH.4.27[5] An address to the Right Worshipful the Mayor and Corporation...of the town of Kingston-upon-Hull, containing...arguments in favour of a Parliamentary reform...To which is added a letter to...C.J. Fox, by J. Cartwright. 8°, London, 1784.

HARWOOD, Edward (1729-1794)
MI.1.24 Discourses on St. Paul's description of death, and its consequences. 8°, London, 1790.

HASTINGS, Rt. Hon. Warren (1732-1818)
MH.4.27[1] A letter to the Honourable the Court of Directors of the East-India Company, dated from Lucnow, April 30, with a postscript, dated May 13, 1784. 8°, London, [1784].

HASTINGS, Rt. Hon. Warren (1732-1818)
MM.5.13[3] A narrative of the Insurrection which happened in the Zemeedary of Banaris in the month of August 1781, and of the transactions of the Governor-General in that district... 4°, Calcutta, 1782.

HASTINGS, Rt. Hon. Warren (1732-1818)
MH.4.28[2] The present state of the East Indies. With notes by the editor (J. Stockdale). 8°, London, 1786.

HASTINGS, Rt. Hon. Warren (1732-1818)
MH.5.12^{4} See REVIEW
A review of the principal charges against Warren Hastings Esquire...[By J. Logan.] 1788.

HAUGHTON, Sir Graves Chamney (1788-1849)
MM.5.7^{1} A short enquiry into the nature of language, with a view to ascertain the original meanings of Sanskrit prepositions...(For private circulation.) 4°, London, 1832.

HAWKINS, Sir John (1719-1789)
ML.3.3 See PROBATIONARY
Probationary odes for the laureatship: with a preliminary discourse, by Sir John Hawkins. [Satirical parodies on Sir J. Hawkins and other Tories. By R. Tickell and others.] 1785.

HAWKINS, Thomas (d. 1772)
ML.1.23-5 The origin of the English drama, illustrated in its various species...with explanatory notes. 3 vols. 8°, Oxford, 1773.

HAY, William (1695-1755)
MH.5.19^{1} Deformity: an essay. 8°, London, 1754.

HAY, William (1695-1755)
MH.5.21^{3} See REMARKS
Remarks on the laws relating to the poor; with proposals for their better relief and employment. By a Member of Parliament [W. Hay]. First published in 1735...1751.

HAYES, Samuel
MG.7.8^{6} Duelling: a poem. 4°, Cambridge, 1775.

HENRY, Robert (1718-1790)
MC.6.1-12 The history of Great Britain, from the first invasion of it by the Romans...12 vols. (Vols. 1-10, 4th ed., vols. 11, 12, 3rd ed.) 8°, London, 1799-1805.

HERAULT DE SECHELLES, Marie Jean (1760-1794)
MI.2.20^{3} Voyage à Montbar, contenant des détails très-interéssans sur...Buffon. 8°, Paris, an IX [1801].

HERBERT, George (1593-1633)
ME.2.19 The Temple; sacred poems and private ejaculations. 8°, London, 1844.*

HERMIT'S
MG.7.8[4] A hermit's tale; recorded by his own hand, and found in his cell. [By S. Lee.] 4°, London, 1787.

HERODOTUS (c. 485-425 B.C.)
MF.1.28-31, 31a, 32-5 Historia. Ex editione J. Gronovii...(Parallel Latin & Greek texts.) 9 vols. 8°, Glasguæ, 1761.

HERRIES, Sir Robert
MH.3.21[3] See SKETCH
Sketch of financial and commercial affairs in the Autumn of 1797...[By Sir R. Herries.] 1797.

HERSCHEL, Sir John Frederick William (1792-1871)
MB.1.33 A preliminary discourse on the study of natural philosophy. 8°, London, 1829.

HEURES
ML.2.8 Heures nouvelles dédiées au Roy, contenant les offices qui se disent dans l'Eglise pendant l'année. En latin & en françois...Nouvelle éd., augmentée... 12°, Paris, 1760.

HEY, John (1734-1815)
MM.3.8[1] Heads of lectures in divinity, delivered in the University of Cambridge. 3rd ed. 8°, Cambridge, 1794.

HEYLYN, Peter (1600-1662)
ML.3.1 The historie of that most famous Saint and souldier of Christ Iesus; St. George of Cappadocia...2nd ed., corrected and enlarged. 4°, London, 1633.

HIEROCLES, Alexandrinus (fl. c. 430)
ML.2.16[1] Commentarius in Aurea Pythagoreorum carmina. J. Curterio interprete...(Greek & Latin.) 8°, London, 1673.

HIEROCLES, Alexandrinus (fl. c. 430)
ML.2.16[2] De providentia & fato; una cum fragmenta ejusdem; et Lillii Gyraldi interpretatione Symbolorum Pythagoræ; notisque Merici Casauboni ad Commentarium Hieroclis in Aurea carmina. 8°, London, 1673.

HIGGINS, John
MH.4.22[6] Report upon the farm of Thomas Greg, Esq. at Coles in Hertfordshire. (Signed J. Higgins, T. Wilson, J. Foster.) 8°, Bedford, 1811.

HILL, Aaron (1685-1750)
ML.1.31[1] The tragedy of Zara. As it is acted at the Theatre-Royal, in Drury-Lane, by His Majesty's servants. 2nd ed. 12°, London, 1758.

HILL, Sir Richard (1732-1808)
MH.5.10[4] The substance of a speech intended to have been delivered in the House of Commons, on Mr. Grey's first motion for peace, on Monday, January 26, 1795... 8°, London, 1795.

HINDS, Samuel, Bp of Norwich (1793-1872)
MF.5.17-18 The history of the rise and early progress of Christianity...2 vols. 8°, London, 1828.

HINTS
MG.5.19[1] Hints towards the formation of a society, for promoting a spirit of independence among the poor. 2nd ed. 12°, Bristol [1812].

HIRZEL, Hans Kaspar (1725-1803)
MK.1.1-2 Le Socrate rustique, ou Description de la conduite économique & morale d'un paysan philosophe. Traduit de l'allemand...par un officier suisse au service de France...4e éd., exactement corrigée...2 vols. 8°, Lausanne, 1777.

HISTOIRE
ML.4.14-15 Histoire des navigations aux Terres Australes. Contenant ce que l'on sçait des mœurs & des productions des contrées découvertes jusqu'à ce jour...[By C. de Brosses.] 2 vols. 4°, Paris, 1756.

[ED. NOTE: Referred to in the later edition of Malthus's *Essay*, Bk. I., Ch. V.]

HISTOIRE
MB.3.12 Histoire des Sévarambes, peuples qui habitent une partie du troisiéme continent, communément apellé la Terre australe...[By D. Veiras.] Nouvelle éd., corrigée & augmentée. 2 vols. in 1. 12°, Amsterdam, 1715-16.

HISTORIÆ
MI.2.11-12 Historiæ Augustæ scriptores VI. ...cum integris notis I. Casauboni, C. Salmasii & J. Gruteri...2 vols. 8°, Lugduni Batav., 1671.

HISTORY
MB.6.61[3] The history of Isaac Jenkins, and Sarah his wife and their three children. [By T. Beddoes.] 2nd ed. 8°, London, 1793.

HISTORY
MJ.1.45-7 The history of the Jews. [By H.H. Milman.] 3 vols. 8°, London, 1829.

HISTORY
ML.5.23 A history of the revolt of Ali Bey, against the Ottoman Porte...By S. L[usignan]. 2nd ed. 8°, London, 1784.

HISTORY
MH.5.7[1] History of the Royal malady, with variety of entertaining anecdotes, to which are added, strictures on the declaration of Horne Tooke, respecting Mrs. Fitzherbert...By a page of the Presence [i.e. P. Withers]. 8°, London, [1789].

HOADLY, Benjamin, Bp of Winchester (1676-1761)
MH.5.20[5] See ENQUIRY
An enquiry into the reasons of the conduct of Great Britain, with relation to the present state of affairs in Europe. [By B. Hoadly.] 1727.

HOADLY, Benjamin, M.D., dramatist (1706-1757)
MI.4.9[5] The suspicious husband. A comedy. As it is acted at the Theatre-Royal in Covent-Garden. 2nd ed. 8°, London, 1747.

HOBBES, Thomas (1588-1679)
MC.7.4 Moral and political works...To which is prefixed the author's life... F°, London, 1750.

HODGSON, Christopher (1784-1874)
MG.7.19 An account of the augmentation of small livings by 'The Governors of the Bounty of Queen Anne, for the augmentation of the maintenance of the poor clergy'...to the end of the year 1825... 8°, London, 1826.

HOGARTH, William (1697-1764)
MG.4.1 Biographical anecdotes of William Hogarth; with a catalogue of his works chronologically arranged; and occasional remarks. [By J. Nichols.] 2nd ed., enlarged and corrected. 8°, London, 1782.

HOLWELL, John Zephaniah (1711-1798)
ME.1.40[3] Dissertations on the origin, nature, and pursuits, of intelligent beings, and on Divine Providence... 8°, Bath, 1786.

HOLWELL, John Zephaniah (1711-1798)
MA.3.19-20 Interesting historical events, relative to the provinces of Bengal, and the Empire of Indostan...2nd ed. corrected, with a supplement. 3 pts. (2 vols.) 8°, London, 1766-7; 1771.

HOLWELL, John Zephaniah (1711-1798)
ME.1.40[2] A new experiment for the prevention of crimes... 8°, Bath, 1786.

HOMERUS (mid 9th C. B.C.)
MJ.1.33-7 The Iliad of Homer. Translated by Mr. Pope. Vols. 2-6. (Vol. 1 wanting.) 8°, London, 1718-21.

HOMERUS (mid 9th C. B.C.)
MA.5.14-18 The Iliad of Homer. Translated by A. Pope, Esq. A new ed. ...by G. Wakefield. 5 vols. 8°, London, 1806.

HOMERUS (mid 9th C. B.C.)
MG.5.11-13 The Odyssey of Homer. Translated by A. Pope. 3 vols. 12°, Dublin, 1766.

HOMERUS (mid 9th C. B.C.)
MA.5.10-13 The Odyssey of Homer. Translated by A. Pope, Esq. A new ed....by G. Wakefield. 4 vols. 8°, London, 1806.

HOMERUS (mid 9th C. B.C.)
MF.3.9-13 Opera omnia ex recensione et cum notis S. Clarkii. Accessit varietas lectionum...cura I.A. Ernesti...Ed. 2^{a} correctior et auctior. 5 vols. 8°, Lipsiae, 1824.

HOMERUS (mid 9th C. B.C.)
ME.5.41-4 Works; translated from the Greek, into English verse, by A. Pope. 7 Vols. in 4. 12°, London, 1794.

HOOKER, Richard (1554-1600)
MB.6.13-15 Works; with an account of his life and death by I. Walton. A new ed. ...by J. Keble. 3 vols. 8°, Oxford, 1836.*

HOOKER, Sir William Jackson (1785-1865)
MA.3.28 Journal of a tour in Iceland in the summer of 1809. (Privately pr.) 8°, Yarmouth, 1811.

HOOLE, John (1727-1803)
MI.4.7^{1} Timanthes: a tragedy. As it is performed at the Theatre Royal in Covent-Garden. [Founded on Metastasio's Demofoonte.] 8°, London, 1770.

HORATIUS FLACCUS, Quintus (65-8 B.C.)
MK.3.1-2 Epistolae ad Pisones, et Augustum: with an English commentary and notes. To which are added, Two dissertations...and A letter to Mr. Mason. [Ed. by R. Hurd.] 3rd ed., corrected and enlarged. 2 vols. 8°, Cambridge, 1757.

HORATIUS FLACCUS, Quintus (65-8 B.C.)
MI.3.5-6 Opera, illustravit C.G. Mitscherlich. 2 vols. 8°, Lipsiae, 1800.

HORATIUS FLACCUS, Quintus (65-8 B.C.)
ME.5.58 Poemata omnia. Exactiori multo fide...recognita: varijsq; adnotationibus aucta. 16°, Lugduni, 1559.

HORATIUS FLACCUS, Quintus (65-8 B.C.)
MF.2.2-5 A poetical translation of the works of Horace: with the original text, and critical notes...By P. Francis. 4 vols. (Vols. 1-3, 4th ed.; vol. 4, 3rd ed.) 12°, London, 1749-50.

HORNE, George, Bp of Norwich (1730-1792)
MH.5.14[1] An apology for certain gentlemen in the University of Oxford, aspersed in a late anonymous pamphlet [by B. Kennicott]... 8°, Oxford, 1756.

HORNE, George, Bp of Norwich (1730-1792)
MH.5.14[3] Considerations on the life and death of St. John the Baptist. 8°, Oxford, 1769.

HORNE, George, Bp of Norwich (1730-1792)
MB.6.54[2];MJ.1.20[2] [2 copies.] See LETTER
A letter to Adam Smith LL.D. on the life, death, and philosophy of his friend David Hume Esq. By one of the people called Christians [i.e. G. Horne]. 1777.

HORNE, George, Bp of Norwich (1730-1792)
MB.6.54[1] See LETTERS
Letters on infidelity. By the author of a Letter to Doctor Adam Smith [i.e. G. Horne]. 1784.

HORNER, Francis (1778-1817)
ME.3.12-13 Memoirs and correspondence. Ed. by L. Horner. 2 vols. 8°, London, 1843.*

HORSE
ME.3.22 The horse [by W. Youatt]; with a treatise on draught [by I.K. Brunel], and a copious index. (Libr. of Useful Knowledge.) 8°, London, 1831.

HOTMAN, Jean, sieur de Villiers Saint-Paul (1552-1636?)
See TURLUPINUS DE TURLUPINIS, Nicodemus, pseud.

HOWARD, Leonard (1699?-1767)
MK.4.10 A collection of letters from the original manuscripts of many princes, great personages and statesmen... 4°, London, 1753.

HOWLETT, John (1731-1804)
MH.5.15[3] An enquiry concerning the influence of tithes upon agriculture... 8°, London, 1801.

HOWLETT, John (1731-1804)
MH.3.22[1] The insufficiency of the causes to which the increase of our poor, and of the poor's rates have been commonly ascribed... 8°, London, 1788.

HUME, David (1711-1776)
MH.3.27-8 Essays and treatises on several subjects. New ed. 2 vols. 8°, Edinburgh, 1800.

[ED. NOTE: Hume was first referred to by Malthus in his 1798 *Essay*, (Ch. IV.). In the later *Essay*, he refers to the 1764 edition (starting w/Bk. I. Ch. V). Hume is also referred to in the Preface to the second edition of the *Essay*, where Hume is cited among the four authors from whom Malthus has "Deduced the Principle." Hume's Essays are referred to as well in Malthus's "Principles of Political Economy," p. 59 n., and p. 406 of the 1820 edition.]

HUME, David (1711-1776)
MF.4.10-17 The history of England, from the Invasion of Julius Cæsar to the Revolution in 1688. New ed., with the author's last corrections...to which is prefixed, A short account of his life, written by himself. 8 vols. 8°, London, 1786.

HUME, David (1711-1776)
MF.5.38-9 Life and correspondence of D. Hume...By J.H. Burton. 2 vols. 8°, Edinburgh, 1846.*

HUME, David (1711-1776)
MH.4.2-3 A treatise of human nature...New ed. 2 vols. 8°, London, 1817.

HUME, David (1711-1776)
MM.3.11 See LETTERS
Letters of eminent persons addressed to David Hume. [Ed. by J.H. Burton.] 1849.*

HURD, Richard, Bp of Worcester (1720-1808)
MH.4.26[2] See OBSERVATIONS
Observations on the Reverend Doctor Hurd's, now Lord Bishop of Worcester's, two dialogues on the constitution of the English government, addressed in a letter to the Right Hon. E. Burke. 1790.

HUTCHINSON, Rt. Hon. John Hely (1724-1794)
MH.4.29[4] A letter from J.H. Hutchinson, Esq., to the Mayor of Cork, &c. [Wants title-page.] 8°, [Dublin, 1785.]

HUTCHINSON, Lucy (b. 1620) [wife of Hutchinson, John (1615-1664)]
MM.5.3 Memoirs of the life of Colonel Hutchinson, Governor of Nottingham Castle and Town...Now first published...by J. Hutchinson... 4°, London, 1806.

HUTTEN, Ulrich von (1488-1523)
ML.2.21 See EPISTOLÆ OBSCURORUM VIRORUM
Duo volumina epistolarum obscurorum virorum, ad Dominum M. Ortuinum Gratium, Attico lepôre referta, denuo excusa, & à mendis repurgata...[By U. von Hutten and others.] (2 pts.) 1581.

HUTTON, George
MH.3.21[5] An appeal to the nation, on the subject of Mr. Gilbert Wakefield's Letter to William Wilberforce, Esq. M.P. To which are subjoined four sermons... 8°, Nottingham, 1798.

I

WASHINGTON IRVING

IDLER
ME.4.27-8 The Idler. [A periodical, by S. Johnson, and others.] 2 vols. 12°, London, 1761.

IGNATIUS, St, Bp of Antioch (35?-107 A.D.)
MG.6.13 Polycarpi et Ignatii epistolæ: una cum vetere vulgata interpretatione Latina...Quibus præfixa est...I. Usserii dissertatio. (Greek & Latin.) (2 pts.). 4°, Oxoniæ, 1644.

IMPARTIAL

MH.5.21[1] An impartial examination of a pamphlet, intitled, Considerations on several proposals lately made for the better maintenance of the poor [by C. Gray]... 8°, London, 1752.

INCHBALD, Elizabeth Simpson, Mrs. J. (1753-1821)

MI.4.6[4] Wives as they were, and maids as they are. A comedy, in 5 acts, performed at the Theatre Royal, Covent-Garden. 8°, London, 1797.

INDEPENDENT

MM.4.10-12 The Independent Whig: or, A defence of primitive Christianity...[By J. Trenchard and T. Gordon.] (Nos. 1-74.) 6th ed. With additions and amendments. 3 vols. 12°, London, 1735.

INGLIS, Henry David (1795-1835)

MA.4.2-3 Ireland in 1834. A journey throughout Ireland, during the Spring, Summer, and Autumn of 1834. 3rd ed. 2 vols. 12°, London, 1835.*

INQUIRY

MH.3.17[1] An inquiry into the causes of popular discontents in Ireland. By an Irish country gentleman [i.e. W. Parnell]. 8°, London, 1804.

INQUIRY

MH.3.20[4] An inquiry into the state of the nation, at the commencement of the present administration. [By Lord Brougham.] 8°, London, 1806.

IRELAND, William Henry (1777-1835)

MJ.1.21-3 See PASSAGES

Passages selected by distinguished personages on the great literary trial of Vortigern and Rowena [by W.H. Ireland]. A comi-tragedy. 2nd ed. 3 vols. (Vol. 1 misbound.) [1795.]

IRVING, Washington (1783-1859)

MA.4.4 A history of New-York, from the beginning of the world to the end of the Dutch dynasty...By Diedrich Knickerbocker [i.e. W. Irving]. 8°, London, 1824.

IMPROVISATRICE

MK.2.30 The improvisatrice; and other poems. By L.E. L[andon]. 8°, London, 1824.

J

THOMAS JEFFERSON

JACHIN

MH.5.24[3] Jachin and Boaz; or, An authentic key to the door of free-masonry, both ancient and modern...By a gentleman belonging to the Jerusalem Lodge...New ed., greatly enlarged and improved. 8°, London, 1797.

JACOB, Joseph

MM.5.10 Observations on the structure and draught of wheel-carriages. 4°, London, 1773.

JACOB, William (1762?-1851)

MM.5.2 A view of the agriculture, manufactures, statistics, and state of society, of Germany, and parts of Holland and France. Taken during a journey through those countries in 1819. 4°, London, 1820.

JAMERAI-DUVAL, Valentin (1695-1775)

MK.4.4 Œuvres de V. Jamerai Duval, précédées des mémoires sur sa vie (par M.F.A. de K*** [i.e. Koch]). 2 vols. in 1. 8°, S. Pétersbourg, 1784.

JAMES, Prince of Wales, Francis Edward Stuart, the Old Pretender (1688-1766)

MH.5.20[3] See REMARKS
Remarks on the Pretender's Declaration and Commission. (2 pts.) 1745.

JAMES, Patricia (1917-)

MX.1.12 Population Malthus, his life and times. 8°, London, (1979).**

[ED. NOTE: Patricia James has an intimate knowledge of the Malthus family, and is among the most documented contemporary Malthus scholars. She is a contributor to the presentations of this catalogue, and is now preparing a variorum edition of the "Essay on Population" for Cambridge University Press.]

JAMES, Patricia (1917-)

MX.1.4 See MALTHUS, Thomas Robert
Travel diaries; ed. by P. James. 1966.**

JEFFERSON, Thomas, President of the U.S. (1743-1826)
MA.5.9 Notes on the State of Virginia. 8°, London, 1787.

JENYNS, Soame (1704-1787)
ML.1.4-5 See MISCELLANEOUS
Miscellaneous pieces. [By S. Jenyns.] 2 vols. 1761.

JESUITS
MC.1.13-36 See LETTRES
Lettres édifiantes et curieuses, écrites des missions étrangères (de la Compagnie de Jésus). Nouvelle éd. 24 vols. 1780-81.

JEVONS, William (1794-1873)
MF.5.36-7 Systematic morality, or A treatise on the theory and practice of human duty, on the grounds of natural religion. 2 vols. 8°, London, 1827.

JOCKEY
MK.4.21 The Jockey Club, or A sketch of the manners of the age. [By C. Pigott.] 3 pts. (Pt 1, 7t. ed.; pt 2, 3rd ed.) 8°, London, 1792.

JOHNSON, Samuel (1709-1784)
MH.4.15[3] Deformities of Dr. Samuel Johnson. Selected from his works. 8°, Edinburgh, 1782.

JOHNSTONE, Charles (1719?-1800?)
MC.2.38-9 See CHRYSAL
Chrysal: or, The adventures of a guinea...By an adept [i.e. C. Johnstone]. 4th ed., greatly inlarged and corrected. 2 vols. 1764.

JOHNSTONE, Charles (1719?-1800?)
ME.2.12-15 See CHRYSAL
Chrysal: or, The adventures of a guinea...By an adept [i.e. C. Johnstone]. 4 vols. (Vols. 1, 2, 5th ed.) 1766-7.

JONES, Richard (1790-1855)
MH.1.17 An essay on the distribution of wealth, and on the sources of taxation. 8°, London, 1831.

JONES, Richard (1790-1855)
MH.3.1 Literary remains, consisting of lectures and tracts on political economy, ed. ...by W. Whewell. 8°, London, 1859.*

JONSON, Ben (1573-1637)
ML.1.13 Plays, viz. I. Volpone: or, The fox. II. The Alchemist. III. Epicoene: or, The silent woman. 8°, Glasgow, 1766.

JOHNSON, Samuel (1709-1784)
MG.6.1-2 A dictionary of the English language...To which are prefixed, A history of the language, and an English grammar. 2 vols. 4°, London, 1786.

JOHNSON, Samuel (1709-1784)
ME.4.27-8 See IDLER
The Idler. [A periodical, by S. Johnson, and others.] 2 vols. 1761.

JOHNSON, Samuel (1709-1784)
MI.4.9[4] Irene: a tragedy. As it is acted at the Theatre Royal in Drury-Lane. 8°, London, 1749.

JOHNSON, Samuel (1709-1784)
MG.3.4 Prayers and meditations, composed by S. Johnson and published from his MSS., by G. Strahan. 8°, London, 1785.

JOHNSON, Samuel (1709-1784)
ME.5.17-26 See WORLD
The world displayed; or, A curious collection of voyages and travels, selected from the writers of all nations... [Introduction by S. Johnson.] 20 vols. in 10. (Vol. 1, 2nd ed.) 1760-61.

JONSON, Ben (1573-1637)
MF.2.31-9 Works. With notes critical, and explanatory, and a biographical memoir, by W. Gifford. 9 vols. 8°, London, 1816.

JORTIN, John (1698-1770)
MK.3.28-32 Remarks on ecclesiastical history. 5 vols. 8°, London, 1751-74.

JOSEPHUS, Flavius (38-c. 100 A.D.)
MA.7.8 Genuine works. Translated from the original Greek, according to Havercamp's accurate edition...[Ed. by] W. Whiston. F°, London, 1737.

JUAN, Jorge (Juan y Santacilia, Jorge) (1713-1773)
ML.4.12-13 Voyage historique de l'Amérique Méridionale fait par ordre du Roi d'Espagne, par George Juan et par Antoine de Ulloa...[Translated by E. Mauvillon.] 2 vols. 4°, Amsterdam, 1752.

[ED. NOTE: It is actually the narrative of Ulloa's voyage which is referred to in the later *Essay*, Bk. I, Ch. IV and Bk. II, Ch. XIII.]

JULIANUS, Roman Emperor (c. 331-363 A.D.)
MB.3.11 Déffense du paganisme par l'Empereur Julien, en grec et en françois avec des dissertations...par Mr. Le Marquis d'Argens. 8°, Berlin, 1764.

JULIANUS, Roman Emperor (c. 331-363 A.D.)
MJ.2.39 Opera quæ extant omnia. A Petro Martinio Morentino & Carolo Cantoclaro...Latina facta, emendata, & aucta...(4 pts.) 8°, Parisiis, 1583.

JUNIUS, pseud.
MG.4.9-11 Junius: including letters by the same writer under other signatures, now first collected. To which are added, his confidential correspondence with Mr. Wilkes, and his private letters addressed to Mr. H.S. Woodfall. 2nd ed. 3 vols. 8°, London, 1814.

JUNIUS, pseud.
ME.4.31-2 The letters of Junius. New ed. 2 vols. 12°, London, 1810.

JUSTIFICATION
MK.5.15[8] The justification: a poem. By the author of The Diaboliad [i.e. W. Combe]. 4°, London, 1777.

JUSTINUS
MF.2.7 Historia ex Trogo Pompeio. Diligentissime recensuit & emendationes addidit T. Faber. Ed. nova. (2 pts.) 12°, Salmurii, 1671.

JUVENALIS, Decimus Junius (c. 60-130 A.D.)
MF.3.1-2 Satirae XVI ad optimorum exemplarium fidem recensitae...a G.A. Ruperti. 2 vols. 8°, Lipsiae, 1801.

[ED. NOTE: Malthus cites the VIth Satire of Juvenal in a note to Bk. I, Ch. XIV of the later *Essay*.]

JUVENALIS, Decimus Junius (c. 60-130 A.D.)
MM.5.12 Satires: translated and illustrated by F. Hodgson. 4°, London, 1807.

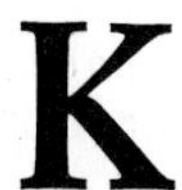

KAEMPFER, Engelbert (1651-1716)
MA.6.9-10 The history of Japan, giving an account of the ancient and present state and government of that Empire... Translated...by J.G. Scheuchzer. With the life of the author, and an introduction. 2 vols. F°, London, 1727.

[ED. NOTE: In his later *Essay*, Bk. I, Ch. XII, Malthus wrote: "The Japanese are distinguished from the Chinese, in being much more warlike, seditious, dissolute and ambitious: and it would appear, from Kaempfer's account, that the check to population from infanticide, in China, is balanced by the greater dissoluteness of manners with regard to the sex, and the greater frequency of wars and intestine commotions which prevail in Japan. With regard to the positive checks to population from disease and famine, the two countries seem to be nearly on a level".]

KALIDASA (1st C. B.C.)
MM.5.13[2] Sacontala; or, The fatal ring: an Indian drama. By Calidas. Translated from the original Sanscrit and Pracrit [by Sir W. Jones]. 4°, London, 1790.

KALM, Peter (1715-1779)
ML.5.18-20 Travels into North America; containing its natural history...Translated into English by J.R. Forster. 3 vols. 8°, Warrington, 1770; London, 1771.

KAMES, Henry Home, Lord (1696-1782)
MM.4.1-2 Elements of criticism. 3rd ed. With additions and improvements. 2 vols. 8°, Edinburgh, 1765.

[ED. NOTE: In his later edition of his *Essay*, (Bk. I, Ch. IV and Bk. III, Ch. XIV), Malthus refers to the more popular Kames work: "Sketches of the History of Man."]

KENT, Nathaniel (1737-1810)
MH.1.8 Hints to gentlemen of landed property. 2nd ed. 8°, London, 1776.

KIDD, John (1775-1851)
MC.4.20 On the adaptation of external nature to the physical condition of man...(Bridgewater Treatises, 2). 8°, London, 1833.

KING, Peter King, Lord, 7th Baron of Ockham (1776-1833)
MF.6.8 The life of John Locke, with extracts from his correspondence, journals, and common-place books. By Lord King. 4°, London, 1829.

KING, Peter King, Lord, 7th Baron of Ockham (1776-1833)
MF.5.16 A selection from the speeches and writings of the late Lord King. With a short introductory memoir, by Earl Fortescue. 8°, London, 1844.*

KING, Peter King, Lord 7th Baron of Ockham (1776-1833)
MH.3.18[4]; MH.5.9[1] [2 copies.] Thoughts on the effects of the Bank restrictions. 2nd ed. enlarged, including some remarks on the coinage. 8°, London, 1804.

KING, William, Abp of Dublin (1650-1729)
ML.5.27-8 An essay on the origin of evil. Translated from the Latin, with notes. 2nd ed. corrected and enlarged...By E. Law. 2 vols. 8°, London, 1732.

KIPPIS, Andrew (1725-1795)
MH.4.15[2] Observations on the late contests in the Royal Society. 8°, London, 1784.

KIRBY, Joshua (1716-1774?)
MG.7.21[6] A syllabus to four lectures on perspective. With remarks for assisting the memory. 4°, [London? 1760?]

KIRBY, William (1759-1850)
MB.1.4-6 An introduction to entomology: or Elements of the natural history of insects...By W. Kirby and W. Spence. Vols. 2-4. (Vol. 2, 2nd ed.; vol. 1 wanting.) 8°, London, 1818-26.

KIRBY, William (1759-1850)
MC.4.27-8 On the power, wisdom and goodness of God, as manifested in the creation of animals and in their history, habits and instincts. (2nd ed.) 2 vols. (Bridgewater Treatises, 7.) 8°, London, 1835.*

KIRWAN, Richard (1733-1812)
MH.5.11[2] The manures most advantageously applicable to the various sorts of soils...8°, London, 1796.

KNICKERBOCKER, Diedrich, pseud.
See IRVING, Washington.

KNIGHT, Richard Payne (1750-1824)
MM.5.6 An analytical essay on the Greek alphabet. 4°, London, 1791.

KNIGHT, Richard Payne (1750-1824)
ML.3.32 An analytical inquiry into the principles of taste. 4th ed. 8°, London, 1808.

KNOWLER, William (1699-1773)
MA.7.1-2 The Earl of Strafforde's letters and despatches, with an essay towards his life by Sir George Radcliffe...By W. Knowler. 2 vols. F°, London, 1739.

KNOX, Vicesimus (1752-1821)
ME.3.2-3 See ELEGANT
Elegant extracts: or, Useful and entertaining passages in prose...[Compiled by V. Knox.] 4 books. 2 vols. 1808.

KNOX, Vicesimus (1752-1821)
ME.3.4-5 See ELEGANT
Elegant extracts: or, Useful and entertaining pieces of poetry...[Compiled by V. Knox.] 4 books. 2 vols. 1809.

KOCH, Christophe Guillaume de (1737-1813)
MA.3.5-7 Tableau des révolutions de l'Europe...3 vols. 8°, Paris, 1807.

KORAN
MG.7.3 The Koran, commonly called the Alcoran of Mohammed, translated into English...with explanatory notes...By G. Sale. 4°, London, 1734.

KOTZEBUE, August von (1761-1819)
MI.4.6[5] The stranger: a comedy. Freely translated from Kotzebue's German comedy of misanthropy and repentance. 4th ed. 8°, London, 1798.

KREBS, Johannes Tobias (1718-1782)
MG.3.2 Observationes in Novum Testamentum e Flavio Iosepho. 8°, Lipsiae, 1755.

L

LINNAEUS

LA BRUYERE, Jean de (1645?-1696)
ME.5.69-70 Les Caractères. 2 vols. 8°, Paris, 1750.

LA CONDAMINE, Charles Marie de (1701-1774)
ML.4.11 Journal du voyage fait par ordre du Roi, à l'Equateur... 4°, Paris, 1751.

LA CONDAMINE, Charles Marie de (1701-1774)
MI.4.28 Relation abrégée d'un voyage fait dans l'intérieur de l'Amérique Méridionale...Nouvelle éd. augmentée... 8°, Maestricht, 1778.

LACRETELLE, Jean Charles Dominique de (1766-1855)
ML.2.6 Précis historique de la Révolution Française, Assemblée Législative. 12°, Paris, 1801.

LACTANTIUS FIRMIANUS, Lucius Coelius (?260-?340)
MF.1.26 Opera quæ extant omnia; ad fidem codicum tam impressorum, quàm manu scriptorum recensita. 8°, Cantabrigiæ, 1685.

LAFFAN, James
MH.4.29[5] Political arithmetic of the population, commerce, and manufactures of Ireland...8°, (London, 1786).

LA FONTAINE, Jean de (1621-1695)
MM.1.2-3 Fables; suivies d'Adonis, poème. Ed. stéréotype. 2 vols. 12°, Paris, an VII [1799].

LA HARPE, Jean François de (1739-1803)
ME.1.11-24 Lycée, ou Cours de littérature ancienne et moderne. 14 vols. 12°, Paris, 1800.

LAING, Malcolm (1762-1818)
MF.5.12-15 The history of Scotland, from the Union of the Crowns...to the Union of the Kingdoms in the reign of Queen Anne. 2nd ed. corrected...4 vols. 8°, London, 1804.

LA MOTRAYE, Aubry de (1674?-1743)
MD.1.4-5 Voyages en Europe, Asie & Afrique... 2 vols. F°, La Haye, 1727.

LANCASTER, Joseph (1778-1838)
MH.5.8[3] Outlines of a plan for educating ten thousand poor children, by establishing schools in country towns and villages; and for uniting works of industry with useful knowledge. 8°, London, 1806.

LANDON, Letitia Elizabeth (1802-1838)
MK.2.30 See IMPROVISATRICE
The improvisatrice; and other poems. By L.E. L[andon]. 1824.

LA ROCHE DU MAINE, Jean Pierre Louis de, Marquis of Luchet (1740-1792)
MI.2.20[1] See ESSAI
Essai sur la Secte des Illuminés. [By J.P.L. de La Roche du Maine, marquis de Luchet.] 1789.

LA ROQUE, Jean de (1661-1745)
MK.2.15 Voyage dans la Palestine...Fait par ordre du Roi Louis XIV... 12°, Amsterdam, 1718.

LAUDERDALE, James Maitland, 8th Earl of (1759-1839)
MH.5.16[1] Observations by the Earl of Lauderdale on the review of his Inquiry into the nature and origin of public wealth, published in the VIIIth number of the Edinburgh review. 8°, Edinburgh, 1804.

[ED. NOTE: Among the definitions which have extended the meaning of the term wealth so far, Lord Lauderdale's may be taken as an example. He defines wealth to be, "All that man desires as useful and delightful to him." - (Malthus, "Principles of Political Economy," 1820 - Ch. I, Sec. I, p. 27.)]

LAVEAUX, Jean Charles Thibault de (1749-1827)
MA.2.15-16 Dictionnaire raisonné des difficultés grammaticales et littéraires de la langue française. 2e éd. revue, corrigée, et considérablement augmentée. 2 vols. 8°, Paris, 1822.

LAVEAUX, Jean Charles Thibault de (1749-1827)
MG.6.6-7 Nouveau dictionnaire de la langue française...2 vols. 4°, Paris, 1820.

LAVINGTON, George (1684-1762)
MF.5.30-31 See ENTHUSIASM
The enthusiasm of Methodists and Papists compared. [By G. Lavington.] (3 pts.) 2 vols. (Vol. 1, 2nd ed.) 1749-51.

LAW, William (1686-1761)
MH.4.6 An appeal to all that doubt, or disbelieve the truths of the Gospel... 8°, London, 1742.

LAW, William (1686-1761)
ML.3.26 A serious call to a devout and holy life...16th ed. corrected... 8°, London, 1810.

LAWRENCE, Sir William, 1st Bart (1783-1867)
MG.4.5 Lectures on physiology, zoology, and the natural history of man... 8°, London, 1819.

LECKIE, Gould Francis
MH.5.9[2] An historical survey of the foreign affairs of Great Britain...(2 pts.) 8°, London, 1808.

LE COURAYER, Pierre François
MA.4.11 Traité oè l'on expose ce que l'Ecriture nous apprend de la Divinité de Jésus Christ. 8°, Londres, 1810.

LEE, Nathaniel (1653?-1692)
ML.1.31[3] Theodosius: or, The force of love: a tragedy. As it is now acted at the Theatres Royal. 12°, London, 1761.

LEE, Sophia (1750-1824)
MG.7.8[4] See HERMIT'S
A hermit's tale: recorded by his own hand, and found in his cell. [By S. Lee.] 1787.

LEGEND
MB.6.61[6] The legend of Saint Robert, the hermit of Knaresbro'. 8°, Knaresbro', 1792.

LELAND, Thomas (1722-1785)
MK.5.5-7 The history of Ireland from the invasion of Henry II. With a preliminary discourse on the antient state of that Kingdom. 3 vols. 4°, London, 1773.

LE MERCIER DE LA RIVIERE, Pierre François Joachim Henri (1761-1838)
MK.2.16-17 See ORDRE
L'ordre naturel et essentiel des sociétés politiques. [By P.F.J.H. Le Mercier de la Rivière.] 2 vols. 1767.

LENGLET DU FRESNOY, Pierre Nicolas (1674-1755)
MH.3.25-6 Chronological tables of universal history... Translated from the last French ed. ...[by T. Flloyd.] 2 vols. 8°, London, 1762.

LEROY, Julien (1686-1759)
MG.7.21[4] Exposé succinct des travaux de MM. Harrison et Le Roy, dans la recherche des longitudes en mer, & des épreuves faites de leurs ouvrages. 4°, Paris, 1768.

LE SAGE, Alain René (1668-1747)
ME.5.27-30 Les avantures de Gil Blas de Santillane. Nouvelle éd. 4 vols. 12°, Londres, 1749.

L'ESTRANGE, Sir Roger (1616-1704)
MG.1.9 See SENECA, Lucius Annaeus
Seneca's Morals by way of abstract...6th ed. To which is added, A discourse, under the title of An after-thought. By Sir R. L'Estrange. (4 pts.) 1696.

LETTER
MH.5.14[2] A letter from a father to his son at the University: relative to a late address to young students, &c. [By R. Graves.] 8°, Oxford, 1787.

LETTER
MH.5.23[7] A letter from a gentleman to his friend concerning the naturalization of the Jews. [Wants title-page.] 8°, [London? 1753?].

LETTER
MI.2.2[7] A letter most humbly and respectfully addressed to His Royal Highness the Prince of Wales [George IV], upon the present state of Ireland... 8°, London, 1798.

LETTER
MH.3.22[9] A letter on the nature, extent, and management, of Poor Rates in Scotland... 8°, Edinburgh, 1807.

LETTER
MH.5.17[2] A letter to a friend in the country, upon the news of the town. 8°, London, [1747].

LETTER
MH.5.22[3] A letter to a Member of the H—-e of C——-s of I——-d [House of Commons of Ireland], on the present crisis of affairs in that Kingdom. 8°, London, [1753].

LETTER
MB.6.54[2]; MJ.1.20[2] [2 copies.] A letter to Adam Smith LL.D. on the life, death, and philosophy of his friend David Hume Esq. By one of the people called Christians [i.e. G. Horne]. 8°, Oxford, 1777.

LETTER
MK.5.15[1]0 A letter to Her Grace the Duchess of Devonshire. [By W. Combe.] 4°, London, 1777.

LETTER
MH.4.25[9] A letter to Miss Hannah More, occasioned by her remarks on the speech which M. Dupont delivered...December 14th, 1792. 8°, London, 1793.

LETTER
MH.5.6[5] A letter to the Earl of Chatham on the Quebec Bill. [By Sir W. Meredith.] 5th ed. 8°, London, 1774.

LETTER
MH.5.22[4] A letter to the King of ***** [i.e. Louis XV, King of France]. By an Englishman, not a Member of the House of Commons. 8°, London, 1756.

LETTER
MH.5.22[6] A letter to the late Recorder of N[ewcastle, C. Fawcett]. From an old friend. 8°, London, [1754.]

LETTER

MI.2.2^{6} A letter to the Prince of Wales [George IV], on a second application to Paliament, to discharge debts wantonly contracted since May, 1787. 10th ed. enlarged... 8°, London, [1795.]

LETTER

MH.5.23^{1} A letter to the Reverend D^{r}. Codex [i.e. E. Gibson], on the subject of his modest instruction to the Crown...[By W. Arnall.] 2nd ed. 8°, London, 1734.

LETTER

MH.4.26^{4} A letter to the Right Hon. Edmund Burke, in reply to his "Reflections on the Revolution in France, &c." 2nd ed., with considerable additions...By a Member of the Revolution Society [i.e. J. Scott, afterwards Scott Waring]. 8°, London, 1790.

LETTER

MH.5.6^{2} A letter to the Right Honourable Willoughby Bertie, by descent Earl of Abingdon, by descent Lord Norreys...In which His Lordship's...treatment of the now Earl of Mansfield is fully vindicated. [By J. Lind.] 8°, London, 1778.

LETTERS

ME.2.2 Letters concerning the present state of Poland...[By J. Lind.] 2nd ed. 8°, London, 1773.

LETTERS

ME.2.1 Letters from Edinburgh; written in the years 1774 and 1775...[By E. Topham.] 8°, London, 1776.

LETTERS

MH.4.19^{2} The letters of an Englishman; in which the principles, and conduct, of the Rockingham Party...are freely, and impartially displayed. 8°, London, 1786.

LETTERS

MM.3.11 Letters of eminent persons addressed to David Hume. [Ed. by J.H. Burton.] 8°, Edinburgh, 1849.*

LETTERS

MB.6.54^{1} Letters on infidelity. By the author of a Letter to Doctor Adam Smith [i.e. G. Horne]. 8°, Oxford, 1784.

LETTERS

MB.6.55^{1} Letters on patriotism. Translated from the French original printed at Berlin. [By Frederick II, the Great.] 8°, London, 1780.

LETTRE

ML.3.14[2] Lettre sur le Discours de M. Le Comte de Windisgraetz...addressée à Monsieur l'Abbé de Bon Conseil, par un vrai patriote, bon citoyen & zélé sujet. 8°, [Brussels?] 1789.

LETTRES

MJ.1.15 Lettres de Mistriss Fanni Butlerd, à Milord Charles Alfred de Caitombridge, comte de Plisinte, duc de Raslingth, écrites en 1735, traduites de l'Anglois en 1756, par A. de Varançai. [By M.J. Riccoboni.] 8°, Paris, 1759.

LETTRES

MB.3.17 Lettres écrites de Londres sur les Anglois et autres sujets. Par M.D.V.*** [i.e. Voltaire]. 8°, 'Basle' [London], 1734.

LETTRES

MC.1.13-36 Lettres édifiantes et curieuses, écrites des missions étrangères (de la Compagnie de Jésus). Nouvelle éd. 24 vols. 12°, Paris, 1780-81.

[ED. NOTE: Frequently referred to by Malthus in the later *Essay*, Bk. I, Ch. IV, V. and XII.]

LETTRES

MB.6.55[2] Lettres turques, et Le temple de Gnide du même auteur [i.e. C. de S. baron de Montesquieu]. (2 pts.) 8°, Cologne, 1748.

LEVAILLANT, François (1753-1824)

MK.4.1-3 Second voyage dans l'intérieur de l'Afrique, par le Cap de Bonne-Espérance, dans les années 1783, 84 et 85. 3 vols. 8°, Paris, an 3 (1795).

[ED. NOTE: "...Vaillant mentions the phlegmatic temperament of the Hottentots as the chief reason of their thin population." (Malthus's *Essay*, Bk. I. Ch. IV.]

LEVIS, Pierre Marc Gaston, duc de (1755-1830)

ME.1.38 See HAMILTON, Antoine, comte
Suite des Quatre Facardins et de Zeneyde, contes d'Hamilton terminés par M. de Levis. 1813.

LEVITA, Elias

See ELIAS, Levita.

LEWESDON

MK.5.15[1] Lewesdon Hill; a poem. [By W. Crowe.] 4°, Oxford, 1788.

LEWIS, Matthew Gregory (1775-1818)
MI.4.5[3] The Castle spectre: a drama. In 5 acts...2nd ed. 8°, London, 1798.

LEWIS, Matthew Gregory (1775-1818)
MB.3.33-6 Romantic tales. 4 vols. 8°, London, 1808.

LIFE
MH.5.19[7] The life of Sir Robt. Cochran, Prime-Minister to King James III. of Scotland. 8°, London, 1734.

LIGHTFOOT, John (1602-1675)
MA.6.6-7 Works. Revised and corrected by G. Bright. 2 vols. F°, London, 1684.

LIND, John (1737-1781)
MH.5.6[2] See LETTER
A letter to the Right Honourable Willoughby Bertie, by descent Earl of Abingdon, by descent Lord Norreys...in which His Lordship's...treatment of the now Earl of Mansfield is fully vindicated. [By J. Lind.] 1778.

LIND, John (1737-1781)
ME.2.2 See LETTERS
Letters concerning the present state of Poland...[By J. Lind.] 2nd ed. 1773.

LINGARD, John (1771-1851)
MF.4.18-31 A history of England from the first invasion by the Romans. 14 vols., (Vols. 1-10, 13, 14, 3rd ed.; vols. 11, 12, 2nd ed.) 8°, London, 1825-31.

LINGUET, Simon Nicolas Henri (1736-1794)
MA.4.10[1] La France plus qu'Angloise, ou Comparaison entre la procédure entamée à Paris le 25 Septembre 1788...et le procès intenté à Londres en 1640... 8°, Bruxelles, 1788.

LINNAEUS, Carl [Carolus] (1707-1778)
MH.4.17 Miscellaneous tracts relating to natural history, husbandry, and physick...[Dissertations from Amœnitates academicæ, by C. Linnaeus; translated.] By B. Stillingfleet. 3rd ed. 8°, London, 1775.

LIST
MH.5.24[9] A list, or Short account, of various charitable institutions in Great-Britain, for the benefit of the poor and infirm, &c. ... 8°, York, 1794.

LITERARY
MM.2.3-4 Literary memoirs of living authors of Great Britain...including a list of their works...[By D. Rivers.] 2 vols. 8°, London, 1798.

LIVIUS, Titus (B.C. 59-A.D. 17)
MI.1.12-14 Historiarum quod extat. Cum perpetuis C. Sigonii et J.F. Gronovii notis. 3 vols. 8°, Amstelodami, 1678-9.

[ED. NOTE: Referred to by Malthus in his later *Essay*, Bk. I, Ch. XIV. (Of the check to Population among the Romans).]

LIVRE
MJ.2.22 Livre d'Eglise pour les laïques, à l'usage du Diocèse de Bourges, imprimé par ordre de Frédéric-Jerosme de Roye de la Rochefoucauld, Patriarche... 12°, Bourges, 1747.

LOCKE, John (1632-1704)
MG.5.25 An abridgment of M^{r}. Locke's Essay concerning humane understanding [by J. Wynne]. 8°, London, 1696.

LOCKE, John (1632-1704)
MG.7.6 A paraphrase and notes on the Epistles of St. Paul to the Galatians, I & II Corinthians, Romans, and Ephesians. To which is prefixed, An essay for the understanding of St. Paul's Epistles...6th ed. 4°, London, 1763.

LOCKE, John (1632-1704)
MF.6.8 See KING, Peter King, Lord, 7th Baron of Ockham
The life of John Locke, with extracts from his correspondence, journals, and common-place books. By Lord King. 1829.

LOGAN, John (1748-1788)
MH.5.12^{4} See REVIEW
A review of the principal charges against Warren Hastings Esquire...[By J. Logan.] 1788.

LONG, Roger (1680-1770)
ME.6.15-16 Astronomy, in 5 books. 2 vols. 4°, Cambridge, 1742-85.

LONGINUS, Cassius (213?-273?)
MM.5.11 De sublimitate commentarius, quem nova versione donavit, perpetuis notis illustravit...Z. Pearce. (Greek & Latin.) 4°, Londini, 1724.

LORIA, Achille (1857-1943)
MX.1.10 Malthus. (Profili, 6.) 8°, Bologna, 1909.**

LOUIS XV, King of France (1710-1774)
MH.5.22[4] See LETTER
A letter to the King of ***** of [i.e. Louis XV, King of France]. By an Englishman, not a Member of the House of Commons. 1756.

LOWE, Joseph
MH.3.17[5] An inquiry into the state of the British West Indies. 8°, London, 1807.

[ED. NOTE: In his later *Essay*, Malthus refers to Lowe's "The Present State of England in Regard to Agriculture, Trade and Finance" (London, 1822). In the 7th Chapter, Lowe supports Simon Gray's views, as opposed to Malthus's theory of population.]

LOWTH, Robert, Bp of London (1710-1787)
MH.4.15[6] See MEMOIRS
Memoirs of the life and writings of the late Robert Lowth...Lord Bishop of London. [By Robert Lowth, Vicar of Halstead.] 1787.

LOWTH, Robert, Vicar of Halstead
MH.4.15[6] See MEMOIRS
Memoirs of the life and writings of the late Robert Lowth...Lord Bishop of London. [By Robert Lowth, Vicar of Halstead.] 1787.

LUCANUS, Marcus Annaeus (39-65 A.D.)
MG.1.18 De bello civili, cum H. Grotii, Farnabii notis integris & variorum selectiss. Accurante C. Schrevelio. 8°, Amstelodami, 1658.

LUCIANUS, Samosatensis (120?-180?)
MG.1.21-2 Opera. Ex versione I. Benedicti cum notis integris I. Bourdelotii [etc.]...(Greek & Latin.) 2 vols. 8°, Amstelodami, 1687.

LUCIEN
ML.2.10-11 Lucien en belle humeur. Ou Nouvelles conversations des morts. [By J.C. Buslé de Montpleinchamp.] Nouvelle éd. augmentée & corrigée. 2 vols. 12°, Amsterdam, 1701.

LUCRETIUS CARUS, Titus (98-55? B.C.)
MG.7.20 De rerum natura libros VI interpretatione et notis illustravit M. Fayus... 4°, Parisiis, 1680.

LUCRETIUS CARUS, Titus (98-55? B.C.)
MK.4.7 De rerum natura libri VI: quibus interpretationem et notas addidit T. Creech. 8°, Oxonii, 1695.

LUCRETIUS CARUS, Titus (98-55? B.C.)
MF.3.24-7 De rerum natura libri VI; ad exemplar Gilberti Wakefield cum ejusdem notis...4 vols. 8°, Glasguæ, 1813.

LUDLOW, Edmund (1617?-1692)
MK.3.25-7 Memoirs. 3 vols. 8°, Switzerland, Vivay pr., 1698-9.

LUDWIG, Christian (1660-1728)
MG.6.10 A dictionary, English, German and French...taken from the best new English dictionaries. 2nd ed. carefully revised... 4°, Leipzig & Francfurt, 1736.

LUDWIG, Christian (1660-1728)
MG.6.11 Teutsch-Englisches Lexicon... 4°, Leipzig, 1716.

LUSIGNAN, Sauveur (ca. 18th C.-beg. 19th C.)
ML.5.23 See HISTORY
A history of the revolt of Ali Bey, against the Ottoman Porte...By S. L[usignan]. 2nd ed. 1784.

LYELL, Sir Charles (1797-1875)
MB.5.21-3 Principles of geology...3 vols. 8°, London, 1830.

LYTTELTON, George Lyttelton, 1st Baron (1709-1773)
MF.4.6-9 The history of the life of King Henry the Second, and of the age in which he lived...3rd ed. Vols. 1-4. (Vols. 5, 6 wanting.) 8°, London, 1769.

LYTTELTON, George Lyttelton, 1st Baron (1709-1773)
MH.5.12[5] See OBSERVATIONS
Observations on the Conversion and Apostleship of St. Paul. In a letter to Gilbert West, Esq. [By George, Lord Lyttelton.] New ed. 1777.

LYTTELTON, George Lyttelton, 1st Baron (1709-1773)
MH.5.19[9] See OBSERVATIONS
Observations on the life of Cicero. [By George, Lord Lyttelton.] 1733.

LYTTELTON, George Lyttelton, 1st Baron (1709-1773)
ME.4.41[2] Poetical works. With the life of the author. (Bell's Edition. The Poets of Great Britain.) 12°, Edinburg, 1781.

MABLY, Gabriel Bonnot de (1709-1785)
ML.2.4-5 Des droits et des devoirs du citoyen. Ed. augmentée...2 vols. 12°, Paris, 1793.

MACAULAY, Catharine (1731-1791)
MH.5.5[3] An address to the people of England, Scotland, and Ireland, on the present important crisis of affairs. 2nd ed. 8°, London, 1775.

McCULLOCH, John Ramsay (1789-1864)
MK.4.11 A dictionary, practical, theoretical, and historical, of commerce and commercial navigation. 8°, London, 1832.

McCULLOCH, John Ramsay (1789-1864)
MB.7.51 The principles of political economy...2nd ed. corrected and greatly enlarged. 8°, London, 1830.

[ED. NOTE: McCulloch apparently disliked Malthus for reasons not necessarily related to his opinions, which he intended to correct. (See letter of McCulloch to Napier, Patricia James, Op. cit. pp. 311 & 315.) Malthus discussed McCulloch's views, in Ch. VII of his "Definitions" entitled: "On the Definition and Application of Terms, by Mr. McCulloch, in his 'Principles of Political Economy.'"

McCULLOCH, John Ramsay (1789-1864)
MK.4.20 See SELECT
A select collection of scarce and valuable tracts on money, from the originals of Vaughan, Cotton, Petty [etc.]. With a preface, notes, and index (by J.R. McCulloch). 1856.*

MACHIAVELLI, Niccolo (1469-1527)
MG.7.16 Tutte le opere, divise in V. parte et di nuovo con somma accuratezza ristampate. 4°, [Geneva?] 1550.

[ED. NOTE: In the later *Essay*, Malthus cites from Machiavelli's Istorie Fiorentine, to indicate that increase in population has forced people to leave "The northern parts that lie between the Rhine and the Danube." (Bk. I, Ch. VI.)]

MACKENZIE, Henry (1745-1831)
ME.5.56-7 See MIRROR
The Mirror. [A periodical published at Edinburgh in 1779-80. By H. Mackenzie and others.] 2 vols., 1794.

[ED. NOTE: "Malthus may have met the man of feeling on some of his many visits to London, and must have regarded him—twenty-one years his senior—with considerable respect...." Patricia James, *Population Malthus*, p. 342.]

MACKINTOSH, Sir James (1765-1832)
MM.5.21 Dissertation on the progress of ethical philosophy, chiefly during the Seventeenth and Eighteenth centuries. 4°, Edinburgh, 1830.

[ED. NOTE: "Among the men conspicious in Whig society in 1813 were...(among others) Sir James Mackintosh, just about to become MP for Nairn, who had stayed with the Malthuses for a fortnight in March, suffering from high fever and erysipelas of the face, and had 'experienced the kindest hospitality.'" (*Op. cit.*, pp. 225-6), citing Sir James Mackintosh by his son, Vol. II., p. 262.]

MACKINTOSH, Sir James (1765-1832)
MB.1.3 A fragment on Mackintosh: being strictures on some passages in the dissertation by Sir James Mackintosh, prefixed to the Encyclopaedia Britannica. [By J. Mill] 8°, London, 1835.*

MACKINTOSH, Sir James (1765-1832)
MH.5.8[1] Vindiciæ Gallicæ. Defence of the French Revolution and its English admirers, against the accusations of the Right Hon. Edmund Burke...2nd ed., corrected. 8°, London, 1791.

[ED. NOTE: This reply was praised among others by Dr. Parr, but the further developments of the 1789 French Revolution had deceived Mackintosh in many respects. According to his son, he was the dupe of his "own enthusiasm," (Sir James Mackintosh, Vol. 1, p. 87). Godwin's "Thoughts Occassioned by the Perusal of Dr. Parr's Spital Sermon, 'being a reply to the attacks of Dr. Parr, Mr. Mackintosh, the Author of An Essay on Population, and Others'" published in 1801, is discussed by Malthus in Bk. III, Ch. III of his subsequent edition of the *Essay* under the heading "Observations on the Reply of Mr. Godwin." In the later editions, however, this chapter has been replaced.]

MACKINTOSH, Sir James (1765-1832)
MG.3.1 Vindiciæ Gallicæ. Defence of the French Revolution and its English admirers, against the accusations of the Right Hon. Edmund Burke...4th ed., with additions. 8°, London, 1792.

MACPHERSON, David (1746-1816)
ME.7.5-8 Annals of commerce, manufactures, fisheries, and navigation...4 vols. 4°, London, 1805.

MACPHERSON, James (1736-1796)
MF.7.7 See FINGAL
Fingal, an ancient epic poem...together with several other poems, composed by Ossian the Son of Fingal. Translated [or rather, largely composed] from the Galic language, by J. Macpherson. 2nd ed. 1762.

MACPHERSON, James (1736-1796)
MH.5.5[6] See RIGHTS
The rights of Great Britain asserted against the claims of America: being an answer to the Declaration of the General Congess. [By J. Macpherson.] 8th ed. ... 1776.

MACROBIUS, Ambrosius Aurelius Theodosius (c. 400 A.D.)
MG.1.13 Opera. Accedunt notis integræ I. Pontani, J. Meursii, J. Gronovii. 8°, Lugd. Batav., 1670.

MADDOX, Isaac, Bp of Worcester (1697-1759)
MH.5.21[6] An epistle to the Right Honourable the Lord-Mayor...of the City of London...concerning the pernicious and excessive use of spirituous liquors. 2nd ed., with additions. 8°, London, 1751.

MAGNUS, Olaus, Abp of Upsala (1490-1558)
MB.6.52[5] Historia de gentibus septentrionalibus... 8°, Antverpiæ, 1558.

MAHABHARATA, Bhagavadgita
MM.5.13[1] The Bhagvat-Geeta, or Dialogues of Kreeshna and Arjoon; in eighteen lectures; with notes. Translated from the original, in the Sanskreet...by C. Wilkins. 4°, London, 1785.

MALONE, Edmund (1741-1812)
MH.1.24[1] See BIOGRAPHICAL
A biographical memoir of the Right Honourable William Windham. [By E. Malone.] 1810.

MALTHUS, Daniel (1730-1800)
MJ.1.24 & 25 [2 copies.] See GIRARDIN, René Louis, Marquis de
An essay on landscape...Translated from the French [by D. Malthus?]. 1783.

[ED. NOTE: In May 1778, Jean Jacques Rousseau moved to Girardin's estate of Ermenonville, where he died on July 2, and was buried on the "Ile des Peupliers." Girardin erected a tomb on this island for Rousseau but his remains were moved to the Pantheon in Paris during the Revolution. "An Essay on Landscape..." by Girardin was published with a frontispiece showing Rousseau's tomb on the island at Ermenonville. The translation is attributed to Daniel Malthus who was both a friend of Rousseau and corresponded with him on botanical matters. (See: Patricia James, "Population Malthus," pp. 77-78).]

MALTHUS, Francis

MK.5.19 Pratique de la guerre. Contenant l'usage de l'artillerie, bombes & mortiers... 4°, Paris, 1650.

MALTHUS, Thomas Robert (1766-1834)

MH.3.9 & 10 [2 copies.] An essay on the principle of population, as it affects the future improvement of society. With remarks on the speculations of Mr. Godwin, M. Condorcet, and other writers. [Published anonymously.] 8°, London, by J. Johnson, 1798.

[ED. NOTE: "Malthus's *Essay* is a work of youthful genius. The author was fully conscious of the significance of the ideas he was expressing. He believed that he had found the clue to human misery. The importance of the *Essay* consisted not in the novelty of his facts but in the smashing emphasis he placed on a simple generalisation arising out of them. Indeed his leading idea had been largely anticipated in a clumsier way by other eighteenth-century writers without attracting attention." (J.M. Keynes.) From this book came both worldwide fame and fierce controversies on the subject of population. This *Essay*, as Malthus said in its preface, "owes its origin to a conversation with a friend, on the subject of Mr. Godwin's Essay, on Avarice and Profusion, in his Enquirer." This friend was suggested to have been his own father. Godwin, who sparked the *Essay*, "was to write with pride of this book, and his subsequent Enquirer, inasmuch as they 'gave the occasion, and furnished the incentive, to the producing so valuable a treatise' as the anonymous Essay on the Principle of Population." (Patricia James). From the very beginning of the *Essay*, Malthus wrote what will remain in most people's minds after reading his book, and what those who never read it will have heard about: "I said that population, when unchecked, increased in a geometrical ratio; and subsistence for man in an arithmetical ratio." Actually most will summarize Malthus's *Essay* by repeating this famous quotation. Malthus first tried to convince his readers of this tendency, and thereafter started to collect proof, which made the objective of the big Quarto of 1803 and subsequent editions: there were six during his lifetime. There are in the Malthus Library, now with Jesus College at Cambridge, two copies of the original 1798 edition of the *Essay*. As indicated in the Paris Exhibition Catalogue, (p. 23), one of the copies has a title-page on which an inscription reads: "Particularly addressed to Young Clergymen." Apparently this may not be Malthus's handwriting and is suggested as having been an ironic comment.]

MALTHUS, Thomas Robert (1766-1834)

ME.6.4 An essay on the principle of population; or, A view of the past and present effects on human happiness; with an inquiry into our prospects respecting the future removal or mitigation of the evils which it occasions. A new ed., very much enlarged. 4°, London, by J. Johnson, 1803.

[ED. NOTE: Considering the difference between the first and the second edition of Malthus's *Essay*, James Bonar's view was that he "had not been sufficiently concrete." Therefore "the second *Essay* applies the theory of the first to new facts and with new purpose. The author, having gained his case against Godwin, ceases to be the critic and became the social reformer." In the view of Patricia James, "The difference between the first and the second editions is so great that it is hard to believe they are separated by only five years." Actually not only facts and figures will support the basic principles laid down in the first *Essay*, but Malthus will show in the "Great Quarto" and the later editions the importance of the powerful check to the increase of population, "The moral restraint."]

MALTHUS, Thomas Robert (1766-1834)

MX.1.16-17 An essay on the principle of population; or, A view of its past and present effects on human happiness... 3rd ed. 2 vols. 8°, London, by J. Johnson, 1806.**

[ED. NOTE: The third edition is slightly different from the second but includes an appendix which was also made available separately, dealing with the Poor Laws and arguing in a long note with those who considered the "Principle of Population in favour of the slave trade."]

MALTHUS, Thomas Robert (1766-1834)

MX.1.1-2 An essay on the principle of population; or, A view of its past and present effects on human happiness; with an inquiry into our prospects respecting the future removal or mitigation of the evils which it occasions. 4th ed. 2 vols. 8°, London, by J. Johnson, 1807.**

[ED. NOTE: The fourth edition is very similar to the third. It includes the Advertisement of the previous edition which includes the principal alterations from the second edition.]

MALTHUS, Thomas Robert (1766-1834)

MX.1.3-5 An essay on the principle of population; or, A view of its past and present effects on human happiness; with an inquiry into our prospects respecting the future removal or mitigation of the evils which it occasions. 5th ed., with important additions. 3 vols. 8°, London, by John Murray, 1817.**

[ED. NOTE: In this edition Malthus has given an additional chapter to the Poor Laws, made alterations to the chapters on Bounties upon

Exportation and added on the Subject of Restrictions upon Importation...New chapters entitled "On the Effects of the Knowledge of the Principal Cause of Poverty on Civil Liberty" and "Different Plans of Improving the Condition of the Poor" are main additions.]

MALTHUS, Thomas Robert (1766-1834)
MH.3.11-12 An essay on the principle of population; or, A view of its past and present effects on human happiness; with an inquiry into our prospects respecting the future removal or mitigation of the evils which it occasions. 6th ed. 2 vols. 8°, London, by John Murray, 1826.

[ED. NOTE: The sixth was the last edition of the *Essay* which Malthus was to correct. As Prof. Wm. Petersen noted, the designation of the author appears only on this edition as "The Rev. T.R. Malthus...." Before 1826, he did not designate himself as a clergyman, although he had been one since 1788. He was, however, styled "The Rev." in the 1807 "Letter to Samuel Whitbread."]

MALTHUS, Thomas Robert (1766-1834)
MX.1.19-21 Essai sur le principe de population, ou Exposé des effets passés et présens de l'action de cette cause sur le bonheur du genre humain...Traduit de l'anglois par P. Prévost. 3 vols. 8°, Paris, 1809.**

MALTHUS, Thomas Robert (1766-1834)
MH.3.7-8 Versuch über die Bedingung und die Folgen der Volksvermehrung; aus dem Englischen von F.H. Hegewisch. 2 vols. 8°, Altona, 1807.

MALTHUS, Thomas Robert (1766-1834)
MH.1.7^{2}, MH.3.15^{5} [2 copies.] The grounds of an opinion on the policy of restricting the importation of foreign corn; intended as an appendix to 'Observations on the Corn Laws.' 8°, London, by John Murray, 1815.

[ED. NOTE: To the astonishment of his Whig friend, Malthus argued in favour of restriction on corn importation. This pamphlet of 48 pages was intended to protect the investments in domestic development of agriculture.]

MALTHUS, Thomas Robert (1766-1834)
MH.1.7^{3}; MH.3.15^{3} [2 copies.] An inquiry into the nature and progress of rent, and the principles by which it is regulated. 8°, London, by John Murray, 1815.

[ED. NOTE: In 1814, David Buchanan published his edition of Smith's "Wealth of Nations" in 4 vols., the last being his own "Observations." Malthus's "The Nature and Progress of Rent" is a brochure intended and published primarily in response to Buchanan's "Observations."]

MALTHUS, Thomas Robert (1766-1834)
MH.3.15[1] An investigation of the cause of the present high price of provisions. By the author of the Essay on the principle of population [i.e. T.R. Malthus.] 8°, London, by J. Johnson, 1800.

[ED. NOTE: Still anonymously as with the 1st ed. of *An Essay...*, this pamphlet indicates the actual facts: The high price of provisions was the result of scarcity and, as Malthus shows, of the population surge. In the later *Essay*, Malthus refers to this pamphlet in a note to Bk. III, Ch. V.]

MALTHUS, Thomas Robert (1766-1834)
MX.1.13.JES.P.JOH.4 [2 copies.] An investigation of the cause of the present high price of provisions. With an introduction by H.G. Johnson. (Repr. from The Canadian Journal of Economics & Political Science, May 1949.) 8°, Toronto, 1949.**

[ED. NOTE: Original pamphlet MH.3.15[1].]

MALTHUS, Thomas Robert (1766-1834)
MH.3.15[2], MH.3.22[6] [2 copies.] A letter to Samuel Whitbread, Esq. M.P. on his proposed Bill for the amendment of the Poor Laws. 8°, London, by J. Johnson, 1807.

[ED. NOTE: Defending his opinion in respect to the Poor Law, and responding to Whitbread's contention, Malthus wrote: "Were it possible to fix the number of the poor and to avoid the further depression of the independent labourer, I should be the first to propose that those who were actually in want should be most liberally relieved, and that they should receive it as a right, and not as a bounty."]

MALTHUS, Thomas Robert (1766-1834)
MH.3.15[7] The measure of value stated and illustrated, with an application of it to the alterations in the value of the English currency since 1790. 8°, London, by John Murray, 1823.

[ED. NOTE: This pamphlet appeared separately instead of being incorporated in an augmented edition of the 1820 "Principles of Political Economy."]

MALTHUS, Thomas Robert (1766-1834)
MH.1.7[1]; MH.3.15[4] [2 copies.] Observations on the effects of the Corn Laws, and of a rise or fall in the price of corn on the agriculture and general wealth of the country. 3rd ed. 8°, London, by John Murray, 1815.

[ED. NOTE: First published in 1814, the "Observations" became very popular. Malthus advocated "Increasing the proportion of the middle classes, that body on which the liberty, public spirit, and good government of every country, must mainly depend." (Observations, p. 31).]

MALTHUS, Thomas Robert (1766-1834)
MX.1.18 The pamphlets of T.R. Malthus. (Repr. of Economic Classics.) 8°, New York, 1970.**

MALTHUS, Thomas Robert (1766-1834)
MX.1.6 Principles of political economy considered with a view to their practical application. 8°, London, by John Murray, 1820.**

[ED. NOTE: On the title page "Rev." Malthus is designated as Professor of History and Political Economy in the East India College, Hertfordshire. The first 1820 edition contradicts what he wrote about rent in 1815, which Mrs. James considered to be "tragic."]

MALTHUS, Thomas Robert (1766-1834)
MH.3.6 Principles of political economy considered with a view to their practical application. 2nd ed. with considerable additions from the author's own MS. and an original memoir [by William Otter]. 8°, London, by William Pickering, 1836.*

[ED. NOTE: Apparently, the contradictory opinions on rent as affecting prices were altered by John Cazenove the editor of the new edition which was supposed to appear as early as 1823, but considered then by John Murray the publisher as too early for its sales potential.]

MALTHUS, Thomas Robert (1766-1834)
MH.3.15^{8} A review article of the Essay on political economy published as supplement to the Encyclopaedia Britannica, Vol. VI, Pt. 1, Edinburgh, 1823. (Extracted from the Quarterly Review, January, 1824, Vol. XXX. no. LX, pp. 297-334.) [With the pencilled initials 'T.R.M.' at end of text.] 8°, London, 1824.

MALTHUS, Thomas Robert (1766-1834)
MH.3.15^{6} Statements respecting the East-India College, with an appeal to facts, in refutation of the charges lately brought against it, in the Court of Proprietors. 8°, London, by John Murray, 1817.

[ED. NOTE: Malthus was involved intimately in the business of the East India College, which went through student disturbances and was about to be closed. Defending its existence, Malthus asked his publisher to produce his MS. without delay and "To advertise it immediately and extensively."]

MALTHUS, Thomas Robert (1766-1834)
MX.1.7 Travel diaries, ed. by Patricia James. 8°, Cambridge, 1966.**

MALTHUS, Thomas Robert (1766-1834)
MX.1.8 See BONAR, James. Malthus and his work. 1885.**

MALTHUS, Thomas Robert (1766-1834)
MX.1.9 See BONAR, James. Malthus and his work. (2nd ed.) (1924).**

MALTHUS, Thomas Robert (1766-1834)
MH.3.22[8] See CARPENTER, Daniel
Reflections suggested by Mr. Whitbread's Bill, and by several publications...on the subject of the Poor-Laws, particularly by...T.R. Malthus, G. Rose, J. Weyland, and P. Colquhuon... 1807.

MALTHUS, Thomas Robert (1766-1834)
MM.5.7[2] See COMTE, François Charles Louis
Notice historique sur la vie et les travaux de M. Thomas-Robert Malthus. (Extr. from Académie des Sciences Morales et Politiques. Recueil des lectures...1836.) [1837].*

MALTHUS, Thomas Robert (1766-1834)
MA.2.24-5 See GANILH, Charles
Des systèmes d'économie politique...2e éd., avec de nombreuses additions relatives aux controverses récentes de MM. Malthus, Buchanan, Ricardo...2 vols. 1821.

MALTHUS, Thomas Robert (1766-1834)
MH.2.26 See GODWIN, William
Of population. An enquiry concerning the power of increase in the numbers of mankind, being an answer to Mr. Malthus's Essay on that subject. 1820.

MALTHUS, Thomas Robert (1766-1834)
MK.4.19 See GRAY, John
The social system: a treatise of the principle of exchange. [Chapter X, a criticism of the principle of Malthus.] 1831.

MALTHUS, Thomas Robert (1766-1834)
MH.2.27 See GRAY, Simon
Gray versus Malthus. The principles of population and production investigated...By George Purves [i.e. Simon Gray].
1818.

MALTHUS, Thomas Robert (1766-1834)
MA.3.31 See HAMILTON, Robert
The progress of society. [Chapter XVIII, 'Population', discusses Malthus.] 1830.

MALTHUS, Thomas Robert (1766-1834)
MX.1.12 See JAMES, Patricia
Population Malthus: his life and times. (1979).**

MALTHUS, Thomas Robert (1766-1834)
MX.1.10 See LORIA, Achille
Malthus. 1909.**

MALTHUS, Thomas Robert (1766-1834)
MX.1.11 See NICKERSON, Jane Soames
Homage to Malthus; with an introduction by R. Kirk. (1975).**

MALTHUS, Thomas Robert (1766-1834)
MX.1.14 See PARIS. Bibliothèque Nationale
De Malthus...au Malthusianisme. Exposition du 27 mai au 26 juin 1980, Bibliothèque Nationale. Catalogue. 1980.**

MALTHUS, Thomas Robert (1766-1834)
MH.2.25 See PLACE, Francis
Illustrations and proofs of the principles of population: including an examination of the proposed remedies of Mr. Malthus, and a reply to the objections of Mr. Godwin and others. 1822.

MALTHUS, Thomas Robert (1766-1834)
MX.1.15 See RICARDO, David
Letters of David Ricardo to T.R. Malthus, 1810-23; ed. by J. Bonar. 1887.**

MALTHUS, Thomas Robert (1766-1834)
MH.1.19 See SAY, Louis
Considérations sur l'industrie et la législation, sous le rapport de leur influence sur la richesse des états... [Chapter VIII a study of Malthus's 'Principles of Political Economy'.] 1822.

MALTHUS, Thomas Robert (1766-1834)
MB.7.45 See TUCKER, George
Essays on various subjects of taste, morals, and national policy. [Pp. 305-36: 'On the theory of Malthus'.] 1822.

MALVASIA, Carlo Cesare, conte (1616-1693)
ML.2.29 Le pitture di Bologna che nella pretesa, e rimostrata sin' ora da altri maggiore antichità, e impareggiabile eccellenza nella pittura, con manifesta evidenza di fatto, rendono il passeggiere disingannato, ed instrutto dell'Ascoso Accademico Gelato (C.C., conte Malvasia). 3ª ed. con nuova e copiosa aggiunta (da G.P.C. Zanotti). 12°, Bologna, 1732.

MANDEVILLE, Bernard (1670-1733)
MG.5.21-2 See FABLE
The fable of the bees: or, Private vices, public benefits. With, An essay

on charity and charity-schools; and, A search into the nature of society. [By B. Mandeville.] 2 vols. (Vol. 1, 9th ed.) 1755.

[ED. NOTE: In the later *Essay* (Appendix), Malthus refers to the Fable of the Bees as a system of morals "which I consider as absolutly false, and directly contrary to the just definition of virtue. The great art of Dr. Mandeville consisted in misnomers."]

MANUEL
MI.4.18 Manuel des amphitryons; contenant un traité de la dissection des viandes à table...Par l'auteur de l'Almanach des gourmands [A.B.L. Grimod de la Reynière]. 8°, Paris, 1808.

MARKLAND, Jeremiah (1693-1776)
MI.1.3[1] Epistola critica ad eruditissimum virum Franciscum Hare in qua Horatii loca aliquot et aliorum veterum emendantur. 8°, Cantabrigiæ, 1723.

MARKLAND, Jeremiah (1693-1776)
MI.1.3[2] Remarks on the Epistles of Cicero to Brutus, and of Brutus to Cicero: in a letter to a friend... 8°, London, 1745.

MARLBOROUGH, Sarah Churchill, Duchess of (1660-1744)
MH.5.20[2] See REMARKS
Remarks upon the Account of the conduct of a certain Dutchess [of Marlborough]. In a letter from a Member of Parliament in the reign of Queen Anne...1742.

MARMONTEL, Jean François (1723-1799)
ME.2.39 Bélisaire, et fragmens de philosophie morale. 3e éd. ...revue et soigneusement corrigée par N. Wanostrocht. 12°, Londres, 1811.

MARTIALIS, Marcus Valerius (43-103?)
MJ.1.29 Epigrammaton libri XIIII. Adiecta Græcarum vocum, quibus autor utitur, interpretatione. 8°, Lugduni, 1553.

MARTIALIS, Marcus Valerius (43-103?)
MG.1.24 Epigrammatum libri XIV. Interpretatione & notis illustravit V. Collesso... 8°, Londini, 1720.

MARTIN, Benjamin (1704-1782)
MG.7.21[5] The nature and construction of a solar eclipse, explained and exemplified in that which will happen on April 1st, A.D. 1764... 4°, London, 1764.

MARTINEAU, Harriet (1802-1876)
ME.1.4-7 A history of the thirty years' peace. A.D. 1816-46. 4 vols. (Bohn's Standard Libr.) 8°, London, 1877-8.*

[ED. NOTE: Better known for her "Illustrations of Political Economy" published in 1832, Harriet Martineau's views were close to Malthus's on the Poor Laws which she also opposed.]

MASERES, Francis (1731-1824)
MK.4.12 See SELECT
Select tracts relating to the Civil Wars in England, in the reign of King Charles the First...[Ed. by F. Maseres.] 2 pts. 1815.

MASERS DE LATUDE, Henri (1725-1805)
MH.4.15[7] Memoirs...containing an account of his confinement thirty-five years in the state prisons of France...Written by himself, and translated from the French... 12°, London, 1787.

MASON, William (1724-1797)
MI.4.14 Poems. New ed. 8°, York, 1771.

MASSINGER, Philip (1583-1640)
MG.4.25-8 Plays, with notes critical and explanatory, by W. Gifford. 2nd ed. 4 vols. 8°, London, 1813.

MATHIAS, Thomas James (1754?-1835)
MK.3.20 Poesie liriche italiane, inglesi e latine. (Privately pr.) 4°, Napoli, 1822.

MATHIAS, Thomas James (1754?-1835)
MB.1.11 See PURSUITS
The pursuits of literature; a satirical poem in four dialogues with notes. [By T.J. Mathias.] 14th ed. 1808.

MAXIMUS, Tyrius (2nd C. A.D.)
ML.2.32 Dissertationes. (Greek & Latin.) 12°, Oxoniæ, 1677.

MAXIMUS, Tyrius (2nd C. A.D.)
MG.1.25 Dissertationes ex recensione I. Davisii. Ed. altera ...cui accesserunt I. Marklandi annotationes, recudi curavit et annotatiunculus de suo addidit I.I. Reiske. (Greek.) 2 pts. 8°, Lipsiae, 1774-5.

MAYO, Charles (1750-1829)
MA.7.7 A chronological history of the European states, with their discoveries and settlements...1678 to...1794. F°, Bath, 1795.

MAYO, Herbert (1796-1852)
MG.4.4 Outlines of human physiology. 3rd ed. 8°, London, 1833.

MELANGES
MB.2.28-9 Mélanges de littérature, d'histoire, et de philosophie. [By J. Le R. d'Alembert.] Nouvelle éd., augmentée...Vols. 1, 2. 12°, Amsterdam, 1763.

MEMOIRS
MM.3.13 Memoirs of the life and ministerial conduct, with some free remarks on the political writings, of the late Lord Visc. Bolingbroke. 8°, London, 1752.

MEMOIRS
MH.4.15[6] Memoirs of the life and writings of the late Robert Lowth...Lord Bishop of London. [By Robert Lowth, Vicar of Halstead.] 8°, London, 1787.

MENANDER, comicus (ca. 343-291 B.C.)
MI.2.6 Menandri et Philemonis reliquiæ, quotquot reperiri potuerunt; Græce et Latine, cum notis H. Grotii et J. Clerici... 8°, Amstelodami, 1709.

MENDELSSOHN, Moses (1729-1786)
MA.3.8 Phédon, ou Entretiens sur la spiritualité et l'immortalité de l'âme. Traduit de l'allemand, par M. Junker. 8°, Paris, 1772.

MENON (18th C.)
MB.3.13 See CUISINIERE
La cuisinière bourgeoise, suive de l'office...[By Menon.] Nouvelle éd., augmentée...1775.

MERCIER, Louis Sébastien (1740-1814)
MB.2.35-8 See TABLEAU
Tableau de Paris. [By L.S. Mercier.] Nouvelle éd., corrigée et augmentée. Vols. 1-4. (Vols. 5-12 wanting.) 1782-4.

MEREDITH, Rt. Hon. Sir William, Bart (d. 1790)
MH.5.6[5] See LETTER
A letter to the Earl of Chatham on the Quebec Bill. [By Sir W. Meredith.] 5th ed. 1774.

MERIAN, Matthaeus (1593-1650)
ML.3.17 See DANCE OF DEATH
La danse des morts, comme elle est dépeinte dans la louable et célebre ville de Basle, pour servir de miroir de la nature humaine. Dessinée et gravée sur l'original de M. Merian... (German & French.) 1789.

MERITON, Henry
MB.6.61[1] A circumstantial narrative of the loss of the Halsewell, East-Indiaman, Capt. Richard Pierce...6th of January, 1786. Compiled

from the communications...of H. Meriton and J. Rogers. 12th ed. 8°, London, 1786.

METASTASIO, Pietro (1698-1782)
MJ.2.1-14 Poesie, giusta le correzioni fatte dall'autore nell'edizione di Parigi...14 vols. 8°, Torino, 1757-88.

MICROCOSM
MM.3.17[2] The Microcosm, a periodical work, by Gregory Griffin [i.e. George Canning, John Smith, Robert Smith and John Hookham Frere], of the College of Eton. Nos. 1-3, 6, 7, 10-12, 14, 16, 20, 23, 25, 36, 38-40. 8°, Windsor, 1786-7.

MIDDLETON, Conyers (1683-1750)
MG.7.21[1] A letter from Rome, shewing an exact conformity between Popery and paganism... 4°, London, 1729.

MIDDLETON, Conyers (1683-1750)
MI.4.2-4 The life of Marcus Tullius Cicero. New ed. 3 vols. 8°, London, 1804

MIGNET, François Auguste Marie (1796-1884)
MA.2.26-7 Histoire de la Révolution française, depuis 1789 jusqu'en 1814. 3e éd. 2 vols. 8°, Paris, 1826.

MILL, James (1773-1836)
MB.1.35-6 Analysis of the phenomena of the human mind. 2 vols. 8°, London, 1829.

MILL, James (1773-1836)
MH.5.16[4] Commerce defended. An answer to the argument by which Mr. Spence, Mr. Cobbett, and others, have attempted to prove that commerce is not a source of national wealth. 2nd ed. 8°, London, 1808.

[ED. NOTE: Malthus refers to the doctrine advocated by Mill, according to which commodities are only purchased by commodities, which he considers an error. ("Principles of Political Economy," 1820 ed., p. 354.)]

MILL, James (1773-1836)
MH.1.9 Elements of political economy. 3rd ed., revised and corrected. 8°, London, 1826.

[ED. NOTE: In his 1827 "Definitions in Political Economy," Malthus discusses Mill's views in Ch. VI: "On the Definition and Application of Terms" by Mr. Mill, in his "Elements of Political Economy."]

MILL, James (1773-1836)
MH.5.15[4] See ESSAY
An essay of the impolicy of a bounty on the exportation of grain; and on the principles which ought to regulate the commerce of grain...[By James Mill.] 1804.

MILL, JAMES (1773-1836)
MB.1.3 See MACKINTOSH, Sir James
A fragment on Mackintosh: being strictures on some passages in the dissertation by Sir James Mackintosh, prefixed to the Encyclopædia Britannica. [By J. Mill.] 1835.*

MILL, John Stuart (1806-1873)
MH.1.10-11 Principles of political economy...2 vols. 8°, London, 1848.*

MILL, John Stuart (1806-1873)
MH.1.12-13 A system of logic, ratiocinative and inductive...3rd ed. 2 vols. 8°, London, 1851.*

MILLAR, John (1735-1801)
MA.1.17-20 An historical view of the English government, from the settlement of the Saxons in Britain to the Revolution in 1688. 4 vols. 8°, London, 1803.

MILLE
ML.2.34-40 Les mille et une nuits; contes arabes, traduits en français par M. Galland. Nouvelle éd., corrigée...7 vols. 12°, Paris, 1811.

MILLER, Johann Martin (1750-1814)
MK.2.24 Beytrag zur Geschichte der Zärtlichkeit...2., rechtmässige, durchgesehene...Aufl. 8°, Frankfurt, 1780.

MILLER, Vincent
MH.5.19[5] The man-plant: or, Scheme for increasing and improving the British breed. 8°, London, 1752.

MILLOT, Claude François Xavier (1726-1785)
MF.4.1-2 Elements of general history. Translated from the French. Pt. 1, Ancient history. 2 vols. 8°, London, 1778.

MILMAN, Henry Hart (1791-1868)
MJ.1.45-7 See HISTORY
The history of the Jews. 3 vols. 1829.

MILNER, Isaac (1750-1820)
ME.2.9 An essay on human liberty. 8°, London, 1824.

MILTON, John (1608-1674)
MF.6.19-20 Paradise Lost...8th ed. with notes of various authors, by T. Newton. 2 vols. 4°, London, 1775.

MILTON, John (1608-1674)
MF.6.21 Paradise regain'd...To which is added Samson Agonistes: and poems upon several occasions. New ed., with notes of various authors, by T. Newton. 4°, London, 1752.

MILTON, John (1608-1674)
ME.4.37-8 Poetical works. From the text of Dr. Newton. With the life of the author and a critique on Paradise Lost, by J. Addison. 4 vols. in 2. (Bell's Edition. The Poets of Great Britain.) 12°, Edinburg, 1776.

MILTON, John (1608-1674)
MM.5.19-20 Works, historical, political and miscellaneous... To which is prefixed, An account of his life and writings (by T. Birch). 2 vols. 4°, London, 1753.

MINGAY, James
MH.5.7[5] See SKETCHES
Sketches of the characters of the Hon. Thomas Erskine, and James Mingay, Esq. interspersed with anecdotes and professional strictures. [Wants title-page.] 1794.

MINUCIUS FELIX, Marcus (c. 200 A.D.)
MF.2.8 Octavius. Ex recensione J. Davisii. 8°, Glasguae, 1750.

[Ed. NOTE: Malthus refers to this work in his later *Essay*, Bk. I, Ch. XIV.]

MIRABEAU, Honoré Gabriel Riquetti, comte de (1749-1791)
MC.2.5-8 Lettres originales, écrites au Donjon de Vincennes ...1777, 78, 79 et 80...Recueillies par P. Manuel. 4 vols. 12°, Paris, 1792.

[ED. NOTE: Malthus refers in his later *Essay* to a 9- volume 12° edition of Mirabeau's father's works published in 1762. (Bk. III, Ch. XIV.) He refers to the "author of L'Ami des Hommes," underlining his recognized error according to which population was considered as a source of revenue.]

MIRROR
ME.5.56-7 The Mirror. [A periodical published at Edinburgh in 1779-80. By H. Mackenzie and others.] 2 vols. 8°, London, 1794.

MISCELLANEOUS
ML.1.4-5 Miscellaneous pieces. [By S. Jenyns.] 2 vols. 8°, London, 1761.

MISCELLANIES
MK.5.22 Miscellanies. [By J. Arbuthnot, A. Pope, J. Swift, and others.] Vol. 2. 8°, London, 1727.

MISCELLANY
MF.1.2-6 Miscellany poems. Containing variety of new translations of the ancient poets: together with several original poems. By the most eminent hands. Publish'd by Mr. Dryden. Pts. 1-3, 5, 6. (Pts. 1, 2, 4th ed.) (Pt. 4 wanting.) 5 vols. 12°, London, 1716.

MODEST
MH.5.19^{2} A modest defence of gaming. 8°, London, 1754.

MOLIERE, Jean Baptiste Poquelin de (1622-1673)
ME.5.53-5 Œuvres. Nouvelle éd. Vols. 1-3. (Vol. 4 wanting.) 12°, Amsterdam et Leipzig, 1750.

MOLIERE, Jean Baptiste Poquelin de (1622-1673)
MA.2.1-6 Œuvres, avec des remarques grammaticales; des avertissemens et des observations sur chaque pièce, par M. Bret. 6 vols. 8°, Paris, 1773.

MONKS
MB.6.58 The monks and the giants: prospectus and specimen of an intended national work, by William and Robert Whistlecraft [i.e. J.H. Frere]. 4th ed. 8°, London, 1821.

MONTAGU, George (1751-1815)
ME.3.20-21 Ornithological dictionary; or, Alphabetical synopsis of British birds. 2 vols. [Interleaved.] 8°, London, 1802.

MONTAIGNE, Michel Eyquem de (1533-1592)
MG.5.6-8 Essays in three books. With notes and quotations, and an account of the author's life...Translated by C. Cotton. 5th ed. corrected and amended. 3 vols. 12°, London (1738).

MONTESQUIEU, Charles de Secondat, baron de (1689-1755)
MB.6.55^{2} See LETTRES
Lettres turques, et Le temple de Gnide du même auteur [i.e. C. de S. baron de Montesquieu]. (2 pts.) 1748.

MONTESQUIEU, Charles de Secondat, baron de (1689-1755)
MA.5.3-7 Œuvres. Nouvelle éd. 5 vols. 8°, Paris, 1796.

[ED. NOTE: Malthus refers to Montesquieu even in the Preface to the second edition of the *Essay*. Numerous references are made in the text to Montesquieu's "Grandeur et Décadence des Romains," (Bk. I, Ch. VI);

"Esprit des Loix," (Bk. I, Ch. V, VII, XI, XII, XIV; Bk. II, Ch. III, IV; Bk. IV, Ch. XIII) and "Lettres Persannes," (Bk. II, Ch. IV).]

MONTESQUIEU, Charles de Secondat, baron de (1689-1755)
MA.5.8 Œuvres posthumes, pour servir de supplément aux différentes éditions in-8°... 8°, Paris, 1798.

MONTOLIEU, Elisabeth Jeanne Pauline, baronne de (1751-1832)
MM.1.31-3 See CAROLINE
Caroline de Lichtfield, par Madame de *** [i.e. the Baronne de Montolieu.] Publié par le traducteur de Werther. 3 vols. [1795.]

MOORE, Edward (1712-1757)
MI.4.9[6] The foundling. A comedy. As it is acted at the Theatre-Royal in Drury-Lane. 2nd ed. 12°, London, 1748.

MOORE, Edward (1712-1757)
ME.4.23-6 See WORLD
The world. 1753-6. [A periodical.] By Adam Fitz-Adam [i.e. E. Moore]. 3rd ed. 4 vols. 1761.

MOORE, James Carrick (1762-1860)
MA.3.32 A narrative of the campaign of the British Army in Spain, commanded by His Excellency Lieut.-General Sir John Moore... 4th ed. 8°, London, 1809.

MOORE, Thomas (1779-1852)
MB.2.13 See ROCK, Captain
Memoirs of Captain Rock, the celebrated Irish chieftain, with some account of his ancestors. Written by himself [or rather, by T. Moore]. 3rd ed. 1824.

MOORE, Thomas (1779-1852)
MB.2.14-15 See TRAVELS
Travels of an Irish gentleman in search of a religion...[By T. Moore.] 2 vols. 1833.

MORAL
MA.1.26 Moral and historical memoirs. [By W.J. Temple.] 8°, London, 1779.

MORAL
MH.5.24[8] Moral annals of the poor, and middle ranks of society, in various situations, of good and bad conduct. [By T. Burgess.] 8°, Durham, 1793.

MORE, Hannah (1745-1833)
MG.7.8[2] See FLORIO
Florio: a tale, for fine gentlemen and fine ladies: and The Bas Bleu; or, Conversation: two poems. [By H. More.] 1786.

MORE, Hannah (1745-1833)
MK.5.15[5] Slavery, a poem. 4°, London, 1788.

MORE, Hannah (1745-1833)
MK.3.22-3 Strictures on the modern system of female education...2 vols. (Vol. 1, 8th ed.; vol. 2, 6th ed.) 8°, London, 1799-1800.

MORE, Hannah (1745-1833)
MJ.1.20[3] See THOUGHTS
Thoughts on the importance of the manners of the great to general society. [By H. More.] 1788.

MORE, Hannah (1745-1833)
MH.4.25[9] See LETTER
A letter to Miss Hannah More, occasioned by her remarks on the speech which M. Dupont delivered...December 14th, 1792. 1793.

MORGAN, William (1750-1833)
MH.5.12[1] An examination of Dr. Crawford's theory of heat and combustion. 8°, London, 1781.

MORGAN, William (1750-1833)
MH.4.24[1] Facts addressed to the serious attention of the people of Great Britain respecting the expence of the War, and the state of the National Debt. 3rd ed., improved. 8°, London, 1796.

MORRIS, Edward (d. 1815)
MH.4.16[3] A short enquiry into the nature of monopoly and forestalling. 3rd ed., with considerable additions. 8°, London, 1800.

MORRISON, John
MH.5.6[3] The advantages of an alliance with the Great Mogul... 8°, London, 1774.

MORSE, Jedidiah (1761-1826)
ML.5.14 The American geography; or, A view of the present situation of the United States of America...2nd ed. 8°, London, 1792.

MORSE, Sidney Edwards (1794-1871)
MK.5.23 A new system of modern geography, or A view of the present state of the world... 8°, Boston [Mass.], 1822.

MORTON, Thomas (1764-1838)
MI.4.6[3] Columbus: or, A world discovered. An historical play. As it is performed at the Theatre-Royal, Covent-Garden. 8°, London, 1792.

MORTON, Thomas (1764-1838)
MI.4.6[2] A cure for the heart-ache; a comedy, in 5 acts, as performed at the Theatre-Royal, Covent-Garden. 8°, London, 1797.

MORTON, Thomas (1764-1838)
MI.4.6[1] Secrets worth knowing; a comedy, in 5 acts. As performed at the Theatre Royal, Covent Garden. 8°, London, 1798.

MORVAN DE BELLEGARDE, Jean Baptiste (1648-1734)
MM.1.1 Les règles de la vie civile, avec des traits d'histoire, pour former l'esprit d'un jeune prince. 12°, La Haye, 1720.

MOSCHUS, Syracusanus (fl. 150 B.C.)
MG.6.16 Musæi, Moschi & Bionis quæ extant omnia: quibus accessere quædam selectiora Theocriti Eidyllia...Autore D. Whitfordo. (Greek & Latin.) 4°, Londini, 1659.

MOSER, Joseph (1748-1819)
MH.5.10[3] Anecdotes of Richard Brothers, in the years 1791 and 1792, with some thoughts upon credulity, occasioned by the testimony of N.B. Halhed... 8°, London, 1795.

MOSHEIM, Johann Lorenz (1694?-1755)
MF.7.8-9 An ecclesiastical history, antient and modern...Translated...and accompanied with notes and chronological tables, by A. Maclaine. 2 vols. 4°, London, 1765.

MOYEN
ME.1.34-6 Le moyen de parvenir. [By F. Béroalde de Verville.] Nouvelle éd. augmentée...3 vols. 12°, Londres, 1781-6.

MUN, Thomas (1571-1641)
MG.5.34 England's treasure by forraign trade...published... by J. Mun. 12°, London, 1669.

MUNCASTER, Sir John Pennington (1737-1813)
MH.4.28[1] Historical sketches of the slave trade, and of its effects in Africa... 8°, London, 1792.

MURPHY, Arthur (1727-1805)
MI.4.7[3] See GRECIAN
The Grecian daughter: a tragedy: as it is acted at the Theatre-Royal in Drury-Lane. [By A. Murphy.] 1772.

MUSÆUS, grammaticus

MG.6.16 Musæi, Moschi & Bionis quæ extant omnia: quibus accessere quædum selectiora Theocriti Eidyllia...Autore D. Whitfordo. (Greek & Latin.) 4°, Londini, 1659.

MUSARUM

MJ.2.25-7;MJ.2.28 [Another copy of Vol. 3.] Musarum Anglicanarum analecta: sive Poemata quædam melioris notæ, seu hactenus inedita, seu sparsim edita. 3 vols. (Vols. 1, 2, Ed. 4^{a}, prioribus auctior.) 8°, Londini, 1721; Oxon., 1717.

MUSGRAVE, Sir Richard, 1st Bart (1757?-1818)

MH.5.8^{2} A letter on the present situation of public affairs. 8°, London, 1794.

MUSHET, Robert (1782-1828)

MH.3.18^{6} An enquiry into the effects produced on the national currency, and rates of exchange, by the Bank Restriction Bill... 8°, London, 1810.

MY

MB.4.25 My pocket-book; or, Hints for 'A ryghte merrie and conceitede' tour...By a Knight errant [i.e. E. Dubois]. 3rd ed. With various additions... 12°, London, 1808.

N

NECKER

NARES, Edward (1762-1841)

MB.4.23-4 See THINKS

Thinks-I-to-myself. A serio-ludicro, tragico-comico tale, written by Thinks-I-to-myself who? [i.e. E. Nares]. 9th ed. ...2 vols. 1813.

NARES, Robert (1753-1829)

MI.4.15-16 Essays, and other occasional compositions, chiefly reprinted. 2 vols. 8°, London, 1810.

NATURE

MH.5.17[1] The nature and use of subsidiary forces fully considered: in answer to a pamphlet [by J. Shebbeare], intitled A second letter to the people of England. 8°, London, 1755.

NEAL, Daniel (1678-1743)

MC.3.23-7 The history of the Puritans, or, Protestant Non-Conformists...New ed., revised...by J. Toulmin. 5 vols. 8°, Bath, 1793-7.

NECKER, Jacques (1732-1804)

MB.2.21-3 De l'administration des finances de la France. 3 vols. 8°, [Paris] 1785.

[ED. NOTE: In the later *Essay*, Malthus refers frequently to this work, especially in Bk. II, Ch. VI, "Of the Checks to Population in France." Other references can be found in Bk. II. Ch. VIII, XIII; Bk. IV, Ch. V, and in the Appendix.]

NECKER, Jacques (1732-1804)

MI.4.17 See SUR

Sur la législation et le commerce des grains. [By J. Necker.] 2e éd. 2 vols. in 1. 1775.

NELSON, Robert (1656-1715)

MC.3.28 A companion for the festivals and fasts of the Church of England...18th ed. 8°, London, 1744.

NEUCHATEL

MB.2.34 See RELATION

Relation exacte et impartielle de tout ce qui s'est passé à Neuchâtel, depuis la naissance des troubles actuels, jusqu'à présent...(With Recueil de diverses pièces survenus dans la principauté...and Robert Covelle, citoyen de Genève, à Monsieur de Voltaire). (3 pts.) 1767.

NEW

MM.4.15-26 A new and general biographical dictionary; containing an historical and critical account of the lives and writings of the most eminent persons in every nation... New ed., greatly enlarged and improved. 12 vols. 8°, London, 1784.

NEW

MK.3.34 The new Bath guide: or, Memoirs of the B——-r—-d [i.e. Blunderhead] family. In a series of poetical epistles. [By C. Anstey.] 4th ed. 8°, London, 1767.

NEW

ME.2.34 The new Bath guide: or Memoirs of the B—n—r—d [i.e. Blunderhead] family. In a series of political epistles. [By C. Anstey.] 10th ed. 8°, London, 1776.

NEWHAVEN, William, Lord (1722-1794)

MH.4.27[6] A short address to the public, containing some thoughts how the National Debt may be reduced, and all home taxes, including Land-tax, abolished. 8°, London, 1786.

NEWMAN, John Henry, Cardinal (1801-1890)

MB.6.7 Apologia pro vita sua: being a reply to a pamphlet... 8°, London, 1864.*

NEWMAN, John Henry, Cardinal (1801-1890)

MB.6.1-6 Parochial sermons. 6 vols. (Vols. 1, 2, 5th ed.; vols. 3, 4, 4th ed.; vols. 5, 6, 2nd ed.) 8°, London, 1842-51.*

NEWMAN, Samuel (1600?-1663)

MA.6.2 The Cambridge concordance to the Holy Scriptures, together with the Books of the Apocrypha... [By S. Newman.] 5th ed.; very accurately corrected. F°, London, 1720.

NEWTON, Sir Isaac (1642-1727)

ME.3.1 The chronology of ancient kingdoms amended... 4°, London, 1728.

NEWTON, Sir Isaac (1642-1727)

MG.7.7 Observations upon the Prophecies on Daniel, and the Apocalypse of St. John. [Ed. by B. Smith.] In 2 pts. 4°, London, 1733.

NEWTON, Sir Isaac (1642-1727)

ME.6.11 Philosophiæ naturalis principia mathematica. Ed. 3^{a} aucta & emendata. 4°, Londini, 1726.

[ED. NOTE: "The grand and consistent theory of Newton will be placed upon the same footing as the wild and eccentric hypotheses of Descartes." Malthus, *Essay* (later edition), Bk. III, Ch. I.]

NEWTON, John (1725-1807)

MH.5.10[6] Thoughts upon the African slave trade. 8°, London, 1788.

NICHOLS, John (1779-1863)

MG.4.1 See HOGARTH, William

Biographical anecdotes of William Hogarth; with a catalogue of his works chronologically arranged; and occasional remarks. [By J. Nichols.] 2nd ed., enlarged and corrected. 1782.

NICKERSON, Jane Soames
MX.1.11 Homage to Malthus; with an introduction by R. Kirk. 8°, Port Washington, N.Y. (1975).**

NICOLSON, William, Abp of Cashel (1655-1727)
MA.6.8 The English, Scotch and Irish historical libraries. Giving a short view and character of most of our historians... F°, London, 1736.

NIEBUHR, Barthold Georg (1776-1831)
MH.1.26-7 The history of Rome...Ed. by L. Schmitz. 2 vols. 8°, London, 1844.*

NITSCH, F. A.
MG.4.6 A general and introductory view of Professor Kant's principles concerning man, the world and the Deity... 8°, London, 1796.

NOBLE, Mark (1754-1827)
MM.2.5-7 A biographical history of England, from the Revolution to the end of George I's reign; being a continuation of J. Granger's work...Editor, M. Noble. 3 vols. 8°, London, 1806.

NORDEN, Frederik Ludvig (1708-1742)
ML.5.21 Travels in Egypt and Nubia. Translated...and enlarged...by P. Templeman. 2 vols. in 1. 8°, London, 1757.

NORTHCOTE, James (1746-1831)
MF.6.10-11 Memoirs of Sir Joshua Reynolds, Knt. ...To which are added, Varieties on art. (With Supplement.) (2 vols.) 4°, London, 1813-15.

NOUVEAU
MF.2.10-11 Nouveau recueil des épigrammistes françois, anciens et modernes...Par Mr. B.L.M. [i.e. A.A. Bruzen de la Martinière]. 2 vols. 12°, Amsterdam, 1720.

O'BRIEN, Sir Lucius (d. 1795)
MH.4.29[2] Letters concerning the trade and manufactures of Ireland... 8°, London, 1785.

OBSERVATIONS
MH.4.27[7] Observations and reflections, on an Act, passed in the year, 1774, for the settlement of the Province of Quebec...By A country gentleman. 8°, London, 1782.

OBSERVATIONS
MH.5.12[5] Observations on the Conversion and Apostleship of St. Paul. In a letter to Gilbert West, Esq. [By George, Lord Lyttelton.] New ed. 8°, London, 1777.

OBSERVATIONS
MH.4.21[2] Observations on the emigration of Dr. Joseph Priestley...[By W. Cobbett.] New ed. 8°, London, 1794.

OBSERVATIONS
MH.5.19[9] Observations on the life of Cicero. [By George, Lord Lyttelton.] 8°, London, 1733.

OBSERVATIONS
ME.2.3 Observations on the present state of Denmark, Russia, and Switzerland. In a series of letters. 8°, London, 1784.

OBSERVATIONS
MH.4.26[2] Observations on the Reverend Doctor Hurd's, now Lord Bishop of Worcester's, two dialogues on the constitution of the English government, addressed in a letter to the Right Hon. E. Burke. 8°, London, 1790.

OBSERVATIONS
MJ.1.20[1] Observations on the three last volumes of the Roman history, by E. Gibbon. [By H.J. Pye?] 8°, London, 1788.

OBSERVATIONS
MI.2.1[2] Observations suggested by a pamphlet entitled 'The question, why do we go to war? temperately discussed...' [by W. Burdon]. In a letter to a friend. 8°, London, 1803.

ODDY, Joshua Jepson (d. 1814)
ME.6.5 European commerce, shewing new and secure channels of trade with the Continent of Europe... 4°, London, 1805.

ODE
MH.4.21[4] An ode, addressed to the Right Honourable William Windham in 1778. (Not published.) 8°, London, 1810.

ODIHAM. Society for the Encouragement of Agriculture and Industry
MH.5.7[3] See ACCOUNT
An account of the proceedings, intentions, rules, and orders, of the Society for the Encouragement of Agriculture and Industry, instituted at Odiham in Hampshire...[1785.]

OLDHAM, John (1653-1683)
ML.1.3 See POEMS
Poems, and translations. By the author of the Satyrs upon the Jesuits [i.e. J. Oldham]. 1683.

OLDHAM, John (1653-1683)
ML.1.1 See SATYRS
Satyrs upon the Jesuits: written in the year 1679. And some other pieces by the same hand. [By J. Oldham.] 2nd ed. more corrected. 1682.

OLDHAM, John (1653-1683)
ML.1.2 See SOME
Some new pieces never before publisht. By the author of the Satyrs upon the Jesuites [i.e. J. Oldham]. 1681.

OPUSCULA
MI.2.7 Opuscula mythologica physica et ethica. Græce et Latine...[Ed. by T. Gale.] 8°, Amstelædami, 1688.

ORDERS
MH.3.21[4] Orders in Council, or An examination of the justice, legality, and policy of the new system of commercial regulations... 8°, London, 1808.

ORDRE
MK.2.16-17 L'ordre naturel et essentiel des sociétés politiques. [By P.F.J.H. Le Mercier de la Rivière.] 2 vols. 8°, Londres, 1767.

OSSIAN
MF.7.7 See FINGAL
Fingal, an ancient epic poem...together with several other poems, composed by Ossian the Son of Fingal. Translated [or rather, largely composed] from the Galic language, by J. Macpherson. 2nd ed. 1762.

OTTER, William, Bp of Chichester (1768-1840)
MM.4.13-14 The life and remains of Edward Daniel Clarke...(2nd ed.) 2 vols. 8°, London, 1825.

[ED. NOTE: At Jesus College, as an undergraduate, Malthus made lifetime friends, chief among them being William Otter, later to become Bishop of Chichester. Otter's Memoir, Malthus's Obituary, published first in "Athenaeum" in January 1835, was incorporated in the posthumous second edition of "Principles of Political Economy" published in 1836. This edition is included in the library.]

OTWAY, Thomas (1652-1685)
ML.1.31[4] The orphan: or, The unhappy marriage. A tragedy. 12°, London, 1751.

OTWAY, Thomas (1652-1685)
ML.1.31[2] Venice preserv'd: or, A plot discover'd. A tragedy. 12°, London, 1753.

OTWAY, Thomas (1652-1685)
MJ.1.49-50 Works. 2 vols. 12°, London, 1717-18.

OVIDIUS NASO, Publius (43 B.C.-17/18 A.D.)
ME.5.60-64 Opera quæ extant. 5 vols. 12°, Londini, 1745.

OVIDIUS NASO, Publius (43 B.C.-17/18 A.D.)
MF.3.3-7 Opera, e textu Burmanni; cum notis Bentleii hactenus ineditis...5 vols. 8°, Oxonii, 1825-6.

OWEN, Robert (1771-1858)
MM.5.5 Report to the County of Lanark, of a plan for relieving public distress... 4°, Glasgow, 1821.

[ED. NOTE: Malthus discussed the work of Owen entitled "A New View of Society" published in 1813, in Bk. III, Ch. III. of his later *Essay* (Of Systems of Equality). In Bk. IV, Ch. XII, Malthus referred to "The Society at the 'Lanerk' Mills" which might also result from the "Report to the County of Lanark." Malthus's opinion was that "Mr. Owen's plan...seems to be peculiarly calculated...to increase and multiply the number of Paupers."]

P

ALEXANDER POPE

PAINE, Thomas (1737-1809)
MH.4.18[1] The case of the Officers of Excise; with remarks on the qualifications of officers... 8°, London, 1793.

PAINE, Thomas (1737-1809)
MH.4.18[2] Common sense; addressed to the inhabitants of America...New ed., with several additions... 8°, London, 1791.

PAINE, Thomas (1737-1809)
MH.4.18[7] The decline and fall of the English system of finance. 5th ed. 8°, London, 1796.

PAINE, Thomas (1737-1809)
MH.4.18[3] Dissertation on first principles of government ...2nd ed. (2 pts.) (The genuine ed., from the Paris copy.) 8°, London, (Paris pr.), 1795.

PAINE, Thomas (1737-1809)
MH.4.18[6] A letter to the Earl of Shelburne, now Marquis of Lansdowne, on his speech, July 10, 1782, respecting the acknowledgement of American Independence. 8°, London, 1791.

PAINE, Thomas (1737-1809)
MH.4.18[5] Prospects on the War and paper currency. 2nd ed., corrected. 8°, London, 1793.

PAINE, Thomas (1737-1809)
MK.3.18[1] Rights of man: being an answer to Mr. Burke's attack on the French Revolution. [Pt. 1.] 8°, London, 1791.

[ED. NOTE: In the later *Essay* Malthus discusses the views of Paine and refers to his "Rights of Man" in Bk. IV, Ch. VI. This book, in Malthus's words "has done great mischief among the lower and middling classes of people in this country."]

PAINE, Thomas (1737-1809)
MH.5.11[3] Rights of man: being an answer to Mr. Burke's attack on the French Revolution. 2nd ed. 8°, London, 1791.

PAINE, Thomas (1737-1809)
MK.3.18[2] Rights of man. Part the second. Combining principle and practice. 3rd ed. 8°, London, 1792.

PAINE, Thomas (1737-1809)
MH.4.18[4] Thoughts on the Peace, and the probable advantages thereof to the United States of America. New ed. 8°, London, 1791.

PALEY, William (1743-1805)
MB.4.37 Natural theology; or Evidences of the existence and attributes of the Deity...Illustrated by...J. Paxton. 2 vols. in 1. 8°, Oxford, 1828.

[ED. NOTE: Cited and referred to by Malthus in his later *Essay*, Bk. IV, Ch. I. and XIII. Malthus notes that Paley "states most justly that Mankind will in every country breed up to a certain point of distress." This indicates a change in his initial opinion according to which a crisis resulting from the increase of population in excess of the means of subsistance cannot occur.]

PALEY, William (1743-1805)

MF.5.22-8 Works, with additional sermons...and a corrected account of the life and writings of the author, by E. Paley. New ed. 7 vols. 8°, London, 1825.

[ED. NOTE: In the chapter "Of the Effect on Society of Moral Restraint" of his later *Essay* (Bk. IV, Ch. II), Malthus cites also from Paley's moral philosophy, "The method of coming at the will of God from the light of nature is, to inquire into the tendency of the action to promote or diminish the general happiness." Paley was eventually converted to Malthus's views.]

PARAPHRASE

MH.4.21[7] A paraphrase in rhyme of the poetical beauties and spirit exhibited in a letter from the Right Hon. Edmund Burke to a Noble Lord. 8°, London, 1796.

PARIS

MH.4.22[4] See EXPLANATION
Explanation of the view of the interior of the City of Paris, now exhibiting in the Large Circle, Barker's Panorama, Strand, near Surrey-Street. 1815.

PARIS. Bibliothèque Nationale

MX.1.14 De Malthus...au Malthusianisme. Exposition du 27 mai au 26 juin 1980, Bibliothèque Nationale. Catalogue. 4°, Paris, 1980.**

[ED. NOTE: This excellent catalogue is actually a concise account of Malthus's life and work, with the contributions of French and English scholars, edited by Margaret Smith.]

PARIS. Hôpital Général

MF.7.5 Code de l'Hôpital-Général de Paris, ou Recueil des principaux édits, arrêts, déclarations & réglements qui le concernent... 4°, Paris, 1786.

PARKHURST, John (1728-1797)

ME.7.4 A Greek and English lexicon to the New Testament... 4°, London, 1769.

PARKINSON, Sydney (1745?-1771)

MC.7.6 A journal of a voyage to the South Seas in His Majesty's Ship, The Endeavour...[Ed. by Stanfield Parkinson.] F°, London, 1773.

PARLIAMENT. Committee of Secrecy
MH.5.7[6] See REPORT
Report of Committee of Secrecy of the House of Commons. Ordered to be printed 15th March, 1799. New ed. 1799.

PARMENTIER, Antoine Augustin (1737-1813)
MI.4.29 Le parfait boulanger, ou Traité complet sur la fabrication & le commerce du pain. 8°, Paris, 1778.

PARNELL, Sir Henry Brooke (1776-1842)
See CONGLETON, Henry Brooke Parnell, 1st Lord.

PARNELL, Thomas (1679-1718)
ME.4.45[1] Poetical works...With the life of the author. 2 vols. in 1. (Bell's Edition. The Poets of Great Britain.) 12°, Edinburg, 1778.

PARNELL, William (d. 1821)
MH.3.17[1] See INQUIRY
An inquiry into the causes of popular discontents in Ireland. By an Irish country gentleman [i.e. W. Parnell]. 1804.

PASSAGES
MJ.1.21-3 Passages selected by distinguished parsonages on the great literary trial of Vortigern and Rowena [by W.H. Ireland]. A comi-tragedy. 2nd ed. 3 vols. (Vol.1 misbound.) 8°, London, [1795].

PATERSON, Daniel (1739-1825)
ME.4.8 A new and accurate description of all the direct and the principal cross roads in Great Britain...3rd ed., corrected... 8°, London, 1776.

PATERSON, Daniel (1739-1825)
MA.1.27 Paterson's roads; being an entirely original and accurate description of all the direct and principal cross roads in England and Wales. With parts of the roads of Scotland. 18th ed. By E. Mogg. 8°, London, (1829).

PAXTON, Peter (d. 1711)
MI.1.11 See CIVIL
Civil polity. A treatise concerning the nature of government...[By P. Paxton.] 1703.

PEARSON, John, Bp of Chester (1613-1686)
MF.5.32-3 An exposition of the Creed. New ed. 2 vols. 8°, Oxford, 1820.

PEARSON, Joseph
MH.5.2[4] Pearson's political dictionary...more particularly appertaining to the House of Commons... 8°, London, 1792.

PECKWELL, Henry (1747-1787)
MB.6.61[4] See PLAIN
A plain narrative of the much lamented death of the Rev. Henry Peckwell, D.D. ...By a visiter of the sick man's friend...2nd ed. [1787.]

PEIRCE, James (1674?-1726)
ML.4.20 Dissertations on six texts of Scripture...2nd ed. 4°, London, 1737.

PELISSON, Paul
See PELLISON-FONTANIER, Paul.

PELLISSON-FONTANIER, Paul (1624-1693)
ME.4.2 Histoire de l'Académie Françoise. Nouvelle éd. augmentée... 12°, Amsterdam, 1717.

PEMBERTON, Henry (1694-1771)
ME.7.11 A view of Sir Isaac Newton's philosophy. 4°, London, 1728.

PENROSE, John (1778-1859)
MF.5.35 An inquiry, chiefly on principles of religion, into the nature and discipline of human motives. 8°, London, 1820.

PENROSE, John (1778-1859)
ME.2.10 Of Christian sincerity. 8°, Oxford, 1829.

PENROSE, John (1778-1859)
MF.5.34 A treatise on the evidence of the Scripture miracles. 8°, London, 1826.

PERCY, Thomas, Bp of Dromore (1729-1811)
MB.4.1-3 See RELIQUES
Reliques of ancient English poetry: consisting of old heroic ballads, songs, and other pieces...[Ed. by T. Percy.] 3rd ed. 3 vols. 1775.

PERFECT
ME.5.16[3] A perfect description of the people and country of Scotland. [A later ed. of 'Terrible news from Scotland', probably written by Sir Anthony Weldon.] 12°, London, 1659.

PERSIUS FLACCUS, Aulus (34-62)
ME.2.11 Satiræ VI. Ad optimorum exemplarium fidem recensitæ...a G.L. Koenig. (Classici Romanorum scriptores, 1ii.) 8°, Gottingæ, 1803.

PERSIUS FLACCUS, Aulus (34-62)
MJ.1.30 Satires, translated into English verse [by T. Brewster]; with some occasional notes; and the original text corrected. 2nd ed. ... 8°, London, 1751.

PETRARCA, Francesco (1304-1374)
MJ.1.11 Les œuvres amoureuses. Traduites en françois, avec l'italien à costé. Par le Sieur Placide Catanusi. 12°, Paris, 1669.

PETRARCA, Francesco (1304-1374)
MK.4.9 Le rime del Petrarca brevemente sposte per L. Castelvetro. (2 pts.) 4°, Basilea, 1582.

PETRARCA, Francesco (1304-1374)
ME.5.45-7 Rime, pubblicate da A. Buttura. 3 vols. (Bibl. poetica italiana, 4-6.] 8°, Parigi, 1820.

PETRONIUS ARBITER (fl. 1st C. B.C.)
MG.1.20[2] Integrum Titi Petronii Arbitri fragmentum...cum Apologia M. Statilii [i.e. P. Petit]. Ed. 2^a...auctior & curatior. (3 pts.) 8°, Amstelodami, 1671.

PETRONIUS ARBITER (fl. 1st C. B.C.)
MG.1.20[1] Satyricon, cum fragmento nuper Tragurii reperto...Omnia commentariis, & notis doctorum virorum illustrata. Concinnante M. Hadrianide. 8°, Amstelodami, 1669.

PETTY, Sir William (1623-1687)
MB.3.38 Several essays in political arithmetick. (6 pts.) 8°, London, 1699.

[ED. NOTE: Malthus refers to "Political Arithmetic" of Petty but does not indicate the edition used. In Bk. I. Ch. I. of the later *Essay*, he indicates that "Sir William Petty supposes a doubling (of population) possible in so short a time as ten years."]

PETTY, Sir William (1623-1687)
MH.1.1 Several essays in political arithmetick. 4th ed., corrected. To which are prefix'd, memoirs of the author's life. 8°, London, 1755.

[ED. NOTE: In the later *Essay*, Bk. II, Ch. XIII, Malthus refers again to "Political Arithmetic," indicating that Petty foresaw the population of London at 5,359,000 inhabitants in 1800...]

PHÆDRUS (fl. 1st C. B.C.)
MI.1.10 Fabularum Æsopiarum libri V. Cum integris commentariis M. Gudii...& excerptis aliorum. Curante P. Burmanno. 8°, Amstelædami, 1698.

PHILEMON, comicus (ca. 361-262 B.C.)
MI.2.6 See MENANDER, comicus
Menandri et Philemonis reliquiæ, quotquot reperiri potuerunt; Græce et Latine, cum notis H. Grotii et J. Clerici...1709.

PHILIDOR, François André Danican, dit (1726-1795)
MB.4.35 Analyse du jeu des échecs; nouvelle éd., considérablement augmentée. 8°, Londres, 1777.

PHILIDOR, François Andre Danican, dit (1726-1795)
MM.4.9 An easy introduction to the game of chess...2 vols. in 1. 12°, London, 1806.

PHILIPON DE LA MADELAINE, Louis (1734-1818)
MK.2.12 See VUES
Vues patriotiques sur l'éducation du peuple, tant des villes que de la campagne...[By L. Philipon de la Madelaine.] 1783.

PHILIPS, John (1676-1709)
MJ.1.48[2] See CYDER
Cyder. A poem in two books. [By J. Philips.] 4th ed. 1744.

PHILIPS, John (1676-1709)
MJ.1.48[1] Poems attempted in the style of Milton. By J. Philips, with his life by Dr. Sewell. 10th ed. 12°, London, 1744.

PHILLIPS, John (fl. 1792)
MF.7.2 A general history of inland navigation, foreign and domestic...New ed. corrected...to 1795. (2 pts.) 4°, London, 1795.

PHILLIPS, William (1775-1828)
ML.3.34 See CONYBEARE, William Daniel
Outlines of the geology of England and Wales...By W.D. Conybeare and W. Phillips. Pt. 1. [No more published.] 1822.

PHOTIUS, Patriarch of Constantinople (c. 820-891)
MM.5.16[1] Epistolæ. Per R. Montacutium Latinè redditæ, & notis subinde illustratæ. (Greek & Latin.) F°, Londini, 1651.

PIGOTT, Charles (d. 1794)
MK.4.21 See JOCKEY
The Jockey Club, or A sketch of the manners of the age. [By C. Pigott.] 3 pts. (Pt. 1, 7th ed.; pt. 2, 3rd ed.) 1792.

PILPAY
MG.5.29 The fables of Pilpay. 12°, London, 1818.

PINDARUS (518-c. 440 B.C.)

MG.7.2 Odes, with several other pieces in prose and verse, translated from the Greek. To which is prefixed a dissertation on the Olympic Games. By G. West. 4°, London, 1749.

PLACE, Francis (1771-1854)

MH.2.25 Illustrations and proofs of the principles of population: including an examination of the proposed remedies of Mr. Malthus, and a reply to the objections of Mr. Godwin and others. 8°, London, 1822.

[ED. NOTE: Place is considered the founder of the modern movement of contraception, while pretending to be a disciple of Malthus. This is the reason why Malthusianism is often assimilated with birth control, a practice unaccepted by Malthus.]

PLAIN

MB.6.61[4] A plain narrative of the much lamented death of the Rev. Henry Peckwell, D.D. ...By a visiter of the sick man's friend...2nd ed. 12°, [London, 1787.]

PLATO (c. 427-347 B.C.)

MG.5.37-8 Works, abrig'd: with an account of his life, philosophy, morals, and politicks...Illustrated with notes. By M. Dacier...2 vols. (Vol. 1, 2nd ed. corrected.) 12°, London, 1719-20.

[ED. NOTE: Plato is referred to in the second edition of the *Essay*. In Bk. I, Ch. XIII, reference is made to Plato's "De Legibus," and to his "Philosophical Republic."]

PLAUTUS, Titus Maccius (c. 250-184 B.C.)

MG.1.16-17 Comoediæ. Accedit commentarius ex variorum notis & observationibus. Ex recensione I.F. Gronovii. Ed. novissima. 2 vols. 8°, Amstelodami, 1684.

PLAUTUS, Titus Maccius (c. 250-184 B.C.)

MJ.1.7-9 Comœdiæ quæ supersunt. 3 vols. 8°, Parisiis, 1759.

PLEADER'S

MC.1.1 The pleader's guide: a didactic poem. ...By the late J.J.S. Esquire [i.e. Anstey]. New ed. 8°, London, 1803.

PLINIUS CÆCILIUS SECUNDUS, Gaius (61-ca. 112 A.D.)

ML.3.8 Epistolæ et Panegyricus, notis illustrata. 8°, Oxonii, 1677.

PLINIUS CÆCILIUS SECUNDUS, Gaius (61-ca. 112 A.D.)

MM.2.24-5 The letters of Pliny the Consul (translated): with occasional remarks. By W. Melmoth. 2nd ed., corrected. 2 vols. 8°, London, 1747.

PLINIUS SECUNDUS, Gaius (23/4-79 A.D.)
MI.2.14-16 C. Plinii Secundi Naturalis historiæ, tomus primus (—-tertius). Cum commentariis & adnotationibus H. Barbari [etc.] ...3 vols. 8°, Lugd. Batav., 1668-9.

[ED. NOTE: Referred to in a note of Malthus's later *Essay*, Bk. I, Ch. XIV.]

PLOWDEN, Francis (1749-1829)
MI.2.2[3] A friendly and constitutional address to the people of Great Britain. 8°, London, 1794.

PLOWDEN, Francis (1749-1829)
MC.3.29 A short history of the British Empire during the last twenty months; viz. from May 1792 to the close of the year 1793. 8°, London, 1794.

PLUTARCHUS (c. A.D. 46-after 119)
MF.1.15 Liber Quomodo juveni audienda sint poemata. Cum interpretatione H. Grotii, variantes lectiones et notas adjecit J. Potter. Ed. 2[a]. 8°, Glasguæ, 1753.

[ED. NOTE: Actually Malthus refers to Plutarch's "De Amore Prolis" in his later *Essay*, Bk. I, Ch. XIV.]

PLUTARCHUS (c. A.D. 46-after 119)
MA.3.13-18 Lives, translated from the original Greek, with notes critical and historical...By J. Langhorne and W. Langhorne. 6 vols. 8°, London, 1770.

PLYMLEY, Peter, pseud.
See SMITH, Sydney.

POEMS
ML.1.3 Poems, and translations. By the author of the Satyrs upon the Jesuits [i.e. J. Oldham]. 8°, London, 1683.

POETÆ
MF.3.28-9 Poetæ minores Græci. Præcipua lectionis varietate et indicibus locupletissimis instruxit T. Gaisford. Vols. 1, 2. (Vols. 3, 4 wanting.) 8°, Oxonii, 1814-16.

POETICAL
MK.5.15[4] A poetical and philosophical essay on the French Revolution. [By J. Courtenay.] Addressed to the Right Hon. E. Burke. 4°, London, 1793.

POETICAL
MG.7.8^{5} A poetical epistle to Sir Joshua Reynolds, Knt. and President of the Royal Academy. [By W. Combe.] 4°, London, 1777.

POETRY
MG.5.40 See ANTI-JACOBIN
The Poetry of the Anti-Jacobin. 1799.

POETRY
ME.2.20&21 [2 copies.] See ANTI-JACOBIN
The Poetry of the Anti-Jacobin. 6th ed. 1813.

POETRY
MF.1.7 The poetry of the world. [Ed. by E. Topham.] 2 vols. in 1. 8°, London, 1788.

POLITICAL
MH.4.27^{3} Political letters, written in March and April M.DCC.LXXXIV. 8°, London, 1785.

POLITICAL
MH.4.27^{1}0 The Political magazine and parliamentary, naval, military and literary journal. For June, 1780. 8°, London, 1780.

POLYBIUS (204-125 B.C.)
MG.2.1-2 General history. In 5 books. Translated from the Greek by Mr. Hampton. 2nd ed. 2 vols. 8°, London, 1761.

POLYBIUS (204-125 B.C.)
MG.2.3-5 Polybii Historiarum quae supersunt, interprete I. Casaubono ex recensione I. Gronovii...Accessit Aeneae Tactici Comm. de obsidione toleranda...(Greek & Latin.) 3 vols. (A made-up set, with vols., 2 & 3 a different ed.) 8°, Lipsiæ, 1764; Vindobonae, 1763.

POLYCARP, St, Bp of Smyrna (c. 70-155 or 156)
MG.6.13 Polycarpi et Ignatii epistolæ: una cum vetere vulgata interpretatione Latina...Quibus præfixa est...I. Usserii dissertatio. (Greek & Latin.) (2 pts.) 4°, Oxoniæ, 1644.

POPE, Alexander (1688-1744)
ML.1.30 The Dunciad. An heroic poem. To Dr. Jonathan Swift. With the prolegomena of Scriblerus, and notes variorum. 8°, London, 1736.

POPE, Alexander (1688-1744)
MK.5.22 See MISCELLANIES
Miscellanies. [By J. Arbuthnot, A. Pope, J. Swift, and others.] Vol. 2. 1727.

POPE, Alexander (1688-1744)
MA.5.19-27 Works. With notes and illustrations by J. Warton, and others. 9 vols. 8°, London, 1797.

POPE, Alexander (1688-1744)
MA.5.28 A supplementary volume to the works of A. Pope, Esq., containing pieces of poetry, not inserted in Warburton's and Warton's editions... 8°, London, 1807.

POPE, Alexander (1688-1744)
MJ.1.33-7 See HOMERUS
The Iliad of Homer. Translated by Mr. Pope. Vols. 2-6. (Vol. 1 wanting.) 1718-21.

POPE, Alexander (1688-1744)
MA.5.14-18 See HOMERUS
The Iliad of Homer. Translated by A. Pope, Esq. A new ed. ...By G. Wakefield. 5 vols. 1806.

POPE, Alexander (1688-1744)
MG.5.11-13 See HOMERUS
The Odyssey of Homer. Translated by A. Pope. 3 vols. 1766.

POPE, Alexander (1688-1744)
MA.5.10-13 See HOMERUS
The Odyssey of Homer. Translated by A. Pope, Esq. A new ed. ...By G. Wakefield. 4 vols. 1806.

POPE, Alexander (1688-1744)
ME.5.41-4 See HOMERUS
Works; translated from the Greek, into English verse, by A. Pope. 7 vols. in 4. 1794.

PORSON, Richard (1759-1808)
MB.7.43 Letters to Mr. Archdeacon Travis, in answer to his Defence of the three heavenly witnesses, I John V. 7. 8°, London, 1790.

POTT, Joseph Holden (1759-1847)
MM.3.8[2] Considerations on the general conditions of the Christian Covenant... 8°, London, 1803.

POWELL, Baden (1796-1860)
MB.1.34 History of natural philosophy, from the earliest periods to the present time. 8°, London, 1834.

POWELL, William Samuel (1717-1775)
ML.3.31 Discourses on various subjects. Published by T. Balguy. 8°, London, 1776.

PRESS CUTTINGS

MA.7.5 [A volume of press cuttings, consisting mainly of letters on various subjects of historical, political, and literary interest, mostly taken from St. James' Chronicle, ca. 1750-90.] F°.

PRETYMAN, George, Bp of Lincoln

See TOMLINE, George Pretyman, Bp of Winchester.

PRICE, Charles (1770?-1806)

MB.6.61[7] See AUTHENTIC
An authentic account of forgeries and frauds of various kinds committed by...Charles Price. Otherwise Patch...1786.

PRICE, James (1752-1783)

MG.7.21[2] An account of some experiments on mercury, silver and gold, made at Guildford in May, 1782. In the laboratory of J. Price. To which is prefixed An abridgment of Boyle's account of a degradation of gold. 4°, Oxford, 1782.

PRICE, Richard (1723-1791)

MH.5.1[3] A discourse on the love of our country, delivered on Nov. 4, 1789...3rd ed., with additions...(2 pts.) 8°, London, 1790.

PRICE, Richard (1723-1791)

MH.1.14 A free discussion of the doctrines of materialism and philosophical necessity, in a correspondence between Dr. Price and Dr. Priestley... 8°, London, 1778.

PRICE, Richard (1723-1791)

MH.3.23-4 Observations on reversionary payments; on schemes for providing annuities for widows, and for persons in old age...4th ed. enlarged...2 vols. 8°, London, 1783.

[ED. NOTE: Malthus discusses the Observations of Dr. Price in the 1798 *Essay*. Ch. XVII. which also covers the "Error of Dr. Price in attributing the happiness and rapid population of America, chiefly, to its peculiar state of civilization." In the Preface of the second edition of his *Essay*, Malthus wrote: "The only authors from whose writings I had deduced the principle, which formed the main argument of the *Essay*, were Hume, Wallace, Dr. Adam Smith, and Dr. Price... ." In the later *Essay*, Price's Observations are referred to in Bk. I, Ch. I; Bk. II, Ch. II, VIII, XI, XIII.]

PRICE, Richard (1723-1791)

MH.5.1[2] Observations on the importance of the American Revolution... 8°, London, 1785.

PRICE, Richard (1723-1791)
MH.5.5[4] Observations on the nature of civil liberty, the principles of government, and the justice and policy of the War with America...2nd ed. 8°, London, 1776.

PRICE, Richard (1723-1791)
MH.5.1[1] Observations on the nature of civil liberty, the principles of government, and the justice and policy of the War with America...6th ed. [Misbound.] 8°, London, 1776.

PRICE, Richard (1723-1791)
MH.5.5[5] Additional observations on the nature and value of civil liberty, and the War with America... 8°, London, 1777.

PRICE, Richard (1723-1791)
ML.3.24 Sermons on the Christian doctrine as received by the different denominations of Christians...2nd ed. corrected... 8°, London, 1787.

PRICE, Sir Uvedale, 1st Bart (1747-1829)
MM.3.15-16 Essay(s) on the picturesque, as compared with the sublime and the beautiful...2 vols. (Vol. 1, New ed., with considerable additions.) 8°, London, 1796; Hereford, 1798.

PRICHARD, Samuel
MH.5.19[3] Masonry dissected. [Wants title-page.] 8°, [London, c. 1730.]

PRIDEAUX, Humphrey (1648-1724)
MK.3.3-5 The Old and New Testament connected in the history of the Jews and neighbouring nations...2 vols. in 3. (Vol. 1, 6th ed.; vol. 2, 3rd ed.) 8°, London, 1718-19.

PRIESTLEY, Joseph (1733-1804)
MM.3.7 An examination of Dr. Reid's Inquiry into the human mind on the principles of common sense, Dr. Beattie's Essay on the nature and immutability of truth, and Dr. Oswald's Appeal to common sense in behalf of religion. 2nd ed. 8°, London, 1775.

PRIESTLEY, Joseph (1733-1804)
MH.1.14 A free discussion of the doctrines of materialism and philosophical necessity, in a correspondence between Dr. Price and Dr. Priestley... 8°, London, 1778.

PRIESTLEY, Joseph (1733-1804)
MF.7.13-14 The history and present state of discoveries relating to vision, light and colours. 2 vols. 4°, London, 1772.

PRIESTLEY, Joseph (1733-1804)
MH.4.21[2] See OBSERVATIONS
Observations on the emigration of Dr. Joseph Priestley...[By W. Cobbett.] New ed. 1794.

PRIOR, Matthew (1664-1721)
MG.5.30-31 Poems on several occasions. 2 vols. (Vol. 1, 6th ed.; vol. 2, 4th ed. to which is prefixed the life of Mr. Prior, by S. Humphreys.) 12°, London, 1741-2.

PRIOR, Matthew (1664-1721)
ME.5.6-7 Poetical works. With the life of the author. 3 vols. in 2. (Bell's Edition. The Poets of Great Britain.) 12°, Edinburg, 1777.

PRIOR, Thomas (1682?-1751)
ML.3.33[2] An authentick narrative of the success of tar-water, in curing a great number and variety of distempers... 8°, London, 1746.

PROBATIONARY
ML.3.3 Probationary odes for the laureatship: with a preliminary discourse, by Sir John Hawkins. [Satirical parodies on Sir J. Hawkins and other Tories. By R. Tickell and others.] 8°, London, 1785.

PROCEEDING
MH.5.22[2] The proceeding of the honourable House of Commons of Ireland, in rejecting the altered Money-Bill, on December 17, 1753, vindicated... [By Sir Richard Cox.] 8°, London, [1754].

PROJET
ML.3.14[5] Projet de requête à présenter à Sa Majesté par les Tiers-Etat de sa province de Brabant. Au sujet des refus de subsides, impôts &c. 8°, [ ] 1789.

PROPERTIUS, Sextus Aurelius (b. 48? B.C.)
MI.3.3-4 Carmina, recensuit, illustravit C.T. Kuinoel. 2 vols. 8°, Lipsiae, 1805.

PROPOSAL
MH.5.22[7] A proposal for uniting the Kingdoms of Great Britain and Ireland... 8°, London, 1751.

PROPOSALS
MG.5.19[2] Proposals for the establishment of a society in Bristol, for the suppression of mendicity, and the promotion of economy and prudence among the labouring classes, to be called The Prudent Man's Friend Society. 12°, Bristol [c. 1812].

PROUT, William (1785-1850)
MC.4.29 Chemistry, meteorology, and the function of digestion considered with reference to natural theology. (Bridgewater Treatises, 8.) 8°, London, 1834.

PSALMANAZAR, George (1679-1763)
MM.3.20 Memoirs of ****. Commonly known by the name of George Psalmanazar; a reputed native of Formosa. Written by himself ...2nd ed. 8°, London, 1765.

PUFENDORF, Samuel von (1632-1694)
MC.7.5 Of the law of nature and nations. 8 books...Done into English by B. Kennett...4th ed., carefully corrected... F°, London, 1729.

PURSUITS
MB.1.11 The pursuits of literature; a satirical poem in four dialogues with notes. [By T.J. Mathias.] 14th ed. 8°, London, 1808.

PURVES, George, pseud.
See GRAY, Simon.

PYE, Henry James (1745-1813)
MJ.1.20[1] See OBSERVATIONS
Observations on the three last volumes of the Roman history, by E. Gibbon. [By H.J. Pye?] 1788.

PYLE, Thomas (1674-1766)
MI.1.21-2 A paraphrase with some notes, on the Acts of the Apostles, and upon all the Epistles of the New Testament... 2nd ed., reviewed...2 vols. 8°, London, 1725-6.

QUESTION
MI.2.1[1] The question, why do we go to war? temperately discussed, according to the official correspondence. [By W. Burdon.] 8°, London, 1803.

QUESTIONS
MH.3.4 Questions in political economy, politics, morals, metaphysics, polite literature... [By S. Bailey.] 8°, London, 1823.

QUINTILIANUS, Marcus Fabius (c. 30-96 A.D.)
MG.7.18 De institutione oratoria libri XII, cum notis et animadversionibus virorum doctorum, summa cura recogniti et emendati per P. Burmannum. 4°, Lugduni Batavorum, 1720.

QUINTILIANUS, Marcus Fabius (c. 30-96 A.D.)
MG.7.10 M. Fabii Quinctiliani, ut ferunt Declamationes XIX majores, et quae ex CCCLXXXVIII. supersunt CXLV minores. Et Calpurnii Flacci Declamationes. Cum notis doctorum virorum; curante P. Burmanno. 4°, Lugduni Batavorum, 1720.

QUINTUS, Smyrnaeus (fl. c. 400)
MI.2.10 Prætermissorum ab Homero libri XIV. Græce cum versione Latina et integris emendationibus L. Rhodomanni; et adnotamentis selectis C. Dausqueji; curante J.C. de Pauw ... 8°, Lugduni Batavorum, 1784.

R

SAMUEL RICHARDSON

RABELAIS, François (1494?-1553)
MM.1.36-7 Œuvres. Augmentées de la vie de l'auteur & de quelques remarques...2 vols. 12°, [Amsterdam?] 1675.

RACINE, Jean (1639-1699)
MM.1.43 Abrégé de l'histoire de Port-Royal... 12°, Paris, 1767.

RACINE, Jean (1639-1699)
MI.4.9[3] Esther, tragédie tirée de l'Ecriture S^{te}. Nouvelle éd., revuë...Par D.D. de la S.R. [i.e. D. Durand.] 8°, Londres, 1745.

RAIMBERT, M.
MH.4.25[1] Glimpse of the political history of the French Revolution. (French & English.) 8°, London, 1793.

RALEGH, Sir Walter (1552?-1618)
MD.1.1 The historie of the world. In 5 bookes. (With A chronologicall table.) F°, (London, 1634. Engraved title dated 1614.)

RAMEL, Jean Pierre (1768-1815)
MI.2.20[2] Journal de l'Adjudant-Général Ramel...l'un des déportés à la Guiane...3e éd., revue, corrigée et augmentée ... 8°, Londres, 1799.

RAMSBOTTOM, Richard
MJ.1.32 Fractions anatomized: or, The doctrine of parts made plain and easy to the meanest capacity... 12°, London, 1762.

RAMUS, Petrus (1515-1572)
MB.6.52[4] Scholæ grammaticæ. 8°, Parisiis, 1559.

RAPIN-THOYRAS, Paul de (1661-1725)
ML.4.1-10 Histoire d'Angleterre. 10 vols. 4°, La Haye, 1724-7.

RAVENSTONE, Piercy, pseud.
MH.2.23 A few doubts as to the correctness of some opinions generally entertained on the subjects of population and political economy. 8°, London, 1821.

RAY, John (1627-1705)
MJ.1.6 A collection of English proverbs...with short annotations...By J.R[ay]. 8°, Cambridge, 1670.

RAY, John (1627-1705)
ME.2.38 A collection of English proverbs...with short annotations. 2nd ed. enlarged... 8°, Cambridge, 1678.

RAY, John (1627-1705)
MI.1.16 Synopsis methodica stirpium Britannicarum...Ed. 3[a] multis locis emendata... 8°, Londini, 1724.

[ED. NOTE: This book of John Ray, as well as the book of François Boissier, obviously belonged to Daniel Malthus. There are speculations that these books were sent to Malthus's father by Jean Jacques Rousseau, who reciprocated for the botanical books received from Daniel. It is heavily annotated by Rousseau.]

RAYNAL, Guillaume Thomas François (1713-1796)
MA.1.9-16 A philosophical and political history of the settlements and trade of the Europeans in the East and West Indies. Revised, augmented, and published. Newly translated from the French, by J.O. Justamond. 8 vols. 8°, London, 1788.

[ED. NOTE: Malthus frequently refers to Raynal in the later *Essay*, especially in Bk. I, Ch. IV: "Of the checks to population among the American Indians." Also, he refers to Raynal in Bk. I, Ch. XI; Bk. III, Ch. IV. and VI. However, the edition referred to by Malthus was an 8°, 10-vol. set of 1795.]

RECUEIL

MB.2.34[2] Recueil de diverses pièces relatives aux troubles survenus dans la principauté de Neuchâtel et Valengin... 12°, [Geneva?] 1767.

REED, Mary

MH.5.24[5] See TRIAL
The trial of Mrs. Mary Reed, upon the charge of poisoning her husband, at Berkeley, in Gloucestershire, in April, 1794...[1796].

REFLECTIONS

MH.5.3[1] Reflections, moral, and political, on the murder of Louis the Sixteenth: in a sermon, preached...February 3rd, 1793...(Jer. IX, 9.) 8°, London, 1793.

REFLECTIONS

ML.5.29[9] Reflections on faith: in which it is shewn, that no difference of religious opinion is any reasonable grounds of disrespect among men and especially among Christians. By Philantropos [i.e. G. Wakefield?]. New ed. ...(2 pts.) 8°, London, 1790.

REFLECTIONS

MH.4.16[2] Reflections on the present scarcity, and high price of provisions...By a Hampshire freeholder. 8°, London, 1801.

REFLECTIONS

MH.4.24[4] Reflections on the propriety of an immediate conclusion of peace. [By N. Vansittart, Lord Bexley.] 8°, London, 1793.

REGNARD, Jean François (1655-1709)

MB.4.29-34 Œuvres complètes, avec des avertissements et des remarques...par M. Garnier. Nouvelle éd. 6 vols. 8°, Paris, 1820.

REJECTED

MB.4.26 Rejected addresses: or, The new Theatrum poetarum. [By J. and H. Smith.] 18th ed. carefully revised... 8°, London, 1833.

RELATION

MB.2.34 Relation exacte et impartielle de tout ce qui s'est passé à Neuchâtel, depuis la naissance des troubles actuels, jusqu'à présent...(With Recueil de diverses pièces survenus dans la principauté...and Robert Covelle, citoyen de Genève, à Monsieur de Voltaire.) (3 pts.) 8°, [Neuchâtel?] 1767.

RELIGION

MK.5.18 The religion of nature delineated. [By W. Wollaston.] 4°, London, 1725.

RELIGION

MK.5.17 The religion of nature delineated. [By W. Wollaston.] [New ed.] 4°, London, 1726.

RELIQUES

MB.4.1-3 Reliques of ancient English poetry: consisting of old heroic ballads, songs, and other pieces...[Ed. by T. Percy.] 3rd ed. 3 vols. 8°, London, 1775.

REMARKS

MH.5.21^{3} Remarks on the laws relating to the poor; with proposals for their better relief and employment. By a Member of Parliament [William Hay]. First published in 1735... 8°, London, 1751.

REMARKS

MH.5.20^{3} Remarks on the Pretender's Declaration and Commission. (2 pts.) 8°, London, 1745.

REMARKS

MH.5.19^{4} Remarks on the sentence given in favour of E—-W—-M—- [Edward Wortley Montagu], and T—-T—- [Theobald Taafe], Esqs; by the L—-t C—-l [Lieutenant Criminal] at Paris. 8°, London, 1752.

REMARKS

MH.5.20^{2} Remarks upon the Account of the conduct of a certain Dutchess [of Marlborough]. In a letter from a Member of Parliament in the reign of Queen Anne... 8°, London, 1742.

REPORT

MH.5.7^{6} Report of Committee of Secrecy of the House of Commons. Ordered to be printed 15th March, 1799. New ed. 8°, London, 1799.

RESOLUTIONS

MH.4.29^{3} The resolutions of England and Ireland relative to a commercial intercourse between the two kingdoms... 8°, London, 1785.

RESSOURCES

MK.2.3 Les ressources de l'amour. [By J.F. de Bastide.] (4 pts.) 12°, Amsterdam, 1752.

RETZ, Jean François Paul de Gondi, Cardinal de (1613-1679)

MF.2.13-15 Mémoires, contenant ce qui s'est passé de remarquable en France pendant les premières années du règne de Louis XIV. Nouvelle éd., revue exactement...3 vols. 8°, Amsterdam, 1731.

REVIEW

MH.5.12[4] A review of the principal charges against Warren Hastings Esquire...[By J. Logan.] 8°, London, 1788.

REVIEW

MH.5.23[4] A review of the proposed naturalization of the Jews...By a merchant [J. Hanway]... 8°, London, 1753.

REYNOLDS, Frederick (1764-1841)

MI.4.5[4] The will: a comedy, in 5 acts. As it is performed at the Theatre-Royal, Drury-Lane. 8°, London, 1797.

REYNOLDS, Sir Joshua (1723-1792)

MG.7.8[5] See POETICAL
A poetical epistle to Sir Joshua Reynolds, Knt. and President of the Royal Academy. [By W. Combe.] 1777.

RICARDO, David (1772-1823)

MH.3.18[7] The high price of bullion, a proof of the depreciation of bank notes. 2nd ed. corrected. 8°, London, 1810.

[ED. NOTE: "A duty on importation not too high, and a bounty nearly such as was recommended by Mr. Ricardo, would probably be best suited to our present situation, and best secure steady prices." Malthus's *Essay*, Bk. III, Ch. XII. n.]

RICARDO, David (1772-1823)

MX.1.15 Letters of David Ricardo to T.R. Malthus, 1810-23; ed. by J. Bonar. 8°, Oxford, 1887.**

[ED. NOTE: The letters of this edition were "printed for the first time from the original manuscripts, kindly lent for the purpose by Colonel Malthus, C.B. The representatives of Ricardo have been good enough to make search for the corresponding letters of Malthus, but without success." (From the Preface.)]

RICARDO, David (1772-1823)

MH.3.2 On the principles of political economy, and taxation. 3rd ed. 8°, London, 1821.

[ED. NOTE: Malthus's "Principles of Political Economy" (1820) extensively discusses Ricardo's "Principles"; but he refers to the third edition of Ricardo's "Principles" in a note on p. 87 and to the first edition in a note on p. 188. However, in Malthus's "Definitions" he refers to Ricardo in Ch. V. entitled "On the Definition and Application of Terms by Mr. Ricardo" and cites the 3rd edition of his basic work, which was actually in his library as per this entry. It is also referred to in Malthus's later *Essay*, Bk. III, Ch. XII.]

RICCOBONI, Marie Jeanne (1714-1792)
MJ.1.15 See LETTRES
Lettres de Mistriss Fanni Butlerd, à Milord Charles Alfred de Caitombridge, comte de Plisinte, duc de Raslingth, écrites en 1735, traduites de l'Anglois en 1756, par A. de Varançai. [By M.J. Riccoboni.] 1759.

RICHARDSON, Samuel (1689-1761)
MB.6.32-9 Clarissa; or, The history of a young lady...A new ed. ... 8 vols. 12°, London, 1810.

RICHARDSON, Samuel (1689-1761)
MB.6.40-46 The history of Sir Charles Grandison; in a series of letters. A new ed. ... 7 vols. 8°, London, 1820.

RICHARDSON, Samuel (1689-1761)
MB.6.28-31 Pamela; or, Virtue rewarded...A new ed., being the 15th...4 vols. 12°, London, 1810.

RICHESSE
MA.3.3-4 La richesse de la Hollande, ouvrage dans lequel on expose l'origine du commerce & de la puissance des Hollandois ... [By J. Accarias de Sérionne.] 2 vols. 8°, Londres, 1778.

RIGHTS
MH.4.26^{6} The rights of Englishmen; or The British constitution of government, compared with that of a Democratic Republic. By the author of the History of the Republic of Athens [i.e. Sir William Young]. 8°, London, 1793.

RIGHTS
MH.5.5^{6} The rights of Great Britain asserted against the claims of America: being an answer to the Declaration of the General Congress. [By J. Macpherson.] 8th ed. ... 8°, London, 1776.

RIVERS, David
MM.2.3-4 See LITERARY
Literary memoirs of living authors of Great Britain... including a list of their works...[By D. Rivers.] 2 vols. 1798.

ROBERT, St, of Knaresborough (?-1235?)
MB.6.61^{6} See LEGEND
The legend of Saint Robert, the hermit of Knaresbro'. 1792.

ROBERTSON, William (1721-1793)
MF.5.9 An historical disquisition concerning the knowledge which the Ancients had of India; and the progress of trade with that country...3rd ed. 8°, London, 1799.

ROBERTSON, William (1721-1793)
MF.5.5-8 The history of America. 3rd ed. 4 vols. 8°, London, 1780-99.

[ED. NOTE: Malthus refers to Robertson's "History of America" (this very edition) in Bk. I, Ch. IV, of the later *Essay*, regarding the "Checks to Population among American Indians," as well as in Bk. III, Ch. IV, regarding "Emigration." Reference to it is made also in Malthus's "Principles of Political Economy" 1820 ed., notes on pp. 56-57.]

ROBERTSON, William (1721-1793)
MF.4.32-3 The history of Scotland during the reigns of Queen Mary and King James VI. till his accession to the Crown of England...14th ed. ... 2 vols. 8°, London, 1794.

ROBERTSON, William (1721-1793)
MF.5.1-4 The history of the reign of the Emperor Charles V. With a view of the progress of society...New ed. 4 vols. 8°, London, 1782.

[ED. NOTE: This edition is referred to by Malthus in his later *Essay*, Bk. I, Ch. VI.]

ROCK, Captain (1779-1852)
MB.2.13 Memoirs of Captain Rock, the celebrated Irish chieftain, with some account of his ancestors. Written by himself [or rather, by Thomas Moore]. 3rd ed. 12°, London, 1824.

RODENHURST, T.
MB.6.53[3] A description of Hawkstone, the seat of Sir Richard Hill, Bart...3rd ed., with several alterations... 8°, [London] Shrewsbury pr., 1786.

ROGERS, John
MB.6.61[1] A circumstantial narrative of the loss of the Halsewell, East-Indiaman, Capt. Richard Pierce...6th of January, 1786. Compiled from the communications...of H. Meriton and J. Rogers. 12th ed. 8°, London, 1786.

ROGET, Peter Mark (1779-1869)
MC.4.23-4 Animal and vegetable physiology considered with reference to natural theology. (2nd ed.) 2 vols. (Bridgewater Treatises, 5.) 8°, London, 1834.

ROLAND, Marie Jeanne Phlipon (1754-1793)
ML.3.15-16 Appel à l'impartiale postérité, ou Recueil des écrits qu'elle a rédigés, pendant sa détention, aux prisons de l'Abbaye et de Sainte-Pélagie...4 pts. 2 vols. 8°, Paris, 1795.

ROLLIN, Charles (1661-1741)
MG.2.6-13 The ancient history of the Egyptians, Carthaginians, Assyrians [etc.]...Translated from the French. 10th ed. 8 vols. 8°, London, 1804.

ROLLIN, Charles (1661-1741)
MB.2.18-20, 20a De la manière d'enseigner et d'étudier les belles-lettres...Nouvelle éd. 4 vols. 12°, Paris, 1748.

ROME
MC.7.9 See VARIE
Varie vedute di Roma Antica, e Moderna disegnate e intagliate da celebri autori. [Plates.] 1748.

ROMILLY, Sir Samuel (1757-1818)
MH.4.7-8 Speeches in the House of Commons. [With a memoir by W. Peter.] 2 vols. 8°, London, 1820.

ROOKE, John (1780-1856)
MH.4.4 An inquiry into the principles of national wealth, illustrated by the political economy of the British Empire. 8°, Edinburgh, 1824.

ROSCOE, William (1753-1831?)
MI.2.1^{3} Considerations on the causes, objects and consequences of the present war, and on the expediency, or the danger of peace with France. 2nd ed. 8°, London, 1808.

ROSCOE, William (1753-1831?)
MG.2.14-19 The life and Pontificate of Leo the Tenth. 2nd ed., corrected. 6 vols. 8°, London, 1806.

ROSCOE, William (1753-1831?)
MI.2.1^{4} Remarks on the proposals made to Great Britain, for opening negotiations for peace in the year 1807. 2nd ed. (2 pts.) 8°, London, 1808.

ROSCOE, William (1753-1831?)
MH.4.25^{6} See THOUGHTS
Thoughts on the causes of the present failures. [By W. Roscoe.] 3rd ed. 1793.

ROSCOMMON, Wentworth Dillon, 4th Earl of (1633?-1685)
MG.1.14 Poems. To which is added, An essay on poetry, by the Earl of Mulgrave, now Duke of Buckingham. Together with poems by Mr. Richard Duke. 8°, London, 1717.

ROSE, Rt. Hon. George (1744-1818)
MH.3.22^{4} Observations on the Poor Laws, and of the Management of the poor, in Great Britain... 8°, London, 1805.

ROSINUS, Johannes (1551-1626?)
MG.7.4 Antiquitatum Romanarum corpus absolutissimum, cum notis doctissimis ac locupletissimis T. Dempsteri...Ed. postrema... 4°, Trajecti ad Rhenum, 1701.

ROUSSEAU, Jean Jacques (1712-1778)
MB.2.24-7 Emile ou de l'éducation. 4 vols. 8°, Amsterdam, 1762.

[ED. NOTE: Likely from Daniel Malthus's Library.]

ROWLEY, Alexander
ML.2.33 The schollers companion, or a little library, containing all the interpretations of the Hebrew and Greek Bible...(3 pts.) 8°, London, 1648.

ROYAL
MH.5.2[2] Royal recollections on a tour to Cheltenham, Gloucester, Worcester, and places adjacent, in the year 1788. [By D. Williams.] 9th ed. 8°, London, 1788.

RUCHAT, Abraham (1680?-1750)
MB.2.30-33 See ETAT
L'état et les délices de la Suisse...Nouvelle éd. corrigée...[A translation of A. Stanyan's Account of Switzerland, together with Les délices de la Suisse, by A. Ruchat. Ed. by J.G. Altman.] 4 vols. 1764.

RUGGLE, George (1575-1622)
ML.2.1 Ignoramus. Comœdia coram Rege Jacobo...Ed. 5a, a MSS. emendatior. 16°, Londini [167-?.]

RULHIERE, Claude Carloman de (1735-1791)
MA.2.28-31 Histoire de l'anarchie de Pologne, et du démembrement de cette République. Suivie des anecdotes sur la révolution de Russie, en 1762...4 vols. 8°, Paris, 1807.

RUSSELL, John Russell, 1st Earl (1792-1878)
MB.7.46 An essay on the history of the English government and constitution...2nd ed. greatly enlarged. 8°, London, 1823.

RUSSELL, Lady Rachel Wriothesley (1636-1723)
MK.4.15 Letters; from the manuscript in the Library at Wooburn Abbey...To which is added, The trial of Lord William Russell for high treason...[Ed. by T. Sellwood.] 5th ed. (2 pts.) 8°, London, 1793.

S

ADAM SMITH

SADLER, Michael Thomas (1780-1835)
MH.2.30 Ireland; its evils, and their remedies: being a refutation of the errors of the Emigration Committee and others, touching that country. 8°, London, 1828.

[ED. NOTE: Sadler is known for his treatise "The Law of Population...in disproof of the superfecundity of human beings, and developing the real principle of their increase," in which he attacks Malthus.]

SADLER, Michael Thomas (1780-1835)
MH.2.28-9 The law of population: a treatise, in 6 books...2 vols. 8°, London, 1830.

SAINT-FOIX, Germain François Poullain de (1698-1776)
MJ.1.38-42 Essais historiques sur Paris. Nouvelle éd. 5 vols. 12°, Londres, 1755-8.

SALMONIA
MB.2.12 Salmonia: or Days of fly fishing. In a series of conversations...By an angler [Sir Humphry Davy]. 3rd ed. 8°, London, 1832.

SANDFORD, Daniel (1766-1830)
MG.3.31-2 Remains of the late Right Rev. D. Sandford...With a memoir by the Rev. J. Sandford. 2 vols. 8°, Edinburgh, 1830.

SANDYS, George (1578-1644)
ME.7.10 Sandys Travailes: containing a history of the original and present state of the Turkish Empire...6th ed. F°, London, 1658.

SATYRS
ML.1.1 Satyrs upon the Jesuits: written in the year 1679. And some other pieces by the same hand. [By J. Oldham.] 2nd ed. more corrected. 8°, London, 1682.

SAUVAGES, François Boissier de
See BOISSIER DE SAUVAGES DE LA CROIX, François.

SAVAGE, Richard (1696/7-1743)
ME.5.1 Poetical works. With the life of the author [by Dr. Johnson]. 2 vols. in 1. (Bell's Edition. The Poets of Great Britain.) 12°, Edinburg, 1780.

SAVAGE, Richard (1696/7-1743)
MB.4.27-8 Works. With an account of the life and writings of the author, by S. Johnson. 2 vols. 8°, London, 1775.

SAY, Jean Baptiste (1767-1832)
MA.2.18-23 Cours complet d'économie politique pratique...6 vols. 8°, Paris, 1828-9.

[ED. NOTE: Malthus actually refers to Say's "Treatise on Political Economy," in his "Principles" (1820 ed. pp. 136, 353, 354), and in his "Definitions" 1821 ed. pp. 21, 251, 252, 258), Malthus refers to Say's "Traité d'Economie Politique, 4th edition." Malthus also refers to the former in his tract "The Nature and Progress of Rent." However for his library, Malthus chose the French extended text.]

SAY, Jean Baptiste (1767-1832)
MA.2.17 Mélanges et correspondance d'économie politique, ouvrage posthume; publ. par C. Comte. 8°, Paris, 1833.

SAY, Louis (1774-1840)
MH.1.19 Considérations sur l'industrie et la législation, sous le rapport de leur influence sur la richesse des états...[Chapter VIII, a study of Malthus's Principles of political economy.] 8°, Paris, 1822.

SCHILLER, Johann Christoph Friedrich von (1759-1805)
MG.7.1 Sämmtliche Werke. 4°, Stuttgart & Tübingen, 1834.

SCHLEUSNER, Johann Friedrich (1759-1831)
MG.6.5 Novum lexicon Græco-Latinum in Novum Testamentum ...Juxta editionem Lipsiensem quartam. 4°, Glasguæ, 1824.

SCOTT, John
See SCOTT WARING, John.

SCOTT, Sir Walter, Bart (1771-1832)
ML.2.20 Letters on demonology and witchcraft, addressed to J.G. Lockhart, Esq. (The Family Libr., 16.) 8°, London, 1830.

SCOTT WARING, John (1747-1819)
MH.4.26[5] A letter from Major Scott to the Right Honourable Edmund Burke. 8°, London, 1791.

SCOTT WARING, John (1747-1819)
MH.4.26[4] See LETTER
A letter to the Right Hon. Edmund Burke, in reply to his 'Reflections on the Revolution in France, &c.' 2nd ed., with considerable additions...By a Member of the Revolution Society [i.e. J. Scott, afterwards Scott Waring]. 1790.

SCROPE, George Poulett (1797-1876)
ML.2.22 Principles of political economy, deduced from the natural laws of social welfare, and applied to the present state of Britain. 12°, London, 1833.

[ED. NOTE: This Treatise includes a rejection of Malthus's theory of population. He actually considered that Malthus's theory had brought great harm.]

SEARCH, Edward, pseud.
See TUCKER, Abraham.

SEARCH, Simon, pseud.
MA.4.1 The spirit of the times. In a series of observations on the important events of the age. Politics (and Literature). 8°, London, 1790.

SEBRIGHT, Sir John Saunders (1767-1846)
MH.4.22[1] The art of improving the breeds of domestic animals. In a letter addressed to Sir Joseph Banks. 8°, London, 1809.

SECHELLES, Hérault de
See HERAULT DE SECHELLES, Marie Jean.

SECKER, Thomas, Abp of Canterbury (1693-1768)
MB.6.19 Fourteen sermons preached on several occasions. 8°, London, 1766.

SECOND
ME.2.7[2] A second letter to the people of England. On foreign subsidies, subsidiary armies, and their consequences to this nation. [By J. Shebbeare.] 4th ed. 8°, London, 1756.

SECOND
MH.5.10[5] A second letter to the Rt. Hon. Charles James Fox, upon the dangerous and inflammatory tendency of his late conduct in

Parliament...By the author of the First letter [T.R. Bentley?]. 8°, London, 1793.

SECOND
MB.6.56 Second travels of an Irish gentleman in search of a religion... [By J. Blanco White.] 2 vols. in 1. 8°, Dublin, 1833.

SEED, Jeremiah (1700-1747)
MG.3.11-12 Discourses on several important subjects. To which are added, eight sermons preached at the Lady Moyer's lecture...2 vols. 8°, London, 1743.

SEGUR, Louis Philippe, comte de (1753-1830)
MI.4.25-7 Tableau historique et politique de l'Europe, depuis 1786 jusqu'en 1796, ou l'an 4...2e éd., revue et corrigée. 3 vols. 8°, Paris, 1801.

SELECT
MK.4.20 A select collection of scarce and valuable tracts on money, from the originals of Vaughan, Cotton, Petty [etc.]. With a preface, notes, and index (by J.R. McCulloch). 8°, London, 1856.*

SELECT
MK.4.12 Select tracts relating to the Civil Wars in England, in the reign of King Charles the First...[Ed. by F. Maseres.] 2 pts. 8°, London, 1815.

SELECT
MB.7.33 Select works of the British poets. With biographical and critical prefaces by Dr. Aikin. 8°, London, 1820.

SELECT
ME.5.31-40 Select works of the British poets. With biographical and critical prefaces. By Dr. Aikin. 10 vols. 12°, London, 1821.

SELKIRK, Thomas Douglas, 5th Earl of (1771-1820)
MI.2.1^{5} On the necessity of a more effectual system of national defence, and the means of establishing the permanent security of the Kingdom. 8°, London, 1808.

SENECA, Lucius Annaeus (3? B.C.-65 A.D.)
MG.1.9 Seneca's Morals by way of abstract...6th ed. To which is added, A discourse, under the title of An after-thought. By Sir R. L'Estrange. (4 pts.) 8°, [London] In the Savoy, 1696.

SENECA, Lucius Annaeus (3? B.C.-65 A.D.)
MG.1.10 Tragœdiæ cum notis J.F. Gronovii... 8°, Amstelodami, 1682.

SEVIGNE, Marie de Rabutin-Chantal, marquise de (1626-1696)
MB.3.1-10 Recueil des lettres de Madame de Sévigné. Nouvelle éd., augmentée...par B. de Vauxcelles...10 vols. 8°, Paris, 1801.

SEVILLE, Treaty of
MH.5.20[7] See TREATY
The Treaty of Seville [between England, France and Spain], and the measures that have been taken for the four last years, impartially considered. In a letter to a friend. [Signed A.B.] 1730.

SEWARD, Anna (1747-1809)
MG.7.8[3] Louisa, a poetical novel, in four epistles. 4°, Lichfield, 1784.

SHADWELL, Thomas (1642?-1692)
ML.1.6-9 Dramatick works. 4 vols. 12°, London, 1720.

SHAFTESBURY, Anthony Ashley Cooper, 3rd Earl of (1671-1713)
MM.4.3-5 Characteristicks of men, manners, opinions, times. 6th ed., corrected...3 vols. 8°, [London] 1737-8.

SHARP, John, Abp of York (1645-1714)
MG.3.13-16 Sermons. 4 vols. (Vol. 1, 5th ed., Fifteen sermons preached on several occasions; Vol. 2, Sermons preached on several occasions...; Vol. 3, Sixteen casuistical sermons...; Vol. 4, Eighteen sermons. ...) 8°, London, 1715-21.

SHEBBEARE, John (1709-1788)
ME.2.7[1] See FIRST
A first letter to the people of England. On the present situation and conduct of national affairs. [By J. Shebbeare.] 4th ed. 1756.

SHEBBEARE, John (1709-1788)
ME.2.7[2] See SECOND
A second letter to the people of England. On foreign subsidies, subsidiary armies, and their consequences to this nation. [By J. Shebbeare.] 4th ed. 1756.

SHEBBEARE, John (1709-1788)
ME.2.7[3] See THIRD
A third letter to the people of England. On liberty, taxes, and the application of public money. [By J. Shebbeare.] 2nd ed. 1756.

SHEBBEARE, John (1709-1788)
ME.2.7[4] See FOURTH
A fourth letter to the people of England. On the conduct of the M—-rs in alliances, fleets, and armies...[By J. Shebbeare.] 2nd ed. 1756.

SHEBBEARE, John (1709-1788)
ME.2.7^{5} See FIFTH
A fifth letter to the people of England, on the subversion of the Constitution: and, the necessity of its being restored. [By J. Shebbeare.] 2nd ed. 1757.

SHEBBEARE, John (1709-1788)
ME.2.7^{6} See SIXTH
A sixth letter to the people of England, on the progress of national ruin...[By J. Shebbeare.] 1757.

SHEFFIELD, John Baker Holroyd, 1st Earl of (1735-1821)
MH.4.16^{5} Remarks on the deficiency of grain, occasioned by the bad harvest of 1799; on the means of present relief, and of future plenty... 8°, London, 1800.

SHERIDAN, Rt. Hon. Richard Brinsley Butler (1751-1816)
MB.3.37 Dramatic works. With some observations upon his personal and literary character. 8°, Greenock, 1828.

SHERIDAN, Rt. Hon. Richard Brinsley Butler (1751-1816)
MH.4.19^{3} The speeches of Mr. Sheridan, Mr. Fox, Mr. Burke [etc.] on the charges brought against Mr. Hastings and on the commercial treaty. 8°, London, 1787.

SHERIDAN, Thomas (1719-1788)
MG.6.9 A general dictionary of the English language...To which is prefixed A rhetorical grammar. 4°, London, 1780.

SHERIDAN, Thomas (1719-1788)
MM.3.12 The life of the Rev. Dr. Jonathan Swift, Dean of St. Patrick's Dublin. 8°, London, 1784.

SHERLOCK, Thomas, Bp of London (1678-1761)
MG.3.10 The use and intent of prophecy, in the several ages of the world. In six discourses, delivered at the Temple Church, in April and May, 1724...5th ed., corrected and enlarged. 8°, London, 1749.

SHERLOCK, William (1641?-1707)
MG.3.29-30 Sermons. 2 vols. (Vol. 1, 3rd ed., Sermons preach'd upon several occasions; Vol. 2, Several sermons upon useful subjects.) 8°, London, 1707-19.

SHIRLEY, William (1739-1780)
MI.4.9^{2} Edward the Black Prince; or, The Battle of Poictiers: an historical tragedy. Attempted after the manner of Shakespear. As it is

acted at the Theatre-Royal in Drury-Lane, by His Majesty's servants. 8°, London, 1750.

SHORT

MH.4.28[3] A short account of the Marratta State. Written in Persian by a Munshy, who accompanied Col. Upton...Translated by W. Chambers. To which is added The voyages and travels of M. Caesar Fredericke... 8°, London, 1787.

SHORT

MH.5.6[6] A short account of the Society for Equitable Assurances on lives and survivorships, established by deed... 8°, London, 1777.

SHORT

MI.2.2[5] A short review of the political state of Great-Britain, at the commencement of the year 1787. [By Sir N.W. Wraxall.] [Wants title-page.] 8°, [London, 1787.]

SHORT

MH.3.21[2] Short state of the present situation of the India Company, both in India and in Europe... 8°, London, 1784.

SILIUS ITALICUS, Gaius (25-100 A.D.)

MF.7.11 Punicorum libri septemdecim...curante A. Drakenborch, cujus etiam annotationes passim additae sunt. 4°, Trajecti ad Rhenum, 1717.

SINS

MH.4.25[7] Sins of government, sins of the nation; or, A discourse for the fast, appointed on April 19, 1793. By a volunteer [i.e. A.L. Barbauld]. 2nd ed. 8°, London, 1793.

SISMONDI, Jean Charles Léonard Simonde de (1773-1843)

MB.7.1-31 Histoire des Français. 31 vols. 8°, Paris, 1821-44. [Vols. 19-31, 1835-44.*]

[ED. NOTE: Neither Sismondi's "Histoire des Français" nor the "Italian Republic" (see next entry), whose extensive volumes were in Malthus's library, are directly referred to in the works of the latter. Instead, Sismondi's "Nouveau Principes d'Economie Politique," published first in 1819 apparently triggered the publication in 1820 of Malthus's "Principles of Political Economy" where he also referred to the "Principles" of Sismondi (p. 420). An early treatise of Sismondi: "De la Richesse Commerciale," published in 1803 was also referred to by Malthus in his "Principles" (p. 136) as well as in his 1815 tract on "The Nature and Progress of Rent."]

SISMONDI, Jean Charles Léonard Simonde de (1773-1843)

MB.1.32 A history of the Italian Republic... 8°, London, 1832.

SIXTH

ME.2.7[6] A sixth letter to the people of England, on the progress of national ruin... [By J. Shebbeare.] 8°, London, 1757.

SKETCH

MH.3.21[3] Sketch of financial and commercial affairs in the Autumn of 1797... [By Sir R. Herries.] 8°, London, 1797.

SKETCH

MH.3.17[3] A sketch of the state of Ireland, past and present. [By J.W. Croker.] 8°, London, 1808.

SKETCHES

MH.5.7[5] Sketches of the characters of the Hon. Thomas Erskine, and James Mingay, Esq. interspersed with anecdotes and professional strictures. [Wants title-page.] 8°, London, 1794.

SMART, Christopher (1722-1771)

ME.6.1[2] Hymn to the Supreme Being, on recovery from a dangerous fit of illness. 4°, London, 1756.

SMITH, Adam (1723-1790)

MA.5.29-32 An inquiry into the nature and causes of the wealth of nations. With a life of the author...By J.R. McCulloch. 4 vols. 8°, Edinburgh, 1828.

[ED. NOTE: Malthus first refers to "The Wealth of Nations" in the 1798 *Essay*, devoting Ch. XVI. to it. He refers to Smith in the Preface of the second edition as one of the four authors from whose writings he has deduced his "Principles," and cites him in the later *Essay* in Bk. II, Ch. XIII; Bk. III, Ch. V, XI, XII, XIII; Bk. IV, Ch. IX and XI. He refers to Smith's "The Wealth of Nations" 93 times in his "Principles" (2nd ed.), and 51 times in his "Definitions." In his tract "Observations on the Effects of the Corn Laws" (1814), Malthus refers to "The Wealth of Nations" on 10 pages out of 27 (of "Observations" according to the reprint), and abundantly in his other tract "The Nature and Progress of Rent" (1815). In this tract, Malthus refers to Buchanan's fourth volume of his own edition of Adam Smith's main work. Thus it is inconcievable for Malthus to have had in his library only a 1828 edition of "The Wealth of Nations." (See also the comments of Mrs. Patricia James in her Introduction.)]

SMITH, Adam (1723-1790)

ME.1.42-3 The theory of moral sentiments...8th ed. 2 vols. 8°, London, 1797.

SMITH, Adam (1723-1790)
MB.6.54^{2};MJ.1.20^{2} [Two copies] See LETTER.
A letter to Adam Smith LL.D. on the life, death, and philosophy of his friend David Hume Esq. By one of the people called Christians [i.e. G. Horne]. 1777.

SMITH, Charles (1713-1777)
MH.4.20 See THREE
Three tracts on the corn-trade and corn-laws...To which is added, a supplement... [By C. Smith.] 1766.

SMITH, Charlotte (1749-1806)
MG.7.8^{1} Elegiac sonnets. 3rd ed. With twenty additional sonnets. 4°, London [1786.]

SMITH, Edmund (1672-1710)
MJ.1.48^{3} Phædra and Hippolitus, a tragedy. 12°, London, 1745.

SMITH, Horace (1779-1849)
MB.4.26 See REJECTED
Rejected addresses: or, The new Theatrum poetarum. [By J. and H. Smith.] 18th ed. carefully revised... 1833.

SMITH, James (1775-1839)
MB.4.26 See REJECTED
Rejected addresses: or, The new Theatrum poetarum. [By J. and H. Smith.] 18th ed., carefully revised...1833.

SMITH, Margaret
See PARIS. Bibliothèque Nationale.

SMITH, Sydney (1771-1845)
MH.1.7^{5} Letters on the subject of the Catholics, to my brother Abraham, who lives in the country. By Peter Plymley [i.e. S. Smith]. 6th ed. 8°, London, 1808.

SMITH, Sydney (1771-1845)
MH.4.22^{2} Two letters on the subject of the Catholics, to my brother Abraham, who lives in the country. By Peter Plymley [i.e. S. Smith]. 4th ed. 8°, London, 1807.

SMITH, Sydney (1771-1845)
MH.4.22^{3} Three more letters on the subject of the Catholics, to my brother Abraham, who lives in the country. By Peter Plymley [i.e. S. Smith]. 3rd ed. 8°, London, 1807.

SMITH, W. C.
ME.4.1 Rambles round Guildford, with a topographical and historical description of the town. 12°, Guildford, 1828.

SMITH, William, of South Carolina (1762-1840?)
MI.2.2[4] An address from William Smith of South-Carolina, to his constituents. 8°, London, (Philadelphia pr.) [1794.]

SMOLLETT, Tobias George (1721-1771)
MB.3.27-8 The adventures of Peregrine Pickle. In which are included Memoirs of a lady of quality. 2 vols. 8°, London, 1831.

SMOLLETT, Tobias George (1721-1771)
MB.3.30 The adventures of Roderick Random. 8°, London, 1831.

SMOLLETT, Tobias George (1721-1771)
MB.3.23[2] The adventures of Sir Launcelot Greaves. 8°, London, 1832.

SMOLLETT, Tobias George (1721-1771)
MB.3.29 The expedition of Humphry Clinker. With a memoir of the author by T. Roscoe. 8°, London, 1831.

SOCIETY FOR EQUITABLE ASSURANCES
MH.5.6[6] See SHORT
A short account of the Society for Equitable Assurances on lives and survivorships, established by deed...1777.

SOME
MH.5.19[6] Some considerations on the establishment of the French Strolers; the behaviour of their bully-champions, and other seasonable matters... 8°, [London, 1749.]

SOME
ML.1.2 Some new pieces never before publisht. By the author of the Satyrs upon the Jesuites [i.e. J. Oldham]. 8°, London, 1681.

SOME
MH.5.22[1] Some observations on the present state of Ireland, particularly with relation to the woollen manufacture... [By John Perceval, Earl of Egmont.] 8°, London, 1731.

SOMERVILLE, Mary (1780-1872)
MC.3.13 On the connexion of the physical sciences. 8°, London, 1834.

SOMERVILLE, William (1675-1742)
MK.2.26[1] The chace. A poem. 5th ed. 8°, London, 1767.

SOMERVILLE, William (1675-1742)
MK.2.26[2] Hobbinol, or The rural games. A burlesque poem, in blank verse. 5th ed. 8°, London, 1768.

SOPHOCLES (495 B.C.?-406 B.C.?)
MF.1.20-21 Tragœdiæ quae extant septem; cum versione Latina. Additae sunt lectiones variantes; et notae T. Johnson...2 vols. 8°, Glasguæ, 1745.

SOPHOCLES (495 B.C.?-406 B.C.?)
MM.1.38-40 See ÆSCHYLUS
Tragoediæ selectæ Aeschyli, Sophoclis, Euripidis. Cum duplici interpretatione Latina, una ad verbu, altera carmine. Ennianae interpretationes locoru aliquot Euripidis. 3 vols. 1567.

SOUTH, Robert (1634-1716)
MG.3.24-7 Twelve sermons preached upon several occasions. 4 vols. (Vols. 1, 2, 3rd ed.; vol. 3, 2nd ed.) 8°, London, 1704-15.

SOUTHERNE, Thomas (1660-1746)
ML.1.21-2 Works. 2 vols. 12°, London, 1721.

SPECTATOR
ME.2.24-31 The Spectator. [By J. Addison, Sir R. Steele, and others.] 5th ed. 8 vols. 12°, London, 1720.

SPECTATOR
MC.3.1-8 The Spectator. [By J. Addison, Sir R. Steele, and others.] 8 vols. 12°, London, [c. 1800.]

SPECTATOR
ME.2.41-3 Selections from the Spectator, Tatler, Guardian, and Freeholder: with a preliminary essay by A.L. Barbauld. 3 vols. 12°, London, 1804.

SPECTATOR
ME.5.15 A general index to the Spectators, Tatlers and Guardians. 12°, London, 1757.

SPENCE, William (1783-1860)
MH.5.16[3] Agriculture, the source of the wealth of Britain; a reply to the objections raised by Mr. Mill...and others... 8°, London, 1808.

[ED. NOTE: In the "Principles of Political Economy" (1820 ed. p. 354), Malthus refers to Mill's reply to Spence, dated 1808. Actually a reply was called forth from James Mill.]

SPENCE, William (1783-1860)
MH.5.16[2] Britain independent of commerce; or, Proofs, reduced from an investigation into the true causes of the wealth of nations...2nd ed. 8°, London, 1807.

SPENCE, William (1783-1860)
MB.1.4-6 An introduction to entomology: or Elements of the natural history of insects...By W. Kirby and W. Spence. Vols. 2-4. (Vol. 2, 2nd ed., Vol. 1 wanting.) 8°, London, 1818-26.

SPENSER, Edmund (1552?-1599)
ML.3.19 Il Cavaliero della Croce Rossa, o La leggenda della santita. Poema in dodici canti, recato in verso italiano detto ottava rima da T.J. Mathias. 8°, Napoli, 1826.

SPENSER, Edmund (1552?-1599)
ML.3.4-7 The faerie queene. A new ed., with notes critical and explanatory, by R. Church. 4 vols. 8°, London, 1758.

SPENSER, Edmund (1552?-1599)
ML.3.18 La mutabilità, poema in due canti; recato in verso italiano detto ottava rima da T.J. Mathias. 8°, Napoli, 1827.

SPENSER, Edmund (1552?-1599)
ME.4.33-6 Poetical works, from the text of Mr. Upton, &c. With the life of the author. 8 vols. in 4. (Bell's Edition. The Poets of Great Britain.) 12°, Edinburg, 1778.

SPIRITUAL
MM.4.6-8 The spiritual Quixote; or, The summer's ramble of Mr. Geoffry Wildgoose. A comic romance. [By R. Graves.] (New ed.) 3 vols. 12°, London, 1792.

SPOTSWOOD, John, Abp of St Andrews (1565-1639)
MD.1.2 The history of the Church and State of Scotland, beginning the year...203, and continued to the end of the reign of King James the VI. ...In 7 books...4th ed. corrected...(2 pts.) F°, London, 1677.

SPRAT, Thomas (1635-1713)
MM.5.14 See TRUE
A true account and declaration of the horrid conspiracy against the late King, his present Majesty, and the government...[By T. Sprat.] 2nd ed. (With Copies of the informations and original papers relating to the proof of the horrid conspiracy against the late King... .) (2 pts.) 1685.

STAEHLIN STORCKSBURG, Jakob von (1710-1785)
MH.5.4[1] An account of the new Northern Archipelago, lately discovered by the Russians in the seas of Kamtschatka and Anadir. Translated from the German original [by C. Heidinger, revised by M. Maty]. (With A narrative of the singular adventures of four Russian sailors...By P.L. Le Roy.) 8°, London, 1774.

STAEL-HOLSTEIN, Anne Louise Germaine, baronne de (1766-1817)
ME.1.39 Delphine. Vol. 1. (Vols. 2-4 wanting.) 12°, Paris, 1803.

STANHOPE, Charles Stanhope, 3rd Earl (1753-1816)
MH.4.26[3] A letter to the Right Honourable Edmund Burke: containing a short answer to his late speech on the French Revolution. 2nd ed. 8°, London, 1790.

STANHOPE, George (1660-1728)
MC.3.19-22 A paraphrase and comment upon the Epistles and Gospels appointed to be used in the Church of England...4 vols. (Vols. 1-3, 5th ed.; vol. 4, 4th ed.) 8°, London, 1732.

STANHOPE, George (1660-1728)
MG.3.7 Twelve sermons preached on several occasions. 8°, London, 1727.

STANYAN, Abraham (1669?-1732)
MB.2.30-33 See ETAT.
L'état et les délices de la Suisse...Nouvelle éd. corrigée...[A translation of A. Stanyan's Account of Switzerland, together with Les délices de la Suisse, by A. Ruchat. Ed. by J.G. Altmann.] 4 vols. 1764.

STATE
MH.5.20[4] The state of the Nation for the year 1747, and respecting 1748. Inscribed to a Member of the present Parliament. [By John Carteret, Earl of Granville.] 3rd ed. 8°, London, 1748.

STATIUS, Publius Papinius (45?-96 A.D.)
MG.1.11 Sylvarum lib. V., Thebaidos lib. X11., Achilleidos lib. II. Notis selectissimis in Sylvarum libros Domitii, Morelli, Bernartii...accuratissime illustrati a J. Veenhusen. 8°, Lugd. Batav., 1671.

STEELE, Sir Richard (1672-1729)
ML.1.35 Dramatick works. Containing, Conscious lover, Funeral, Tender husband, Lying lover. 12°, London, 1736.

STEELE, Sir Richard (1672-1729)
MG.5.42 See GUARDIAN
The Guardian. [A periodical by Sir R. Steele, J. Addison and others.] 5th ed. Vol. 1. (March 12 to June 15, 1713.) 1729.

STEELE, Sir Richard (1672-1729)
The lucubrations of Isaac Bickerstaff [i.e. Sir Richard Steele, J. Addison, and others]. [Other editions called The Tatler.] See TATLER.

STEELE, Sir Richard (1672-1729)
For the Spectator, by J. Addison, Sir R. Steele, and others, See SPECTATOR.

STERNE, Laurence (1713-1768)
MB.3.31-2 The life and opinions of Tristram Shandy, gentleman. To which is added The sentimental journey. 2 vols. 8°, London, 1832.

STERNE, Laurence (1713-1768)
MF.2.24-30 The sermons of Mr. Yorick [i.e. L. Sterne]. 7 vols. (Vols. 1, 2, 5th ed.; vols. 3, 4, New ed.; vols. 5-7, called Sermons by the late Rev. Mr. Sterne.) 8°, London, 1763-9.

STEUART, Sir James (1712-1780)
MK.5.1-2 An inquiry into the principles of political œconomy...2 vols. 4°, London, 1767.

[ED. NOTE: In the Preface to his second *Essay*, Malthus refers to "Sir James Steuart" as one of our outstanding writers who dealt with population problems. Malthus notes that Steuart "has explained many parts of the subject of population very ably." (Bk. I, Ch. II.) Reference to Steuart's work is made also in Bk. I, Ch. IX. and Bk. III, Ch. XIV of the later *Essay*.]

STEWART, Dugald (1753-1828)
MF.6.9 Biographical memoirs, of Adam Smith, LL.D., of William Robertson, D.D., and of Thomas Reid, D.D. ... 4°, Edinburgh, 1811.

STEWART, Dugald (1753-1828)
MM.5.8-9 Dissertation first: exhibiting a general view of the progress of metaphysical, ethical, and political philosophy, since the revival of letters in Europe. 2 vols. (From the Supplement to the Encyclopaedia Britannica, Vol. 5i.) 4°, [London, c. 1825.]

[ED. NOTE: Malthus refers to the preliminary dissertation as supplement to E.B. by Dugald Stewart when rediscussing the "Systems of Equality" in the later *Essay*, being Bk. III, the continuation to Ch. III.]

STEWART, Dugald (1753-1828)
ME.6.13 Philosophical essays. 4°, Edinburgh, 1810.

STILLINGFLEET, Benjamin (1702-1771)
MH.4.17 See LINNÆUS, Carl
Miscellaneous tracts relating to natural history, husbandry, and physick...[Dissertations from Amœnitates academicæ, by C. Linnæus; translated.] By B. Stillingfleet. 3rd ed. 1775.

STONECASTLE, Henry, pseud.
See BAKER, Henry.

STRABO (63 B.C.?-21 A.D.)
MA.7.3-4 Strabonis rerum geographicarum libri XVII. Græce et Latine...Codicum Mss. collationem annotationes et tabulas geographicas adjecit T. Falconer...2 vols. F°, Oxonii, 1807.

STRAFFORD, Thomas Wentworth, 1st Earl of (1593-1641)
MA.7.1-2 See KNOWLER, William
The Earl of Strafforde's letters and despatches, with an essay towards his life by Sir George Radcliffe...By W. Knowler. 2 vols. 1739.

SUETONIUS TRANQUILLUS, Gaius (65?-?)
MI.1.19 Opera omnia quæ extant, interpretatione et notis illustravit A. Babelonius... 8°, Londini, 1718.

SULLY, Maximilien de Béthune, duc de (1560-1641)
MF.2.16-23 Mémoires, mis en ordre: avec des remarques. Par M.L.D.L.D.L. Nouvelle éd., revûe & corrigée. 8 vols. 12°, Londres, 1752.

SULPICIUS SEVERUS (d. 410?)
MF.1.24 Sulpicii Severi quæ exstant opera omnia...cum notis J. Vorstii...ex recensione...J. Clerici. 8°, Lipsiæ, 1719.

SUMNER, Charles Richard, Bp of Winchester (1790-1874)
ML.3.29 The ministerial character of Christ, practically considered. 8°, London, 1824.

SUR
MI.4.17 Sur la législation et le commerce des grains. [By J. Necker.] 2e éd. 2 vols. in 1. 8°, Paris, 1775.

SWIFT, Jonathan (1667-1745)
MH.5.19[8] A libel on Dr. D—-ny, and a certain Great Lord [i.e. on Doctor Delany, occasioned by his 'Epistle to...John Lord Carteret']. By Dr. Sw—t [Swift]... 8°, London, 1730.

SWIFT, Jonathan (1667-1745)
MK.5.22 See MISCELLANIES
Miscellanies. [By J. Arbuthnot, A. Pope, J. Swift, and others.] Vol. 2. 1727.

SWIFT, Jonathan (1667-1745)
MB.6.62-81 Works...With some account of the author's life, and notes...by J. Hawkesworth. 20 vols. 12°, London, 1765-7.

SWINBURNE, Henry (1743-1803)
MA.3.9-12 Travels in the Two Sicilies, in the years 1777, 1778, 1779, and 1780. 2nd ed. 4 vols. 8°, London, 1790.

T

WILLIAM TEMPLE

TABLEAU
MB.2.35-8 Tableau de Paris. [By L.S. Mercier.] Nouvelle éd., corrigée et augmentée. Vols. 1-4. (Vols. 5-12 wanting.) 12°, Amsterdam, 1782-4.

TACHARD, Guy (1650?-1712)
MF.7.1 Dictionnaire nouveau françois-latin... 4°, Paris, 1689.

TACITUS, Gaius Cornelius (55?-120)
MI.2.17-18 Opera, ex recensione I.A. Ernesti cum notis integris I. Lipsii et I.F. Gronovii quibus et suas adiecit. 2 vols. 8°, Lipsiae, 1752.

TACITUS, Gaius Cornelius (55?-120)
MF.1.14 C. Cornelii Taciti quæ exstant opera; juxta accuratissimam D. Lallemant editionem. 12°, Parisiis, 1779.

TACITUS, Gaius Cornelius (55?-120)
ML.3.13 A treatise on the situation, manners, and inhabitants of Germany; and the life of Agricola; translated into English by J. Aikin. 8°, Warrington, 1777.

[ED. NOTE: In Bk. I, Ch. VI. of the later *Essay*, entitled "Checks to Population among the ancient inhabitants of the North of Europe,"

Malthus frequently refers to "Tacitus de Moribus Germanorum," which is included in the previous "Opera" as well as this translation. He also refers to the same treatise when discussing the "Checks to Population among the Romans." (Bk. I, Ch. XIV.]

TALLEYRAND-PERIGORD, Charles Maurice de, Prince of Benevento (1754-1838)

MH.3.17[2] Mémoire sur les relations commerciales des Etats-Unis avec l'Angleterre. Suivi d'un essai... 8°, Londres, 1805.

[ED. NOTE: The financial laws presented by Talleyrand, appointed president of the provisional government (1814), were under heavy criticism. At the same time, the theories of Malthus on the nature of rent were also criticized by an anonymous English writer.]

TASSO, Torquato (1544-1595)

MJ.1.10 Aminta; favola boscareccia. 8°, Glasgua, 1753.

TASSO, Torquato (1544-1595)

MM.1.34-5 La Gerusalemme liberata. 2 vols. 16°, Firenze, 1813.

TASSO, Torquato (1544-1595)

MI.1.1 Godfrey of Bulloigne: or The recovery of Jerusalem. Done into English heroical verse, by E. Fairfax. Together with the life of the said Godfrey. 8°, London, 1687.

TATLER

ME.5.15 A general index to the Spectators, Tatlers and Guardians. 12°, London, 1757.

TATLER

ME.5.8-11 The lucubrations of Isaac Bickerstaff Esq. [i.e. Sir Richard Steele, J. Addison, and others]; revised and corrected by the author. (The Tatler.) 4 vols. 12°, London, 1710-16.

TATLER

ME.5.12-14 The lucubrations of Isaac Bickerstaff Esq. [i.e. Sir Richard Steele, J. Addison, and others]; revised and corrected by the author. (The Tatler.) Vols. 1-3. 12°, London, 1712-13.

TATLER

MG.5.43-5 The lucubrations of Isaac Bickerstaff Esq. [i.e. Sir Richard Steele, J. Addison, and others]; revised and corrected by the author. Vols. 2-4. (Vols. 1, 5 wanting.) (The Tatler, August 6, 1709 - January 1710.) 8°, London, 1733.

TATLER
ME.2.41-3 Selections from the Spectator, Tatler, Guardian, and Freeholder: with a preliminary essay by A.L. Barbauld. 3 vols. 12°, London, 1804.

TAYLOR, Sir Henry (1800-1886)
MB.2.16-17 Philip van Artevelde; a dramatic romance. 2 vols. 8°, London, 1834.

TAYLOR, John, LL.D. (1704-1766)
MF.6.3 Elements of the civil law. 2nd ed. 4°, London, [1756].

TAYLOR, John, of Norwich (1694-1761)
ML.4.19 A paraphrase with notes on the Epistle to the Romans... 4°, London, 1745.

TEMMINCK, Coenraad Jacob (1778-1858)
ME.3.16-17, 18-19 [2 copies.] Manuel d'ornithologie...2e éd. considérablement augmentée...Vols. 1, 2. (Vols. 3, 4 wanting from both sets.) 8°, Paris, 1820.

TEMPLE, Sir William (1628-1699)
MC.7.1-2 Works. To which is prefixed, The life and character of Sir William Temple. Written by a particular friend [i.e. Lady Giffard]. 2 vols. F°, London, 1740.

[ED. NOTE: Discussing the commercial system of Holland, Malthus refers in the later *Essay*, to the opinion of Sir William Temple who was in that country "as early as 1669 and 1670," and who considered that their trade had started to decay. (Bk. III, Ch. IX.)]

TEMPLE, William Johnston (1739-1796)
MA.1.26 See MORAL
Moral and historical memoirs. [By W.J. Temple.] 1779.

TEN
MH.4.24[6] Ten minutes reflection on the late events in France. Recommended by a plain man to his fellow citizens. 8°, London, 1792.

TERENTIUS, Publius, Afer (190-159 B.C)
MF.1.11-13 Les comédies; avec la traduction et les remarques de Madame Dacier. Nouvelle éd. corrigée...3 vols. 12°, Hambourg, 1732.

TERENTIUS, Publius, Afer (190-159 B.C)
MI.3.2 Comoediae ad codices Mss. et optimas editiones recognovit, varietate lectionis commentario perpetuo... instruxit F.C.G. Perlet...8°, Lipsiae, 1821.

TERTULLIANUS, Quintus Septimius Florens (160?-222?)
MG.1.5 Apologeticus...recognitus, castigatus, emendatus ut et perpetuo commentario...studio & industria S. Havercampi... (Greek & Latin.) (With J.L. Mosheim, Disquisitio chronologico-critica de vera aetate Apologetici...) (2 pts.) 8°, Lugduni Batavorum, 1718-20.

TERTULLIANUS, Quintus Septimius Florens (160?-222?)
MA.7.16 Tertulliani omniloquium alphabeticum rationale, sive Tertulliani opera omnia...Autore Carolo Moreau. Vol. 2. (Vols. 1, 3 wanting.) F°, Parisiis, 1657.

THELWALL, John (1764-1834)
MH.5.25^{5} The rights of nature, against the usurpations of establishments. A series of letters...on the state of public affairs, and the recent effusions of...E. Burke. Letter the 1st. 8°, London, 1796.

THEOCRITUS (fl. 283-263? B.C.)
MJ.2.37 Theocriti quae extant. Ex editione D. Heinsii expressa. (Greek & Latin.) 8°, Glasguae, 1746.

THINKS
MB.4.23-4 Thinks-I-to-myself. A serio-ludicro, tragico-comico tale, written by Thinks-I-to-myself who? [i.e. E. Nares]...9th ed. 2 vols. 12°, London, 1813.

THIRD
ME.2.7^{3} A third letter to the people of England. On liberty, taxes, and the application of public money. [By J. Shebbeare.] 2nd ed. 8°, London, 1756.

THOMAS, Antoine Léonard (1732-1785)
MK.2.5^{2} Esprit, maximes et principes de Thomas, de l'Académie Française. 8°, Paris, 1788.

THOMAS, Antoine Léonard (1732-1785)
MK.2.5^{1} Essai sur le caractère, les moeurs et l'esprit des femmes dans les différens siècles. 12°, Amsterdam, 1772.

THOMPSON, Benjamin (1776-1816)
MC.1.2-7 See GERMAN
The German theatre, translated by B. Thompson. 4th ed. 6 vols. 1811.

THOMSON, James (1700-1748)
ME.1.44 Il Castello dell'Ozio; poema in duo canti, recato in verso italiano...da T.J. Mathias. 8°, Napoli, 1826.

THOMSON, James (1700-1748)
ME.4.40 Poetical works. With his last corrections and improvements. With the life of the author. 2 vols. in 1. (Bell's Edition. The Poets of Great Britain.) 12°, Edinburg, 1777.

THOMSON, James (1700-1748)
ML.2.27 Seasons. [Imperfect: wants title-page and all before sign. B.] 8°, [London? 1790?]

THOMSON, John
ME.2.16 The universal calculator; or, The merchant's, tradesman's, and family's assistant...New ed. 12°, Edinburgh, 1793.

THORNTON, Bonnell (1724-1768)
ME.4.16-19 See CONNOISSEUR
The Connoisseur. By Mr. Town, critic and censor-general [i.e. G. Colman and B. Thornton]. [A periodical, 1754-6.] 2nd ed. 4 vols. 1755-7.

THOUGHTS
MH.4.25[6] Thoughts on the causes of the present failures. [By W. Roscoe.] 3rd ed. 8°, London, 1793.

THOUGHTS
MH.4.24[5] Thoughts on the defence of these Kingdoms. (2 pts.) 8°, London, 1796.

THOUGHTS
MJ.1.20[3] Thoughts on the importance of the manners of the great to general society. [By Hannah More.] 8°, London, 1788.

THREE
MH.4.20 Three tracts on the corn-trade and corn-laws...To which is added a supplement...[By C. Smith.] 8°, London, 1766.

THUCYDIDES (471-402 B.C.)
MJ.2.29-36 Bellum Peloponnesiacum. Ex editione Wassii et Dukeri. (Greek & Latin.) 8 vols. 8°, Glasguae, 1759.

THUCYDIDES (471-402 B.C.)
MD.1.3 Eight bookes of the Peloponnesian Warre. Interpreted...out of the Greeke by T. Hobbes. F°, London, 1629.

THUCYDIDES (471-402 B.C.)
MH.2.21-2 The history of the Grecian War: in 8 books. Faithfully translated...by T. Hobbes. 3rd ed., corrected and amended. 2 vols. 8°, London, 1723.

TIBULLUS, Albius (fl. 54?-19)
MI.3.1 Albii Tibulli carmina libri tres cum libro quarto Sulpiciae et aliorum. C.G. Heynii ed. 4[a] nunc aucta notis et observationibus E.C.F. Wunderichii. (With Supplementum... edidit L. Dissenius.) (3 pts.) 8°, Lipsiae, 1817-19.

TICKELL, Richard (1751-1793)
MK.5.15[6] See EPISTLE
Epistle from the Honourable Charles Fox, partridge-shooting, to the Honourable John Townshend, cruising. [By R. Tickell.] 1779.

TICKELL, Richard (1751-1793)
ML.3.3 See PROBATIONARY
Probationary odes for the laureatship: with a preliminary discourse, by Sir John Hawkins. [Satirical parodies on Sir J. Hawkins and other Tories. By R. Tickell and others.] 1785.

TIMBERLAKE, Henry (d. 1626)
MA.3.30 The memoirs of Lieut. Henry Timberlake, who accompanied the three Cherokee Indians to England in the year 1762... 8°, London, 1765.

TINDAL, Nicholas (1687-1774)
MD.1.6-7 Remarques historiques et critiques sur l'Histoire d'Angleterre de Mr. de Rapin Thoyras, par N. Tindal. Et Abrégé historique du recueil des acts publics d'Angleterre de T. Rymer; par Mr. de Rapin Thoyras...2 vols. 4°, La Haye, 1733.

TISSOT, Samuel Auguste André David (1728-1797)
MF.2.9[2] De la santé des gens de lettres. 8°, Lausanne, 1768.

TISSOT, Samuel Auguste André David (1728-1797)
MF.2.9[1] Essai sur les maladies des gens du monde. 8°, Lausanne, 1770.

TOMLINE, George Pretyman, Bp of Winchester (1750-1827)
ML.3.27-8 Elements of Christian theology...3rd ed. 2 vols. 8°, London, 1800.

TOMLINS, Sir Thomas Edlyne (1762-1841)
MG.6.3-4 The law-dictionary: explaining the rise, progress, and present state of the British law...3rd ed., with considerable additions. 2 vols. 4°, London, 1820.

TOOKE, John Horne (1736-1812)
MH.4.15[1] A letter to a friend on the reported marriage of His Royal Highness the Prince of Wales. 8°, London, 1787.

TOOKE, John Horne (1736-1812)
MH.5.2[3] Two pairs of portraits, presented to all the unbiassed electors of Great-Britain; and especially to the electors of Westminster. 8°, London, 1788.

TOOKE, Thomas (1774-1858)
MB.1.2 Thoughts and details of the high and low prices of the thirty years, from 1793 to 1822. In 4 pts. 2nd ed. 8°, London, 1824.

[ED. NOTE: Malthus refers to this work in the later *Essay*, Bk. III, Ch. XII. entitled: "Of Corn-Laws. Restrictions upon Importation."]

TOPHAM, Edward (1751-1820)
ME.2.1 See LETTERS
Letters from Edinburgh; written in the years 1774 and 1775...[By E. Topham.] 1776.

TOPHAM, Edward (1751-1820)
MM.3.17 The life of the late John Elwes, Esquire; member in three successive Parliaments for Berkshire...7th ed. 8°, London, 1790.

TOPHAM, Edward (1751-1820)
MF.1.7 See POETRY
The poetry of the world. [Ed. by E. Topham.] 2 vols. in 1. 1788.

TORCY, Jean Baptiste Colbert, marquis de
See COLBERT, Jean Baptiste, Marquis of Torcy.

TOUR
MH.5.4[3] A tour in Ireland in 1775. [By R. Twiss.] 8°, London, 1776.

TOUR
ML.5.17 A tour through the South of England, Wales, and part of Ireland, made during the summer of 1791. [By E.D. Clarke.] 8°, London, 1793.

TOUR
MB.6.53[2] A tour to Ermenonville; containing besides an account of...Chantilly...a particular description of the tomb of J.J. Rousseau... 8°, London, 1785.

TOWERS, Joseph (1737-1799)
MI.2.2[8] See DIALOGUE
A dialogue between an associator and a well-informed Englishman, on the grounds of the late associations, and the commencement of a war with France. [By J. Towers.] 1793.

TOWERS, Joseph (1737-1799)
MH.4.26[1] Thoughts on the commencement of a new Parliament ... 8°, London, 1790.

TOWN, Mr, pseud.
See COLMAN, George, and THORNTON, Bonnell.

TOWNSEND, Joseph (1739-1816)
ML.5.2-4 A journey through Spain in the years 1786 and 1787; with particular attention to the agriculture, manufactures, commerce, population, taxes, and revenue of that country... 2nd ed., with additions and corrections. 3 vols. 8°, London, 1792.

[ED. NOTE: Malthus refers to Townsend in the Preface to the second edition of the *Essay*. He later refers to his "Dissertation on the Poor Laws," 2nd ed., of 1787 (Bk. IV, Ch. X, XI.), as well as to his "Journey Through Spain." Townsend was actually a precursor of Malthus since he considered similarly the problem of population and was also opposed to the Poor Laws. Regarding the monograph on Spain, Malthus wrote: ·"..I refer the reader to the valuable and entertaining travels of Mr. Townsend in that country, in which he will often find the principle of population very happily illustrated." (Bk. II, Ch. VI.)]

TRAVELS
MB.2.14-15 Travels of an Irish gentleman in search of a religion...[By T. Moore.] 2 vols. 8°, London, 1833.

TREATISE
MH.5.17[4] A treatise concerning the Militia, in 4 sections ...By C.S. [i.e. Charles Sackville, Duke of Dorset.] 8°, London, 1752.

TREATISE
MH.1.20 A treatise on the police of the Metropolis...By a magistrate [i.e. P. Colquhoun]. 3rd ed., revised and enlarged. 8°, London, 1796.

TREATY
MH.5.20[7] The Treaty of Seville [between England, France and Spain], and the measures that have been taken for the four last years, impartially considered. In a letter to a friend. [Signed A.B.] 8°, London, 1730.

TRENCHARD, John (1662-1723)
MM.4.10-12 See INDEPENDENT
The Independent Whig: or, A defence of primitive Christianity ...[By J. Trenchard and T. Gordon.] (Nos. 1-74.) 6th ed. With additions and amendments. 3 vols. 1735.

TRENT, Council of

MK.2.29 See CATECHISM

The Catechism for the curats, compos'd by the decree of the Council of Trent, and publish'd by command of Pope Pius the Fifth. Faithfully translated into English. 1687.

TREVELYAN, Sir Charles Edward, 1st Bart (1807-1886)

MK.5.21 A report upon the inland customs and town-duties of the Bengal Presidency. 4°, Calcutta, 1834.

TRIAL

MH.5.24[5] The trial of Mrs. Mary Reed, upon the charge of poisoning her husband, at Berkeley, in Gloucestershire, in April, 1794... 8°, [London, 1796.]

TROTTER, Alexander

MH.4.1 Observations on the financial position and credit of such of the states of the North American Union as have contracted public debts... 8°, London, 1839.*

TRUE

MM.5.14 A true account and declaration of the horrid conspiracy against the late King, his present Majesty, and the government...[By T. Sprat.] 2nd ed. (With Copies of the informations and original papers relating to the proof of the horrid conspiracy against the late King...) (2 pts.) 4°, In the Savoy, 1685.

TRYALS

MH.4.9-14 Tryals for high-treason, and other crimes. With proceedings on Bills of Attainder, and impeachments...6 vols. 8°, London, 1720.

TSCHIFFELI, Johann Rudolf (1716-1780)

MG.5.24[2] Lettres sur la nourriture des bestiaux à l'étable. 8°, Berne, 1775.

TUCKER, Abraham (1705-1774)

MM.3.14 Freewill, foreknowledge and fate. A fragment. By Edward Search, Esq; [i.e. Abraham Tucker]. 8°, London, 1763.

TUCKER, George (1775-1861)

MB.7.45 Essays on various subjects of taste, morals, and national policy. [Pp. 305-36: 'On the theory of Malthus.'] 8°, Georgetown, D.C., 1822.

TUCKER, Josiah (1712-1799)

MH.5.6[4] An humble address and earnest appeal to those...who...are ablest to judge, and fittest to decide, whether a connection with, or separation from the Continental colonies of America, be most for the national advantage... 2nd ed., corrected. 8°, Gloucester, 1775.

[ED. NOTE: In Bk. IV, Ch. XI. of the later *Essay*, Malthus refers to various plans for improving the condition of the poor and on "Dean Tucker's" remarks that there should be only voluntary association to this effect. In this address, Tucker proposed that the colonies be "separate from England, because trade laws were the only link, and that link was rotten." (Palgrave.) In 1755 Tucker published his great work, "Elements of Commerce and Theory of Taxes."]

TUCKER, Josiah (1712-1799)
MH.4.29[7] Reflections on the present matters in dispute between Great Britain and Ireland... 8°, London, 1785.

TURGOT, Anne Robert Jacques (1727-1784)
MA.4.12-20 Oeuvres, précédées et accompagnées de mémoires et de notes sur sa vie, son administration et ses ouvrages. 9 vols. (Vol.1, 2e éd.) 8°, Paris, 1808-11.

[ED. NOTE: Malthus refers to this very edition of Turgot's "Oeuvres" in the later *Essay*, Bk. III, Ch. XII: "Of Corn Laws. Restrictions upon Importation."]

TURLUPINUS DE TURLUPINIS, Nicodemus, pseud.
ML.2.26 Anti-Choppinus, imo potius Epistola congratulatoria M. Nicodemi Turlupini de Turlupinis, a M. Renatum Choppinum de Choppinis... 8°, Carnuti (1592).

TWISS, Richard (1747-1821)
MH.5.4[3] See TOUR
A tour in Ireland in 1775. [By R. Twiss.] 1776.

TWO
MH.4.21[3] Two apologetical odes, and an elegy. [By J. Courtenay.] (Privately pr.) 8°, London, 1808.

U

ULLOA, Antonio de (1716-1795)
ML.4.12-13 Voyage historique de l'Amérique Méridionale fait par ordre du Roi d'Espagne, par George Juan et par Antoine de Ulloa...[Translated by E. Mauvillon.] 2 vols. 4°, Amsterdam, 1752.

[ED. NOTE: Entered usually as a narration of Juan and Ulloa, this title actually pertains only to the latter author. Malthus refers to this voyage in the later *Essay*, Bk. I, Ch. IV: "Of the Checks to Population among American Indians," and in his "General Deductions" (Bk. II, Ch. XIII.)]

URE, Andrew (1778-1857)
MB.7.34 A dictionary of chemistry and mineralogy, with their applications. 4th ed., with numerous improvements. 8°, London, 1830.

V

VOLTAIRE

VALERIUS FLACCUS, Gaius (1st C.)
MK.2.25 Argonauticon libri VIII. Ex recensione N. Heinsii et P. Burmanni. 8°, Patavii, 1720.

VALERIUS FLACCUS, Gaius (1st C.)
MI.1.20 Argonauticon libri VIII ad optimas editiones collati præ mittitur notitia literaria accedit index studiis Societatis Bipontinæ. Ed. accurata. 8°, Biponti, 1786.

VANDERSTRAETEN Ferdinand
MH.4.22[5] A supplement to the work entitled Improved agriculture, &c. [Wants title-page.] 8°, [London, 1816].

VARIE
MC.7.9 Varie vedute di Roma Antica, e Moderna disegnate e intagliate da celebri autori. [Plates.] Oblong F°, Roma, 1748.

VEIRAS, Denis (fl. 1675?)
MB.3.12 See HISTOIRE
Histoire des Sévarambes, peuples qui habitent une partie du troisiéme continent, communément apellé la Terre australe... [By D. Veiras.] Nouvelle éd., corrigée & augmentée. 2 vols. in 1. 1715-16.

VERNON, Edward (1684-1757)
MH.5.18[2] Original papers relating to the Expedition to Carthagena. (By E. Vernon.) 8°, [London] 1744.

VERNON, Edward (1684-1757)
MH.5.18[3] Original papers relating to the Expedition to the Island of Cuba. (By E. Vernon.) 8°, London, 1744.

VERNON, Edward (1684-1757)
MH.5.18[1] Original papers relating to the Expedition to Panama. (By E. Vernon.) 8°, London, 1744.

VERRAL, William
MK.3.19 A complete system of cookery. 8°, London, 1759.

VERRI, Alessandro, conte (1741-1816)
ME.4.20-21 Le notti romane. 2 vols. 12°, Parigi, 1820.

VERTOT, René Aubert de (1655-1735)
MK.2.19-21 Histoire des révolutions arrivées dans le gouvernement de la République Romaine. 3e éd. augmentée. 3 vols. 12°, La Haye, 1721.

VERTOT, René Aubert de (1655-1735)
MK.1.20 Origine de la grandeur de la Cour de Rome: et de la nomination aux évechés et aux abbaïes de France. 12°, La Haye, 1737.

VINDICATION
A vindication of the rights of woman (Author of)
See GODWIN, Mary Wollstonecraft.

VOGHT, Caspar, Baron von (1752-1839)
MH.3.22[2] Account of the management of the poor in Hamburgh, since the year 1788... 8°, London, 1796.

[ED. NOTE: Malthus refers to this work in his later *Essay*, Bk. IV, Ch. IV.]

VOLTAIRE, François Marie Arouet de (1694-1778)
MA.4.9 See DICTIONNAIRE
Dictionnaire philosophique, portatif. [By F.M.A. de Voltaire.] 1765.

VOLTAIRE, François Marie Arouet de (1694-1778)
MK.4.5 La Henriade. 2e éd. revûe, corrigée, & augmentée de remarques critiques sur cet ouvrage. 8°, Londres, 1728.

VOLTAIRE, François Marie Arouet de (1694-1778)
ME.2.18 The history of Charles XII, King of Sweden. Translated from the French. 8th ed. 12°, London, 1755.

VOLTAIRE, François Marie Arouet de (1694-1778)
MB.3.17 See LETTRES
Lettres écrites de Londres sur les Anglois et autres sujets. Par M.D.V*** [i.e.Voltaire]. 1734.

VOLTAIRE, François Marie Arouet de (1694-1778)
MA.2.32-4 Romans. 3 vols. 8°, Paris, 1821.

VOLTAIRE, François Marie Arouet de (1694-1778)
MI.3.23-30 Théâtre, nouvelle édition, avec des notes. 8 vols. 8°, Paris, an 6 [1798].

VUES
MK.2.12 Vues patriotiques sur l'éducation du peuple, tant des villes que de la compagne...[By L. Philipon de la Madelaine.] 12°, Lyon, 1783.

WADE, John (1788-1875)
MB.6.57 History of the middle and working classes...2nd ed. 8°, London, 1834.

WAKEFIELD, Gilbert (1756-1801)
ML.5.29[5] An address to the inhabitants of Nottingham occasioned by a letter lately sent to the Mayor...of that town... 8°, London, 1789.

WAKEFIELD, Gilbert (1756-1801)
ML.5.29[7] An address to the Right Reverend Dr. Samuel Horsley, Bishop of St. David's, on the subject of an apology for the liturgy and clergy of the Church of England. 8°, Birmingham, 1790.

WAKEFIELD, Gilbert (1756-1801)
ML.5.29[8] See COUNTRY
A country curate's observations on the advertizement...from the Leeds Clergy, relative to the Test Act, &c. ...[By G. Wakefield?] [1790.]

WAKEFIELD, Gilbert (1756-1801)
ML.5.29[1] An essay on inspiration: considered chiefly with respect to the Evangelists. 8°, Warrington, 1781.

WAKEFIELD, Gilbert (1756-1801)
MH.4.24[7] A letter to William Wilberforce, Esq., on the subject of his late publication. 8°, London, 1797.

WAKEFIELD, Gilbert (1756-1801)
ML.5.29^{2} A new translation of the First Epistle of Paul the Apostle to the Thessalonians offered to the public as a specimen of an intended version of the whole New Testament. 8°, Warrington, 1781.

WAKEFIELD, Gilbert (1756-1801)
ML.5.29^{3} A new translation of those parts only of the New Testament, which are wrongly translated in our common version. 8°, London, 1789.

WAKEFIELD, Gilbert (1756-1801)
ML.5.29^{9} See REFLECTIONS
Reflections on faith: in which it is shewn, that no difference of religious opinion is any reasonable grounds of disrespect among men and especially among Christians. By Philanthropos [i.e. G. Wakefield?]. New ed. ...(2 pts.) 1790.

WAKEFIELD, Gilbert (1756-1801)
ML.5.29^{6} Remarks on Dr. Horsley's ordination-sermon; in a letter to the Lord Bishop of Gloucester. 8°, London, 1788.

WAKEFIELD, Gilbert (1756-1801)
ML.5.29^{4} Remarks on the internal evidences of the Christian religion. 8°, Warrington, 1789.

WAKEFIELD, Gilbert (1756-1801)
MI.2.2^{2} A reply to some parts of the Bishop of Landaff's [i.e. R. Watson's] Address to the people of Great Britain. 8°, London, 1798.

WALLACE, Robert (1697-1771)
MH.1.21 See DISSERTATION
A dissertation on the numbers of mankind in antient and modern times: in which the superior populousness of antiquity is maintained...[By R. Wallace.] 1753.

[ED. NOTE: Malthus refers to Wallace as being among the four authors whose writings conduced him to The Principle of Population (Preface to the second edition of the *Essay*). He also refers to this Treatise in Bk. I, Ch. XIV: "Of the Checks to Population among the Romans," and discusses Wallace's arguments in Bk. III, Ch. I. & III: "Of Systems of Equality. Wallace, Condorcet." Reference to Wallace is also made in Malthus's Appendix to the later *Essay*, while in the 1798 first edition he discusses "Mr. Wallace's error of supposing that the difficulty arising from population is at a great distance."]

WALLER, Edmund (1606-1687)
ME.4.42 Poetical works. From Mr. Fenton's quarto edit. 1729. With the life of the author. 2 vols. in 1. (Bell's Edition. The Poets of Great Britain.) 12°, Edinburg, 1777.

WALLS, Edward
MH.4.21^{6} A letter to the Right Honourable Sir Joseph Banks. 2nd ed., with considerable additions. 8°, Louth [1804].

WALPOLE, Horace, 4th Earl of Orford (1717-1797)
MK.3.21 A catalogue of the royal and noble authors of England, with lists of their works. (By H. Walpole.) New ed. 8°, Edinburgh, 1796.

WALPOLE OF WOLTERTON, Horatio Walpole, 1st Baron (1678-1757)
MH.5.20^{8} See CASE
The case of the Hessian forces, in the pay of Great Britain, impartially and freely examined...[By Horatio, Lord Walpole.] 1731.

WALTON, Izaak (1593-1683)
MA.3.33-4 The lives of Dr. John Donne; Sir Henry Wotton; Mr. Richard Hooker; Mr. George Herbert; and Dr. Robert Sanderson ...With notes, and the life of the author. By T. Zouch. 3rd ed. 2 vols. 8°, York, 1817.

WARBURTON, William, Bp of Gloucester (1698-1779)
MC.4.1-5 The divine legation of Moses demonstrated. In 9 books. 5 vols. (Vols. 1, 2, 5th ed...vols. 3-5, 4th ed.) 8°, London, 1765-6.

WATSON, Richard, Bp of Llandaff (1737-1816)
MI.2.2^{1} An address to the people of Great Britain. 12th ed. 8°, London, 1798.

WATSON, Richard, Bp of Llandaff (1737-1816)
MB.6.47-51 Chemical essays. 5 vols. (Vols. 1, 2, 4th ed.; vols. 3, 4, 3rd ed.) 8°, London, 1785-9.

WATSON, Richard, Bp of Llandaff (1737-1816)
MM.2.17-22 See COLLECTION
A collection of theological tracts. [Ed.] By R. Watson. 6 vols. 1785.

WATTS, Isaac (1674-1748)
ME.2.5 The improvement of the mind: or, A supplement to the art of logick...(Pt. 1.) 8°, London, 1741.

WATTS, Isaac (1674-1748)
ME.2.4 Logick: or, The right use of reason in the enquiry after truth...7th ed., corrected. 8°, London, 1740.

WATTS, Isaac (1674-1748)
MG.5.33 A short view of the whole Scripture history: with a continuation of the Jewish affairs...19th ed. 12°, London, 1800.

WEBB, Daniel (1719?-1798)
MK.2.33 Remarks on the beauties of poetry. 8°, London, 1762.

WELDON, Sir Anthony (16th C.-1649?)
ME.5.16^{3} See PERFECT
A perfect description of the people and country of Scotland. [A later ed. of 'Terrible news from Scotland,' probably written by Sir A. Weldon.] 1659.

WESLEY, John (1703-1791)
MF.7.10 Explanatory notes upon the New Testament. [With the text.] 4°, London, 1757.

WEST, Gilbert (1703-1756)
MH.5.12^{5} See OBSERVATIONS
Observations on the Conversion and Apostleship of St. Paul. In a letter to Gilbert West, Esq. [By George, Lord Lyttelton.] New ed. 1777.

WEST INDIAN
MI.4.7^{2} The West Indian: a comedy. As it is performed at the Theatre-Royal in Drury-Lane. By the author of The Brothers [R. Cumberland]. 8°, London, 1771.

WEYLAND, John (1774-1854)
MH.3.22^{7} Observations on Mr. Whitbread's Poor Bill, and on the population of England... 8°, London, 1807.

WEYLAND, John (1774-1854)
MH.2.24 The principles of population and production, as they are affected by the progress of society; with a view to moral and political consequences. 8°, London, 1816.

[ED. NOTE: In 1817 Malthus responded to the attack of Weyland in his fifth edition of the *Essay*, in the Appendix under "1817."]

WHEWELL, William (1794-1866)
MC.4.21 Astronomy and general physics considered with reference to natural theology. (Bridgewater Treatises, 3.) 8°, London, 1833.

WHISTLECRAFT, William and Robert, pseud.
See FRERE, Rt. Hon. John Hookham.

WHITBREAD, Samuel (1785-1815)
MH.3.22^{5} Substance of a speech on the Poor Laws: delivered in the House of Commons...1807... 8°, London, 1807.

[ED. NOTE: The bill of 1807 which became the Poor Laws was a hot topic in Malthus's Discussions. The speech of Whitbread mentions Malthus's influence in opposition to the Poor Laws.]

WHITE, Gilbert (1720-1793)
MF.7.16 The natural history and antiquities of Selborne, in the County of Southampton...New ed., with engravings. 4°, London, 1813.

WHITE, Gilbert (1720-1793)
MK.2.27 A naturalist's calendar, with observations in various branches of natural history; extracted from the papers of the late G. White. 8°, London, 1795.

WHITE, Henry Kirke (1785-1806)
ML.2.7 The life and remains of Henry Kirke White, late of St. John's College, Cambridge. 12°, London [1825].

WHITE, Joseph (1745-1814)
MH.5.11[4] A sermon preached before the University of Oxford, July 4, 1784... 8°, London, 1785.

WHITE, Joseph (1745-1814)
MG.3.6 Sermons preached before the University of Oxford, in the year 1784, at the lecture founded by the Rev. John Bampton. 2nd ed. ...8°, London, 1785.

WHITE, Joseph Blanco (1775-1841)
MB.6.26 Letters from Spain. By Don Leucadio Doblado [i.e. J. Blanco White]. 2nd ed. Revised and corrected by the author. 8°, London, 1825.

WHITE, Joseph Blanco (1775-1841)
MB.6.56 See SECOND
Second travels of an Irish gentleman in search of a religion...[By J. Blanco White.] 2 vols. in 1. 1833.

WHITEHEAD, William (1715-1785)
MI.4.9[1] The Roman father, a tragedy. As it is acted at the Theatre Royal in Drury-Lane, by His Majesty's servants. 2nd ed. 8°, London, 1750.

WILLETT, Edward
MH.4.15[4] Letters addressed to Mrs. Bellamy, occasioned by her apology. 8°, London [1785].

WILLIAMS, David (1738-1816)
MH.5.2[2] See ROYAL
Royal recollections on a tour to Cheltenham, Gloucester, Worcester, and places adjacent, in the year 1788. [By D. Williams.] 9th ed. 1788.

WILLIAMSON, William
MH.4.27[9] Trial of an action for thirty seven thousand pounds, brought by Paul Benfield, Esq; against Samuel Petrie, Esq; upon a charge of bribery. Tried at Salisbury... 1782... 8°, London, 1782.

WILSON, Jasper, pseud.
See CURRIE, James.

WINDHAM, Rt. Hon. William (1750-1810?)
MH.1.24[1] See BIOGRAPHICAL
A biographical memoir of the Right Honourable William Windham. [By E. Malone.] 1810.

WINDHAM, Rt. Hon. William (1750-1810?)
MH.4.21[4] See ODE
An ode, addressed to the Right Honourable William Windham in 1778. (Not published.) London, 1810.

WINDISCH-GRAETZ, Joseph Niklas, Graf von (1744-1802)
ML.3.14[1] Discours dans lequel on examine les deux questions suivantes: 1°. Un monarque a-t-il le droit de changer de son chef une constitution évidemment vicieuse? 2°. Est-il prudent à lui, est-il de son intérêt de l'entreprendre?... 8°, [Brussels?] 1789.

WINDISCH-GRAETZ, Joseph Niklas, Graf von (1744-1802)
ML.3.14[3] Objections aux sociétés secretes. 8°, [Brussels?] 1789.

WINDISCH-GRAETZ, Joseph Niklas, Graf von (1744-1802)
ML.3.14[2] See LETTRE
Lettre sur le Discours de M. Le Comte de Windisgraetz... addressée à Monsieur l'Abbé de Bon Conseil, par un vrai patriote, bon citoyen & zélé sujet. 1789.

WITHERS, Philip (d. 1790)
MH.5.7[4] See ALFRED
Alfred, or A narrative of the...measures to suppress a pamphlet intituled, Strictures on the declaration of Horne Tooke, Esq. respecting...Mrs. Fitzherbert...[By P. Withers.] 4th ed. [Imperfect: wants all after p. 46.] 1789.

WITHERS, Philip (d. 1790)
MH.5.7[1] See HISTORY
History of the Royal malady, with variety of entertaining anecdotes, to which are added, strictures on the declaration of Horne Tooke, respecting Mrs. Fitzherbert...By a page of the Presence [i.e. P. Withers]. [1789.]

WOLLASTON, William (1660-1724)
MK.5.18 See RELIGION
The religion of nature delineated. [By W. Wollaston.] 1725.

WOLLASTON, William (1660-1724)
MK.5.17 See RELIGION
The religion of nature delineated. [By W. Wollaston.] New ed. 1726.

WOLLSTONECRAFT, Mary
See GODWIN, Mary Wollstonecraft.

WOOD, Anthony à (1632-1695)
MA.7.15 Athenæ Oxonienses. An exact history of all the writers and bishops who have had their education in the... University of Oxford, from...1500, to...1690...2 vols. in 1. F°, London, 1691-2.

WORDSWORTH, William (1770-1850)
MB.4.14-20 Poetical works. 7 vols. (Vols. 1-6, New ed.) 8°, London, 1842-43.*

WORLD
ME.4.23-6 The world. 1753-6 [A periodical.] By Adam Fitz-Adam [i.e. E. Moore]. 3rd ed. 4 vols. 12°, London, 1761.

WORLD
ME.5.17-26 The world displayed; or, A curious collection of voyages and travels, selected from the writers of all nations ...[Introduction by Dr. Johnson.] 20 vols. in 10. (Vol. 1, 2nd ed.) 12°, London, 1760-61.

WORMULL, Thomas
MG.5.36 A short and easy introduction to heraldry, in two parts. By H. Clark and T. Wormull. 6th ed., with considerable improvements. 8°, London, 1788.

WRAXALL, Sir Nathaniel William, 1st Bart (1751-1831)
MI.2.2^{5} See SHORT
A short review of the political state of Great Britain, at the commencement of the year 1787. [By Sir N.W. Wraxall.] [Wants title-page.] [1787.]

WRAY, Sir Cecil (1734-1805)
MH.4.27^{8} A letter to the independent electors of Westminster, in the interest of Lord Hood, and Sir Cecil Wray. (Signed Cecil Wray.) 8°, London, 1784.

WYCHERLEY, William (1640?-1716)
MG.5.9 Plays. Containing The plain dealer, The country wife, Gentleman dancing master, Love in a wood. 12°, London, 1731.

WYVILL, Christopher (1740-1822)
MH.4.25^{3} A letter to the Right Hon. William Pitt. 8°, York [1793].

WYVILL, Christopher (1740-1822)
MH.5.25^{4} A state of the representation of the people of England, on the principles of Mr. Pitt in 1785... 8°, York 1793.

XENOPHON

XENOPHON (430?-355? B.C.)
MG.1.3 De Cyri expeditione libri VII...Notas H. Stephani, Leunclavii, Æ. Porti & Mureti recensitas & castigatas, & variantium lectionum delectum, adjunxit T. Hutchinson. Ed. 2^{a}. (Greek & Latin.) 8°, Oxonii, 1745.

XENOPHON (430?-355? B.C.)
MG.1.4 De Cyri institutione libri VIII... Notas H. Stephani, Leunclavii, Æ. Porti & Mureti recersitas & castigatas, variantium lectionum delectum, indiceque necessarios adjunxit T. Hutchinson. Ed. 4^{a}. (Greek & Latin.) 8°, Londini, 1747.

XENOPHON (430?-355? B.C.)
MG.1.8 Memorabilium Socratis dictorum libri IV, Græce & Latine. Cum notis integris Ernesti... 8°, Oxonii, 1741.

XENOPHON (430?-355? B.C.)
MK.2.6 La retraite des dix mille. Ou L'expédition de Cyrus contre Artaxerxes. Avec des remarques. De la traduction de N. Perrot, Sieur d'Ablancourt. Nouvelle éd. 12°, Paris, 1706.

XENOPHON (430?-355? B.C.)
MK.2.1-2 Trois ouvrages. (La retraite des dix mille, traduite par M. Perrot d'Ablancourt, Portrait de la condition des rois, traduit par M. Coste, Les choses mémorables de Socrate, ouvrage traduit par M. Charpentier.) 2 vols. 12°, Amsterdam, 1758.

XENOPHON, Ephesius
MG.6.14 De Anthia et Habrocome Ephesiacorum libri V. Graece et Latine recensuit...A.E. Liber Baro Locella. 4°, Vindobonae, 1796.

YEARSLEY, Ann (1756-1806)
MF.6.17[2] Earl Goodwin, an historical play. 4°, London, 1791.

YEARSLEY, Ann (1756-1806)
MF.6.17[1] Poems on various subjects...being her second work. 4°, London, 1787.

YOUATT, William (1776-1847)
ME.3.22 See HORSE
The horse [by W. Youatt]; with a treatise on draught [by I.K. Brunel], and a copious index. 1831.

YOUNG, Arthur (1741-1820)
MH.3.22[3] An inquiry into the propriety of applying wastes to the better maintenance and support of the poor... 8°, Bury, 1801.

[ED. NOTE: In a long note to the later edition of the *Essay* (Bk. IV, Ch. XI) Malthus refers to this pamphlet of Arthur Young which suggested support for the poor, ineffective according to the former.]

YOUNG, Arthur (1741-1820)
MH.4.16[4] The question of scarcity plainly stated, and remedies considered... 8°, London, 1800.

[ED. NOTE: Arthur Young is among the writers Malthus mentioned in the Preface of the second edition of the *Essay* as being foremost in considering the problem of population. In his later *Essay*, Malthus refers to this very Treatise of 1800 in Bk. IV, Ch. XI which covers "Different Plans of Improving the Condition of the Poor."]

YOUNG, Arthur (1741-1820)
ML.5.15-16 A tour in Ireland: with general observations on the present state of that kingdom: made in the years 1776, 1777, and 1778. And now brought down to the end of 1779. 2nd ed. 2 vols. 8°, London, 1780.

YOUNG, Arthur (1741-1820)

ME.6.9-10 Travels during the years 1787, 1788 and 1789. Undertaken more particularly with a view of ascertaining the cultivation, wealth, resources, and national prosperity of the Kingdom of France. 2 vols. (Vol. 2, 2nd ed.) 4°, Bury St. Edmunds, 1792-4.

[ED. NOTE: In the later *Essay*, Malthus refers to this famous monograph frequently. Special reference is made to these travels in Bk. II, Ch. VI. "Of the Checks to Population in France." Reference to these travels is also made in Bk. IV, Ch. XI. regarding "Different Plans of Improving the Condition of the Poor," as well as in the Appendix of the later *Essay*.]

YOUNG, Edward (1683-1765)

MK.5.20 See COMPLAINT

The complaint: or, Night-thoughts on life, death, and immortality. [By E. Young.] (Nights 5-8.) (4 pts.) [Misbound.] 1743-5.

YOUNG, Edward (1683-1765)

ME.6.1[1] See CONSOLATION

The consolation. Containing, among other things, I. A moral survey of the nocturnal heavens. II. A night-address to the Deity...[By E. Young.] 1745.

YOUNG, Edward (1683-1765)

ME.4.46-7 Poetical works. With the life of the author. 4 vols. in 2. (Bell's Edition. The Poets of Great Britain.) 12°, Edinburg, 1777.

YOUNG, John

MH.5.13[1] Essays on the following interesting subjects: viz I. Government. II. Revolutions. III. The British Constitution ...4th ed. 8°, Glasgow, 1794.

YOUNG, Sir William (1749-1815)

MH.4.26[6] See RIGHTS

The rights of Englishmen; or The British constitution of government, compared with that of a Democratic Republic. By the author of the History of the Republic of Athens [i.e. Sir William Young]. 1793.

Z

ZANOTTI, Giampetro Cavazzoni (1674-1765?)
ML.2.29 See MALVASIA, Carlo Cesare, conte
Le pitture di Bologna che nella pretesa, e rimostrata sin' ora da altri maggiore antichità, e impareggiabile eccellenza nella pittura, con manifesta evidenza di fatto, rendono il passeggiere disingannato, ed instrutto dell' Ascoso Accademico Gelato (C.C., conte Malvasia). 3ª ed. con nuova e copiosa aggiunta (da G.P.C. Zanotti). 1732.

ZIMMERMANN, Eberhard August Wilhelm von (1743-1815)
MH.3.19 A political survey of the present state of Europe, in 16 tables, illustrated with observations... 8°, London, 1787.

ZOSIMUS, Panopolitanus (5th C.)
MG.1.19 Historiæ novæ libri VI, notis illustrati. (Greek & Latin.) 8°, Oxonii, 1679.

SUPPLEMENTARY LIST OF BOOKS PUBLISHED BEFORE 1835 REGISTERED IN THE DALTON HILL CATALOGUE BUT NOT FORMING PART OF THE JESUS COLLEGE COLLECTION

ESTABLISHED BY JOHN HARRISON

AESCHYLUS (525/4-456 B.C.)
F4 Prometheus vinctus. Emendavit, notas et glossarium adjecit C.J. Blomfield. 8°, Cantabrigiæ, 1810.

AESCHYLUS (525/4-456 B.C.)
H3 Tragœdiæ septem, cum versione Latina. [Ed. by R. Porson.] 2 vols. 8°, Londini, 1794.

AINSWORTH, Robert (1660-1743)
H8 Dictionary, English and Latin. New ed. By T. Morell. 2 vols. 4°, London (1773).

ALFIERI, Vittorio (1749-1803)
A2 Tragedies. Translated from the Italian by C. Lloyd. 3 vols. 12°, London, 1806.

ANDREWS, John (fl. 1766-1809)
H9 A new and accurate map of the country twenty-five miles round London... F°, London, 1783.

ANECDOTES
G2 (Vols. 1&3); H3 (Vol. 2). Anecdotes littéraires... [By G.T.F. Raynal.] Nouv. éd. augmentée. 3 vols. 8°, Paris, 1752.

ARISTOPHANES (ca. 445-ca. 386 B.C.)
E5 Comedies. By T. Mitchell. Vol. 1. 8°, London, 1820.

BACON, Francis, Viscount St. Albans (1561-1626)
E8 Works. 5 vols. 4°, London, 1778.

BAILLY, Jean Sylvain (1736-1793)
D8 Histoire de l'astronomie ancienne... 4°, Paris, 1775.

BAILLY, Jean Sylvain (1736-1793)
D8 Histoire de l'astronomie moderne... Vols. 1, 2. 4°, Paris, 1779.

BATHER, Edward (1779-1847)
B6 Sermons, chiefly practical. Vols. 1, 2. 8°, London, 1827-9.

BAYLE, Pierre (1647-1706)
A8 The dictionary historical and critical of Mr. P. Bayle. 2nd ed. ...revised, corrected, and enlarged, by Mr Des Maizeaux. 5 vols. F°, London, 1734-8.

BELL, John (1691-1780)
G10 Observations on Italy. 4°, Edinburgh, 1825.

BENSON, Christopher (1789-1868)
B6 The chronology of Our Saviour's Life... 8°, Cambridge, 1819.

BENSON, George (1669-1762)
G10 The history of the first planting of the Christian religion... 2nd ed. 3 vols. in 1. 4°, London, 1756.

BERKSHIRE
In CB See KENT
Maps of Kent and Berkshire. [Part of Ordnance Survey publ. by Mudge.] 1819.

BEWICKE, Thomas (1735-1828)
E5 History of British birds. Vol. 1. 8°, Newcastle, 1797.

BIBLE. English
F9 The Holy Bible. [Bishop Otter's copy.] F°, London, 1798.

BIBLE. English
E7 The Holy Bible. [Ed. by J. Reeves.] Vols. 1-5. 8°, London, 1802.

BIBLE. English
G6 The Holy Bible. 8°, Oxford, 1821.

BIBLE. English. Matthew
B6 A new version of the Gospel according to Saint Matthew; with a commentary...by Messieurs De Beausobre and Lenfant. 8°, London, 1819.

BIBLE. Greek. New Testament
F4 Novum Testamentum (ad editionam Buckianam recusam). 8°, Londini, 1728.

BIBLE. Greek-English. New Testament
E2 The New Testament (Gr.-Eng. Mill's text.) London, 1823. *Not identified.*

BICKERSTETH, Edward (1786-1850)
E3 A treatise on the Lord's Supper. 5th ed. 8°, London, 1824.

BINGLEY, William (1774-1823)
D3 Animal biography; or Authentic anecdotes of the lives, manners, and economy of the animal creation... 4th ed. ... 3 vols. 8°, London, 1813.

BIOGRAPHIA
A8 Biographia Britannica: or, The lives of the most eminent persons who have flourished in Great Britain and Ireland... 6 vols. in 7. F°, London, 1747-56.

BLUNT, John James (1794-1855)
E2 Sketch of the Reformation in England. 8°, London, 1832.

BOYDELL, John (1719-1804)
D8 An alphabetical catalogue of plates, engraved...after the finest pictures and drawings...which compose the stock of John and Josiah Boydell. 4°, London, 1803.

BREWSTER, Sir David (1781-1868)
E2 Letters on natural magic addressed to Sir Walter Scott. 12°, London, 1832.

BREWSTER, John (1753-1842)
B6 Lectures on the Acts of the Apostles... 2nd ed. 8°, London, 1830.

BRITISH MUSEUM
E2 The British Museum. Egyptian antiquities. [By G. Long.] Vol. 1. 8°, London, 1832.

BROWN, Thomas (1778-1820)
G7 Lectures on the philosophy of the human mind. 4 vols. 8°, Edinburgh, 1820.

BUFFON, Georges Louis Leclerc, comte de (1707-1788)
E2 Histoire naturelle générale et particulière. Vol. 7 only in 2 parts. 4°, Paris, 1753.

BUFFON, Georges Louis Leclerc, comte de (1707-1788)
E3 Histoire naturelle générale et particulière. 28 vols. [of a 31 vol. set.] 8°, Paris, 1762-8.

[ED. NOTE: Malthus cited this work in the later edition of his *Essay* (Bk. I, Ch. VIII).]

CARR, George (1705-1776)
C5 Sermons. 6th ed. 2 vols. 8°, London, 1787.

CARRERA, Pietro (1571-1647)
E6 A treatise on the game of chess... Translated from the Italian...by W. Lewis. 8°, London, 1822.

CARY, John (1754?-1835)
E9 Map of England and Wales. F°, London, 1816.

CATTLE
A5 Cattle; their breeds, management, and diseases. (Libr. of Useful Knowledge.) 8°, London, 1834.

CHALMERS, Thomas (1780-1847)
E6 A series of discourses on the Christian Revelation... 7th ed. 8°, Glasgow, 1817.

CHANNING, William Ellery (1780-1842)
E6 Discourses. 8°, London, 1833.

CHANNING, William Ellery (1780-1842)
E6 Works. 8°, London, 1829.

CICERO, Marcus Tullius (106-43 B.C.)
E1 Opera quæ supersunt omnia. Ad fidem optimarum editionum diligenter expressa. 20 vols. 8°, Glasguæ, 1748-9.

CICERO, Marcus Tullius (106-43 B.C.)
C7 Sex orationum partes ineditæ... Ed. 2^{a} quam recensuit...A. Maius. 4°, Mediolani, 1817.

CLASSICI
F2 Classici Romanorum scriptores. [Ed. by G.A. Ruperti, etc.] Vol. 1. 8°, Gottingæ, 1803.

CLAUDIAN, Claudius (d.c. 404)
E2 Cl. Claudiani quæ exstant; ex emendatione N. Heinsij. 16°, Amstelodami, 1677.

CONVERSATIONS
F2 Conversations on chemistry... [By J. Marcet.] 6th ed. ...Vol. 2. 12°, London, 1819.

CONVERSATIONS
B3 Conversations on vegetable physiology... By the author of Conversations on chemistry [J. Marcet]. 2 vols. 8°, London, 1829.

COOPER, James Fenimore (1789-1851)
H9 The prairie; a tale. Revised, corrected, and illustrated... 8°, London, 1832.

COOTE, Charles (1761-1835)
E5 The history of Europe, from...1763 to...1802. 8°, London, 1817.

CORNEILLE, Pierre (1606-1684)
E2 Chefs d'œuvres. Vol. 1. 8°, Paris, 1822.

DAMIANO, da Odemira (fl. 1512)
E6 The works of Damiano, Ruy Lopez and Salvio, on the game of chess; translated...by J.H. Sarratt. 8°, London, 1813.

DAVY, Sir Humphry (1778-1829)
D6 Elements of chemical philosophy. Pt. 1, Vol. 1. [*No more published.*] 8°, London, 1812.

DESHOULIERES, Antoinette du Ligier de La Garde (1637-1694)
E1 Œuvres. Nouvelle éd. ... Vol. 1. 8°, Paris, 1768.

DESTOUCHES, Philippe Néricault (1680-1754)
E2 Œuvres dramatiques. Nouvelle éd. ... Vol. 4. 12°, Paris, 1774.

DISCURSORY
C4 Discursory considerations on the hypothesis of Dr. Macknight and others, that St. Luke's Gospel was the first written. By a country clergyman [C. Dunster]. 8°, London, 1808.

DUNSTER, Charles (1750-1816)
C4 See DISCURSORY
Discursory considerations on the hypothesis of Dr. Macknight and others, that St. Luke's Gospel was the first written. By a country clergyman [C. Dunster]. 1808.

ENFIELD, William (1741-1797)
C5 Sermons on practical subjects. To which are prefixed, memoirs of the author, by J. Aikin. 3 vols. 8°, London, 1798.

EUGENIUS

F2 Eugenius, or Anecdotes of the Golden Vale. [By R. Graves.] Vol. 1. 12°, London, 1785.

EURIPIDES (480-406 B.C.)

E9 Tragedies. Translated [by R. Potter]. Vol. 1. 4°, London, 1781.

EVELYN, John (1655-1699)

E8 Memoirs illustrative of the life and writings of John Evelyn...comprising his diary... Ed. by W. Bray. 2 vols. F°, London, 1818.

FRANKLIN, Benjamin (1706-1790)

D2 Works... 2 vols. 8°, London, 1793.

FREDERICK II, the Great, King of Prussia (1712-1786)

E1 Œuvres du philosophe de Sans-Souci [Frederick the Great]. Nouvelle éd. Vols. 2 & 4. 12°, Neuchâtel, 1760.

GRAVES, Richard (1715-1804)

F2 See EUGENIUS
Eugenius, or Anecdotes of the Golden Vale. [By R. Graves.] Vol. 1. 1785.

GROTIUS, Hugo (1583-1645)

D3 Of the rights of war and peace... Done into English by several hands. [Ed. by J. Morrice.] Vol. 2. 8°, London, 1715.

HEBER, Reginald, Bp of Calcutta (1783-1826)

D7 Sermons preached in England. [Ed. by A. Heber.] 8°, London, 1829.

HEY, John (1734-1815)

B7 Lectures in divinity, delivered in the University of Cambridge. 4 vols. 8°, London, 1796-8.

HINDS, Samuel, Bp of Norwich (1793-1872)

H6 The Catechists' manual and family lecturer, being an arrangement and explanation...of St. Mark's Gospel... 8°, Oxford, 1829.

HINDS, Samuel, Bp of Norwich (1793-1872)
H6 An inquiry into the proofs, nature, and extent of inspiration, and into the authority of Scripture. 8°, Oxford, 1831.

HODGSON, Christopher (1784-1874)
E6 Instructions for the use of candidates for Holy Orders, and of the Parochial Clergy... 4th ed. 8°, London, 1829.

HOFFMANN, Karl Friedrich Vollrath (1796-1842)
E4 Die Erde und ihre Bewohner...3...vermehrte Aufl. 8°, Stuttgart, 1833.

HOMERUS (c. 850 B.C.)
E2 The Iliad of Homer. Translated by Mr. Pope. Vol. 1. 8°, London, 1718.

HORNE, George, Bp of Norwich (1730-1792)
C4 A commentary on the Book of Psalms. [With the text.] 2 vols. 8°, London, 1816.

HORNE, George, Bp of Norwich (1730-1792)
C4 Discourses on several subjects and occasions. Vols. 1, 2. 8°, London, 1794.

HORNE, Thomas Hartwell (1780-1862)
B6 An introduction to the critical study and knowledge of the Holy Scriptures... 5th ed., corrected. 4 vols. 8°, London, 1825.

HUGO, Victor Marie (1802-1885)
H9 The hunchback of Notre-Dame... Translated...by F. Shoberl. New ed., revised. 8°, London, 1833.

IRVING, Edward (1792-1834)
C4 For the Oracles of God, four orations. For judgement to come, an argument, in nine parts. 8°, London, 1823.

JEBB, John, Bp of Limerick (1775-1883)
E6 Piety without asceticism, or The Protestant Kempis... 8°, London, 1830.

JOHNSON, Samuel (1709-1784)
E5 A dictionary of the English language...Abridged... 8°, London, 1824.

KENT
In CB Maps of Kent and Berkshire. [Part of Ordnance Survey publ. by Mudge.] F°, London, 1819.

KNEBEL, Karl Ludwig von (1744-1834)
C1 See SAMMLUNG
Sammlung kleiner Gedichte. [By K.L. von Knebel.] 1815.

LA FONTAINE, Jean de (1621-1695)
E1 Œuvres. 8°, Paris, 1826.

LE BAS, Charles Webb (1779-1861)
F6 Considerations on miracles... 8°, London, 1828.

LE BAS, Charles Webb (1779-1861)
D7 Sermons, delivered chiefly in the Chapel of the East India College. 3 vols. 8°, London, 1822-34.

LEIGHTON, Robert, Abp of Glasgow (1611-1684)
D6 A practical commentary upon the First Epistle of St. Peter, and other expository works... New ed. 2 vols. 8°, London, 1825.

LEIGHTON, Robert, Abp of Glasgow (1611-1684)
B7 The select works of Robert Leighton... 2 vols. 8°, London, 1823.

LEMPRIERE, John, D.D. (1765?-1824)
H8 Bibliotheca classica: or, A classical dictionary... [5th ed.] 4°, London, 1804.

LEWIS, William (1787-1870)
E6 The games of the match at chess played by the London and Edinburgh Chess Clubs between the years 1824 and 1828... 8°, London, 1828.

LEWIS, William (1787-1870)
E6 A series of progressive lessons on the game of chess. 2nd series. 8°, London, 1832.

LINNAEUS, Carl (1707-1778)
D3 Select dissertations from the Amœnitates academicæ... transl. by F.J. Brand. 2 vols. 8°, London, 1781.

LIVES
A5 Lives of eminent persons. (Libr. of Useful Knowledge.) 8°, London, 1833.

LOCKE, John (1632-1704)
B6 A common-place book to the Holy Bible... [Ascribed to J. Locke.] 8°, London, 1824.

LOCKE, John (1632-1704)
E8 Works. 8th ed. [Ed. by E. Law.] 4 vols. 4°, London, 1777.

LONG, George (1800-1879)
E2 See BRITISH MUSEUM
The British Museum. Egyptian antiquities. [By G. Long.] Vol. 1. 1832.

LOPEZ DE SIGURA, Ruy (fl. 1561)
E6 See DAMIANO, da Odemira
The works of Damiano, Ruy Lopez, and Salvio, on the game of chess; translated...by J.H. Sarratt. 1813.

MACKNIGHT, James (1721-1800)
D7 A new literal translation...of all the Apostolical Epistles, with a commentary and notes... 4 vols. 4°, London, 1821.

MAGEE, William, Abp of Dublin (1766-1831)
C5 Discourses on the scriptural doctrines of atonement and sacrifice...3 vols. 4°, London, 1830.

MALTHUS, Thomas Robert (1766-1834)
F6 Definitions in political economy... 8°, London, 1827.

[ED. NOTE: This copy presented to Jesus College in 1949, catalogued as MH.3.14, but later missing.]

MALTHUS, Thomas Robert (1766-1834)
D6 MS notes. 1822. *Not identified.*

[ED. NOTE: Listed in Dalton Hill Catalogue under Malthus, H (sic), but in view of the given date this seems likely to be a mistake for Malthus, T.R. The MS has not been located.]

MALTHUS, Thomas Robert (1766-1834)
F6 Principles of political economy considered with a view to their practical application. 8°, London, 1820.

[ED. NOTE: Presented to Marshall Library, Cambridge, by R.A. Bray, 1949, now on deposit in Cambridge University Library. Imperfect, with numerous MS corrections and marginal notes by the author with 17 loose sheets of his MS revisions for the 2nd ed., 1836. On title-page: 'H^{y} Dalton Esqr. from the Author'.]

MARCET, Jane (1769-1858)
F2 See CONVERSATIONS
Conversations on chemistry... [By J. Marcet.] 6th ed. ... Vol. 2. 1819.

MARCET, Jane (1769-1858)
B3 See CONVERSATIONS
Conversations on vegetable physiology... By the author of Conversations on chemistry [J. Marcet]. 2 vols. 1829.

MILTON, John (1608-1674)
F9 De doctrina Christiana libri duo posthumi, quos...curavit C.R. Sumner. 4°, Cantabrigiæ, 1825.

MOOR, James (1712-1779)
G2 Elementa linguæ Græcæ. Ed. 2^{a}. Emendavit...J. Tate. 12°, Glasguæ, 1824.

NATURAL
A5 Natural philosophy. Vols. 1-3. (Libr. of Useful Knowledge.) 8°, London, 1829-34.

PARIS
E2 Guide aux environs de Paris. Vol. 1. Paris, 1788. *Not identified.*

PARIS. Conseil Général des Hospices
E9 Rapport au Conseil Général des Hospices. Paris, 1816. *Not identified.*

PASCAL, Blaise (1623-1662)
H3 Les Provinciales. Vols. 2 & 3. 12°, [Paris] 1712.

PENROSE, John (1778-1859)
E3 Explanatory lectures on the Gospel according to St. Matthew. 12°, London, 1832.

PHILLIPS, John (1800-1874)
E2 A guide to geology. 8°, London, 1834.

PLATO (428-348 or 347 B.C.)
E9 A synopsis or general view of the works of Plato. [By F. Sydenham.] 4°, London, 1759.

PLAUTUS, Titus Maccius (254-184 B.C.)
E2 Comédies; traduites en françois par Mlle Le Fèvre...Dernière éd., avec l'original latin... Vol. 1. 12°, Paris, 1691.

PLUTARCHUS (50-ca. 125)
H3 Liber quomodo juveni audienda sint pœmata...Variantes lectiones et notas adjecit J. Potter. 2 pts. 8°, Oxoniæ, 1694.

POPE, Alexander (1688-1744)
E2 See HOMERUS
The Iliad of Homer. Translated by Mr. Pope. Vol. 1. 1718.

PORTUGAL
A5 See SPAIN
The history of Spain and Portugal. From B.C. 1000 to A.D. 1814. (Libr. of Useful Knowledge.) 1833.

RAYNAL, Guillaume Thomas François (1713-1796)
G2 (Vols. 1 & 3); H3 (Vol. 2) See ANECDOTES
Anecdotes littéraires... [By G.T.F. Raynal.] Nouv. éd. augmentée. 3 vols. 1752.

RECUEIL
H10 Recueil de pièces graves antiques. Paris, 1737. *Not identified.*

ROPER, William (1496-1578)
D4 The life of Sir Thomas More... New ed. 8°, Chiswick, 1817.

ROSSETTI, Gabriele Pasquale Giuseppe (1783-1854)
E6 Sullo spirito antipapale che produsse la riforma... 8°, Londra, 1832.

ROUSSEAU, Jean Jacques (1712-1778)
E1 Les confessions. 4 vols. in 2. 8°, Paris, 1813.

ROUSSEAU, Jean Jacques (1712-1778)
E1 Emile, ou De l'éducation. 3 vols. 8°, Paris, 1813.

ROUSSEAU, Jean Jacques (1712-1778)
E1 Julie, ou La nouvelle Héloïse. 4 vols. in 2. 8°, Paris, 1806.

ROYAL SOCIETY OF LITERATURE
E9 Transactions. [Vol. 1.] 1827, 1829, 1832. 4°, London, 1832.

SALVIO, Alessandro (fl. 1604-1634)
E6 See DAMIANO, da Odemira
The works of Damiano, Ruy Lopez, and Salvio, on the game of chess; translated...by J.H. Sarratt. 1813.

SAMMLUNG
C1 Sammlung kleiner Gedichte. [By K.L. von Knebel.] 4°, Leipzig, 1815.

SCHLEIERMACHER, Friedrich Daniel Ernst (1768-1834)
B6 A critical essay on the Gospel of St. Luke. With an introduction by the translator [C. Thirlwall]... 8°, London, 1825.

SCOTT, Sir Walter, Bart (1771-1832)
A1 The Abbot. 2 vols. (Waverley Novels.) 8°, Edinburgh, 1831.

SCOTT, Sir Walter, Bart (1771-1832)
A1 Anne of Geierstein. 2 vols. (Waverley Novels.) 8°, Edinburgh, 1833.

SCOTT, Sir Walter, Bart (1771-1832)
A1 The Antiquary. 2 vols. (Waverley Novels.) 8°, Edinburgh, 1829.

SCOTT, Sir Walter, Bart (1771-1832)
A1 The Betrothed. (Waverley Novels.) 8°, Edinburgh, 1832.

SCOTT, Sir Walter, Bart (1771-1832)
A2 Biographical memoirs of eminent novelists, and other distinguished persons. 2 vols. (Prose Works, 3, 4.) 8°, Edinburgh, 1834.

SCOTT, Sir Walter, Bart (1771-1832)
A2 Bridal of Triermain... (Poetical Works.) 8°, Edinburgh [183-?].

SCOTT, Sir Walter, Bart (1771-1832)
A1 The Bride of Lammermoor. 2 vols. (Waverley Novels.) 8°, Edinburgh, 1830.

SCOTT, Sir Walter, Bart (1771-1832)
A1 Castle dangerous. (Waverley Novels.) 8°, Edinburgh, 1833.

SCOTT, Sir Walter, Bart (1771-1832)
A1 Count Robert of Paris. (Waverley Novels.) 8°, Edinburgh, 1833.

SCOTT, Sir Walter, Bart (1771-1832)
A2 Dramas. (Poetical Works.) 8°, Edinburgh [183-?].

SCOTT, Sir Walter, Bart (1771-1832)
A2 Essays on chivalry, romance and the drama. (Prose Works, 6.) 8°, Edinburgh, 1834.

SCOTT, Sir Walter, Bart (1771-1832)
A1 The fair maid of Perth. 2 vols. (Waverley Novels.) 8°, Edinburgh, 1832.

SCOTT, Sir Walter, Bart (1771-1832)
A1 The fortunes of Nigel. 2 vols. (Waverley Novels.) 8°, Edinburgh, 1831.

SCOTT, Sir Walter, Bart (1771-1832)
A1 Guy Mannering. 2 vols. (Waverley Novels.) 8°, Edinburgh, 1829.

SCOTT, Sir Walter, Bart (1771-1832)
A1 The Heart of Mid-Lothian. 2 vols. (Waverley Novels.) 8°, Edinburgh, 1830.

SCOTT, Sir Walter, Bart (1771-1832)
A1 The Highland Widow &c. (Waverley Novels.) 8°, Edinburgh, 1832.

SCOTT, Sir Walter, Bart (1771-1832)
A1 Ivanhoe. 2 vols. (Waverley Novels.) 8°, Edinburgh, 1830.

SCOTT, Sir Walter, Bart (1771-1832)
A1 Kenilworth. 2 vols. (Waverley Novels.) 8°, Edinburgh, 1831.

SCOTT, Sir Walter, Bart (1771-1832)
A2 The Lady of the Lake. (Poetical Works.) 8°, Edinburgh [183-?].

SCOTT, Sir Walter, Bart (1771-1832)
A2 The lay of the last minstrel. (Poetical Works.) 8°, Edinburgh [183-?].

SCOTT, Sir Walter, Bart (1771-1832)
A1 A legend of Montrose. (Waverley Novels.) 8°, Edinburgh, 1830.

SCOTT, Sir Walter, Bart (1771-1832)
A2 The life of John Dryden. (Prose Works, 1.) 8°, Edinburgh, 1834.

SCOTT, Sir Walter, Bart (1771-1832)
A2 The Lord of the Isles &c. &c. (Poetical Works.) 8°, Edinburgh [183-?].

SCOTT, Sir Walter, Bart (1771-1832)
A2 Marmion. (Poetical Works.) 8°, Edinburgh [183-?].

SCOTT, Sir Walter, Bart (1771-1832)
A2 Memoirs of Jonathan Swift, D.D. (Prose Works, 2.) 8°, Edinburgh, 1834.

SCOTT, Sir Walter, Bart (1771-1832)
A1 The Monastery. 2 vols. (Waverley Novels.) 8°, Edinburgh, 1830.

SCOTT, Sir Walter, Bart (1771-1832)
A1 Old Mortality. 2 vols. (Waverley Novels.) 8°, Edinburgh, 1829.

SCOTT, Sir Walter, Bart (1771-1832)
A2 Paul's letters to his kinsfolk, and Abstract of the Eyrbiggia-Saga. (Prose Works, 5.) 8°, Edinburgh, 1834.

SCOTT, Sir Walter, Bart (1771-1832)
A1 Peveril of the Peak. 3 vols. (Waverley Novels.) 8°, Edinburgh, 1831.

SCOTT, Sir Walter, Bart (1771-1832)
A1 The Pirate. 2 vols. (Waverley Novels.) 8°, Edinburgh, 1831.

SCOTT, Sir Walter, Bart (1771-1832)
A1 Quentin Durward. 2 vols. (Waverley Novels.) 8°, Edinburgh, 1831.

SCOTT, Sir Walter, Bart (1771-1832)
A1 Redgauntlet. 2 vols. (Waverley Novels.) 8°, Edinburgh, 1832.

SCOTT, Sir Walter, Bart (1771-1832)
A1 Rob Roy. 2 vols. (Waverley Novels.) 8°, Edinburgh, 1829.

SCOTT, Sir Walter, Bart (1771-1832)
A2 Rokeby and the vision of Don Roderick. (Poetical Works.) 8°, Edinburgh [183-?].

SCOTT, Sir Walter, Bart (1771-1832)
A1 St Ronan's Well. 2 vols. (Waverley Novels.) 8°, Edinburgh, 1831.

SCOTT, Sir Walter, Bart (1771-1832)
A2 Sir Tristram. (Poetical Works.) 8°, Edinburgh [183-?].

SCOTT, Sir Walter, Bart (1771-1832)
A2 Surgeon's daughter. (Waverley Novels.) 8°, Edinburgh, 1833.

SCOTT, Sir Walter, Bart (1771-1832)
A1 The Talisman. (Waverley Novels.) 8°, Edinburgh, 1832.

SCOTT, Sir Walter, Bart (1771-1832)
A1 Waverley. 2 vols. (Waverley Novels.) 8°, Edinburgh, 1829.

SCOTT, Sir Walter, Bart (1771-1832)
A1 Woodstock. 2 vols. (Waverley Novels.) 8°, Edinburgh, 1832.

SHAFTESBURY, Anthony Ashley Cooper, 3rd Earl of (1671-1713)
E2 Characteristicks of men, manners, opinions, times. [By Anthony Ashley Cooper, 3rd Earl of Shaftesbury.] Vol. 3. 8°,[London] 1749.

SHAKESPEARE, William (1564-1616)
E3 Dramatic Works. Printed from the text of the corrected copies of Steevens and Malone. 8°, London, 1827.

SHAKESPEARE, William (1564-1616)
H4 Plays and poems. With the corrections and illustrations of various commentators...and an enlarged history of the stage by the late E. Malone. [Ed. by J. Boswell.] 21 vols. 8°, London, 1821.

SHEPHERD, Lady Mary
F2 Essays on the perception of an external universe... 12°, London, 1827.

SHERLOCK, Thomas, Bp of London (1678-1761)
G6 Several discourses preached at the Temple Church. [Vol. 1?]. 8°, London, 1755.

SMITH, Thomas Southwood, M.D. (1788-1861)
H6 Illustrations of the Divine Government. 3rd ed. 8°, London, 1822.

SPAIN
A5 The history of Spain and Portugal. From B.C. 1000 to A.D. 1814. (Libr. of Useful Knowledge.) 8°, London, 1833.

STEWART, Dugald (1753-1828)
E5 Outlines of moral philosophy ...5th ed. 8°, Edinburgh, 1829.

SUMNER, John Bird, Abp of Canterbury (1780-1862)
C5 A treatise on the records of the Creation, and on the moral attributes of the Creator... 2 vols. 8°, London, 1816.

[ED. NOTE: Malthus cited this work in Bk. III, Ch. III of his later *Essay*.]

SYDENHAM, Floyer (1710-1787)
E9 See PLATO
A synopsis or general view of the works of Plato. [By F. Sydenham.] 1759.

TAYLOR, Jeremy, Bp of Down and Connor (1613-1667)
B7 The whole works of Jeremy Taylor. With a life of the author, and a critical examination of his writings, by R. Heber. 15 vols. 8°, London, 1828.

THOMSON, James (1700-1748)
E2 Poetical works. Vol. 2. 8°, London, 1780.

TURNER, Sharon (1768-1847)
C7 The history of England during the Middle Ages... 2nd ed. 5 vols. 8°, London, 1825.

TURNER, Sharon (1768-1847)
G5 The history of the Anglo-Saxons from their first appearance above the Elbe to the Norman Conquest. 4 vols. 8°, London, 1802-5.

VANBRUGH, Sir John (1664-1726)
D2 Plays. 2 vols. 12°, London, 1759.

VERGILIUS MARO, Publius (70-19 B.C.)
E2 Opera. N. Heinsius...recensuit. [*Wants title-page. Edition not identified.*]

VERGILIUS MARO, Publius (70-19 B.C.)
F4 P. Virgilius Maro varietate lectionis et perpetua adnotatione illustratus à C.G. Heyne...Ed. (3a) novis curis emendata... 6 vols. 8°, Lipsiæ, 1800.

VERGILIUS MARO, Publius (70-19 B.C.)
E2 Publii Virgilii Maronis opera...emendata...cura J. Hunter... Vol. 2. 8°, Andreapoli, 1799.

VILLENEUVE, François Alberti de (1737-1801)
H8 Nouveau dictionnaire françois-italien. 2 vols. 4°, Marseille, 1772.

WADDINGTON, George (1793-1869)
A5 A history of the Church, from the earliest ages to the Reformation. (Libr. of Useful Knowledge.) 8°, London, 1833.

WALLACE, Robert (1697-1771)
F6 Various prospects of mankind, nature and providence. 8°, London, 1761.

[ED. NOTE: This copy presented to Jesus College in 1949, catalogued as MH.3.16, but later missing.]

WARBURTON, William, Bp of Gloucester (1698-1779)
E9 Letters from a late eminent Prelate (W. Warburton) to one of his friends (R. Hurd)... 4°, Kidderminster [1808].

WATSON, Richard, Bp of Llandaff (1737-1816)
D6 A collection of theological tracts. 6 vols. 8°, Cambridge, 1785.

WILSON, Thomas, Bp of Sodor and Man (1663-1755)
G6 Sermons. 4th ed. 4 vols. 8°, London, 1785.

WITHERING, William (1741-1799)
E7 A botanical arrangement of all the vegetables naturally growing in Great Britain... 2 vols. in 1. 8°, London, 1776.

WOLF, Christian Wilhelm Friedrich August (1759-1824)
F4 Prolegomena ad Homerum... Vol. 1. [*No more published.*] 8°, Halis Saxonorum, 1795.

Monographs Referred to
by Malthus in his
An Essay on the Principle of Population

-Preliminary Listings-

At the time this monograph was concluded, no scholar had yet published a list of authorities for Malthus's works. Moreover, although the second and later editions of the *Essay* on Population cover titles of utmost interest, their indexes record at best only a few of the authorities cited.

We understand that in the variorum edition of the *Essay* now being prepared by Mrs. Patricia James, such a listing will be made available. Since this might not be ready before 1985, however, we consider it of interest to include the information the Editor has gathered while preparing this Catalogue for publication, with the belief that the variorum edition of the *Essay*, when published, will complete this attempt.

The following listings cover most of the monographs Malthus referred to, mainly in the First (1798) *Essay* and in the Sixth (1826) *Essay*—-the last edition he was to correct. [The Fourth (1807) *Essay* has, however, often been used in establishing the listings.]

Papers published other than as independent monographs have been listed under the heading "Uncorroborated Entries of References." This list also includes a few other titles on which we have not been able to check bibliographical information. Following this section is an addendum of the classics of antiquity cited by Malthus but not included in the previous section.

When the monographs listed are a part of Malthus's Library at Jesus College, the corresponding shelf numbers are indicated. Generally, additional information is given against these titles in the body of the Catalogue.

In each instance, we have added to the listings the Book (Bk.) and Chapter (Ch.) of the *Essay* in which Malthus made the reference.

ABULGHAZI, KHAN (1605-1660)
Genealogical History of the Tartars translated into English from the French with Additions.
2 vols. 8°, [London, 1729/30.]
6th *ESSAY*, Bk. I, Ch. VII

ACCARIAS DE SERIONNE, Jacques (1706-1792)
MA. 3.3-4 La richesse de la Hollande, ouvrage dans lequel on expose l'origine du commerce & de la puissance des Hollandois... [By J. Accarias de Serionne.] 2 vols. 8°, Londres, 1778
6th *ESSAY*, Bk. III, Ch. IX

AIKIN, John (1747-1822)
A description of the country from thirty to forty miles round Manchester. London, 1795.
6th *ESSAY*, Bk. III, Ch. XIII

ANDERSON, James (1739-1808)
MH.5.15^{2} A calm investigation of the circumstances which have led to the present scarcity of grain in Britain...
2nd ed. 8°, London, 1801.
6th *ESSAY*, Bk. III, Ch. XIV

BESCHREIBUNG VON BERN
2 vols. 8°, Bern, 1796. (See: Prevost)
6th *ESSAY*, Bk. II, Ch. V

BOUGAINVILLE, Louis Antoine de (1729-1811)
ML.4.17 Voyage autour du monde, par la frégate du Roi La Boudeuse, et la flute L'Etoile; en 1766, 1767, 1768 & 1769. 4°, Paris, 1771.
6th *ESSAY*, Bk. I, Ch. V

BRIDGE, Rev. Bewick (1767-1833)
Elements of Algebra. 8°, London, 1810.
6th *ESSAY*, Bk. II, Ch. IX

[ED. NOTE: In Bk. II, Ch. XI Malthus added in 1825 a Table calculated by Rev. Bridge of "Peter House, Cambridge," where he indicated the rate of increase or period of doubling of population, based on the proportion of deaths to births.]

[BROSSES, Charles de (1709-1777)]
ML.4.14-15 Histoire des navigations aux Terres Australes...
2 vols. 4°, Paris, 1756.
6th *ESSAY*, Bk. I, Ch. V

BRUCE, James (1730-1794)
Travels to discover the source of the Nile, in the years 1768, 1769, 1770, 1771, 1772, and 1773. 5 vols. Edinburgh, 1790.
6th *ESSAY*, Bk. I, Ch. VIII

BUFFON, Georges Louis Leclerc (1707-1788)
Histoire naturelle générale et particulière.
5th ed., 31 vols. 12°, (Paris, 1752-1778).
6th *ESSAY*, Bk. I, Ch. VIII

[ED. NOTE: Malthus cites a section of this edition: "Histoire Naturelle de l'Homme," with the given information, except place and date.]

BURKE, Rt. Hon. Edmund (1729-1797)
MH.2.1-16 (from his "Works") Account of European Settlements in America. 2 vols. 8°, London, 1757.
6th *ESSAY*, Bk. I, Ch. IV; Bk. III, Ch. IV

CHARDIN, Sir John (1643-1713)
The travels of Sir John Chardin...into Persia (A new collection). London, 1767.
6th *ESSAY*, Bk. I, Ch. VII & XI

[ED. NOTE: Malthus refers to Harris's Collection.]

CHARLEVOIX, Pierre François Xavier (1682-1761)
Histoire et déscription générale de la nouvelle France... 6 vols. 12°, Paris, 1744 (should have 28 maps).
6th *ESSAY*, Bk. I, Ch. IV

COLEBROOKE, Henry Thomas (1765-1837)
Remarks on the husbandry and internal commerce of Bengal. London, c. 1795 (reprinted 1806).
6th *ESSAY*, Bk. III, Ch. XII

[ED. NOTE: In the *Essay*, Malthus refers to "Husbandry of Bengal" by "Sir George Colebrooke."]

COLLINS, David (1756-1810)
Account of the English colony of New South Wales. 4°, London, 1798/1802.
6th *ESSAY*, Bk. I, Ch. III

[ED. NOTE: Malthus refers to the appendix which was not published until 1808.]

[COLQUHOUN, Patrick (1745-1820)]
MH.1.20 A treatise on the police of the Metropolis...By a magistrate. 3rd ed., revised and enlarged. London, 1796.
6th *ESSAY*, Bk. IV, Ch. IV

CONDORCET, Marie Jean Antoine de Caritat, Marquis de (1743-1794)
Esquisse d'un tableau historique des progrès de l'esprit humain. 8°, Paris, 1795.
1st *ESSAY*, Ch. IV;
6th *ESSAY*, Bk. III, Ch. I; Bk. IV, Ch. XII

COOK, James (1728-1779)
MK.5.3-4 A voyage towards the South Pole, and round the world. Performed in His Majesty's ships the Resolution and Adventure, in the years 1772, 1773, 1774, and 1775... 2 vols. 4°, London, 1777.
6th *ESSAY*, Bk. I, Ch. III, IV & V

[ED. NOTE: Malthus also refers to the first and third voyages. We have listed only this second voyage, found in the Malthus library.]

COXE, William (1747-1828)
See DECOUVERTES RUSSES

CREUXIUS, Franciscus (1596-1666) (also as François du Creux)
Historiae canadiensis seu nova Franciae. 4°, Paris, 1664.
6th *ESSAY*, Bk. I, Ch. IV

CROME, August Friedrich Wilhelm (1753-1833)
Uber die Grösse und Bevölkerung der sämtlichen Europäische Staaten. Leipzig, 1785 (revised 1792).
6th *ESSAY*, Bk. II, Ch. IV, VII, XI

[ED. NOTE: Mrs. Patricia James wrote: "There are French, Dutch and English translations of this work, but I have not been able to find a copy of one which Malthus might have used." ("Population Malthus," p. 471). It is also known that Malthus did not read German. Curiously, the title is not in the Kress, Goldsmith nor even the R.S.S. library.]

CRUMPE, Samuel (1766-1796)
MH.1.18 An essay on the best means of providing employment for the people... 8°, Dublin, 1793.
6th *ESSAY*, Bk. IV, Ch. XI

CURRIE, Dr. James (1756-1805)
MG.5.28/ML.2.28 The Life of Burns - included in Robert Burns's "Poetical Works" and in his "Poems." 8°, Alnwick, 1808/12; Edinburgh, 1802.
6th *ESSAY*, Bk. IV, Ch. II

CURWEN, John Christian (1756-1828)
Hints in agricultural subjects, and on the best means of improving the condition of the labouring classes. London, 1809.
6th *ESSAY*, Bk. IV, Ch. XII

[ED. NOTE: Malthus actually refers to Curwen's plan "For bettering the condition of the labouring classes of the community."]

D'AVENANT, Charles (1656-1714)
The Political and Commercial Works... 8°, London, 1771.
6th *ESSAY*, Bk. II, Ch. VIII

DECOUVERTES RUSSES
4 vols. 8°, Berne & Lausanne, 1781, 1784.
6th *ESSAY*, Bk. I, Ch. VII, IX, X

[ED. NOTE: In Bk. I, Ch. VII, referring to this work, Malthus said: "Not having been able to procure the work of Pallas on the history of the Mongol nations, I have here made use of a general abridgement of the works of the Russian travellers, in 4 vols. oct. published at Berne and Lausanne in 1781 and 1784, entitled 'Découvertes Russes, tom. iii. p. 399.' We have not been able to locate this title in the bibliographies that we have consulted. However, William Coxe's "Nouvelles découvertes de Russes..." was published in Neuchâtel in 1781. Apparently Malthus was familiar with Coxe's works and we assume that the 4-volume "Découvertes Russes" also contained Coxe's works.]

DIACONUS, Paul
See: PAULUS DIACONUS

DU HALDE, Jean Baptiste (1674-1743)
The General History of China...Translated by R. Brookes.
2 vols. F°, London, 1738.
6th *ESSAY*, Bk. I, Ch. XII

DURAND, François Jacques (1727-1816)
MK.1.15-18 Statistique élémentaire, ou Essai sur l'état géographique, physique et politique de la Suisse. 4 vols. 8°, Lausanne, 1795-1796.
6th *ESSAY*, Bk. II, Ch. V

EDEN, Sir Francis Morton (1766-1809)
An estimate of the number of inhabitants in Great Britain and Ireland. London, 1800.
6th *ESSAY*, Bk. II, Ch. VIII; Bk. III, Ch. VI

EDEN, Sir Francis Morton (1766-1809)
State of the poor, or an history of the labouring classes in England, from the conquest to the present period... 3 vols. 4°, London, 1797.
6th *ESSAY*, Bk. IV, Ch. VIII

ELLIS, Henry (1721-1806)
A voyage to Hudson's-Bay, by the "Dobbs Galley," and "California" in the years 1746 and 1747, for discovering a northwest passage... 8°, London, 1748.
6th *ESSAY*, Bk. I, Ch. IV

ESTCOURT, Thomas (late 18th-early 19th C.)
An account of an Effort to Better the Condition of the Poor in a Country Village (Long Newton) and some Regulations suggested by which the same might be extended to other parishes of similar description. London, 1804.
6th *ESSAY*, Appendix

[ED. NOTE: Printed by the board of Agriculture. (Palgrave)]

ETON, William
A survey of the Turkish Empire. 2nd ed. 8°, London, 1799.
6th *ESSAY*, Bk. II, Ch. XII; Bk. III, Ch. IV

[ED. NOTE: Apparently Malthus used the first edition. His actual reference to page 282 is on page 292 in the 2nd edition.]

EULER, Leonhard (1707-1783)
Table of Mortality.
6th *ESSAY*, Bk. I, Ch. I; Bk. II, Ch. XI

[ED. NOTE: The work of the mathematician Leonhard Euler and his son Johann Albrecht (1734-1800) has been published as "Opera Omnia" since 1911; from 74 Vols. of the project, 60 were released.]

FRANKLIN, Benjamin (1706-1790)
MH.1.23 Political, miscellaneous and philosophical pieces... 8°, London, 1779.
6th *ESSAY*, Bk. I, Ch. I, IV, VIII; Bk. III, Ch. IV

GARNIER, Comte Germain (1754-1821)
Annotated translation of Adam Smith's "Wealth of Nations": as "Recherches sur la nature et les causes de la richesse des nations." 5 vols. 8°, Paris, 1802.
6th *ESSAY*, Bk. II, Ch. VI

GIBBON, Edward (1737-1794)
MG.2.20-31 The history of the decline and fall of the Roman Empire. New ed., 12 vols. 8°, London, 1783-1790.
6th *ESSAY*, Bk. I, Ch. VI, VII

GODWIN, William (1756-1836)
MI.2.5 The enquirer. Reflections on education, manners, and literature. In a series of essays. 8°, London, 1797.
1st *ESSAY*, Preface

GODWIN, William (1756-1836)
MI.2.3-4 Enquiry concerning political justice...2nd ed., 2 vols. 8°, London, 1796.
1st *ESSAY*, Ch. X-XV;
6th *ESSAY*, Bk. III, Ch. II

[ED. NOTE: Malthus may have used the 1st and 3rd editions of "Political Justice" for his early *Essay*.]

GRAHAME, James (1790-1842)
An inquiry into the principle of population. Edinburgh, 1816.
6th *ESSAY*, 1817 Appendix

GRAUNT, John (1620-1674)
Natural and political observations, mentioned in a following index and made upon the bills of mortality. 4°, London [1662.]
6th *ESSAY*, Bk. II, Ch. VIII

[ED. NOTE: Other editions in 8° are dated 1665 and 1676.]

HANWAY, Jonas (1712-1786)
MI.1.7-8 Letters on the importance of the rising generation of the laboring part of our fellow-subjects... 2 vols. 8°, London, 1767.
6th *ESSAY*, Bk. III, Ch. VI

HARRIS, John (1666-1719)
MA.7.12-13 Navigantium atque intinerantium bibliotheca, or a compleat collection of voyages and travels... 2 vols. F°, London, 1705.
6th *ESSAY*, Bk. I, Ch. V, VII, X

HAYGARTH, Dr. John (1740-1827)
An inquiry on how to prevent small-pox... London, 1784.
6th *ESSAY*, Bk. IV, Ch. V

HEBERDEN, Dr. William (1767-1845)
Observations on the increase and decrease of different diseases and particularly of the plague. London (?), 1801.
6th *ESSAY*, Bk. II, Ch. VIII; Bk. IV, Ch. V

HENNEPIN, Louis (1640-1701)
Description de la Louisiane...avec les moeurs et manières de vivre des sauvages. Paris, 1688.
6th *ESSAY*, Bk. I, Ch. IV

[ED. NOTE: For both Hennepin and Lafitau, Malthus refers to a title listed as "Moeurs des Sauvages."]

HOWLETT, Rev. John (1731-1800)
An examination of Dr. Price's Essay on the Population of England and Wales, and the doctrine of an Increased Population in this Kingdom established by Facts. Maidstone, 1781.
1st *ESSAY*, Ch. XVI
6th *ESSAY*, Bk. III, Ch. VI

[ED. NOTE: Mrs. Patricia James mentions Rev. Howlett's book in "Population Malthus," p. 57 (note 28, p. 467).]

HUMBOLDT, Alexander, Freiherr von (1769-1859)
Essai politique sur le royaume de la Nouvelle Espagne. Paris, 1811.
6th *ESSAY*, Bk. III, Ch. XIII

[ED. NOTE: Humbolt's great "Voyage aux Régions Equinoxiales du Nouveau Continent, fait de 1799 a 1804" was published in 30 Vols., (20 Folio, 10 4°,) Paris, 1805-1832.]

HUME, David (1711-1776)
MH.3.27-8 Essay and treatises on several subjects. New ed. 2 vols. 8°, Edinburgh, 1800.
1st *ESSAY*, Ch. IV
6th *ESSAY*, Bk. I, Ch. V, XIII, XIV; Bk. IV, Ch. XIII

[ED. NOTE: The references are basically from Hume's essay "Of the Populousness of Ancient Nations" published originally in 1752 in his "Political Discourses."]

HUME, David (1711-1776)
Dialogues on natural religion. London, 1779.
6th *ESSAY*, Bk. II, Ch. XIII

IVERNOIS, Sir Francis D' (1757-1842)
Tableau historique et politique des pertes... London, 1799.
6th *ESSAY*, Bk. II, Ch. VI

[ED. NOTE: In the same year (1799), a translation appeared in London under the title "Historical and Political Survey of the Losses Sustained by the French Nation, in Population, Agriculture, Colonies, Manufactures, and Commerce, in Consequence of the Revolution and the Present War."]

JONES, Sir William (1746-1794)
Works. 6 vols. London, 1799.
6th *ESSAY*, Bk. I,, Ch. XI

KAEMPFER, Engelbert (1651-1716)
MA.6.9-10 The history of Japan, giving an account of the ancient and present state and government of that Empire... 2 vols. F°, London, 1727.
6th *ESSAY*, Bk. I, Ch. XII

KAMES, Henry Home (1696-1782)
Sketches of the history of Man. 2nd ed. 8°, London, 1788.
6th *ESSAY*, Bk. I, Ch. IV and Bk. III, Ch. XIV

[ED. NOTE: Malthus refers to "Lord Kaimes" and to the 1788 edition of "Sketches."]

KING, Gregory (1648-1712)
Natural and Political Observations upon the State and Conditions of England. London, 1696.
1st *Essay* Ch. VII
6th *Essay* Bk. II, Ch. VIII

LA BILLARDIERE [Jacques Julien Houton de] (1755-1834)
An account of a voyage in search of Perouse ... performed in the years 1791, 1792, and 1793, in the Recherche and Esperance, Ships of War, under the command of Rear-Admiral Bruni d'Entrecasteauz. London, 1800. 6th *Essay*, Bk. I, Ch. V

[ED. NOTE: Malthus refers to a "Voyage in search of Perouse—English translation 4to."

LAFITAU, Joseph François (1681-c. 1746)
Moeurs des sauvages ameriquains, comparées aux moeurs des premiers temps. Ouvrage enrichi de figures en taille douce. 2 vols. Paris, 1794.
6th *ESSAY*, Bk. I, Ch. IV

[ED. NOTE: Apparently this is the closest edition that Malthus could have used.]

LA PEROUSE, Jean François de Galaup, Comte de (1741-1788)
A Voyage Around the World. Performed in the Years 1785, 1786, 1787, and 1788, by the Boussole and Astrolabe... 2 vols. 4°, London, 1799.
6th *ESSAY*, Bk. I, Ch. IV, V

[ED. NOTE: Malthus refers to a 4to English translation; the original French appeared in 1797.]

LESSEPS, Jean Baptiste Barthelmy, Baron de (1766-1834)
Travels in Kamtschatka during the years 1787 & 1788 (English translation). 8°, London, 1790.
6th *ESSAY*, Bk. I, Ch. IX

[ED. NOTE: Malthus cited the 1790 edition.]

LETTRES EDIFIANTES ET CURIEUSES, ECRITES DES MISSIONS ETRANGERES (De la Companie de Jésus)
MC.I.13-36 New ed., 24 vols. 12°, Paris, 1780-1781.
6th *ESSAY*, Bk. I, Ch. IV; XII

LE VAILLANT, François (1753-1824)
MK.4.1-3 Second voyage dans l'intérieur de l'Afrique, par le Cap de Bonne-Esperance, dans les années 1783, 1784 et 1785. 3 vols. 8°, Paris, AN III (1795).
6th *ESSAY*, Bk. I, Ch. IV
[Apparently Malthus referred to the first Voyage, Paris, 1790.]

LOWE, Joseph (Early 19th century)
The Present State of England in regard to Agriculture, Trade and Finance. 8°, London, 1822.
6th *ESSAY*, Bk. III, Ch. XII

MACHIAVELLI, Nicolo (1469-1527)
MG.7.16 Istorie Fiorentine. [Geneva?] 1550.
6th *ESSAY*, Bk. I, Ch. VI

[ED. NOTE: See in Malthus's Library under "Tutte le Opere..."]

MACKINTOSH, Sir James (1765-1832)
Discourse on the Study of the Law of Nature and Nations. Introductory Discourse. London, 1798/1799.
4th *ESSAY*, Bk. III, Ch. III

[ED. NOTE: Actually this is a course of lectures where Mackintosh attacked Godwin in an "Introductory Discourse."]

MALLET, Paul Henri (1730-1807)
Introduction à l'Histoire de Dannemarc. 12°, Copenhagen, 1766.
6th *ESSAY*, Bk. I, Ch. VI

[MALTHUS, Thomas Robert (1766-1834)]
MH.3.15[1] An investigation of the cause of the present high price of provisions... 8°, London, 1800.
6th *Essay*, Bk. III, Ch. V

MANDEVILLE, Bernard (1670-1733)
MG.5.21-2 The fable of the Bees. 2 vols. 12°, Edinburgh, 1755.
6th *ESSAY*, Appendix

MEARES, John (1756-1809)
Voyages made...1788 & 1789, from China to the Northwest Coast of America... London, 1791.
6th *ESSAY*, Bk. I, Ch. IV, XII

MIRABEAU, Victor Riquetti, comte de (1715-1789)
[Œuvres.] 9 vols. 12°, Paris, 1762.
6th *ESSAY*, Bk. III, Ch. XIV

[ED. NOTE: Malthus specifically refers to Vol. VIII, p. 84 of this edition.]

MOHEAU (fl. 1778)
Recherches et considerations sur la population de la France. Paris, 1778.
6th *ESSAY*, Bk. II, Ch. VI

[ED. NOTE: Malthus wrote: "According to Necker and Moheau, the mortality in France, before the revolution, was 1 in 30 or 31 1/8."]

MONTESQUIEU, Charles Louis de Secondat (1689-1755)
MA.5.3-7 Œuvres. New ed., 5 vols. 8°, Paris, 1796.
6th *ESSAY*, Bk. I, Ch. VI, for "Grandeur et Decadence des Romains." Bk. I, Ch. V, VII, XI, XII, XIV; Bk. II, Ch. III; Bk. IV, Ch. XIII; for "Esprit des Loix" Bk. II, Ch. IV for "Lettres Persannes."

[ED. NOTE: The edition of " Œuvres " as extant in the Malthus Library evidently includes the references Malthus made to the indicated titles.]

MURET, Jean Louis (1715-1796)
Mémoire sur l'état de la population dans le Pays de Vaud... Yverdon, 1766
Mémoires, &c. par la Société Economique de Berne. Année 1766.
6th *ESSAY*, Bk. II, Ch. V, XI; Appendix.

[ED. NOTE: Malthus refers to Muret and the Mémoires in Chapter V as follows: "About 35 or 40 years ago, a great and sudden alarm appears to have prevailed in Switzerland respecting the depopulation of the country; and the transactions of the Economical Society of Berne, which had been established some years before, were crowded with papers deploring the decay... A paper containing very valuable materials was, however, about this time published by M. Muret, minister of Vevay..." The paper may have been independently published, therefore we have presented both titles. Mr. Prevost (vide) seems to have been the translator of the Mémoires which is listed with the uncorroborated entries.]

NECKER, Jacques (1732-1804)
MB.2.21-3 De l'Administration des Finances de la France. 3 vols. 8°, [Paris], 1785.
6th *ESSAY*, Bk. II, Ch. VI, VII, VIII; Bk. II, Ch. XIII; Bk. IV, Ch. V and Appendix

NIEBUHR, Carsten
Travels in Arabia. London, 1808-1814.
6th *ESSAY*, Bk. I, Ch. VII

[ED. NOTE: Originally published in German. Copenhagen, 1772.]

OWEN, Robert (1771-1858)
A New View of Society: or, Essays [1-4] on the Principle of the Formation of the Human Character... 8°, London, 1813.
6th *ESSAY*, Bk. III, Ch. III; Bk. IV, Ch. XII

PAINE, Thomas (1737-1809)
MK.3.18[1] Rights of Man... 8°, London, 1791.
6th *ESSAY*, Bk. IV,, Ch. VI

PALEY, William (1743-1805)
MB.4.37 Natural theology...2 vols. in 1. 8°, Oxford, 1828.
6th *ESSAY*, Bk. IV, Ch. I, XIII

PALEY, William (1743-1805)
MF.5.22-8 Moral philosophy. Works, with additional sermons. 7 vols. 8°, London, 1825.
6th *ESSAY*, Bk. IV, Ch. II

[ED. NOTE: Malthus refers to both Paley's "Natural Theology" and "Moral Philosophy." For the former there is a separate book in his library. The latter is included in Paley's "Works," as listed.]

PALLAS, Peter Simon (1741-1811)
Voyages de M. P.S. Pallas en différentes provinces de l'empire de Russie et dans l'Asie septentrionale. 5 vols. 4°, Paris, 1788.
6th *ESSAY*, Bk. I, Ch. IX

PARK, Mungo (1771-1806)
Travels in the Interior Districts of Africa...in the years 1795, 1796 & 1797. 4°, London, 1799.
6th *ESSAY*, Bk. I, Ch. VIII; Appendix

[ED. NOTE: Patricia James refers to this book in her "Population Malthus," pp. 269-70.]

PARR, Rev. Samuel (1747-1825)
Spital Sermon. (London), 1801.
4th *ESSAY*, Bk. III, Ch. III

[ED. NOTE: The published version of the 1800 sermon contains many notes. In this sermon Parr joined Mackintosh against Godwin. The note referring to "Dr. Parr, Mr. Mackintosh...and others" did not appear in the 6th *Essay*.]

PAULUS, Diaconus (c. 720-c. 797)
De Gestis Langobardorum. Milan, 1723-1751.
6th *ESSAY*, Bk. I, Ch. VI

[ED. NOTE: Malthus cites Diaconus, from whom Machiavelli is supposed to have taken a description of a people who diminish their population by casting lots; the losers then move to a less populated area. The edition listed may be the one used by Malthus.]

PEROUSE
See LA PEROUSE.

PETTY, William (1623-1687)
MB.3.38 & MH.1.1 Several Essays in Political Arithmetick. (6 pts.) 8°, (London), 1699; also 4th edition corr. 8°, London, 1755.
6th *ESSAY*, Bk. I, Ch. I; Bk. II, Ch. XIII

[ED. NOTE: Malthus actually refers to "Political Arithmetick" without indicating edition or publishing date. However the information he refers to, i.e.: a) "Sir William Petty supposes a doubling possible in so short a time as ten years"; and b) "Sir William Petty calculated that in the year 1800 the city of London would contain 5,359,000 inhabitants..." is at the indicated pages (14 and 17) of the 1755 edition of "Several Essays" which is in Malthus's Library, donated to Jesus College.]

PEUCHET, Jacques (1758-1830)
Essai d'une Statistique Générale. Paris, 1800.
6th *ESSAY*, Bk. II, Ch. VI

PEUCHET, Jaques (1758-1830)
Statistique élémentaire de la France... 8°, Paris, 1805.
6th *ESSAY*, Bk. II, Ch. VII

PRICE, Rev. Richard (1723-1791)
MH.3.23-4 Observation on Reversionary Payments. 4th ed., enlarged. 2 vols. 8°, London, 1783.
1st *ESSAY*, Ch. VI, VII, and especially Ch. XVII
6th *ESSAY*, Bk. I, Ch. I; Bk. II, Ch. II, VIII, XI, XIII

RAYNAL, Guillaume Thomas François (1713-1796)
MA.1.9-16 A Philosophical and Political History of the Settlements and Trade of the Europeans in the East and West Indies. 8 vols. 8°, London, 1788.
6th *ESSAY*, Bk. I, Ch. IV, XI; Bk. III, Ch. IV, VI

[ED. NOTE: This edition is as listed in Malthus's Library. He actually quoted a French 10-volume 1795 edition.]

REYNIER, Jean-Louis Ebenezer, comte (1771-1814)
Considerations Générales sur l'Agriculture de l'Egypte. ("Mémoires sur l'Egypte" Vol. IV) (Paris, 1802?).
6th *ESSAY*, Bk. I, Ch. VIII

RICARDO, David (1772-1823)
MH.3.2 On the Principles of Political Economy, and Taxation. 3rd ed. 8°, London, 1821.
6th *ESSAY*, Bk. III, Ch. XII

RICKMAN, John (1771-1840)
Population Abstracts - Preliminary Observations. London, 1811.
6th *ESSAY*, Bk. II, Ch. IX

ROBERTSON, William (1721-1793)
MF.5.5-8 The History of America. 3rd ed., 4 vols. 8°, London, 1780-1799.
6th *ESSAY*, Bk. I, Ch. IV; Bk. III, Ch. IV

ROBERTSON, William (1721-1793)
MF.5.1-4 The History of the Reign of the Emperor Charles V... New ed., 4 vols. 8°, London, 1782.
6th *ESSAY*, Bk. I, Ch. VI

ROGERS, Robert, Major (1731-1795)
A concise account of North America; containing a description of the several British colonies... London, 1765.
6th *ESSAY*, Bk. I, Ch. IV

RUBRUQUIS, William (1215-1295)
Travels of Wm. Rubruquis (Harris's "Collection of Voyages and Travels.") London, 1705.
6th *ESSAY*, Bk. I, Ch. VII

[ED. NOTE: The more common edition was published in 1900 under "Ruysbroek, Willem van, The journey...to the Eastern parts of the World, 1253-1255."]

RUMFORD, Sir Benjamin Thompson, count (1753-1814)
Essay, political, economical, and philosophical. 3 vols. London, 1716-1802.
6th *ESSAY*, Bk. IV, Ch. XI

[ED. NOTE: Malthus refers to "the cheap soups of Count Rumford" in his plan for improving the condition of the poor.]

SELKIRK, Thomas Douglas, 5th Earl of (1771-1820)
On the present state of the highlands, and on the causes and the probable consequences of emigration. London, 1805.
6th *ESSAY*, Appendix

SHORT, Thomas, M.D. (1690-1772)
New Observations, Natural, Moral, Civil, Political, and Medical, on City, Town, and Country Bills of Mortality... London, [1750.]
1st *ESSAY*, Ch. VII
6th *ESSAY*, Bk. II, Ch. VIII, XIII

SHORT, Thomas, M.D. (1690-1772)
A General Chronological History of the Air... 2 vols. 1749.
6th *ESSAY*, Bk. II, Ch. XII, XIII

[ED. NOTE: Best known is his "Comparative History of the Increase and Decrease of Mankind in England... To which is added a Syllabus of the General States of Health, Air, Seasons and Food for the last three hundred years..." 4°, London, 1767.]

SIMOND, Louis (1767-1831)
A Journal of a Tour & Residence in Great Britain, during 1810 & 1811, by a French traveller. With remarks on the Country, its Arts, Literature & Politics, & on the Manners & Customs of its Inhabitants. New York, 1815.
6th *ESSAY*, Bk. III, Ch. VIII

[ED. NOTE: Malthus describes Mr. Simond as "a French Gentleman, who had resided above twenty years in America."]

SINCLAIR, Sir John, Bart. (1754-1835)
The statistical account of Scotland. Drawn up from the communications of the ministers of the different parishes... 21 vols. 8°, Edinburgh, 1791-99.
6th *ESSAY*, Bk. I, Ch. II; Bk. II, Ch. X

[ED. NOTE: Malthus refers to the above title; Mrs. Patricia James indicates that Malthus was given a copy of the "General Report of Scotland" by Sir John Sinclair.]

SMITH, Adam (1723-1790)
MA.5.29-32 An Inquiry into the Nature and Causes of The Wealth of Nations. 3rd ed. 8°, London, 1784.
1st *ESSAY*, Especially Ch. XVI
6th *ESSAY*, Bk. II, Ch. XIII; Bk. III, Ch. V, XI, XII, XIII; Bk. IV, Ch. IX, XI

[ED. NOTE: Malthus's Library at Jesus College has only the McCulloch, 4 vols., 1828 Edinburgh edition. It is included in the body of the catalogue having the shelfmark MA. 5.29-32. Checking Malthus's references, however, it follows that he used the 3rd edition of 1784. The following example would indicate this conclusion. In the *Essay*'s 4th edition, Vol. II, p. 174, Malthus wrote: ."..Dr. Smith says, that...no bounty upon exportation, no monopoly on the home market, can raise that value (Corn real value), nor the street competition lower it..." Reference is given to "Wealth of Nations," Vol. II, Bk. IV, Ch. V, p. 278. In the "Wealth of Nations," 3rd edition, Vol. II, p. 278, Smith wrote: "No bounty upon exportation, no monopoly of the home market, can raise that value (Corn real value). The street competition cannot lower it."]

STAUNTON, Sir George Leonard (1737-1801)
An authentic account of an embassy from the King of Great Britain, to the Emperor of China... London, 1797.
6th *ESSAY*, Bk. I, Ch. XII

[ED. NOTE: Referred to by Malthus as "Embassy to China," w/o edition. A second edition was published in London in 1798.]

STEUART, Sir James (1712-1780)
MK.5.1-2 An Inquiry into the principles of Political Economy. 2 vols. 4°, London, 1767.
6th *ESSAY*, Bk. I, Ch. II, IX; Bk. III, Ch. XIV

STYLES, John (1782-1849)
A Discourse on Christian Union. Boston, 1761.
1st *ESSAY*, Ch. X
6th *ESSAY*, Bk. II, Ch. XIII

[ED. NOTE: Malthus refers to a sermon by Dr. Styles "from which Dr. Price has taken some facts." These facts were actually from this Discourse, cfm. note of Dr. Price in his "Observations,"(p. 203 n, of the 1772 ed.). Malthus looked for this "hard to get" book as early as 1799 (Patricia James, "Population Malthus," p. 70).]

SUMNER, John Bird, Abp of Canterbury (1780-1862)
A treatise on the records of the creation and on the moral attitudes of the creator... London, 1816.
6th *ESSAY*, Bk. III, Ch. III; Appendix

SUSSMILCH, Johann Peter (1707-1767)
Die Göttliche Ordnung in den Veränderungen des menschlichen Geschlechts aus der Geburt, dem Tode, und der Fortpflanzung desselben Erwiesen. 2 vols. 8°, (Tables), Berlin, 1761.
1st *ESSAY*, Especially Ch. VII
6th *ESSAY*, Bk. II, Ch. II, IV, VIII, XI, XII

[ED. NOTE: First published in 1741 in a single volume (Goldsmith 7825). Subsequent versions were published in 1761, 1765 and posthumously in 1775. Malthus first refers to Süssmilch, as cited by Richard Price, and "may have only known of his work through Price's 'Reversionary Payments,'" according to Mrs. James. Although Price did not indicate the edition of Süssmilch's work, since the tables are recordings through 1756, the edition used cannot be the one of 1741.]

SYMES, Michael (1753?-1809)
An account of an embassy to the Kingdom of AVA, sent by the governor general of India, in the year 1795. 2nd ed. London, 1800.
6th *ESSAY*, Bk. I, Ch. III

TEMPLE, Sir William (1628-1699)
MC.7.1-2 Works (Includes his "Life" by Lady Giffard). 2 vols. F°, London, 1740.
6th *ESSAY*, Bk. III, Ch. IX

THAARUP, Frederik (1766-1845)
Statistik der Dänischen Monarchie. 2 vols. Copenhagen, 1765.
6th *ESSAY*, Bk. II, Ch. I, II, IV

[ED. NOTE: A second Danish edition appeared in 1794 entitled "Veiledning til det Danske Monarkies Statistik," the only one listed in NUC.]

THUNBERG, Karl Peter (1743-1828)
Voyages de C.P. Thunberg, au Japon par le Cap de Bonne-Esperance... 2 vol. ed. in 4°; 4 vol. ed. in 8°, Paris, 1796.
6th *ESSAY*, Bk. I, Ch. XII

TOOKE, Thomas (1774-1858)
MB.1.2 Thoughts and details of the high and low prices of the thirty years, from 1793 to 1822. 2nd ed. 8°, London, 1824.
6th *ESSAY*, Bk. III, Ch. XII

TOOKE, William (1744-1820)
View of the Russian Empire during the reign of Catharine the Second, and the close of the eighteenth century. 2nd ed., 3 vols. London, 1800.
6th *ESSAY*, Bk. I, Ch. VII, IX; Bk. II, Ch. III

TOTT, François, Baron de (1733-1793)
Mémoires sur les Turcs et les Tartares. 4 vols. Amsterdam, 1784.
6th *ESSAY*, Bk. I, Ch. VII

[ED. NOTE: Apparently Malthus refers to this French edition as his note reads, "Mémoires du Baron de Tott"; however an English translation was published in London in 1785.]

TOWNSEND, Rev. Joseph (1739-1816)
A Dissertation on the Poor Laws. 2nd ed. (London), 1787.
6th *ESSAY*, Bk. IV, Ch. XI

[ED. NOTE: The first edition of this pamphlet was published in 1785; Malthus refers to the 1787 ed.]

TOWNSEND, Rev. Joseph (1739-1816)
ML.5.2-4 Journey through Spain. London, 1791.
6th *ESSAY*, Bk. II, Ch. VI

[ED. NOTE: There were three editions: 1791, 1792 and 1814. Palgrave compared them with Arthur Young's "Travels in France."]

TUCKER, Josiah (1712-1799)
The elements of Commerce & Theory of Taxes. (Gloucester), 1755.
6th *ESSAY*, Bk. IV, Ch. XI

[ED. NOTE: Malthus may have referred to another of Tucker's writings. He also refers to a tax proposed by Mr. Pew.]

TURGOT, Anne Robert Jacques (1727-1781)
MA.4.12-20 Œuvres... 9 vols. (Vol. 1, 2nd ed.) 8°, Paris, 1808-1811.
6th *ESSAY*, Bk. III, Ch. XII

[ED. NOTE: The reference by Malthus is from Vol. VI of this edition.]

TURNER, Samuel (1749?-1802)
An account of an embassy, to the court of Teshoo Lama, in Tibet; containing a narrative of a journey through Bootan and part of Tibet... 4°, London, 1800.
6th *ESSAY*, Bk. I, Ch. XI

[ED. NOTE: A second edition as listed in NUC was published in 1806; in 1800 a French translation also appeared, and in 1801 a German version. This is the only published account of a journey to Great Tibet written by an Englishman until the 1875 narratives of Bogle and Manning. (D.N.B.)]

ULLOA, Don Antonio (1716-1795)
ML.4.12-13 Voyage historique de l'Amérique Méridionale fait par ordre du Roi d'Espagne... 2 vols. 4°, Amsterdam, 1752.
6th *ESSAY*, Bk. II, Ch. XIII

VANCOUVER, George (1757-1798)
A voyage of discovery to the North Pacific Ocean, and round the World... 3 vols. & Atlas. London, 1798.
6th *ESSAY*, Bk. I, Ch. III, IV, V

VOGHT, Caspar, Baron von (1752-1839)
MH.3.22[2] Account of the management of the poor in Hamburgh, since the year 1788... 8°, London, 1796.
6th *ESSAY*, Bk. IV, Ch. IV

VOLNEY, Constantin François Chasseboeuf, Comte de (1757-1820)
Voyage en Syrie et en Egypte, pendant les Années 1783-1785 par M.C.F. Volney. 2nd ed., 2 vols. Paris, 1787.
6th *ESSAY*, Bk. I, Ch. VII, VIII, X

WALLACE, Rev. Robert (1697-1771)
MH.1.21 Dissertation on the Numbers of Mankind in antient and modern times... [8°, Edinburgh], 1753.
6th *ESSAY*, Bk. I, Ch. XIV
Various Prospects of Mankind, Nature and Providence. London, 1761
1st *ESSAY*, Ch. VIII; 6th *ESSAY*, Bk. III, Ch. I & III

WARGENTIN, P. Wilhelm (1717-1787)
Tables of Mortality based upon the Swedish population; prepared & presented in 1766 by Per Wilhelm Wargentin... Stockholm, 1930 (A Reprint).

[ED. NOTE: 6th Essay refers to "Mémoires abrégés de l'Académie Royale des Sciences de Stockholm," published in Paris in 1772 (Bk. II, Ch. II, III & VIII). The reprint listed covers the information Malthus used, being a translation from the Swedish Academy Memoires for 1766.]

WEBSTER, Alexander (1707-1784)
First Census of the Kingdom (Scotland) in 1755, (A Webster's Survey). Edinburgh, ?
6th *ESSAY*, Bk. II, Ch. X

WEYLAND, John (1774-1854)
MH.2.24 The principle of population and production, as they are affected by the progress of Society... 8°, London, 1816.
6th *ESSAY*, 1817 Appendix

[ED. NOTE: One of the contemporary critics of Malthus, in 1807 Weyland also wrote "A Short Inquiry into the Policy, Humanity...of the Poor Laws."]

WILKIE
See: Sinclair, Sir John. (Vol. XXI, p. 383).
6th *ESSAY*, Bk. II, Ch. X

[WITT, John de] (1623-1672)
Interest Van Hollandt, Ofte Gronden Van Hollandtswelvaren... Amsterdam, 1662.
6th *ESSAY*, Bk. III, Ch. IX

[ED. NOTE: This book, written by Pieter de la Court (Kress 1092), contains a complete defense of de Witt's policy. The manuscript was corrected by him, and Ch. XXXIX was written by de Witt (Palgrave). Malthus indicates the English translation, citing John de Witt's "Interest of Holland." Actually, in 1702 a translation was published under the title "The true interest and political maximus of the Republick of Holland and West-Friesland...Written by John de Witt and other great men in Holland." (Kress 2344)]

YOUNG, Arthur (1741-1820)
ME.6.9-10 Travels during the years 1787, 1788 and 1789. Undertaken more particularly with a view of ascertaining the cultivation, wealth, resources, and national prosperity of the Kingdom of France. 2 vols. (Vol. 2, 2nd ed.) 4°, Bury St. Edmunds, 1792-1794.
6th *ESSAY*, Bk. II, Ch. VI; Bk. IV, Ch. XI, Appendix

[ED. NOTE: Referred to by Malthus as "Young's Travels in France."]

YOUNG, Arthur (1741-1820)
MH.4.16[4] The question of scarcity plainly stated, and remedies considered. 8°, London, 1800.
6th *ESSAY*, Bk. IV, Ch. XI

YOUNG, Arthur (1741-1820)
MH.3.22[3] An inquiry into the propriety of applying wastes to the better maintanance and support of the poor... 8°, Bury, 1801.
6th *ESSAY*, Bk. IV, Ch. XI

[ED. NOTE: In his *Essay* Malthus made still another reference to Young regarding articles published in the "Annals of Agriculture."]

UNCORROBORATED ENTRIES OF REFERENCES
from
An Essay on the Principle of Population

Analyse des Procès Verbaux des Conseils Généraux de Département: [Account of the internal state of France for the year VIII (1799).]
6th *ESSAY*, Bk. II, Ch. VI, VII

Annals of Agriculture: Gourlay, Robert: "Inquiry into the state of cottagers in the Counties of Lincoln and Rutland" (Vol. XXXVII, p. 514).
6th *ESSAY*, Bk. IV, Ch. XIII

[ED. NOTE: Annals of Agriculture appeared in 46 vols. in all, from 1784-1815. Gourlay made his survey in 1801.] See also: Young

Annuaire: (Bureau des Longitudes): See: Bureau...

Asiatic Researches: (Vol. IV, pp. 401, 354 and Vol. V, p. 14).
6th *ESSAY*, Bk. I, Ch. III, Ch. XI. [Asiatic Researches, or, Transactions of the Asiatic society. Calcutta. Published in 20 vols. during 1788-1839.]

Barton: Observations on the probability... See: Society at Philadelphia

Bernard, Sir Thomas: Society for bettering the condition of the poor: Prefaces to the Reports.
6th *ESSAY*, Bk. IV, Ch. XIII. See also: Society...

Bibliothèque Britannique: (Vol. IV, p. 328). Geneva
6th *ESSAY*, Bk. II, Ch. V

Birbeck: Agricultural Tour in France: (p. 13).
6th *ESSAY*, Bk. II, Ch. VII

Board of Agriculture: Communications. Mann, (Abbé): Memoir on the Agriculture of the Netherlands (Vol. I, p. 225).
6th *ESSAY*, Bk. III, Ch. XIV

Bureau des Longitudes, Paris: Annuaire (founded 1796): Year 1825.
6th *ESSAY*, Bk. II, Ch. VII

Busching: Marrieds, Widows & Widowers: (referred to in Süssmilch, Vol. III, tables, p. 95).
6th *ESSAY*, Bk. II, Ch. XI

Cantzlaer: Mémoires pour servir à la connoissance des affaires politiques et économiques du Royaume de Suède. 4°, 1776.
6th *ESSAY*, Bk. II, Ch. II

Chaptal: Births in France : See: Peuchet in the previous section.
6th *ESSAY*, Bk. II, Ch. VII

Comité de Mendicité: Statements on system of poor laws & its rejection.
6th *ESSAY*, Bk. IV, Ch. VIII

Commons: House of Commons, Committee: Report (Re: Corn Laws, in 1814).
6th *ESSAY*, Bk. III, Ch. XI

Defoe, Daniel: Giving Alms no charity (address to Parliament; extracts in Sir F.M. Eden's "Work on the poor") (Vol. I, p. 261).
6th *ESSAY*, Bk. III, Ch. VI

Descartes: (cited...).
6th *ESSAY*, Bk. III, Ch. I

Economical Society of Berne: Transactions. See: Société economique de Berne
6th *ESSAY*, Bk. II, Ch. V

Encyclopedia Britannica: Supplement [Articles on: Prussia; population (2 articles); the Preliminary Dissertation by Dugald Stewart; Corn-Laws.]
6th *ESSAY*, Bk. II, Ch. IV, XIII, Appendix Year 1825; Bk. III, Ch. III, XII

Foe, Daniel de: See: Defoe, Daniel

Gourlay, Robert: See: Annals of Agriculture

Herman, B. F.: See: Nova Acta Academiae

House of Commons: Committee. See: Commons, House of...

Howard: Society for bettering the condition of the poor: Prefaces to the Reports (Vol. III, p. 32).
6th *ESSAY*, Bk. IV, Ch. XIV. See also: Society...

Krafft, W.L.: See: Nova Acta Academiae

Lords. House of Lords: Reports (p. 51, evidence preceding the Corn-Bill of 1815, brought before the House...).
6th *ESSAY*, Bk. III, Ch. XIII

Mann, (Abbé): See: Board of Agriculture...

Mémoires par la Société économique de Berne See: Société...

Milne: (Actuary to the "Sun Life Assurance Society").
6th *ESSAY*, Bk. II, Ch. II, XI, XIII (reference to article on "Population" in the Supplement of Encyclopedia Britannica, p. 308).

Missionary Voyage.
6th *ESSAY*, Bk. I, Ch. V

Newton: (cited...).
6th *ESSAY*, Bk. III, Ch. I

Nova Acta Academiae: Herman, B.F.: Paper on Births, Deaths & Marriages...of the Empire; presented 1768 to the Academy of Sciences of Petersburg (Vol. IV).
6th *ESSAY*, Bk. II, Ch. III

Nova Acta Academiae: Memoirs. Krafft, W.L. (Vol. IV, relating to an ennumeration of population in 1784).
6th *ESSAY*, Bk. II, Ch. III

Observations on the results of the population Act: (pp. 6, 8-9).
6th *ESSAY*, Bk. II, Ch. VIII

Pew: (Some plan of improving the condition of the poor):
See: Tucker, Josiah (in the previous listings).
6th *ESSAY*, Bk. IV, Ch. XI

Population Abstracts, Parish Registers (1720-1811).
6th *ESSAY*, Bk. II, Ch. VIII, IX; Bk. III, Ch. XI

Portland, (Duke of): in: Malthus, "An investigation of the cause of the present high price of Provisions" (1800) (in the previous listings).
6th *ESSAY*, Bk. III, Ch. V

[Prévost, Pierre? (1751-1839)]

Translator (?) of Société économique de Berne: Mémoires.
6th *ESSAY*, Bk. II, Ch. V, VII

[ED. NOTE: Malthus refers to this title as follows: "M. Prévost, of Geneva, in his translation of this work, gives some account of the small

Canton of Glavis, in which the cotton-manufacture had been introduced." Considering the translation activity of Pierre Prévost of Geneva, we assume he was the actual translator of Muret's work on the "Mémoires" which we were unable to locate.]

Registers for Russia....
6th *ESSAY*, Bk. II, Ch. I

Revue Encyclopédique, Year 1825/March.
6th *ESSAY*, Bk. II, Ch. II

Royal Academy of Science at Stockholm: Transactions (1809).
6th *ESSAY*, Bk. II, Ch. II

Société économique de Berne: Mémoires Année 1766
See: Muret in previous listing.

Society at Philadelphia: Transactions. Barton: "Observations on the probability of Life in the United States." (Vol. 3 no. 7, p. 25).
6th *ESSAY*, Bk. II, Ch. XI

Society for bettering the condition of the poor (Vol. II, p. 21).
(see also: Howard and Bernard, Thomas)
6th *ESSAY*, Bk. IV, Ch. VIII, XIII, XIV

Spencean System (Spencean "Plan," published in Spence's: "Pig meat," 1793-5. Founder of: Society of Spencean Philantropists [1812].)
6th *ESSAY*, Bk. III, Ch. III

Statistique générale et particulière de la France, et de ses colonies (Regarding population in the year VI-1797).
6th *ESSAY*, Bk. II, Ch. VI, VII, Appendix (p. 548)

Stewart, Dugald: Preliminary Dissertation to Supplement of the Encyclopedia Britannica. (p. 121).
6th *ESSAY*, Bk. III, Ch. III cont.

Table Statistique des Etats Danois.
6th *ESSAY*, Bk. II, Ch. I

Westminster Review: Year 1825, No. 6, (...effect of the Corn-Laws).
6th *ESSAY*, Bk. III, Ch. XII

CLASSICS OF ANTIQUITY CITED IN THE 6th ESSAY

Aristotle: (Opera) de Republica: (Lib. II, Ch. X); (Lib. VII, Ch. XVI): Gillies's translation. (Vol. II, Bk. II, pp. 87, 91, 107, 113).
6th *ESSAY*, Bk. I, Ch. XIII

Bible: Genesis.
6th *ESSAY*, Bk. I, Ch. VI

Caesar, Gaius Julius: De bello gallico.
6th *ESSAY*, Bk. I, Ch. VI

Dionysius Halicarnassus: (Lib. II, p. 15).
6th *ESSAY*, Bk. I, Ch. XIV

Gellius, Aulus (c. 123-165 A.D.): Noctium Atticarum...
6th *ESSAY*, Bk. I, Ch. XIV

Jordanes: (fl. mid 6th C.) (also as: Jordandes: De Rebus Geticis. p. 83). "De Origine Actibusque Getarum" (On the origin of deeds of the Getae) A.D. 551.
6th *ESSAY*, Bk. I, Ch. VI

Juvenalis, Decimus Junius (c. 60-130 A.D.): Satires
6th *ESSAY*, Bk. I, Ch. XIV

Livius (Livy), Titus: (Liber VI, ch. XII).
6th *ESSAY*, Bk. I, Ch. XIV

Minucius Felix, Marcus (ca. 200 A.D.): Octavius.
6th *ESSAY*, Bk. I, Ch. XIV

Plato, De Legibus: (Vol. II, p. 54 n).
6th *ESSAY*, Bk. I, Ch. XIII

Plato, De Republica: (pp. 277, 279).
6th *ESSAY*, Bk. I, Ch. XIII

Plinius Gaius, (Pliny) Secundus (A.D.23-79): (Pliny, the elder) Naturalis historia (Lib. XXIX, Ch. IV).
6th *ESSAY*, Bk. I, Ch. XIV

Plutarch, (A.D. 46-119 etc.): De Amore Prolis (from: Moralia).
6th *ESSAY*, Bk. I, Ch. XIV

Tacitus, Gaius Cornelius: De Moribus Germanorum (p. 37, sections: V, XVI, XVIII, XX).
6th *ESSAY*, Bk. I, Ch. VI, XIV